£20.99

Studying Culture

This book is to be returned on or before

Studying Culture

A Practical Introduction

Second Edition

Judy Giles and Tim Middleton

Blackwell
Publishing

© 1999, 2008 by Judy Giles and Tim Middleton

BLACKWELL PUBLISHING
350 Main Street, Malden, MA 02148-5020, USA
9600 Garsington Road, Oxford OX4 2DQ, UK
550 Swanston Street, Carlton, Victoria 3053, Australia

The right of Judy Giles and Tim Middleton to be identified as the Authors of this Work has been asserted in accordance with the UK Copyright, Designs, and Patents Act 1988.

Designations used by companies to distinguish their products are often claimed as trademarks. All brand names and product names used in this book are trade names, service marks, trademarks, or registered trademarks of their respective owners. The publisher is not associated with any product or vendor mentioned in this book.

This publication is designed to provide accurate and authoritative information in regard to the subject matter covered. It is sold on the understanding that the publisher is not engaged in rendering professional services. If professional advice or other expert assistance is required, the services of a competent professional should be sought.

First edition published 1999
Second edition published 2008 by Blackwell Publishing Ltd

1   2008

Library of Congress Cataloging-in-Publication Data

Giles, Judy.
    Studying culture : a practical introduction / Judy Giles and Tim Middleton. — 2nd ed.
        p. cm.
    Includes bibliographical references and index.
    ISBN 978-1-4051-5592-2 (pbk. : alk. paper)   1. Culture.   2. Culture—Study and teaching.
I. Middleton, Tim, 1962–   II. Title.

HM621.G55 2008
306—dc22

2007032637

A catalogue record for this title is available from the British Library.

Set in 10.5 on 13 pt Minion
by SNP Best-set Typesetter Ltd., Hong Kong
Printed and bound in Singapore
by Utopia Press Pte Ltd

The publisher's policy is to use permanent paper from mills that operate a sustainable forestry policy, and which has been manufactured from pulp processed using acid-free and elementary chlorine-free practices. Furthermore, the publisher ensures that the text paper and cover board used have met acceptable environmental accreditation standards.

For further information on
Blackwell Publishing, visit our website:
www.blackwellpublishing.com

Contents

List of Figures   viii
List of Tables   ix
Acknowledgements   x

Introduction   1

1   What is Culture?   6
   Introduction   6
   The 'culture and civilization' debate   8
   The 'mass culture' debate   13
   Social definitions of culture   18
   Culture and power   25
   Conclusions   30

2   Identity and Difference   31
   Introduction   31
   Who am I?   32
   Social constructivist approaches to identity   40
   'Identity crisis' and the modern world   49
   Representing and narrating identity   57
   Conclusions   60

3   Representation   62
   Introduction   62
   Language and representation   63
   Communicating meaning   65

Representation and discourse 72
Representation, discourse and resistance 83
Conclusions 87

4   **History** 90
Introduction 90
The past 'as it really was'? 92
Challenges to objectivity: post-structuralist theories of history 98
The past and popular memory 102
History as 'heritage' 116
Conclusions 119

5   **Location, Location, Location: Cultural Geographies** 120
Place and identity: a brief introduction 121
Mapping realities? 127
Going shopping 130
Case study: mapping Los Angeles 137
Conclusions 146

6   **Case Study: Global Tourism** 149
The story of tourism 152
Tourism as social practice 156
Tourist places 159
Tourism and identities 162
Tourism and heritage 168
Cultural imperialism or cultural globalization? 174
Conclusions 177

7   **Cultural Value: High Culture and Popular Culture** 179
Defining culture 180
Discriminations 181
Versions of literary culture 189
Rereading literature 196
Rereading texts: *The Wind in the Willows* (1908) and
   English masculinity 197
Conclusions 209

8   **Subjects, Bodies, Selves** 212
Introduction 212
Fragmented or multiple selves? 215

Language and subjectivity 220
Discourse and the subject 225
Embodied selves 228
Conclusions 236

9 **Consumption** 238
Introduction 238
What is a consumer? 239
Buying a newspaper 240
My high street and your high street 243
Theories of consumption 246
Selling identities 257
Agency, appropriation and ethics 261
Conclusions 265

10 **Technology** 266
The place of the personal: ethnography and the practice of
  cultural studies 269
Twentieth-century technology: cultural studies of TV 271
Living with technology 277
Working with the Web 280
Conclusions 284

Conclusion 285

References and Further Reading 288
Bibliography 305
Index 307

Figures

1.1	Hereford Cathedral	21
3.1	Old rose-tinted spectacles/New dark shades, by Posy Simmonds	78
3.2	*Madonna and Child*, 1982, by Jo Spence and Terry Dennett (from the series The History Lesson)	88
4.1	Firefighters raise the American flag on 11 September 2001	111
4.2	Marines raise the American flag on Iwo Jima on 23 February 1945	112
4.3	'The Battle for Civilisation'	115
5.1	Bath Spa University's Newton Park Campus	128
5.2	Rand McNally local map of Westlake	140
6.1	'Junk room', Mr Straw's house, Nottinghamshire	172
8.1	An illustration from *Fit Body*, number 16	235
9.1	A suburban shopping area	244
9.2	'New Men'	256
9.3	Advertisement for Tilda sauces	260

Tables

5.1 Population, median income and country of birth for Los
     Angeles in 1990   139
5.2 LAPD crime statistics for 2004, for stations in the Central
     Division, including Rampart   147
6.1 International tourist arrivals 1995–2003, in thousands   155
10.1 Log of personal technology usage   281

Acknowledgements

Tim Middleton

I would like to thank Blackwell for commissioning a second edition of this book and Judy Giles for being a patient and insightful co-author.

At Bath Spa University I should like to thank my colleagues Dr Jenni Lewis and Dr Jo Gill – now at the University of Exeter – for their input to the module 'Sex & the City: Sexualities & subjectivities in modern American urban writing', from which aspects of chapter 5 are derived. I'd also like to thank my students from this module for their contribution to the development of my thinking about how you teach city cultures and for their willingness to try things out even when they seemed a long way removed from their prior experience of literary study.

I should also like to thank Bath Spa University for supporting my attendance at conferences in the UK and Europe at which aspects of the revised material in this book have been given airing.

My final thanks are to Gaynor for her support, encouragement and patience.

Judy Giles

I have worked with Tim Middleton over many enjoyable and productive years. He is a stimulating and enthusiastic co-author whose motivation and enormous good humour have always encouraged me in the inevitable troughs involved in writing and publishing. In addition I owe a particular debt of gratitude to Steve Purcell, Stuart Page, David Richmond, and all the participants in the 'Theory and Cakes discussion group' who have constantly urged me, even when they were unaware that they were doing so, to think harder and deeper about the topics covered in this book. Thanks are also due to the many students on whom the material in this book has been piloted and who, over many years, have shared with me the aspects of study that they found interesting, difficult or just dull. Ken Provencher, our editor, tolerated with infinite good humour the delays and confusions that accompanied this project. Glynis Baguley proved a marvellous copy-editor: her attention to detail, her scrupulous reading of the text, and her helpful suggestions made this a much improved manuscript. All errors that remain are, of course, the responsibility of the authors.

The authors and publishers gratefully acknowledge the following for permission to reproduce copyright material:

Figure 1.1: Hereford Cathedral by A. F. Kersting. © Pitkin Unichrome.

Figure 3.1: Old rose-tinted spectacles/New dark shades, courtesy of Posy Simmonds.

Figure 3.2: *Madonna and Child*, courtesy of the Jo Spence Memorial Archive.

Figure 4.1: Firefighters raise the American flag on 11 September 2001. © *The Record* (Bergen Co., NJ).

Figure 4.2: Marines raise the American flag on Iwo Jima on 23 February 1945. Photograph © AP Photo/Joe Rosenthal/Empics.

Figure 4.3: 'The Battle for Civilisation'. © Crown Copyright, courtesy of Her Majesty's Stationery Office.

Figure 5.1: Bath Spa University's Newton Park Campus. *Source:* www.bathspa. ac.uk/contact/map-newton-park.asp.

Figure 5.2: Local map of Westlake. Map © Rand McNally, R.L.07-S-25.

Figure 6.1: 'Junk room', Mr Straw's house, Nottinghamshire. © National Trust Photographic Library/Geoffrey Frosh.

Figure 8.1: An illustration from *Fit Body*, 16. Courtesy of Carol Day, IHBC, BABTAC.

Figure 9.2: Text by Kathy Marks, *The Independent*, 21 October 1997; photograph courtesy of North News and Pictures, Newcastle-upon-Tyne.

Figure 9.3: Advertisement for Tilda sauces reproduced by courtesy of Tilda Foods.

Reading 1.5: R. Williams, 'Culture is Ordinary', pp. 5–6 from A. Gray and J. McGuigan (eds), *Studying Culture: An Introductory Reader* (London: Edward Arnold, 1958). Reprinted with permission of Verso.

Reading 2.1: G. Jordan and C. Weedon, pp. 439–40 from *Cultural Politics: Class, Gender, Race and the Postmodern World* (Oxford: Blackwell, 1995). Reprinted with permission of Blackwell Publishing.

Reading 3.1: Catherine Belsey, pp. 39–45 from *Critical Practice* (London: Methuen and Co., 1980). Reprinted with permission of Thomson Publishing UK.

Reading 3.2: Stuart Hall (ed.), pp. 4–5 from *Representation: Cultural Representations and Signifying Practices* (Milton Keynes: Open University, 1997). Reprinted by permission of Sage Publications Ltd.

Reading 3.8: Richard Dyer, pp. 20–21 from *The Matter of Images: Essays on Representation* (London: Routledge, 1993). Reprinted with permission.

Reading 4.4: Hayden White, pp. 7–8 from *Metahistory: the Historical Imagination in Nineteenth Century Europe* (Baltimore: The Johns Hopkins University Press, 1973). © 1973 The Johns Hopkins University Press. Reprinted with permission of The Johns Hopkins University Press.

Reading 4.7: Raphael Samuel, pp. 139–40 from *Theatres of Memory* (London: Verso, 1994). Reprinted by permission of Verso.

Reading 7.7: From *English in the National Curriculum: Draft Proposals 1994.* © Crown Copyright, reproduced with the permission of the Controller of Her Majesty's Stationery Office.

Reading 8.2: Carol Ann Duffy, 'Recognition', pp. 40–1 from *Selling Manhattan* (London: Anvil Press Poetry, 1987). Reprinted with permission of Anvil Press Poetry.

Reading 8.4: Rosalind Minsky, 'Lacan', pp. 191–3 from Helen Crowley and Susan Himmelweit (eds), *Knowing Women: Feminism and Knowledge* (Milton Keynes: Open University, 1992).

Reading 8.5: Julia Kristeva, 'A Question of Subjectivity (interview with Susan Sellers)', from *Women's Review*, 12, 1986 (also extracted in Eagleton, 1996). Reprinted with kind permission of the author.

Reading 8.6: Stuart Hall, 'Signification, Representation, Ideology: Althusser and the Post-Structuralist Debates', pp. 4–5 from J. Curran, D. Morley and V. Walkerdine (eds), *Cultural Studies and Communications* (London: Edward Arnold, 1996). Reprinted with permission of Sage Publications.

Reading 8.7: Emily Martin, 'Body narratives, body boundaries', from Lawrence Grossberg, Cary Nelson and Paula Triechler (eds), *Cultural Studies* (London: Routledge, 1992).

Reading 8.8: Susan Bordo, 'Reading the slender body', pp. 96–7 from M. Jacobus, E. Fox Keller and S. Shuttleworth (eds), *Body/Politics: Women and the Discourse of Science* (London: Routledge, 1990).

Reading 9.5: Pierre Bourdieu, extract from 'Sport and social class', pp. 819–40 from *Social Science Information* 17(6), 1978. © 1978 Sage Publications & Foundation of the Maison des Sciences de l'Homme. Reprinted by permission of Sage Publications.

Reading 10.2: R. Johnson et al., pp. 206–8 from *The Practice of Cultural Studies* (London: Sage, 2004). Reprinted with permission of Sage Publications Ltd.

Reading 10.5: M. Gillespie, 'Technology and tradition – audio-visual culture among South Asian families in West London', from *Cultural Studies*, 3(2), 1989.

Reading 10.7: Anmol Madan, Research Profile: Jerk-O-Meter. www.media.mit.edu/press/jerk-o-meter/.

The publishers apologize for any errors or omissions in the above list and would be grateful to be notified of any corrections that should be incorporated in the next edition or reprint of this book.

Introduction

This book is intended as a starting point for those who are newcomers to the study of culture, whether it be in the area of sociology, literature, history, geography, communication, media or cultural studies. Our aims are threefold. First, to offer an accessible and 'beginner's' route through the sometimes bewildering mass of material, theories and information that currently constitutes the study and analysis of culture. Second, to provide you with an introductory taste of some key areas that you may encounter in your studies. Third, as you will soon discover, this is not a book to be read passively: its format is interactive, engaging you, the reader, in activities at various points. Culture is something that all of us are engaged with in our everyday lives, and is the process by which we make sense of the world we inhabit. Everyone is knowledgeable in different ways about the cultures that surround us, and you should not be deterred, because you are now 'studying' culture in an academic environment, from using your own experience as a valuable resource. We want you to bring your own ideas and thoughts to the readings and discussions we offer. In return, it is our intention to offer you a vocabulary in which to express the complex ideas towards which you may be grasping.

One of the problems as well as one of the pleasures of studying culture is that almost everything seems to be cultural and therefore available for study. Cultural studies as an area of knowledge has grown rapidly in recent years, often in tandem with other subjects such as communication, media and film studies, and there is an enormous diversity of topics that lend themselves to cultural studies approaches. However, while cultural studies may seem, at first sight, to be everywhere and nowhere, it does have a distinctive history which has emphasized its interdisciplinary nature and its commitment to appropriating from other disciplinary areas whatever theories or methods are most appropriate to its purposes. Cultural studies, in Britain, began as a wide-ranging critique of dominant views of culture and of the modes of study and academic canons that maintained this dominance. This original challenge to cultural elitism in Britain has widened since the 1960s and 1970s to encompass political interventions in a variety of international contexts. Cultural studies now thrives, for example, in South East Asia, France, the United States and Australia. Its particularly British focus on class has extended to analyses of gender, 'race', ethnicity, nationality and the power relations that shape and are shaped by cultural practices wherever they are found. In this book we have tried to offer a range of dimensions that can be brought to the study of culture – for example, issues of time and space that have their roots in the disciplines of history and geography. As well, we focus on so-called 'high' cultural forms, such as the literary, which are often, although by no means always, excluded from a cultural studies approach and which can, therefore, tend to remain the discrete subject matter of literary critics, art historians and music scholars, for example.

We believe this book will be useful to newcomers to the area by offering an entry point to the field of cultural studies. At the same time, it needs to be acknowledged that our particular version of this field is one that has been shaped by our teaching and thinking about cultural studies and the requirements of students over a number of years. For example, the scope of this book thus conceived has not allowed us to focus in as much detail as some might wish on the import of the ethnographic work that has been produced as part of the process of cultural studies. However, this does not mean that we would wish to favour the textual and the abstract over the lived. Implicit in the interactive format of the book is our belief that the knowledge and experiences of 'ordinary' people are an important starting point for any consideration of culture.

The impetus for writing this book came directly from our teaching of first- and second-year undergraduate students. We found that, while there are a number of excellent readers available, much of the material in these requires familiarity with a vocabulary that most newcomers do not possess. Our experience has shown that students, new to the area, have difficulty assimilating and applying many of the ideas and concepts without guidance. This book is an attempt to offer the kind of help which most readers are unable to provide. We would stress, however, that the activities and readings with which we invite you to engage should not be taken as a substitute for reading and thinking about the articles to be found in many of these collections. Rather, we suggest you use this book as a complement to your wider reading, and to this end we have provided lists of further reading for each chapter.

One of the problems in writing a book of this nature is what to include and what to leave out. We have not included comprehensive accounts of particular areas of knowledge – for example, psychoanalytic theory, media theory and film theory – not because we believe these areas are of lesser import to the study of culture, but because there are excellent, detailed introductions to these topics already available. We have chosen to concentrate on areas that are less accessibly covered elsewhere, and to offer a taste of the variety and diversity of approaches that constitute contemporary cultural studies. We hope that you will find much to interest you, but we also hope that the book's format will encourage you to question and take further areas that you find particularly stimulating.

The origins of this book are to be found in the core modules we teach on the cultural and critical studies programme. Identity and difference, representation, cultural history, heritage and geography are our starting points, and have proved a firm basis for more complex work at higher levels. More recently, we have begun to introduce students to theories and ideas of material and consumer cultures and to ways of thinking about new electronic information technologies. The activities we suggest have grown out of seminar-based discussions and exercises, but can be done individually and will help you to clarify points of debate as well as your own thoughts.

Throughout the book we have addressed 'you', the reader. We can, of course, have very little idea of who 'you' might be. We have, necessarily, assumed that there is a 'typical' student whom we are addressing. However, we remain aware that all of you who read this book will bring to it your individual histories, backgrounds, your preferences and interests, and your own needs. We cannot control how you will read this book or what use you will make of it, but we have tried to allow space for as wide a range of views and preoccupations as we can, at the same time as offering what we believe to be helpful suggestions. This would also be the point at which to say something about 'we': 'we' are lecturers in higher education, one female, one male, both British and both white. Most of the time we speak collectively but occasionally, when using an example specific to one of us, we use 'I'. When we do so we have indicated which of us is speaking at that particular point. Many of our examples are taken from British culture because this is what is most accessible to us and what we know best. However, there is no intention to insist that our particular (white European/British) knowledge of the world is all there is to know, and we would urge you, as readers, to seek out and think about cultures other than the one you know best. Our aim is to suggest possible approaches to studying and analysing culture and it should prove possible to apply the ideas developed in each chapter to a range of different cultures and artefacts.

Occasionally, in the readings, you will come across the male pronouns 'he', 'his', 'him', or the noun 'man', used generically to denote 'human beings'. We do not subscribe to this sexist usage of language. Rather than interrupting the flow of the text by marking each occasion, we have chosen to draw attention to this here in the introduction. Wherever such usage occurs you should get into the habit of mentally inserting, 'she', 'her', 'hers' alongside the male pronoun. You might also consider what difference this insertion makes to the meaning of any particular sentence.

How to Use this Book

Chapters 1 to 5 deal with what we would suggest are some key areas for the study of culture. If you work through these chapters and complement this with wider reading around each area you will be well on the way to acquiring a firm foundation for further study. Chapter 6 comprises a case study in which we draw on the key areas already introduced. Bringing them together in this way illustrates, we hope, how it is possible to apply abstract concepts to empirical material but, equally, demonstrates the value of working across a range of disciplines to produce an interdisciplinary piece of cultural analysis.

The remaining chapters introduce ideas, debates, theories and information that, we think, are more readily understood once the key areas of the earlier chapters have been introduced. In this sense, they build on the foundation established already but, at the same time, continues the objective of introducing you to key areas in the study of culture, in this case extending the debate about culture and introducing theories about the subject and consumption.

We recognize that undergraduate courses, while concentrating on many of the topics we have identified, are unlikely to structure the material in the same way as we have done here. We suggest that you dip into sections as and when these are relevant to your current study. There is no necessity to work through the book as we have organized it – it should be possible to move around the sections and topics as your needs and interests dictate. On occasion we link activities across the chapters or we draw your attention to connections that can be made between topics, but we also hope that you will find your own links and connections as you move around the book.

Throughout the book we offer you short readings and invite you to engage in activities that will clarify the readings or our discussions.

You will find it productive if you do make serious attempts at the suggested activities, even if you do not always write down your thoughts. Don't worry if you find the questions difficult to answer; the purpose is to get you thinking even if you don't come up with a final answer. Some of the activities are best carried out with another person, and we hope this will encourage you to engage in discussion with your peers outside as well as inside the seminar room. Try to get into the habit of problematizing the terms and ideas you encounter by asking questions such as 'what', 'why', 'how', 'when' and 'where'. Neither should you feel you have to agree either with us or with the authors of the various readings. If you disagree, try to work out with what in particular you disagree and why. The aim is to engage in a dialogue or conversation through which you will find it becomes possible to clarify your own thoughts and to develop an individual response to the material.

In each chapter we can offer only a taste of the various debates and you would be advised, as we have already suggested, to follow these up with wider reading. At the end of the book we have provided lists of references from each chapter and suggested further reading, as well as a list of introductory texts and readers. These make good starting points as they offer a range of material and most of them can be found in any academic library. You will always find it helpful to read, in full, the article or chapter from which the extracted readings have been taken. At the same time you might also wish to read something that offers a different perspective. If you find the material you are reading difficult, try to see it as a challenge rather than rejecting it out of hand. Take from it what you do understand or the bits that interest you, and return to it at a later date. Often you will be surprised to find that what seemed impenetrable before has started to become clearer as you have developed and extended your capacity for study. We suggest too that you acquire the habit of using reference books to fill in factual gaps in your knowledge: these can be a valuable source of information of all kinds and we have tried to suggest some titles you may find useful along with the further reading.

One final point: some words have been printed in **bold type**. The intention is to draw your attention to these concepts, as you will find they crop up regularly in your study. We would suggest you compile your own glossary of these terms, and any others that seem to you important. Attempting to produce your own glossary and your own definitions is another way of assimilating and clarifying complex concepts. You could get into the habit of adding to such a glossary and revising your initial definitions as you read more widely.

Above all, we hope this book will prove the starting point for a continuing commitment to and enjoyment of the study of culture in all its diversity and variety. Now read on . . .

Chapter 1

What is Culture?

Introduction

When you start to study any topic or subject it is always useful to think about how that topic or subject has been defined by others and what questions are raised about the subject in the process of attempting to define it. **Culture** is no exception. Raymond Williams, the British cultural critic, famously asserted that 'culture is one of the two or three most complicated words in the English language' (Williams, 1976, p. 87). It is undoubtedly one of the central concepts in our understanding of how modern societies work, and for this reason it is worth spending some time considering the different ways in which the term 'culture' has been and is used. In this chapter we want to introduce you to the variety of ways in which the term can be understood and to suggest how tensions between different meanings have informed current debates about the place of culture in the social sciences and the humanities. We also want to introduce you to a way of understanding culture that is widely accepted and used among contemporary cultural theorists and students of culture. This is not to suggest that the 'true' meaning of culture has finally been defined: because culture is one of the key concepts in our knowledge of societies both past and present, definitions are constantly being developed and refined. We can only make a start in this chapter. You, too, may want to revisit, rethink and develop your understanding of the term as you engage with the material in this book.

It would be useful to begin by noting in a sentence or two what you understand by the term culture. When you have completed this chapter you could look again at your definition and think about whether and how you would change or refine it. It would be useful to continue this exercise at various points in your studies.

ACTIVITY 1.1

You can continue to explore what is meant by the concept 'culture' by examining a number of statements using the term 'culture'. Look at the following statements and note what you think is meant by 'culture' in each. You could try to suggest an example of culture that would be appropriate in each case:

- There are enormous cultural differences between Asia and America.
- She is such a cultured person.
- Pop music is often used by sub-cultures to assert their identity.
- There is a danger that mass culture may destroy the values of our society.
- This course will examine Victorian society and culture.
- Culture is the network of shared meanings in any society.
- McDonald's fosters a distinctive culture based on certain values.

As Raymond Williams points out in *Keywords* (1976), the word culture originally meant the tending or cultivation of something, in particular animals or crops – hence the noun 'agriculture'. From the eighteenth century onwards, this sense of culture as cultivation was particularly associated with the spiritual and moral progress of humanity. Involved in this meaning of culture was the idea of a process, unlike some meanings of the term, which suggest an end product. For example, the term culture is often used to mean actual products, such as opera, concerts, literature, drama and paintings; mass culture is often applied to television, Hollywood, magazines, 'pulp' fiction and newspapers; and the term 'Victorian culture' implies a body of material already available for study. However, as Williams reminds us, from the nineteenth century onwards, with the growth of nation states and the Romantic interest in 'folk art', it became necessary 'to speak of cultures in the plural' in order to distinguish between the particular cultures of different nations, but also between 'the specific and variable cultures of social and economic groups within a nation' (Williams, 1976, p. 89). Moreover, anthropology, as an academic discipline, became established in the early years of the twentieth century, with its sub-branch of cultural anthropology generally understood to be 'the comparative study of preliterate people', in which culture is defined as the whole way of life of a particular society (Kuper and Kuper, 1985, p. 27). As a result, by the twentieth century, there were three broad categories of definition in general usage. Williams identifies these as follows:

- a general process of intellectual, spiritual and aesthetic development;
- a particular way of life, whether of a people, a period, a group or humanity in general;
- the works and practices of intellectual and especially artistic activity (Williams, 1976, p. 90).

What is important for our purposes is not to select one of these definitions as the 'true' meaning of the concept culture, but to begin to think about (a) the ways in which these varied definitions overlap and (b) the points of emphasis that are of interest to contemporary social and cultural theorists. In the following sections we look more closely at the ways in which these different definitions have been expressed and how these have contributed to what is often referred to as 'the contemporary turn to culture' not only in academia, but also in the worlds of business, economics and politics (du Gay et al., 1997, p. 2).

The 'Culture and Civilization' Debate

You should now read the following extract from *Culture and Anarchy* (1869) by Matthew Arnold. Arnold (1822–88) was a British inspector of schools from 1851 to 1887. He was elected Professor of Poetry at the University of Oxford in 1857 and is probably best known today as a poet. Among his most anthologized poems are 'The Scholar-Gipsy' (1853) and 'Dover Beach' (1867). As you read, try to answer the following questions:

- What do you think Arnold means when he claims that culture is 'a study of perfection'?
- Why does Arnold believe culture is so important in 'our modern world'?
- What kinds of things do you think would constitute for Arnold 'the best that has been thought and known in the world'?

Reading 1.1

I am a Liberal, yet I am a Liberal tempered by experience, reflexion, and renouncement, and I am above all, a believer in culture. Therefore I propose now to try and enquire, in the simple unsystematic way which best suits both my taste and my powers, what culture really is, what good it can do, what is our own special need of it; and I shall seek to find some plain ground on which a faith in culture – both my own faith in it and the faith of others, – may rest securely . . .

There is a view in which all the love of our neighbour, the impulses towards action, help and beneficence, the desire for removing human error, clearing human confusion, and diminishing human misery, the noble aspiration to leave the world better and happier than we found it, – motives eminently such as are called social – come in as part of the grounds of culture, and the main and pre-eminent part. Culture is then properly described not as having its origin in curiosity, but as having its origin in the love of perfection: it is a *study of perfection*. It moves by the force, not merely or primarily of the scientific passion for pure knowledge, but also of the moral and social passion for doing good . . .

If culture, then, is a study of perfection, and of harmonious perfection, general perfection, and perfection which consists in becoming something rather than in having something, in an inward condition of the mind and spirit, not in an outward set of circumstances, – it is clear that culture . . . has a very important function to fulfil for mankind. And this function is particularly important in our modern world, of which the whole civilisation is . . . mechanical and external, and tends constantly to become more so . . .

The pursuit of perfection, then, is the pursuit of sweetness and light. He who works for sweetness and light works to make reason and the will of God prevail. He who works for machinery, he who works for hatred, works only for confusion. Culture looks beyond machinery, culture hates hatred; culture has one great passion, the passion for sweetness and light . . . It is not satisfied till we *all* come to a perfect man, it knows that the sweetness and light of the few must be imperfect until the raw and unkindled masses of humanity are touched with sweetness and light . . . Again and again I have insisted how those are the happy moments of humanity, how those are the marking epochs of people's life, how those are the flowering times for litera- ture and art and all the creative power of genius, when there is a *national* glow of life and thought, when the whole of society is in the fullest measure permeated by thought, sensible to beauty, intelligent and alive. Only it must be *real* thought and *real* beauty; *real* sweetness and *real* light. Plenty of people will try to give the masses, as they call them, an intellectual food prepared and adapted in the way they think proper for the actual condition of the masses. The ordinary popular literature is an example of this way of working on the masses. Plenty of people will try to indoctri- nate the masses with the set of ideas and judgements constituting the creed of their own profession or party. Our religious and political organisations give an example of this way of working on the masses. I condemn neither way; but culture works differently. It does not try to teach down to the level of inferior classes; it does not try to win them for this or that sect of its own, with ready-made judgements and watchwords. It seeks to do away with classes; to make the best that has been thought and known in the world current everywhere; to make all men live in an atmosphere of sweetness and light, where they may use ideas, as it uses them itself, freely, – nourished, and not bound by them. (Arnold, 1869, Introduction and chapter 1)

'The pursuit of perfection', for Arnold, is a moral, intellectual and spiritual journey 'to make reason and the will of God prevail'. Opportunities to achieve 'perfection' in this sense cannot be restricted to a privileged minority, but must be available to 'the raw and unkindled masses of humanity'. Culture, in the sense of the 'best that has been thought and known', is the conduit through which 'real thought and real beauty' will be given to 'the masses'. In modern industrial society, Arnold believes, it is the duty of those already possessing 'culture' to ensure its transmission to 'the masses' who are in danger of being offered inferior 'intellectual food': for example, 'ordinary popular literature'.

Arnold's view of culture has to be understood in the context of his time. Arnold, like other nineteenth-century commentators – for example, Thomas Carlyle, John Ruskin and William Morris – believed that mechanization, urbanization and *laissez-faire* economics would inevitably lead to a morally bankrupt society that would eventually collapse into anarchy. The 1867 Reform Act, which extended the franchise to urban working-class males, was further cause for anxiety: granting political power to an uneducated, undeferential mass of urban dwellers could, it was believed, hasten the anarchy that commentators, such as Arnold, feared. Culture offered through education – remember Arnold was a schools inspector as well as professor of poetry – is the solution because, for Arnold, it generates both a moral and spiritual aspiration to know 'the best that has been known and thought in the world'. For Arnold, to be 'cultured' means having a familiarity with that body of knowledge – philosophy, literature, painting, music – which, for him, constitutes the 'best'. In *Culture and Anarchy* culture understood as a process of humanization becomes conflated with the products through which humanization will be achieved.

<table>
<tr><td rowspan="1" style="vertical-align:middle">ACTIVITY 1.2</td><td>

- Can you suggest any ways in which Arnold's view of culture was a progressive view?
- Use a general history of Victorianism to find out more about the ideas of Arnold, Carlyle, Ruskin and Morris. For example, *The Cambridge Cultural History of Britain: Victorian Britain, Volume 9*, edited by Boris Ford, would be a useful source. For a more detailed account try the relevant chapters in Walter Houghton, *The Victorian Frame of Mind*.
- Arnold sees 'culture' and 'anarchy' as two opposing concepts. The question, as he sets it, is *either* culture *or* anarchy. How do you respond to this? What might be the political effects of this way of thinking? You could return to this when you read the extract from Said later in the chapter.
</td></tr>
</table>

The idea that 'the best that has been known and thought' should be available to all and not simply to an educated elite is potentially democratic in that it implies a widening of access to certain forms of culture. Art galleries, theatre, opera, museums and 'great' literature should be available and accessible to all, and not the preserve of the rich or powerful. In this sense a 'cultured' person is educated and knowledgeable about history, literature, art and philosophy, with the corollary that such knowledge is both civilizing and humanizing. However, you might want to question the claim that culture, in this sense, teaches humane values: some Nazi leaders, as we know, enjoyed and understood art, literature and music. Equally, it is worth noting that the Arnoldian perspective on culture is a restrictive one. It limits the meaning of culture to scholarship and the arts: 'high' culture as opposed to 'popular' or 'mass' culture; Mozart but not Eminem. Nevertheless, Arnold's belief in the beneficial aspects of certain forms of culture was highly influential in determining policies towards education and the arts in Britain until the 1950s, and traces still persist today in discussions about what forms of culture society should value and support. For example, the debate about a national curriculum in British schools has, from time to time, invoked an Arnoldian view of the humanizing effects of teaching 'high' culture (see chapter 7).

ACTIVITY 1.3

In order to explore further the consequences of defining 'culture', along the lines taken by Arnold, try the following activities:

1　Make a list of those products or activities which would and would not count as 'culture' according to Arnold. We have started you off.

Would count	Would not count
• Production of *Hamlet*	TV soap opera
• Sculpture	Knitting
• Paintings	Wallpaper designs
•	

2　Can you identify any common elements amongst the items on each list? If there are commonalities do these suggest why some things might count as culture and others not?

3　Look out for articles in newspapers or magazines which seem to you to offer an Arnoldian perspective, particularly with regard to the arts or education.

4　Try to construct a set of criteria for deciding what is the best that has been thought and known. Note down any problems you have in arriving at a set of criteria.

Now read the extract from an influential essay by James Clifford.

Reading 1.2

Since the turn of the century [1900] objects collected from non-Western sources have been classified in two major categories: as (scientific) cultural artefacts or as (aesthetic) works of art. Other collectables – mass-produced commodities, 'tourist art', curios, and so on – have been less systematically valued; at best they find a place in exhibits of 'technology' or 'folklore'.

The ['modern art-culture system'] classifies objects and assigns them relative value. It establishes the 'contexts' in which they properly belong and between which they circulate. . . . These movements select artefacts of enduring worth or rarity, their value normally guaranteed by a 'vanishing' cultural status or by the selection and pricing mechanisms of the art market. The value of Shaker crafts reflects the fact that Shaker society no longer exists: the stock is limited. In the art world work is recognized as 'important' by connoisseurs and collectors according to criteria that are more than simply aesthetic. . . . Indeed, prevailing definitions of what is 'beautiful' or 'interesting' sometimes change quite rapidly. . . .

While the object systems of art and anthropology are institutionalized and powerful, they are not immutable. The categories of the beautiful, the cultural, and the authentic have changed and are changing. . . .

It is perhaps worth stressing that nothing said here about the historicity of these cultural or artistic categories should be construed as claiming that they are false or denying that many of their values are worthy of support. Like any successful discursive arrangement the art-culture authenticity system articulates considerable domains of truth and scientific progress as well as areas of blindness and controversy. By emphasizing the transience of the system I do so out of a conviction . . . that the classifications and generous appropriations of Western art and culture categories are now much less stable than before. This instability appears to be linked to the growing interconnection of the world's populations and to the contestation since the 1950s of colonialism and Eurocentrism. Art collecting and culture collecting now take place within a changing field of counterdiscourses, syncretisms, and reappropriations originating both outside and inside 'the West'. (Clifford, 1993)

ACTIVITY 1.4

- Who do you think classifies objects into the categories identified above?
- Visit a museum or art gallery and try to identify the ways in which objects are categorized as 'works of art' or 'cultural artefacts', as 'technology' or 'folklore'.

- How are the paintings of Picasso categorized? Are they seen as 'master-pieces' or as examples of Spanish painting? What are the implications of such classification?
- Can you think of any examples of when what is seen as beautiful has changed?

Clifford is particularly concerned with the ways in which non-Western objects have been classified within the system he describes. He is arguing that, in the past, Western ideals of beauty and aesthetics have been imposed on objects from other cultures. Such objects have often been seen as cultural artefacts rather than works of art. Clifford's discussion widens the definition of culture from that used by Arnold. Here it is being used in the sense of all the objects generated by a society or a particular way of life, or at least those that are considered collectable by museums and art galleries. Cultural artefacts such as masks, furniture, cooking equipment, quilts, spears and pots are more likely to be classified according to anthropological criteria in which the purpose is to understand what these objects can reveal about the society from which they originate. On the other hand paintings, sculptures, literature, music and theatre are discussed in terms of their aesthetic values. Of course, as Clifford points out, cultural artefacts such as Shaker furniture can over time become classified as works of art. Another example of such movement from one category to another is that of the beautiful quilts stitched by black Americans. Once seen as examples of 'folklore', these now hang in art galleries and are seen as 'works of art'.

The 'Mass Culture' Debate

An extension of Arnold's thesis on culture was the debate about 'mass culture' that gathered momentum in the 1920s and 1930s and continued throughout the 1940s and 1950s. Developing technologies in the early twentieth century made possible a wider range of media through which communication was possible – cinema, radio, television, equipment for listening to music, newspapers, magazines and commercially produced fiction – with, as a result of compulsory universal education, an increasingly literate audience or readership. The growth of a mass media producing cultural products for a growing market of consumers created concern among those who believed in the civilizing effects of 'high' art. Arnold's fear that 'people will try to indoctrinate the masses' was one response to the spread of a so-called 'mass culture', particularly in the context of the growth of totalitarian states in, for example, Germany and Russia. Others, like F. R. Leavis, an academic in the English Literature Department at the University of Cambridge from the 1930s to the 1960s, and the literary critic Q. D. Leavis, condemned the preference of the majority of the population for the products of the mass media. In *Fiction and the Reading Public*, published in 1932, Q. D. Leavis referred to the reading of popular fiction as 'a drug addiction' which could lead to 'a habit of fantasying [which] will lead to maladjustment in actual life' (pp. 152, 54). F. R. Leavis, in his book *Mass Civilization and Minority Culture*, attacked cinemas for offering films that 'involve surrender, under conditions of hypnotic receptivity, to the cheapest emotional appeals' (Leavis, 1930, p. 10). For cultural critics like the Leavises the concept of culture implied a distinction between culture and mass culture, an opposition in which the term 'mass culture' signified an inferior and debased form of culture (often associated with the US and American influence).

In the years following the Second World War, as Cold War ideologies established themselves, intellectuals in the US continued this debate in relation to concerns about 'the enemies within' American society. Mass culture, it was feared, produced fertile ground for the growth of 'un-American' ideologies (in particular, communism) and threatened the liberalism and pluralism on which it was believed an enduring political and cultural consensus had been built. This apparent consensus was to collapse with the rise of the black civil rights movement and the countercultures of the late 1960s and 1970s (Storey, 1993, pp. 33–4). Now read the following extract from an influential essay by the American critic Dwight Macdonald, written in the 1950s. This essay is part of an anthology published in 1957, *Mass Culture: the Popular Arts in America*, edited by Bernard Rosenberg and David Manning White, which attacked what they saw as the dehumanizing effects of mass culture. As you read bear in mind the following questions and at the end note down your responses:

- What does Macdonald see as the differences between 'folk art' and 'mass culture'?
- What does Macdonald see as the dangers of 'mass culture'?
- What does Macdonald see as the characteristics of 'the mass man'?

Reading 1.3

Folk art grew from below. It was a spontaneous, autochthonous expression of the people, shaped by themselves, pretty much without the benefit of High Culture, to suit their own needs. Mass Culture is imposed from above. It is fabricated by technicians hired by businessmen; its audience are passive consumers, their participation limited to the choice between buying and not buying. The Lords of *kitsch*, in short, exploit the cultural needs of the masses in order to make a profit and/or to maintain their class rule – in Communist countries, only the second purpose obtains . . . Folk art was the people's own institution, their private little garden walled off from the great formal part of their masters; High Culture. But Mass Culture breaks down the wall, integrating the masses into a debased form of High Culture and thus becoming an instrument of political domination . . .

For the masses in historical time are what a crowd is in space: a large quantity of people unable to express themselves as human beings because they are related to one another neither as individuals nor as members of communities – indeed, they are not related to each other at all, but only to something distant, abstract, non-human: a football game or bargain sale in the case of a crowd, a system of industrial production, a party or a State in the case of the masses. The mass man is a solitary atom, uniform with and undifferentiated from thousands and millions of other atoms who go to make up 'the lonely crowd' as David Reisman well calls American society. A folk or a people, however, is a community, i.e., a group of individuals linked to each other by common interests, work, traditions, values, and sentiments. (Macdonald, 1957, p. 60)

For those, like Macdonald, who bemoaned the stultifying and manipulative effects of a commercially produced culture, individuals in modern industrial society were perceived as fragmented, atomized and alienated from a sense of community which had once bestowed identity and belonging. In the same year that Macdonald's essay was published (1957), Richard Hoggart, a Senior Staff Tutor in Literature in the Department of Adult Education at Hull University, England, published *The Uses of Literacy*, in which he argued that the urban working-class cultures of his youth were being destroyed by an Americanized mass-produced culture. Hoggart was born in Leeds in 1918 and spent his childhood in the working-class areas of that city. He gained scholarships to secondary school and later to the University of Leeds, where he gained a first class honours degree in English literature. In the 1960s, Hoggart established the Centre for Contemporary Cultural Studies at the University of Birmingham and was its first director.

Reading 1.4

I suggested earlier that it would be a mistake to regard the cultural struggle now going on as a straight fight between, say, what *The Times* and the picture-dailies respectively represent. To wish that a majority of the population will ever read *The Times* is to wish that human beings were constitutionally different, and is to fall into an intellectual snobbery. The ability to read the decent weeklies is not a *sine qua non* of the good life. It seems unlikely at any time, and is certainly not likely in any period which those of us now alive are likely to know that a majority in any class will have strongly intellectual pursuits. There are other ways of being in the truth. The strongest objection to the more trivial popular entertainment is not that they prevent their readers from becoming highbrow, but that they make it harder for people without an intellectual bent to become wise in their own way . . .

Most mass-entertainments are in the end what D. H. Lawrence described as 'anti-life', They are full of a corrupt brightness, of improper appeals and moral evasions . . . they tend towards a view of the world in which progress is conceived as a seeking of material possessions, equality as a moral levelling, and freedom as the ground for endless irresponsible pleasure. These productions belong to a vicarious spectators' world; they offer nothing which can really grip the brain or heart. They assist a gradual drying-up of the more positive, the fuller, the more co-operative kinds of enjoyment, in which one gains much by giving much. They have intolerable pretensions; and pander to the wish to have things both ways, to do as we want and accept no consequences. A handful of such productions reaches daily the great majority of the population: their effect is both widespread and uniform. (Hoggart, 1957, pp. 281–3)

ACTIVITY 1.5

- What is your response to Macdonald's belief that people are 'passive consumers' of the products offered by a mass media? Think about how you and others known to you respond to TV programmes, what you read in the newspapers, what you see at the cinema. What about readers of the tabloid newspapers? What about those who appear on television game shows? Are they 'passive consumers'?
- Does Hoggart see the people he is discussing as 'passive consumers'? If so, are there any differences between his view and Macdonald's? If not, how would you describe his attitude to 'the great majority of the population'?

You may have thought that Hoggart is more optimistic than Macdonald. Hoggart appears to allow that, despite the fragmentation of modern urban life, 'people without an intellectual bent' can 'become wise in their own way' if they can remain untainted by the blandishments of 'mass culture', whereas for Macdonald the 'large quantity of people unable to express themselves as human beings' appear already doomed to 'a narcotized acceptance of Mass Culture' (Macdonald, 1957, p. 73). The idea that the mass of population in modern society consumes passively, accepting without question the diet of ideas, images, stereotypes offered by the mass media, needs to be questioned, and we shall return to this in more detail in later chapters (see chapters 7 and 9). For now it is worth noting that, while Hoggart is concerned about the possibly enervating effects of a mass culture on the British working class, he does allow them wisdom and intelligence. Macdonald, on the other hand, appears to have little faith that people have any resources to resist their positioning as the 'passive dupes' of an all-encompassing mass media. In order to appreciate more fully the similarities and differences between the two arguments you should consider these extracts in context by reading more widely in the books from which they are taken.

Although Hoggart follows Arnold in a concern for cultural decline and a belief in education as the means of stemming this, he uses a wider concept of culture than cultural critics like the Leavises or Macdonald. For Hoggart, culture is not simply 'the best that has been thought and known' but *all* those activities, practices, artistic and intellectual processes and products that go to make up the culture of a specific group at a particular time. Hoggart argues that the British urban working class developed certain cultural forms through which it could express itself at a particular historical moment (the 1930s), and that these forms were now (in the 1950s) in danger of disappearing. Hoggart's work is justly important because it paved the way for later cultural theorists to study a broader version of culture, which included mass as well as 'high' culture.

Although you are unlikely to encounter ideas about culture in the precise form expressed by Arnold, Macdonald or Hoggart in the work of contemporary cultural theorists, traces of these definitions may persist in general works, in newspaper articles and in general usage. We have introduced you to these ideas because you will find it useful to be able to distinguish these traces from the theories of culture currently employed in the academic study of culture. In the next section we shall begin to consider how theories of culture have developed in recent years. Before you move on you could try the following activities.

ACTIVITY 1.6

- Use the list of suggested reading for this chapter to find out more about the debates over culture in the early part of the twentieth century. John Storey's *An Introductory Guide to Cultural Theory and Popular Culture* would be a useful starting point. We have focused on British and American responses but the debate was carried on with different emphases in other European countries. In chapter 9 we look at the contribution of the Frankfurt School, represented here by the German exiles Theodor Adorno and Max Horkheimer.

- We have, in passing, mentioned the working classes. Are there other groups in society who might have a stake in a particular culture? Do they appear in any of the analyses above?
- Does the term 'mass' adequately describe the population of a society? Make a list of the senses in which the term is used and compare the differences. Whenever you come across the word 'mass' or 'masses' in your reading check it against your list of meanings and think about how it is being used.

Social Definitions of Culture

Of the three definitions of culture that we quoted in the introduction to this chapter, we have so far been concerned with two:

- a general process of intellectual, spiritual and aesthetic development;
- the works and practices of intellectual and especially artistic activity (Williams, 1976, p. 90).

In *The Long Revolution* (1961), Raymond Williams outlines a theory of culture that attempts to link these two definitions with the third: that is, 'a particular way of life, whether of a people, a period, a group, or humanity in general' (Williams, 1976, p. 90). Williams called this:

a 'social' definition of culture, in which culture is a description of a particular way of life, which expresses certain meanings and values not only in art and learning but also in institutions and ordinary behaviour. The analysis of culture, from such a definition, is the clarification of the meanings and values implicit and explicit in a particular way of life, a particular culture. Such analysis will include . . . historical criticism . . . in which intellectual and imaginative works are analysed in relation to particular traditions and societies, but will also include analysis of elements in the way of life that to followers of the other definitions are not 'culture' at all: the organization of production, the structure of the family, the structure of institutions which express or govern social relationships, the characteristic forms through which members of the society communicate. (Williams, 1961, p. 57)

Like Richard Hoggart's, Raymond Williams's origins were working-class. Williams was born in the Welsh border village of Pandy and his father was a railway signalman. Like Hoggart, Williams gained scholarships, enabling him to continue his education at Abergavenny Grammar School and later at Trinity College, Cambridge. He became Professor of Drama at Cambridge University and is a central figure in the development of ideas about the relationship between culture and society.

Williams's definition above proposes that culture is a system by which meanings and ideas are expressed, not only in 'art and learning', but also in 'ordinary behaviour'. This breaks with Arnold's version of culture as 'the best that has been thought and known', and posits culture as a more inclusive and wider-ranging phenomenon. The purpose of cultural analysis, according to Williams, is to clarify and identify the meanings that are expressed in not only 'art and learning', but also 'ordinary behaviour', 'the structure of the family' and the institutions of a society. Now read the following extract from an earlier essay by Williams, first published in 1958.

Reading 1.5

The bus stop was outside the cathedral. I had been looking at the Mappa Mundi, with its rivers out of Paradise, and at the chained library, where a party of clergymen had got in easily, but where I had waited an hour and cajoled a verger before I even saw the chains. Now, across the street, a cinema advertised the *Six-Five Special*[1] and a cartoon version of *Gulliver's Travels*. The bus arrived, with a driver and a conductress deeply absorbed in each other. We went out of the city, over the old bridge, and on through the orchards and the green meadows and the fields red under the plough. Ahead were the Black Mountains, and we climbed among them, watching the steep fields end at the grey wall, beyond which the bracken and heather and whin had not yet been driven back. To the east, along the ridge, stood the line of grey Norman castles; to the west, the fortress wall of the mountains. Then, as we still climbed, the rock changed under us. Here, now, was limestone, and the line of the early iron workings along the scarp. The farming valleys, with their scattered white houses, fell away behind. Ahead of us were the narrower valleys: the steel-rolling mill, the gasworks, the grey terraces, the pitheads. The bus stopped, and the driver and conductress got out, still absorbed. They had done this journey so often, and seen all its stages. It is a journey, in fact, that in one form or another we have all made.

I was born and grew up halfway along that bus journey. Where I lived is still a farming valley, though the road through it is being widened and straightened, to carry the heavy lorries to the north. Not far away, my grandfather, and so back through the generations, worked as a farm labourer until he was turned out of his

---

[1] A musical (1958) based on the popular TV programme of the same name.

cottage and, in his fifties, became a road man. His sons went at thirteen or fourteen on to the farms, his daughters into service. My father, his third son, left the farm at fifteen to be a boy porter on the railway, and later became a signalman, working in a box in this valley until he died. I went up the road to the village school, where a curtain divided the two classes – Second to eight or nine, First to fourteen. At eleven I went to the local grammar school, and later to Cambridge.

Culture is ordinary: that is where we must start. To grow up in that country was to see the shape of a culture, and its modes of change . . .

Culture is ordinary: that is the first fact. Every human society has its own shape, its own purposes, its own meanings. Every human society expresses these, in institutions, and in arts and learning. The making of a society is the finding of common meanings and directions, and its growth is an active debate and amendment under the pressures of experience, contact and discovery, writing themselves into the land . . . We use the word culture in . . . two senses: to mean a whole way of life – the common meanings; to mean the arts and learning – the special processes of discovery and creative effort. Some writers reserve the word for one or other of these senses; I insist on both, and on the significance of their conjunction. The questions I ask about our culture are questions about our general and common purposes, yet also questions about deep personal meanings. Culture is ordinary, in every society and in every mind. (Williams, 1958a, pp. 5–6)

ACTIVITY 1.7

1   Why do you think Williams stresses and repeats the phrase 'culture is ordinary'? Can you think of examples from your own knowledge of culture as the ordinary?

2   Make a list of the things Williams identifies as culture. Can you suggest some of the meanings that might be expressed by the cultures he identifies? We have started this off for you; you carry on.

- The cathedral[2] expresses ideas about religion and worship, Christianity, the importance of religion and worship in the past.
- The steel-rolling mill expresses the significance of heavy industry to Britain's economic prosperity now and in the past.
- The Norman castles express. . .
- The life stories. . .

If we take one example from the list above we can explore further what Williams has in mind when he talks about 'meanings and values'. A cathedral is a large building in which people congregate for an act of worship. If we

---

[2]   The cathedral referred to in Williams's article is Hereford Cathedral. Herefordshire is an English county on the border with Wales.

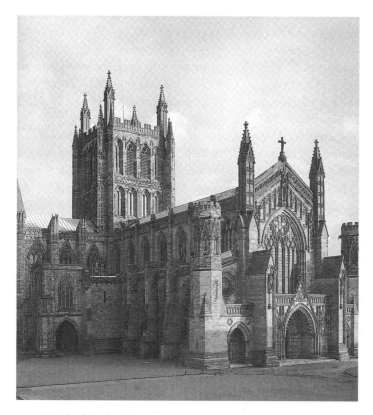

Figure 1.1   Hereford Cathedral

belong to a European or Western society, we will probably recognize a cathedral as a specifically Christian house of worship. If we come from a society that has very different kinds of religious buildings we know what it stands for by relating it to similar buildings in our own cultures – temple, mosque etc. We may also understand a cathedral as a place of historic interest: it tells us about the importance of Christianity in society in the past and the ways in which it was practised. Equally, a cathedral can be understood as a work of art. Visitors come from all over the world to study its architecture, to look at its fine art, to appreciate the beauty and craftsmanship of its stained-glass windows. A cathedral can also mean a tourist attraction, spawning tea rooms, gift shops, guided tours – a piece of heritage that can be marketed at home and abroad. Moreover, specific cathedrals may have another layer of local and particular meanings. Think, for example, of St. Patrick's Cathedral, New York or Sacré Coeur in Paris. You may well be able to think of other meanings that attach themselves to the idea of a cathedral.

The diverse meanings that come to mind when we think or read about cathedrals do not present themselves as intrinsic to the physical presence of the building. We can think about cathedrals, as you are probably doing now, without actually looking at or being present in one. The meanings that attach themselves to physical objects as well as abstract concepts grow out of the ways in which objects or concepts are used by a particular group or society. There was no pre-existent idea of cathedral that preceded the actual design and building of one, although there were strong religious feelings and creative impulses which found their expression in the physical construction of a cathedral. Equally, the ways in which an object or concept may be used can be shaped by the meanings that have grown up around that object or concept. If we take cathedrals as an example, the growth of cathedrals as tourist attractions has come about in part because they have been and are perceived as places of great beauty. An understanding of cathedrals as works of art has led to the practice of making them accessible as places to visit as well as places of worship. You may also have noted that different meanings conflict with and contradict each other. For example, there is surely a tension between understanding a cathedral as a sacred place of worship for the believers of a particular religion and understanding it as a place of beauty that should be accessible to all, or as a marketable tourist attraction. Thinking about this tension and analysing how the tension manifests or resolves itself in actual behaviour and practice can help us to understand the complex relations between religion, the arts, economics and consumerism in secular, contemporary society. The processes by which meanings evolve and interact with behaviour and practice is one that we shall return to thoughout this book.

> **ACTIVITY 1.8**
>
> Try thinking about some other forms of culture in the way we have discussed cathedrals. Consider the meanings that attach to these. Good examples would be: the cinema, the cluster of industrial images (steel-rolling mill, gasworks, terraces, pitheads), 'the Wild West', the main street.

In *The Long Revolution*, Williams expands and develops his assertion that 'culture is ordinary'. At the same time, he spells out very clearly the task of cultural analysis. Now read the following extract from chapter 2 of *The Long Revolution*.

Reading 1.6

Again, such analysis ranges from an 'ideal' emphasis, the discovery of certain absolute or universal, or at least higher and lower, meanings and values, through the 'documentary' emphasis, in which clarification of a particular way of life is the main end in view, to an emphasis which, from studying particular meanings and values, seeks not so much to compare these, as a way of establishing a scale, but by studying their modes of change to discover certain general 'laws' or 'trends', by which social and cultural development as a whole can be better understood . . .

I think we can best understand this if we think of any similar analysis of a way of life that we ourselves share. For we find here a particular sense of life, a particular community of experience hardly needing expression, through which the characteristics of our way of life that an external analyst could describe are in some way passed, giving them a particular and characteristic colour. We are usually most aware of this when we notice the contrasts between generations, who never talk quite 'the same language', or when we read an account of our lives by someone from outside the community, or watch the small differences in style, of speech or behaviour, in someone who has learned our ways yet was not bred in them . . .

The term I would suggest to describe it is *structure of feeling*: it is as firm and definite as 'structure' suggests, yet it operates in the most delicate and least tangible parts of our activity. In one sense, this structure of feeling is the culture of a period: it is the particular living result of all the elements in the general organization . . . I do not mean that the structure of feeling, any more than the social character, is possessed in the same way by the many individuals in the community. But I think it is a very deep and very wide possession, in all actual communities, precisely because it is on it that communication depends. (Williams, 1961, pp. 42, 48)

Here, Williams is concerned to offer a form of cultural analysis that does not have evaluation or comparison as its function but seeks to 'discover certain general "laws"'. Later in the chapter from which this extract is taken, Williams uses Sophocles' *Antigone* to illustrate his point. Let's take two contemporary examples: a production of Shakespeare's *Hamlet* and a pop concert. The aim of the analysis, according to Williams, would not be to produce a comparison of the two events in which one or other is discovered to be superior. Instead, the task would be to seek out similarities as well as differences in content, form and production, and to relate these to the wider structures of the society or community which produced these performances. In so doing, the analysis might reveal the shared attitudes and values of a particular society, community or group. For example, the cultural analyst might be interested in the links between Hamlet, as cynical outsider and/or tormented rebel, and the similar identities often attributed to pop stars, and might then go on to suggest how these identities function in modern societies. However, in order for these identities to be recognized, it is necessary for a group or society to share certain, often tacitly understood, values and attitudes – in this case the various connotations of the rebel/loner/misfit figure – what Williams refers to as 'structure of feeling'.

ACTIVITY 1.9

- Can you think of any values, attitudes in your family, or community, or social group, that could illustrate Williams's 'structure of feeling'?
- Can you widen this to identify examples of structures of feeling in your own society, or other societies more generally?

Williams stresses that it is structures of feeling that enable communication. If we did not share certain common understandings of the world, we would find it extremely difficult to communicate. We used the example of the cathedral, in our discussion above, because we were able to assume that most readers would share with us certain ideas about what a cathedral stands for.

Language, of course, is central to any theory of communication: language is the medium through which shared meanings or structures of feeling are communicated. Verbal language is not the only medium of communication; we also use visual, musical and body languages, often in conjunction with words. Recent developments in sociology and cultural studies have developed Williams's emphasis on the links between culture, language and meaning. However, rather than seeing culture (meanings, beliefs, language) as a reflection of economic and social conditions, which Williams tends to do, these have stressed the ways in which culture itself creates, constructs and constitutes social relations (such as those between men and women, children and parents) and economic relations (for example, those between business and the arts or between industry and environmentalism). Moreover, subsequent developments in the disciplinary areas most concerned with the analysis of culture (social sciences, cultural studies, literary studies, history) have begun to ask questions about how meanings are produced, how they are communicated, which meanings are shared and by which groups, what happens when meanings are contested by different groups. One contemporary definition is that culture is 'the production and circulation of meaning' – the processes by which culture is produced and the forms it takes, rather than simply the 'structure of feeling' or 'way of life' it reveals.

Recent theorists in social theory and cultural studies have put much greater stress on the centrality and the relative autonomy of culture. We cannot just 'read off' culture from society. We need to analyse the role of 'the symbolic' sphere in social life in its own terms . . . This critique gives the production of meaning through language – what is sometimes called *signification* – a privileged place in the analysis of culture. All social practices, recent critics would argue, are organized through meanings – they are *signifying practices* and must therefore be studied by giving greater weight to their cultural dimension. (du Gay et al., 1997, p. 13)

Culture and Power

Whether we choose to see culture as 'the production and circulation of meaning' or as 'a particular way of life', we need to consider carefully its place in constructing, sustaining and reproducing structures and relations of power. A 'structure of feeling' – a particular way of seeing the world – has political implications. The ways in which societies or groups see the world have direct results for how members of a particular society or group treat non-members and are themselves treated. For example, a 'structure of feeling' based on certain ideas about the nature and roles of women and men or on concepts of 'racial' difference can produce practices and behaviours which lead to oppression and discrimination. **Discourses** of gender or race – the ways in which sexual and 'racial' differences are defined, talked about, represented visually – create the conditions in which men and women experience their lives. If we see culture as 'the production and circulation of meaning' then culture is a significant site for the formation of discourses by which one social group or community (a sex, 'race', nation or society) legitimates its power over another group or community.

Equally, culture becomes an important place where power, and the meanings that uphold power, can be resisted. We shall explore the concept of discourse further in chapter 3. Now read the following extract from Edward Said's *Culture and Imperialism*. It may help you to know that 'the administrative massacre' Said refers to occurred in 1865, when the British Governor of Jamaica, F. J. Eyre, ordered the killing of many black people in Jamaica as a means of 'controlling' social unrest and rioting among Jamaican blacks. Said's use of the term 'narrative' is close in meaning to the term 'discourse' used above, and very broadly speaking can be taken to mean the stories we tell, the stories we are told, the stories that circulate in a particular culture through literature, art, music. He is, it should also be noted, mainly concerned with those elements of culture that Arnold would have categorized as 'the best that has been thought and known', and has less to say about the narratives or discourses constructed in other forms of culture.

Reading 1.7

Introduction

. . . The main battle in imperialism is over land, of course; but when it came to who owned the land, who had the right to settle and work on it, who kept it going, who won it back, and who now plans its future – these issues were reflected, contested, and even for a time decided in narrative. As one critic has suggested, nations themselves *are* narrations. The power to narrate, or to block other narratives from forming and emerging, is very important to culture and imperialism, and constitutes one of the main connections between them. Most important, the grand narratives of emancipation and enlightenment mobilized people in the colonial world to rise up and throw off imperial subjection; in the process, many Europeans and Americans were also stirred by these stories and their protagonists, and they too fought for new narratives of equality and human community . . .

Arnold believed that culture palliates, if it does not altogether neutralize, the ravages of a modern, aggressive, mercantile, and brutalizing urban existence. You read Dante or Shakespeare in order to keep up with the best that was thought and known, and also to see yourself, your people, society, and tradition in their best lights. In time, culture comes to be associated, often aggressively, with the nation or state; this differentiates 'us' from 'them', almost always with some degree of xenophobia. Culture in this sense is a source of identity . . .

Chapter 2

. . . Most modern readers of Matthew Arnold's anguished poetry, or of his celebrated theory in praise of culture, do not also know that Arnold connected the 'administrative massacre' ordered by Eyre [the British Governor of Jamaica in 1865] with tough British policies towards colonial Eire [Ireland] and strongly approved both; *Culture and Anarchy* is set plumb in the middle of the Hyde Park Riots of 1867, and what Arnold had to say about culture was specifically believed to be a deterrent to rampant disorder – colonial, Irish, domestic. Jamaicans, Irishmen, and women, and some historians bring up these massacres at 'inappropriate' moments, but most Anglo-American readers of Arnold remain oblivious, see them – if they look at them at all – as irrelevant to the more important cultural theory that Arnold appears to be promoting for all the ages. (Said, 1993, pp. xiii, 157–8)

ACTIVITY 1.10

- Try to express in your own words why Said is critical of Arnold's theory of culture.
- How would you respond to the statement 'culture is civilizing' in the light of Said's argument?
- Can you find or think of any stories of cultural forms which appear to uphold imperialism? The nineteenth-century novel, old films, travel writing, poetry or news reports could prove illuminating. You could ask whether there are forms of imperialism operating in the world today. How are these upheld by contemporary narratives? Comic strips are a good source of material. We will look in more detail at cultural imperialism in chapter 6.
- Said states that culture is 'a source of identity': what do you understand him to mean by this?

In chapter 2 we shall explore the relationship between culture and identity further. For now, it is enough that you begin to be aware of how culture ('the production and circulation of meanings') can play a part in constructing a sense of who 'we' are in relation to 'them' – in European imperialism this is the colonial encounter between European and non-European. And the act of writing, as we have done, 'European' and 'non-European' is itself complicit in the production and circulation of certain meanings which legitimate the idea of the European as superior. To identify someone as 'non-European' is to define her or him against the implicit normality of 'European' and to consolidate that 'structure of feeling' in which Europe is represented as the centre of the world, around which other countries and identities place themselves.

You may also have noted that even those who theorize about culture and the purpose of its study are involved in the legitimation of certain ways of understanding and knowing the world. Said argues that Arnold's defence of culture had a political aim that was specific to the historical moment that produced *Culture and Anarchy*. He suggests that sections of Victorian Britain believed that the civilizing effects of 'the best that has been thought and known' would act as a deterrent to the growing unrest among diverse groups, both at home and abroad. This unrest took the form of demands for political and civil rights and/or independent status from Britain: Arnold, Said suggests, was concerned that these democratic demands would threaten social stability and therefore required suppression by political as well as cultural means. Said, himself of Palestinian origin, is committed to rendering visible the repressive and oppressive nature of Western imperialism, and the ways in which cultural products, particularly the novel, sustain this. Williams, whose ideas we looked at in the previous section, writes from a socialist and Marxist position, in which he seeks to redress the inequalities and injuries of the British class system. Feminist cultural theorists have in mind the particular subordination of women. There is nothing inherently sinister in developing theories from within, or to serve a particular political purpose. Indeed, it could be argued that all academic theories are grounded in struggles over power. Knowledge, Pierre Bourdieu has argued, is part of that 'cultural capital' which, along with financial resources, enables certain groups in society to exert and maintain a privileged position (Bourdieu, 1984; see chapters 7 and 9). In order to challenge dominance and privilege it is necessary to produce 'new' knowledge, as both Said and Williams have done. If you read further in the writings of Williams or Said you will find that both of them make their own political position clear and explicit – the same cannot be said of all theorists. Cultural theories, like all cultural forms, are always related, albeit in complex ways, to the particular historical moment when they are produced and the political climates in which they circulate. As a student of culture you will learn to contextualize the material you encounter, both historically and politically.

The final extract in this chapter is from an essay by the feminist anthropologist Sherry Ortner, published in 1974: 'Is female to male as nature is to culture?' Use the following questions as a guide to your reading:

- What is the problem that Ortner identifies as in need of explanation?
- In what senses is the concept of culture used in this extract?

Reading 1.8

The secondary status of woman in society is one of the true universals, a pancultural fact. Yet within that universal fact, the specific cultural conceptions and symbolizations of woman are extraordinarily diverse and even mutually contradictory. Further, the actual treatment of women and their relative power and contribution vary enormously from culture to culture, and over different periods in the history of particular cultural traditions. Both these points – the universal fact and the cultural variation – constitute problems to be explained . . .

It is important to sort out the levels of the problem. The confusion can be staggering. For example, depending on which aspect of Chinese culture we look at, we might extrapolate any of several entirely different guesses concerning the status of women in China. In the ideology of Taoism, *yin*, the female principle, and *yang*, the male principle, are given equal weight . . . Hence we might guess that maleness and femaleness are equally valued in the general ideology of Chinese culture. Looking at the social structure, however, we see the strongly emphasized patrilineal descent principle, the importance of sons, and the absolute authority of the father in the family. Thus we might conclude that China is the archetypal patriarchal society. Next, looking at the actual roles played, power and influence wielded, and material contributions made by women in Chinese society – all of which are, upon observation, quite substantial – we would have to say that women are allotted a great deal of (unspoken) status in the system. Or again, we might focus on the fact that a goddess, Kuan Yin, is the central (most worshipped, most depicted) deity in Chinese Buddhism, and we might be tempted to say, as many have tried to say about goddess-worshipping cultures in prehistoric and early historical societies, that China is actually a sort of matriarchy. In short, we must be absolutely clear about *what* we are trying to explain before explaining it. (Ortner, 1974, pp. 86–7)

ACTIVITY 1.11

- Can you list the different aspects of Chinese society and culture that Ortner draws on to make her point?
- Use a similar list to attempt the same exercise with regard to your own society. Do you find a similar range of diverse and contradictory meanings about 'woman in society'?

Ortner, rightly, draws attention to the often contradictory ways in which woman is represented in Chinese culture. At this stage in her analysis she doesn't attempt to connect the 'actual roles' played by women in China to the 'symbolization' of woman in culture, but she does stress the importance of being clear about precisely what is being explained. As students of culture you too should aspire to this kind of clarity. Make sure when you read, write or speak about women, or indeed any other social group, that you are clearly distinguishing between **symbolizations** and lived experience. Beware of assuming that films, TV, novels, paintings, advertisements and newspaper reports offer a direct reflection of the actual roles played and experience lived. In chapter 3 we shall take up further the points just made, by exploring what we mean by representation and how it works to produce meaning.

Conclusions

For now, we hope that this chapter has enabled you to begin thinking about how the concept of culture is defined. The process of definition that you have engaged in here should continue as you read and study. You will, we hope, want to revisit and refine your understanding of the term culture as an on-going process. You could begin this now by returning to the sentences about culture that you wrote at the very beginning of this chapter. Have your ideas altered? Would you add to or qualify your original statement?

Chapter 2
Identity and Difference

Introduction

In chapter 1 we examined a range of meanings for the term 'culture'. Culture, as we saw, is inextricably linked with the social groupings and social institutions which constitute society at any given time and in any specific place. Hence culture requires and implies interactions between people, between groups of people and between institutions. All of this might seem to suggest that individuals, you and I as unique, autonomous human subjects, have very little to do with the workings of culture. None the less, although the cultural forms and practices produced in any society are shaped by the structures of that society, they are also shaped by the **subjectivities** of individual women and men in our roles as social actors. For example, in chapter 1 we suggested that Matthew Arnold was part of the social grouping (the gender and class positions he occupied at a specific historical moment) whose interests his version of culture expressed. Yet he was also an individual who experienced himself in daily life as a unique human being with the ability to act autonomously, despite the social structures within which he was necessarily located. This ability to act independently is often referred to as **agency**. Equally, the **identities** that individuals adopt in order to define themselves are produced, at least in part, from the cultural and social contexts in which we find ourselves and from which we draw certain assumptions about 'human nature', 'individuality' and 'the self'.

By the end of this chapter we shall have explored more precisely what is meant by the concepts of identity and difference and why they are significant for the study of culture. (Although we have mentioned subjectivity here we shall deal with this more fully in chapter 8.) You will also have a brief opportunity to consider how these differing ideas about individual identity are represented in a specific representational form: the personal life narrative or autobiography. This will lead into the next chapter, which takes up and develops further the idea of representation and its relation to reality.

Who am I?

> **ACTIVITY 2.1**
>
> Write a short paragraph – no more than two or three lines – describing yourself. Alternatively make a list of things which comprise the way you see yourself.

It would be impossible to cover all the possibilities you may have included but the following are probably some of the things you mentioned. You may well have mentioned things not listed here. If so, try to identify which aspects of identity they are concerned with. Here is our list:

- sex, age, occupation, ethnicity, sexual orientation (social);
- hair colour, skin colour, eye colour, bodyshape, physical disabilities, height, kind of clothes worn (physical appearance);
- lively, quiet, shy, concerned for others, morose, a loner, gregarious (personality);
- Irish, Chinese, American, Nigerian (nationality);
- Catholic, Jewish, Muslim (religion);
- mother, father, daughter, son, niece, grandfather (family relationships);
- barman, waitress, postman, student, teacher, architect (occupation);
- interested in music, a film goer, football-mad, politically committed (cultural).

These categories, as you have probably realized by now, are not watertight. Skin colour can also be a mark of social identity; physical disability may not simply be about appearance, but may have ramifications for all other aspects of identity; sex may have some bearing on how far appearance is important to identity (women are more likely to experience their identity as linked to how they look); political commitment may derive from being born into a certain class or nationality. Some of you may have defined yourselves according to a specific religious faith, and this could be linked to nationality, to ethnicity, to personality and to cultural markers. Or you may have felt that your occupational identity (for example, 'student') is currently the most significant marker of who you are. On the other hand, you may feel that none of these categories captures the 'real you'. You might see yourself as a self detached from society, nation, faith – an individual defined less by the categories above than by an inner sense of a unique self that is the 'true' you and that cannot be fitted easily into these external categories. We shall return to the ways in which identities are marked, but for now we want to explore further the idea that at the heart of each individual there is a 'real' self in which resides some essence of authentic personhood.

However we describe ourselves and however many categories we draw upon (social, personal, biological, cultural etc.), we tend and want to believe that there is a 'real me' in which resides the essence or core of our nature. We want to believe that this 'real' self pre-exists or is independent of the categories mentioned above. We sometimes believe that this 'real me' is hidden or suppressed by the demands of social roles or cultural conventions that require a public facade. A persistent narrative found in novels, films, TV and plays is the man or woman whose story traces a quest for this kind of private, inner identity. How often have you heard people say, and you may well have said it yourself, 'I need time to find myself'? This belief that a unique 'true' self-hood lies within the psyche of each individual and that each individual has the right to express and protect that uniqueness has provided the basis of **humanism**, the predominant philosophy of the individual over the past two centuries in the Western world.

Matthew Arnold appealed to humanist beliefs when he argued that culture could offer every human being the means to a fully realized moral life. Arnold assumed that human beings, more or less evolved, are the same everywhere and in all times, and that culture, as defined by him, would speak to some essential human nature that transcends social, historical and biological differences. Arnold also espoused **liberalism**, in that he believed that education and 'Culture' were the keys which would unlock individual potential and that such opportunities should be open to all, regardless of social distinctions.

> **ACTIVITY 2.2**
>
> How far do you think this is true, i.e. that access to culture (as defined by Arnold) will provide opportunities for self-fulfilment? Can you see any problems with this argument? Can you think of any examples where culture, in Arnold's sense, might have different meanings for different groups? Look at reading 2.3. How are the experiences narrated here linked to a sense of identity?

It does seem that a belief in a fundamental, ahistorical human nature is problematic. Historical moment, nationality, ethnicity, sex and social circumstances do make a difference, and therefore do determine the way we see ourselves and the way we think and act. Yet we continue to experience ourselves as individuals with the feelings, beliefs and attitudes that make us autonomous, unique beings, and prefer to believe that we are not simply the products of external forces such as social structures or historical circumstances. Perhaps it is more accurate to understand identity as the interface between a private sense of self that includes conscious and unconscious feelings, rational and irrational motivations, personal beliefs and values, and those factors that constitute the social context in which we experience those feelings and motivations (for example, age, ethnicity, sex). If our deepest desires and our most personal experiences constitute an individual consciousness, then identity is the way we may choose to represent ourselves and act out our thoughts, beliefs and emotions in the social world.

One of the differences between individual consciousness and identity is that individual consciousness, despite its acquisition in a social context, is an internalized combination of ideas and feelings, while identity may be bestowed by others as well as chosen by ourselves. For example, a woman experiencing her first childbirth may find herself identified by medical experts, midwives and health visitors as a mother, long before she herself has consciously adopted this identity. Another example is the identity of patient which is conferred upon those in hospital; an identity which requires and expects certain behaviours which may be at odds with other aspects of the individual. Throughout our lives we are offered a variety of possible social identities as part of our experience of work, family, sexuality, culture and leisure. Sometimes different identities are contradictory and seemingly impossible to reconcile; nearly always identity positions are located in relations of power, in the binary opposition 'us/them'. Now read the following extract by the artist Rasheed Araeen. Araeen is the founding editor of a quarterly journal, *Third Text*, published in Britain since 1987. *Third Text* provides a space in which 'Third World perspectives on contemporary art and culture' can be expressed, debated and heard (Jordan and Weedon, 1995, pp. 316, 435–42).

Reading 2.1

I was born in India, when India was under the British Raj. As a teenager I grew up, spent my early youth and was educated in Pakistan. At the age of 29, inspired by the West's achievement in art in the 20th century, and to fulfil my own aspirations to be a modern artist, I left my country to live in Europe. I have now lived and worked in London for 27 years. I often travel to Pakistan to see my mother, brothers and sisters, and also some friends. I can say I'm Asian, Indian, Pakistani, British,

European, Muslim, Oriental, secular, modernist, postmodernist, and so on . . . But what do these things mean? Do they define my identity? Can I accept all of them as part of my life, or must I choose one thing or another according to someone else's notion about my identity? I have no problem in saying that I'm all of these things, and perhaps none of these things at the same time . . .

In the summer of 1970 we had a grand party, to which hundreds of people from the art world were invited . . . As I was having drinks and chatting with my friends in my studio, an elderly well-dressed gentleman moved toward us . . . 'I like your work very much' he said as we began to talk. I thanked him and we moved around together in the studio. As we were looking at various works something suddenly occurred to me, and I asked him. 'How did you know that this was my work?' 'Aren't you an Arab?' he replied looking at my face. 'No, I'm from Pakistan,' I said, becoming rather puzzled by all this: 'Oh, it's all the same. You are Muslim.' 'Yes,' I said reluctantly. 'You see, this kind of work could have been conceived only by a Muslim. I cannot imagine a European doing this work,' he began to explain politely.

Next day somebody told me that the person I had met was the Professor of Fine Art at the Slade School of Art, and that he was an important member of the art establishment . . . It was the first time that I became aware that my work had something to do with Islamic tradition. It was a disturbing discovery, because I have never made any connection between my work and my being a Muslim. They were two different things. Moreover I was never interested in Islamic art, or concerned with the expression of my cultural identity. My interest was in modernism. (Rasheed Araeen, 'How I discovered my Oriental soul in the wilderness of the West', cited in Jordan and Weedon, 1995, pp. 439–40)

As Jordan and Weedon suggest, Rasheed Araeen is forced to confront the way in which his work and, by extension, his identity is defined by others. He aspires to be 'a modern artist' working in the European tradition of modernism. However, the professor of fine art sees him as 'Arab', producing Islamic art, and insists that his work cannot be seen as 'European'. The professor's comments, despite his praise and kindness, fix Araeen in a particular identity that by definition excludes him from other possible identities. Because he is perceived as 'Muslim' he cannot, at the same time, be 'European'. To be identified as 'Muslim' is to be identified as 'not-European', 'not-Christian'. Identity definitions function to classify and categorize: the identity 'Muslim' is a marker of **difference** from those who are categorized as 'European' or 'Christian'. That Araeen sees himself as both non-religious and Muslim, as Pakistani, Indian and British, and his work as modernist, doesn't matter. Because the professor represents the British art establishment he has the power to define what is and what is not art, how it should be valued and how Araeen and his art fit into this. The binary logic of Western thought insists that it is impossible to be simultaneously 'Oriental' and 'Western' – each identity depends upon the other for its meaning. Identity and difference are about inclusion and exclusion. If you are British you cannot also be Japanese, if you are male you cannot also be female, if you are young you cannot also be old. Or can you?

ACTIVITY 2.3

Can you think of any occasions when you have been given an identity that did not fit? Have the identity labels you use changed over your lifetime?

The point to grasp is that identities are relational and contingent rather than permanently fixed. They depend upon what they are defined against, and this may change over time or be understood differently in different places. In Britain in the 1960s, Araeen is defined by the professor as 'Arab', a generic identity that signifies his difference from Europeans. In other circumstances, possibly when he visits his family in Pakistan, he might find himself defined as Pakistani in order to mark his difference from Indians. The other point to note is that the identity positions within which we locate ourselves or are located by others are neither neutral nor equal. The act of naming, as we saw with the professor of fine art, is, however liberal and kindly meant, an act of power. It is he who defines and places Araeen from his position as a representative of Western Eurocentric knowledge, and it is Western logic and knowledge that have defined the ways in which it is possible for us to think about who we are. For example, have you ever heard Europeans described as non-Asians, have you ever heard white people described as non-blacks? Yet the terms 'non-European' and 'non-white' are frequently used to define those from Asia or Africa.

Going back to the account by Araeen, did you notice how the professor of fine art was able to define Araeen by reference to his appearance ('"Aren't you an Arab?" he replied looking at my face')? Differences are marked symbolically as well as experienced socially. In the case of Araeen, the symbolic marker of difference is his physical appearance and skin colour. Henry Louis Gates Jr, a professor of African-American studies in the United States, argues, in the extract that follows, that 'race' is not a biological given but a linguistic construct that functions to mark symbolically difference and 'otherness'. Race, Gates insists, is not an objective term of categorization but 'a dangerous trope'. As he comments, later in the article from which this extract is taken, 'who has seen a black or red person, a white, yellow, or brown? These terms are arbitrary constructs, not reports of reality' (Gates, 1986, p. 5).

Reading 2.2

Race, as a meaningful criterion within the biological sciences, has long been recognized to be a fiction. When we speak of 'the white race' or 'the black race,' 'the Jewish race' or 'the Aryan race,' we speak in biological misnomers and, more generally, in metaphors . . .

The sense of difference defined in popular usages of the term 'race' has both described and *inscribed* differences of language, belief system, artistic tradition, and gene pool as well as all sorts of supposedly natural attributes such as rhythm, athletic ability, cerebration, usury, fidelity, and so forth. The relation between 'racial character' and these sorts of characteristics has been inscribed through tropes of race, lending the sanction of God, biology, or the natural order to even presumably unbiased descriptions of cultural tendencies and differences . . . In 1973 I was amazed to hear a member of the House of Lords describe the differences between Irish Protestants and Catholics in terms of their 'distinct and clearly definable differences of race.' 'You mean to say that you can tell them apart?' I asked incredulously. 'Of course,' responded the Lord. 'Any Englishman can.' (Gates, 1986, p. 4)

Identity also operates through social and material conditions. The symbolic markers of difference will have real effects on the lived experience of people's social relations. So, for example, in eighteenth- and nineteenth-century Europe and America black Africans were symbolically and socially marked by their colour as 'inferior' to white people. As a result, they were treated as less than human, sold into slavery and transported from their homelands, prevented from learning to read and write, physically abused and materially and socially disadvantaged long after the specific practices of slavery were abolished. The ways in which groups are symbolically marked (represented) will shape the social relations and practices that constitute lived experience. Equally, social practices of inclusion and exclusion are based on classification systems (e.g. man/woman, black/white, European/American/Eastern, First World/Third World, lesbian/homosexual/heterosexual) that rely on symbolic representation for their maintenance. For example, the assertion of national identities is frequently represented symbolically by national flags or songs. The 'Stars and Stripes', the US flag, is a powerful global marker of American identity. In some countries the carrying of a small handbag by a man would be seen as a symbol or marker of his 'effeminacy': 'real' men don't carry handbags. Femininity has been symbolically marked in a variety of ways at different times and in different places. In nineteenth-century Europe and America a tiny waist was a mark of femininity. In the 1950s blonde hair and an hourglass figure were the symbols of femininity, with Marilyn Monroe as its cinematic epitome. The things people use, the rituals they follow, the way they dress and appear function to define who they are and, importantly, who they are not. Symbolic markers are vital to the construction and maintenance of identities and differences and are inextricably intertwined and interdependent with social processes and practices. Thus, the man carrying a handbag can be seen to be 'effeminate' and can therefore be treated in certain ways; Araeen can be seen to be 'Oriental' and this, in the eyes of the art establishment, legitimates the exclusion of his work from the modernist tradition of European art and his exclusion from the category 'European modern artist'.

This discussion of identity would not be complete without considering the tension between **essentialist** and **non-essentialist** perspectives on identity. By essentialist we mean the idea that identity is fixed in an originating moment, that there is a 'true', authentic, unchanging set of characteristics that belong to, say, Asians, and an equally authentic, fixed set of characteristics that can be attributed to Europeans. An essentialist perspective would maintain that these characteristics do not change across time and are shared by all Asians and all Europeans. An essentialist perspective would maintain that there is something intrinsically 'Asian' or 'British' or 'Japanese' that transcends history or is inherent in the person. The English lord cited by Gates had adopted an essentialist position with regard to Irish Protestants and Catholics. A non-essentialist perspective questions whether it is possible to speak of a 'true' identity that is fixed for all time and in all places. For example, in what sense is it possible to define a third-generation Japanese woman, living in America, who is unable to speak Japanese, as 'Japanese'. What is it that determines her identity as Japanese or not-Japanese? Is it biological genes, citizenship in the sense, for example, of holding an American or Japanese passport as a naturalized citizen, language, place of birth, place of current residence or a personal and subjective sense of herself as 'Japanese' or 'American'?

Now read the following by Suheir Hammad who is an author and a poet. The piece was written in the aftermath of 9/11.

Reading 2.3

Composites

I am packing my backpack with an eye towards minimalism. I want to travel with as little as possible. I left New York a few weeks ago, and the distance has been mostly good for me. I will travel to Morocco from Gibraltar, like countless pilgrims before me, searching for peace of mind in the amazing landscape. I am a woman in travel alone. I am an American woman whose passport is valid. I am a woman raised a Muslim, who knows both the beauty and the weaknesses that I will come across in a Muslim nation. I am a New Yorker whose horizon was forever altered on a brilliant Tuesday morning. I am an Arab woman, unmarried, who knows how not to engage with strangers. I am a poet who loves strangers.

And, so I have to pack lightly, because you see, I already have to carry so much with me. And those who would say, 'Unpack the American, leave behind the gender for once,' I ask them, 'What would you leave behind?' I can pretend I am not a feminist, I can keep quiet about it, but my analysis does not go away. And in feminist circles, where the fear of anti-Jewish racism has become a muzzle on any critique of Zionism, I can't not be me – a Palestinian whose ancestry traces itself to the 1948 territories, whose existence undermines the legitimacy of the state of Israel. Complicated? Not really. We are all composites of where we come from and where we want to go. I want to go to a better, more just world. I have to bring all of me there. I want you to bring all of you. (Hammad, 2002, pp. 470–1).

ACTIVITY 2.4

- How does Hammad identify herself?
- Is she adopting an essentialist, non-essentialist or anti-essentialist perspective?
- How do other people identify Hammad?
- What difficulties might this give rise to?
- What is her solution?

To complete your work on this section you should now read the following extract from Trinh T. Minh-ha's *Woman, Native, Other: Writing, Postcoloniality, and Feminism*. Trinh T. Minh-ha is a filmmaker and composer, as well as a writer and teacher, living in the USA.

Reading 2.4

A critical difference from myself means that I am not i, am within and without i. I/i can be I or i, you and me both involved. We (with capital W) sometimes include(s), other times exclude(s) me. You and I are close, we intertwine, you may stand on the other side of the hill once in a while, but you may also be me, while remaining what you are and what i am not. The differences made *between* entities comprehended as absolute presences – hence the notions of *pure origin* and *true self* – are an outgrowth of a dualistic system of thought peculiar to the Occident (the 'onto-theology' which characterizes Western metaphysics). They should be distinguished from the differences grasped *both between* and *within* entities, each of these being understood as multiple presence. Not One, not two either. 'I' is, therefore, not a unified subject, a fixed identity, or that solid mass covered with layers of superficialities one has gradually to peel off before one can see its true face. 'I' is, itself, *infinite layers*. Its complexity can hardly be conveyed through such typographic conventions as I, i, or I/i. Thus, I/i am compelled by the will to say/unsay, to resort to the entire gamut of personal pronouns to stay near this fleeing *and* static essence of Not-I. Whether I accept it or not, the natures of *I, i, you, s/he, We, we, they,* and *wo/man* constantly overlap. They all display a necessary ambivalence for the line dividing I and *Not-I, us* and *them,* or *him* and *her* is not (cannot) always (be) as clear as we would like it to be. Despite our desperate, eternal attempt to separate, contain, and mend, categories always leak. Of all the layers that form the open (never finite) totality of 'I', which is to be filtered out as superfluous, fake, corrupt, and which is to be called pure, true, real, genuine, original, authentic? Which, indeed, since all interchange, revolving in an endless process? . . . *Authenticity* as a need to rely on an 'undisputed origin,' is prey to an obsessive fear: that of *losing* a *connection*. Everything must hold together. (Minh-ha, 1989, p. 90)

ACTIVITY 2.5

- What do you think Minh-ha means when she says that the 'line dividing *I* and *Not-I, us* and *them,* or *him* and *her* is not (cannot) always (be) as clear as we would like it to be'?
- Think about the pronouns Minh-ha refers to: what meanings are associated with these? Can you think of circumstances in which the use of these pronouns and their meanings might shape how a person is treated or treats others? Try to find specific examples from your own experience.
- Why do you think Minh-ha distinguishes between 'I' and 'i'?
- Do you think Minh-ha is right when she says we make a 'desperate, eternal attempt to separate, contain, and mend'? If you agree with her, why do you think this is? Who is the 'our' she refers to here?
- How might Minh-ha's ideas link to what Suheir Hammad says in reading 2.3?

Social Constructivist Approaches to Identity

Individuals experience their lives within a particular society at a particular time. The ways in which we act and experience ourselves are shaped by the social environment within which we exist and our relations with others. We are defined and define ourselves in terms of how others see us, how we see others, how we act with other people and how other people respond to us, not only on an individual basis but also within social institutions such as the family, the workplace, the school. Equally, the ways in which we are able to act, respond and see ourselves may be shaped by the material and economic circumstances of our environment. Karl Marx famously asserted that 'It is not the consciousness of men that determines their being, but, on the contrary, their social being that determines their consciousness' (Marx, 1859). Marx was particularly concerned with the relationship people had to modes of economic production and exchange, but in order to argue this he first had to show that human consciousness did not pre-exist the actual circumstances and experiences of people's lives, but was produced by those circumstances and experiences, what is sometimes called a **materialist** view of society. In order to clarify for yourself what this means you should attempt the exercise below.

> **ACTIVITY 2.6**
>
> Imagine you are a woman with no educational qualifications, a low-paid job and a family to care for, living in a rural area, many miles from the nearest city, and you want to become a writer. In what ways might these circumstances influence your realization of this ambition? Be as specific as possible in detailing the ways in which you might be constrained or aided in your aspirations.

You may have noted any of the following:

- Lack of money might make it impossible to purchase the equipment you would need, e.g. computer, typewriter, books, paper.
- The necessity of earning an income, however small, might make it impossible to find the time to write.
- The lack of formal education might mean limited access to other books from which to discover the tricks of the trade. It might also mean difficulties with reading and writing generally.
- The lack of formal education might have developed a sense that 'people like me don't become writers' and a consequent lack of confidence.
- A sense of guilt might be felt that the time being used to write rightfully belongs to the family; the belief that it is a mother's role to give time and care to her family and that spending time in activities outside this role is 'selfish'.
- The physical isolation and distance from the centres of publishing would be an obstacle to getting anything into print.

It does seem, doesn't it, as if material circumstances would determine the way in which this woman viewed herself and could militate against her becoming a writer. It does seem as if 'her social being' would foster a consciousness of her own limitations and 'the place' she should occupy in society. Yet . . .

Women with similar circumstances to those detailed above have written and published books. For example, Evelyn Haythorne, who grew up in a mining village during the Second World War, wrote and published an autobiographical account of her childhood (Haythorne, 1990). She kept diaries, despite her mother's discouragement, wrote in secret and only showed the book to her husband when it was ready to be published. While Evelyn Haythorne may have been an exceptional woman, her story does suggest that while consciousness is, in part, formed from material circumstances, this does not preclude individuals from acting against the grain of the structures which shape and determine consciousness. Social forces might predispose individuals like our fictional woman or Evelyn Haythorne not to realize their ambitions, but that does not mean no one in such circumstances will ever become a writer. The possibility of some human agency, choice and self-determination remains, however constrained by social structures.

The point we are making is that social factors have an impact on our sense of identity in a variety of complex ways. Little girls, it is claimed, learn what it means to be women as a result of their experience in the family, at school and later in the workplace, as well as from books, magazines, newspapers, TV, films and other media. Feminist approaches to gender have argued that girls align themselves with femininity and men with masculinity as a result of the social relations experienced in childhood and adolescence. Girls are not 'naturally' feminine, nor boys 'naturally' masculine. These are learned identities. **Social constructivist** approaches to gender have been justifiably influential in breaking the link between sex and biological destiny – all women are not inherently 'maternal', for example. However, more recently writers have questioned the idea that masculinity and femininity are polarized constructs into which individuals are neatly slotted as a result of the lessons learned at school and home. Rather than there being a single form of femininity or masculinity, it has been suggested that we should think in terms of a range of femininities or masculinities that may be taken up by individuals. Moreover, rather than being socialized into one specific gender identity that remains fixed and unchanging, it is possible for individuals to change their sense of identity over time (Crowley and Himmelweit, 1992). Again, the idea that we achieve a stable gender identity at maturity is at odds with many people's experience: both women and men resist some elements of gender identity, while accepting others. Many women gain satisfaction and enjoyment from their maternal and caring roles, but react strongly against the idea that this should be their primary role, while at the same time feeling guilty if they are not 'perfect' mothers. Many men reject the idea that to be masculine they need to be dominant and aggressive, yet complain of feeling 'threatened' by assertive women. Material and social factors can explain the construction of particular identities at specific historical moments, but they do not explain why individuals invest in identity positions that are not always in their best interests, or the depth of attachment to a particular identity, to the extent that an individual is willing to die or kill to maintain that identity.

Louis Althusser developed Marx's work on ideologies in order to try to explain why particular positions are taken up by individuals. In his essay 'Ideology and ideological state apparatuses', Althusser revises Marx's model in which the base – the economic mode of production of a society – is seen as determining the superstructure – social relations, ideologies, political and social institutions (Althusser, 1971). In place of the Marxist model, Althusser emphasizes the ways in which individuals are **interpellated** into subject positions by a process of identification. For example, the new mother sees herself in a variety of representations of motherhood within her society, and is 'recruited' to the subject position 'mother' by an act of recognition: 'yes, that's me, yes, that's how it is'. For Althusser, ideology exists in everyday commonplaces, in what we call 'common sense', as well as in religious, political and philosophical systems of thought. Ideology is apparent in all that strikes us as self-evident and 'obvious', in what Althusser calls 'obviousnesses which we cannot fail to recognize and before which we have the inevitable and natural reaction of crying out (aloud or in the "still, small voice of conscience"): "That's obvious! That's right! That's true!"' (Althusser, 1971, p. 161). This process of interpellation takes place at the level of the unconscious as well as consciously, and is the means by which subjects are constructed. For Althusser, the subject is not the same as the individual. Subjectivity is a constructed category produced by ideology, 'the category of the subject is constitutive of all ideology, but at the same time and immediately I add that the category of the subject is only constitutive of all ideology in so far as all ideology has the function (which defines it) of "constituting" concrete individuals as subjects' (Althusser, 1971, p. 160).

Althusser's essay emphasizes the role of symbolic systems in the production of identities. In particular, he drew on the work of Jacques Lacan (see chapter 8) in order to link the psychoanalytic and material dimensions in explanations of why individuals take up, attach themselves to and invest in particular identity positions. In chapter 8 you will have the opportunity to explore further the ideas of Lacan and the concept of subjectivity. Now read the following by bell hooks, writer and essayist. This is taken from her memories of her childhood, growing up in the southern states of the USA.

Reading 2.5

When they talk about same-sex love they use the word *funny*. They never say the word *homosexual*. As small children we think to be called funny is a nice way of talking about something grown-ups are uncertain about, ashamed and even a bit afraid of. Growing older we learn to be afraid of being called funny because it can change everything. Mostly men we know are funny. Everyone knows who they are and everyone watches and talks about their business. They are good men, kind men, respected men in the community and it is not their fault, not their choice that they are funny – they are just that way. They had to accept themselves and we had to accept them. We do not make fun of them. We know better.

Funny men are different from other men because they want secretly to be able to do the things that women do. They want to care about people, about how they dress themselves, about how the insides of their houses look, about the food they eat. They do not need women in their lives to care about these things for them the way men with wives and girlfriends do. They are only interested in talking to women. Fascinated by their lives, grown-ups watch them as if they were at a circus watching something incredible. Sometimes when a new male, a young male, joins the group that gathers at certain houses, the community blames it on his mother. They talk about how she made him learn to cook, to clean, to take care of small children – all the things that real men should never learn. We don't like real men. We don't like the way our brother never has to iron, wash dishes, or take care of babies. We don't like the contempt he seems to feel for us girls as he watches us doing those things, as he sweet-talks us into doing his chores, mopping the floor, putting out the trash. Since he shows all the right interest in girls mama does not mind his going around the men who are funny as long as he does not go too often, does not make a habit of it. (hooks, 1996, pp. 136–7)

ACTIVITY 2.7

- What, according to hooks, are the markers of homosexual men in her community?
- How does the community view them?
- hooks says 'growing older we learn to be afraid of being called funny because it can change everything'. What do you think she means? Can you relate this to the idea of interpellation discussed above?
- What does this passage also tell us about the markers of femininity and 'real' men?
- Throughout *Bone Black* hooks refers to her blackness. Did you know that she was black? If you didn't, does this information change the way in which you understand the above?

Taking the question 'What is a woman?' or 'What is a man?', brainstorm as many possible answers as you can. We have started you off.

What is a woman?	*What is a man?*
• Someone with long hair	Physically strong
• Career girl	New man
• Lesbian	Lover of football

Simone de Beauvoir famously asserted that 'one is not born but rather becomes a woman' but, if you have completed this activity, it may have surprised you to see how many different, and sometimes contradictory, versions of 'becoming a woman' are possible. Do you think this is equally true of 'becoming a man'?

Social constructivism is the term used to describe approaches that reject essentialist explanations of identity. A social constructivist perspective claims that gender identity is formed through interaction with social factors, and is not simply the result of biological differences. Such an approach does not deny biological differences, but attempts to understand and explain them in terms of social context, rather than seeing individuals as limited and bounded by their biology. In order to complete your work on this section, we want to introduce you briefly to some ideas from sociobiology. Read the following short extract from an article by Richard Stevens. According to Stevens, what do sociobiologists identify as the origin of human behaviour and what function does this serve?

Reading 2.6

A useful principle is that, if you want to understand something, it is worth looking at its origins, its history. One approach to understanding human behaviour is to look at it as a species pattern. Can we gain any insights into identity by considering how human behaviour might have evolved?

The theory which argues that we can is called sociobiology. This is an approach concerned with understanding the social behaviour of animals. Humans are regarded as another animal species and as being, like them, the product of evolutionary development. Sociobiologists are interested in understanding why social behaviours evolved in the way that they did – what functions did they serve in ensuring the survival of the species and passing on genes to future generations? . . .

> Their [sociobiologists'] position is that psychological and behavioural characteristics have been shaped by the process of evolution. Those behaviours which in the past have facilitated survival and reproduction are those which have been selected for. (Stevens, 1994, pp. 158, 166)

Sociobiological explanations of behaviour take as their starting point the idea that humans are a highly complex and evolved species of animal life. 'Even if we allow for major differences between ourselves and other species, given the continuity of evolution, is it not arrogant, the sociobiologist might argue, to presume that we should be *totally* exempt' (Stevens, 1994, p. 168). If, as research has shown, genes and genetic development determine, at least in part, the behaviour and responses of animals, might they not also determine human behaviour? The sociobiological approach argues that biological imperatives, and in particular the impulse to ensure survival of the species, ensured that those behaviours which facilitated survival and reproduction of the species were the behaviours most likely to be adopted and most likely to evolve into highly complex patterns of response.

Explanations of human actions which are rooted in biology will have particular relevance for theories of gender identity because of the significance such theories place on sexual reproduction. Thus, it may be argued, as women are limited in the number of children they can bear, the characteristics and behaviours of our female ancestors might have been those most likely to ensure the survival of their (relatively few) offspring, whereas men, who are able to father as many offspring as they can find partners, might have developed those responses most likely to produce an optimal number of descendants. You may well want to reject such arguments on the grounds that they appear to justify inequalities between the sexes, and biology has often been used as an explanation for the different behaviours of men and women. For example, in the nineteenth century it was argued that women's reproductive capacity rendered them physiologically unfit for the kind of intellectual study required in higher education except at enormous cost to their potential motherhood. Sociobiology is contentious because it does suggest that human responses are more determined than most of us like to imagine. It seems to claim that our actions are the result of deep-seated and innate natural factors over which we may have little control. However, sociobiologists do acknowledge the limitations of their claims. As Stevens goes on to say, a 'more intermediate position sees human social life as a complex interplay between social process and biological predispositions, each affecting the other in complex interaction' (Stevens, 1994, p. 168) He gives the example of crying: weeping is a spontaneous act for children, it is not something they are required to learn; what they do learn is when and where it is inappropriate to cry. 'The meanings attributed to weeping are shaped by social practice and convention rather than by biology' (ibid.). In the same way, we might want to say that the meanings attributed to masculine and feminine behaviours are shaped by social practice and cultural expectations and that these are linked in certain ways to the biological functions of the sexes, male and female.

Biological differences between people have often been used as the basis for social divisions and the injustices which can stem from these. For example, genetic arguments were used until recently to explain alleged differences between the intelligence of white and black people and, as we saw above, arguments from biology were used to hinder women's access to higher education in nineteenth-century Britain and America. Yet we cannot deny our biological selves – our bodies and their workings do shape how we feel about ourselves, what we are able to do and how we are seen by others. We may want to argue that social and cultural environment plays a greater part in how we develop as human beings (the nature/nurture debate as it is often called), but we cannot forget that we do have biologically programmed bodies, that we are not simply the sum of our thoughts and emotions. For example, the inevitability of ageing and the prospect of our own mortality may shape our consciousness and our sense of personal identity in profound ways, and many people explain their desire to have children as a way of leaving some trace of their existence for future generations. Such responses to mortality do not stem simply from either biological imperatives or cultural conventions, but include elements of both. Lynda Birke has argued that we need to think outside the conventionally accepted polarizations biology/culture, body/mind, animal/human. We end this section by asking you to read the following extract and to consider carefully your response.

Reading 2.7

[One] problem with denying our biological selves has to do with the relationship between humans and animals. We know, of course, that we have some things in common with other animals: all female mammals, including women, produce milk with which to feed their young. But we usually draw the line when it comes to behaviour; human behaviour, it is generally assumed, is not really the concern of biology. Indeed, this is why biological determinism is a problem for feminism – we do assume that human (and specifically women's) behaviour is shaped by culture.

The behaviour of animals, by contrast, is included squarely within the domain of 'biology'. Everything about animals, that is, constitutes *their* biology, while only some things in feminist accounts (our anatomy or physiology) constitute ours. As far as behaviour is concerned, we thereby imply that we are not like other animals.

This distinction is not very satisfactory. Are we to assume that evolution has shaped our bodies, but not our minds, while shaping both bodies *and* minds for other species? This is simply another way of recasting the distinction (so prevalent in Western culture) between body and mind. Animals are basically bodies with little in the way of mind; we are minds busily denying that we have bodies.

Yet we cannot simultaneously hold two contrasting positions. If animals' behaviour *is* their biology, then we have to assume that the behaviour is caused directly by something inside the animal. If this was said about women, we would immediately cry foul and accuse someone of biological determinism. But if it is only animals, it is all right. Isn't it?

My short answer is no – I do not think that other mammals (at least) are mere puppets of their genes, any more than I think people are. But biologically determinist arguments always rely on drawing parallels between human and animal societies. . . .So, as long as animals are wholly seen as 'biological', then the parallel will lead inevitably to seeing humans in the same way. An alternative way of drawing parallels would be to point to the extent to which individuals learn to be social – in both humans and other animals. This possibility is rarely considered, so we are left with either (a) accepting parallels based on biological determinism, or (b) denying any parallels or similarity at all. (Birke, 1992, pp. 72–3)

Recent work in sociology and cultural studies has begun to suggest alternative ways in which we can understand the relationship between the physical bodies people inhabit and the formation of identities. These perspectives reject the idea of the body as simply a biological organism, and stress instead that people's experience of their physical bodies is shaped by social structures and expectations, as well as 'natural' functions. For example, we consume food in order to survive, but what we eat, when and how, as well as how far we can choose (or not) to shape our body through eating, is a result of a range of social variables. These might include which part of the globe we inhabit (the industrialized or developing world), whether we are male or female, and historically specific 'ideal' body shapes. The current vogue for body-building is another example of the links between cultural practice and physical bodies. Our bodies, recent writers have argued, are an integral part of our identities, shaping and shaped by the meanings ascribed to them. They are more than a physical shell within which is contained the non-physical 'real' self, as anyone who has suffered anorexia or experienced obesity can testify (Featherstone et al., 1991; Bordo, 1993; Shilling, 1993; and chapter 8 in this book).

Hence the classifying categories that are used to distinguish between people – for example, 'race' and gender – are not immutable aspects of the natural world but social constructs. Racial difference, as the reading from Gates (above) argued, is not a biological phenomenon but a means of categorizing people that uses certain bodily characteristics as markers of 'race'. The persecution and mass slaughter of Jews in Nazi extermination camps during the Second World War is an extreme example of the barbarous practices that can be legitimated by reference to socially constructed 'racial' differences. Differences based on social constructs, such as 'race', gender, sexual orientation, age or disability, can be construed so as to exclude, marginalize or, in extreme forms, slaughter those perceived as 'different' or 'other'. In the 1990s, the Indian government planned to offer financial incentives to families who produce daughters in order to halt the widespread practice of aborting female fetuses. The recognition that 'race', gender, sexual orientation and disability are socially constructed has enabled new social movements, such as black civil rights, the women's liberation movement, gay and lesbian rights and disability rights, to challenge the negative stereotyping that reinforces 'otherness' and difference. Instead, differences have been celebrated as enriching sources of energy and diversity, as in slogans such as 'Glad to be gay' and 'Black is beautiful'.

ACTIVITY 2.9

You could keep a file of images, articles, TV programmes etc. in which stereotyping is used to reinforce a particular social category, e.g. Asian, French, English, Irish, single parent, homosexual, lesbian, AIDS sufferer, feminist, secretary, drug addict. There is more on stereotyping in chapters 3 and 9. Try to identify the precise elements that create recognizable stereotypes of your chosen category.

'Identity Crisis' and the Modern World

Identity, however, is not only experienced at the level of the individual. Collective, ethnic and national identities are important ways in which people negotiate a sense of belonging and, often allied to this, political solidarity. Asserting national, religious or ethnic identities can lead to political conflict, as in the case of the 'war against terrorism', where identities based on religion have the potential to divide the world. In the former Yugoslavia, established identities fragmented under the pressures of economic and political conflict, and the re-emergence of national identities around older forms of ethnicity

– Serb and Croat – led to devastating upheaval and war. In Britain, right-wing politicians have been concerned to reaffirm a sense of national identity in the face of what they perceive as threats from European unity. In many countries, international migration and a loss of certainty about what constitutes national identity have brought with them the possibility of new identities that are less firmly aligned to the older boundaries of nation states. Since the 1950s immigration has produced Asian communities in many parts of Britain that were previously the province of white working-class groups, notably in Bradford (Yorkshire) and parts of London. Many young people whose parents or grandparents came to Britain in the 1950s or the 1970s from the Caribbean or Asia do not see themselves as either wholly British or wholly West Indian or Indian. In his novel *The Buddha of Suburbia*, Hanif Kureishi has his narrator begin with a discussion of his identity:

> My name is Karim Amir, and I am an Englishman born and bred, almost. I am often considered to be a funny kind of Englishman, a new breed as it were, having emerged from two old histories. But I don't care – Englishman I am (though not proud of it), from the South London suburbs and going somewhere. Perhaps it is the odd mixture of continents and blood, of here and there, of belonging and not, that makes me restless and easily bored. (Kureishi, 1990, p. 3)

Karim sees himself as English but not in the way 'English' has been defined in the past. He sees himself as a 'new breed' – a hybrid produced by his Indian background and his English upbringing (his father is a first-generation Indian in Britain and his mother is white, British, working-class). He reflects on the effects of this both in terms of biology (blood) and in terms of the groups he can and cannot belong to. He wonders if the consequences of this 'mixing' have produced the sense of restlessness and boredom he feels. The following reading is from a series of articles in the *Independent* between 17 and 22 November 1997, in which the findings of a large-scale survey of young people, aged 17–24, were discussed and analysed.

Reading 2.8

The extent of isolation felt by this generation is astonishing in a country that until recently called itself Christian and prided itself on local loyalties. Just one in five feels part of a community, while only one in ten identifies with a religion or race. Two per cent see themselves as belonging to a political party, while 13 per cent feel part of a social class.

'I'm very much a creature of the planet,' says Mr Reza, born in Glasgow of Mauritian parents. 'I don't belong to any particular land mass. My skin is brown but I don't feel Mauritian. I feel more British when I go abroad. I don't belong to any religion. I'm open to the existence of anything but I don't believe in God. Some of the Buddhist philosophies I find quite palatable. I don't want to be a member of a class. I'm a person. I've never followed one political party. I'm not a believer in one though if you had to label me I would probably fall somewhere between Labour and the Liberal Democrats'. (*Independent*, 22 November 1997)

ACTIVITY 2.10

- What do you see as the advantages and disadvantages of belonging to an identifiable grouping such as gender, ethnic group, class, political allegiance, religion, nationality?
- The *Independent* report suggests that the loss of clear-cut cultural identities is a cause for concern. How do you respond to this?

The idea that contemporary societies are characterized by crises of identity, such as those exemplified in the former Yugoslavia or, in a different form, by Kureish's narrator and Mr Reza, is one that has been argued by a number of social and cultural theorists in recent years. In a collection of essays on this topic, published in 1990, Kobena Mercer comments,

> Just now everybody wants to talk about 'identity'. As a keyword in contemporary politics it has taken on so many different connotations that sometimes it is obvious that people are not even talking about the same thing. One thing at least is clear – identity only becomes an issue when it is in crisis, when something assumed to be fixed, coherent and stable is displaced by the experience of doubt and uncertainty. (Mercer, 1990, p. 43)

Let us consider some of the features of contemporary life that have been suggested as reasons for a 'crisis of identity'. Some recent writers have argued that the search for collective and individual identities has become more intense in the face of increasing **globalization** (Giddens, 1990; Robins, 1997). The modes of economic production and consumption that have placed McDonald's, the burger chain, in almost every city in the world, made it possible to buy a can of Coca-Cola in the remotest corner of the globe and allowed us to cross continents in hours rather than weeks have led, it is argued, to a fragmentation of the characteristics that once distinguished specific identities and nationalities. According to some writers, instead of identities based on groupings of community or nation, we all now share a common identity as global consumers, as a consequence of what Kevin Robins calls the 'transnationalization of economic and cultural life' (Robins, 1997, p. 12). For example, the management consultant Kenichi Ohmae believes that national boundaries and the identities aligned to these are no longer significant in a world dominated by global corporations and organized around a global economy: 'The nation state has become an unnatural, even dysfunctional, unit for organizing human activity and managing economic endeavour in a borderless world. It represents no genuine, shared community of economic interests; it defines no meaningful flows of economic activity' (Ohmae, cited in Robins, 1997, p. 26).

In the face of these global movements people may feel detached from the older identities that defined previous generations and may, like Mr Reza, see themselves as 'creatures of the planet'. This may express a sense of alienation and detachment or it may involve resistance to the socio-cultural effects of global capitalism through the assertion of a new ethics based on a sense of global citizenship and responsibility. An example of such citizenship would be allegiance to environmental and ecological movements concerned with the future of the planet. There is further consideration of this in chapter 9, but for now the point to grasp is that increasing global trends in terms of the goods that are produced and consumed, the speed and accessibility (for some) of world travel, the development of electronic technologies that allow us to communicate immediately with Tokyo or New York and the movement of people, as a result of occupation, poverty or war, will have far-reaching consequences for the ways in which we define ourselves and are defined by others. Before going any further, you could attempt the following activity in order to extend your understanding of what is being argued in debates about globalization.

ACTIVITY 2.11

- Use a dictionary or reference book to find out what is meant by the term 'nation-state'.
- Can you think of any examples of how the 'transnationalization of economic and cultural life' has shaped the area you live in? Who lives in your neighbourhood? Do you have a sense of belonging to a particular community that bestows identity in your neighbourhood, in the workplace or elsewhere?
- Has globalization had any impact on your work, your family, your neighbourhood?

The trend towards a global economy has led to changes in the migration of labour. Often forced by poverty, and sometimes by war as well, people have moved across the globe. Of course, migration has always occurred, but the contemporary world has seen an acceleration of this phenomenon. Most large cities in the industrialized world have an ethnically diverse population. For example, as mentioned above, London and Bradford in Britain have large, well-established Asian communities that have brought to Britain their own cultures and religious faiths. This dispersal of people across the globe produces new forms of identity, as well as tensions as a result of cross-cultural differences. For example, in the extract above from *The Buddha of Suburbia*, the narrator, Karim, describes himself as 'a funny kind of Englishman, a new breed as it were'. For many centuries Jewish people have been dispersed across the globe. Since the Second World War Jews have struggled to create 'a home' in the Middle East. One of the consequences of this has been to displace Palestinians from what they perceived as their home. Yet for many Jewish people 'home' is the USA or France or wherever they were born and have lived for most of their lives. Thus, for some, Jewish identity is closely aligned to a specific place, a particular geographic area, a bounded land mass; for others, their sense of identity may be created from their upbringing as American (or British or Polish) as well as their Jewish culture and religion. And all Jewish people in the present day live in the shadow of the Holocaust, whether they see their roots in Israel, Europe or America.

The term **diaspora** is used to conceptualize the forced dispersal of people across the globe. Literally the term means: *dia*, through, apart, across; *spora*, from the Greek 'to scatter'; therefore to scatter apart, across, through. The Africans who were brought to the Caribbean or to North America to be sold as slaves from the late sixteenth to the early nineteenth centuries were displaced and dispersed in multiple ways, and the experience of transportation, colonization and slavery caused a profound discontinuity in terms of cultural identity. Taken from different villages, different parts of Africa, different tribes, speaking different tongues, worshipping different gods, the African people of the Caribbean and North America nevertheless shared the experience of exile and slavery. The cultures and identities developed by black Africans in the Caribbean and North America may draw on their African 'roots', but they also draw on a shared history of slavery *and* the experience of living in the industrialized North or under European colonization. Edouard Glissant has commented on this as follows:

There is a difference between the transplanting (by exile or dispersion) of a people who continue to survive elsewhere and the transfer (by the slave trade) of a population to another place where they change into something different, into a new set of possibilities . . . I feel that what makes this difference between a people that survives elsewhere, *that maintains its original nature*, and a population that is transformed elsewhere *into another people* . . . is that the latter has not brought with it, not collectively continued, the methods of existence and survival, both material and spiritual, which it practiced before being uprooted. These methods leave only dim traces or survive in the form of spontaneous impulses. This is what distinguishes, besides the persecution of one and the enslavement of the other, the Jewish Diaspora from the African slave trade. (Glissant, 1992, p. 14)

In more recent times, the wars in Vietnam or in the former Yugoslavia, in the Middle East, South America or Africa have resulted in myriad displacements. In the contemporary world this process of dispersal and displacement has accelerated, and produces cultural identities that are shaped by different places and located in diverse parts of the world. Identities produced in these circumstances cannot be traced back to a single origin or homeland (Africa of Indochina), but are produced from a range of cultures, locations and experiences.

ACTIVITY 2.12

Think about the ways in which the following groups might *share* a sense of cultural identity and the ways in which their different experiences might have produced *variations* of identity.

- South African blacks in the 1990s.
- Jamaicans living in Jamaica.
- Third-generation black British whose grandparents emigrated from Jamaica in the 1950s.
- Black Americans living in the southern states of the USA.
- Black Americans living in New York.
- Tutsi refugees from Rwanda now living in Zaire (1994 conflict).

You may need to find out more about these groups from newspaper reports, reference books or the following texts (full details are in the further reading): Fanon (1986), Gilroy (1987), Rutherford (1990), African Rights (1994).

The third feature that can be linked to the idea of 'identity crisis' is the political disruption in Eastern Europe and the former USSR. The break-up of the USSR and the collapse of communism in 1989 left a political void that was quickly filled by the re-emergence of earlier forms of national identity, ethnicity and religion. Without communism as a central reference point, people in the USSR and Eastern Europe found themselves fragmented and uncertain or in a position to claim identities that had been lost or suppressed under communism. The collapse of communism also had consequences for the ways in which writers and academics saw the future. The spread of capitalism across the globe and the end of the Cold War made it difficult to think and talk in terms of two structuring and opposing centres: capitalism and communism. In the 1960s and 1970s, conflict was frequently discussed and analysed in terms of a small number of 'master' ideologies, such as communism and capitalism. In the opening years of the twenty-first century it has become more tenable to seek explanations for conflict in terms of competing identities, whether between large social groupings or at the level of the individual.

Since the 1960s there has been a growth in social movements based on **identity politics**: feminism, the black civil rights movement, gay and lesbian movements have used a sense of collective identity as women, black people, homosexual men and lesbians to challenge subordination and oppression. Some strands of these movements base their politics and strategies on the uniqueness of a particular identity. For example, some members of the Greenham Common Peace Camp movement that actively protested against nuclear warfare and American missile bases in Britain during the 1980s based their politics on a radical feminism that held that women as women have a greater investment in peace as a consequence of, among other things, their social and biological role as mothers. Attempts on the part of white, Western feminists to advocate a universal female identity have been criticized by black feminists for failing to recognize the differences between women of different cultures, classes and ethnicities. Black feminist critiques have shown how the class and ethnic identities of some white, middle-class feminists are frequently at odds with the desire of such feminists to speak to and for a universal female identity,

> Many black women had been alienated by the non-recognition of their lives, experiences and herstories in the WLM [women's liberation movement]. Black feminists have been, and are still, demanding that the existence of racism must be acknowledged as a structuring feature of our relationships with white women. Both white feminist theory and practice have to recognize that white women stand in a power relation as oppressors of black women. (Carby, 1982, p. 215)

Now read the following extract, by Jeffrey Weeks.

Reading 2.9

Identity is about belonging, about what you have in common with some people and what differentiates you from others. At its most basic it gives you a sense of personal location, the stable core to your individuality. But it is also about your social relationships, your complex involvement with others, and in the modern world these have become ever more complex and confusing. Each of us live with a variety of potentially contradictory identities, which battle within us for allegiance; as men or women, black or white, straight or gay, able-bodied or disabled, 'British' or 'European' . . . The list is potentially infinite, and so therefore are our possible belongings. Which of them we focus on, bring to the fore, 'identify' with, depends on a host of factors. At the centre, however, are the values we share or wish to share with others . . . Identities are not neutral. Behind the quest for identity are different and often conflicting values. By saying who we are, we are also striving to express what we are, what we believe and what we desire. The problem is that these beliefs, needs and desires are often patently in conflict, not only between different communities but within individuals themselves.

All this makes debates over values particularly fraught and delicate: they are not simply speculations about the world and our place in it; they touch on fundamental, and deeply felt, issues about who we are and what we want to be and become. They also pose major political questions: how to achieve a reconciliation between our collective needs as human beings and our specific needs as individuals and members of diverse communities, how to balance the universal and the particular. (Weeks, 1990, pp. 88–9)

Bonding around ethnic, national, racial or religious identities has paradoxically become fiercer the more that social, political, cultural and economic changes appear to be moving in a global direction. Rather than the world becoming one, fragmentation into smaller communities and local identities appears to be increasing. For example, forty per cent of the world's states have more than five different ethnic communities, and by 1996, there were one hundred on-going conflicts within nation-states. Over the last fifty years, while there has been no 'world' war, the United Nations has had increasingly to spend huge sums of money on peacekeeping activities across the globe (Cohen and Kennedy, 2000, p. 342). In recent years social theorists have attempted to explain this paradox by seeing the resurgence of localized conflicts as an explicable reaction to the growing pace of globalization. Fear and uncertainty, it is argued, lead to a need for the familiar and the known. In a rapidly changing world dominated by forces seemingly beyond their control, people are more, not less, likely to turn to 'the communities where they find familiar faces, voices, sounds, smells, tastes and places' (ibid., p. 343). This, in turn, may lead to **heterophobia** (the fear of difference) in which those who are different or unknown are perceived as a threat and, 'sensing attack, people seek a bond with their friends and a clearer definition of their enemies' (ibid.). This may lead to attacks on those perceived as threats, who in turn attack back, thus confirming the first group's fears that this is the enemy. Fiercer attacks are then justified and so the spiral of attack, recrimination, vengeance, atrocities and their historical justification escalates. This psychological process, which is undoubtedly irrational but nevertheless explicable, can be seen in the current relations between the West and Islam. For example, Janice Haaken discusses this in relation to gender.

> In the political choreographing of the war on terrorism, Muslim men are cast in the role of the 'bad' patriarchs and the United States in the role of the 'good' protectors, the guardians of women's freedom. . . . The further one moves from 'ground zero', however, the more complex and murky the picture becomes. Under conditions of crisis, it is difficult to hold this wider picture in view, particularly as graphic images in the media hypnotically fixate on the bad boys on the ground. Victimized women and children are introduced as silent props, present to vivify the barbarism of dark men cast as threatening other. (Haaken, 2002, pp. 456–7)

ACTIVITY 2.13

- Look back at the description you wrote of yourself at the start of this chapter. Try to identify which aspects of your description are about collective identity in the sense discussed by Weeks above. Consider how significant these are for your sense of yourself, which ones 'you bring to the fore'.
- Look out for newspaper reports or news items on TV that refer to collective identities and/or reveal signs of heterophobia. You could collect a portfolio of such material.

Representing and Narrating Identity

The extract from bell hooks in reading 2.5 was from a piece of **autobiographical** writing. The word 'autobiography' is made up of three distinct parts, each with its own meaning: auto meaning 'self', bio meaning 'life' and 'graphy' meaning writing. Autobiography is therefore generally understood as the written account of an individual's own life. As such, it offers a self-representation: a representation of a particular identity created by the self who is thus represented. The writer looks back (usually) on the past and narrates that past from the standpoint of the present. Of course, not all self-representations are literary or even written. People tell stories about their lives in many ways: in conversation, in oral accounts, in therapeutic case histories, in visual images, even in a CV for a job application. Personal narratives, whether produced as written autobiographies or in other forms, are an attempt to impose meaning and coherence on the often random and chaotic experiences which constitute lives as they are lived, to order experiences by placing them within a narrative frame. Telling or writing a life story involves interpretation. The act of selecting, from the mass of lived experience, which events and people to include and emphasize is itself an act of interpretation. If you read bell hooks's memoir you will see how she constructs a specific identity for herself and a particular set of meanings to which her life testifies. The personal narratives we tell are never simply mirror reflections of a lived reality, but are mediated by the need to represent the self as possessing a sense of identity and control. Think about the result if you tried to tell a friend about every event, emotion or person you could recall encountering. Apart from the fact that your friend would undoubtedly quickly tire of listening, wouldn't you feel the account was incoherent, contradictory and meaningless? Autobiographical representation is one of the ways in which we shape our experiences into some form of meaning and construct particular identities for ourselves. Now read the extract below, in which Margaret Woollard, a London teenager, gives her reasons for writing autobiography.

Reading 2.10

I chose to write an autobiography basically because I just love writing about myself. I have kept a detailed diary now for four years because I want my children and my children's children to look back on it and find out what I was like as a teenager and what life was like in the 1980s. I also keep it for my own personal records as to how I have changed. But not only that; even if I never looked back on it again I shall never forget the satisfaction it gave me to put down my deepest thoughts on paper.

It took me a while to work out what to include in my autobiography: how personal I should make it, and what aspects of my personality I should portray. My life has been fairly uneventful compared to some; apart from moving to London and my parents' separation. There are few single events that I can pinpoint as landmarks in it, so I decided to write about the periods I went through and my attitudes and opinions, rather than tell a straight narrative from the day I was born up until the present day.

I have been very frank in my autobiography. I may come across as 'weird': I don't think my life is in fact very different to the average London teenager and I have maybe exaggerated the differences to make a more interesting story. I am not afraid to portray myself as an individual and express what I really feel. I would like other young readers to enjoy reading about my life: to laugh at the funny incidents and be moved by the sad ones, and to try to accept and understand me and see me as a young person similar to themselves. (Simons and Bleiman, 1987, p. 81)

ACTIVITY 2.14

- Why does Margaret want to write about herself?
- What decisions does she make about the story she will tell?
- What message or meanings is she trying to convey about herself?

As we have suggested, there may be a gap between identity as it is represented and identity as it is lived, but this does not mean that representation and reality are two mutually exclusive categories. Personal life narratives may be informed by the ways in which we think 'tales of lives should be told'; that is, they require moments of drama, interesting characters and a coherent meaning in order to communicate with a reader/listener (Stanley, 1992, p. 12) At the same time, a personal life narrative, whatever form it takes, does involve a real rather than a fictional life, it is about people who actually existed rather than imaginary characters and it does refer to events which did occur, however mediated these are by the narrator's shaping influence.

And more complex still, 'lives as they are lived' exist symbiotically with the written representation of lives: we expect our and other people's lives to have troughs and peaks, to have 'meaning', to have major and minor characters, heroes and villains, to be experienced as linear and progressive, and for chronology to provide the most important means of understanding them, all of which are characteristics of fiction. (Stanley, 1992, p. 14)

Many of the issues introduced in this section will be taken up in chapters 3 and 8. There are connections too with the discussion about history in chapter 4.

Conclusions

This chapter has introduced you to the concepts of identity and difference. You will have the opportunity to consider further some of the ideas raised here in later chapters. For now we offer you a summary of the main ideas introduced here.

- Social as well as individual factors create people's sense of themselves, the ways in which they can be seen by others and the lives they may expect to live. Although social factors provide the parameters within which lives are lived and identities experienced, these may not be inevitably determining; there remains scope for individual action and agency. We are able to construct identities from a diverse and sometimes conflicting range of possibilities. However, identities are bestowed as well as chosen, and this may give rise to conflicting identities.
- At the same time, however, material factors alone cannot explain the investment that individuals have in specific identities. Althusser's theory of the subject attempts to incorporate psychoanalytic explanations into a materialist perspective.
- The formation of identities can involve essentialist claims about biology (e.g. the statement 'I have Japanese genes'). Non-essentialist perspectives argue that identity is relational and contingent, and depends upon the symbolic marking of one group as different from another (e.g. man/woman or Asian/European).
- Identities are formed through classification systems that attempt to define social groups in terms of similarities and differences. Thus, in Western classification systems, to be Asian is to be not-European, although, of course, in practice, many people are Asian in terms of ancestry but European in terms of where they live and where they hold citizenship. Such classification systems play a part in shaping how people think but they always remain fluid and contestable.
- Identities and differences can shift over time, circumstances and place. For example, the assertion of national identity during wartime may attempt to transcend those gender, age, class, religious and ethnic differences that in peacetime may have engendered conflict. Thus identities are **contingent** upon time, circumstance and place.
- Social and material effects follow from the symbolic marking of one group as different from another.

- Identities may be formed collectively as well as individually, and can be used for political purposes: for example, the women's liberation movement, 'Glad to be gay', Black Power. They may also lead to heterophobia.
- Accelerated globalization, increased migration and the collapse of an alternative ideology to capitalism have led to what some writers see as 'a crisis of identity' in the contemporary world.
- The perspectives we explored also raised the question of a conceptual split between body/mind, animal/human, nature/culture. Lynda Birke suggests that this conceptual polarization constrains the ways in which we are able to understand the relationship between biological imperatives and cultural identity.
- Cultural representations, in this context autobiography and personal life narratives, are one of the ways in which we can construct self-definitions and identities out of the 'raw material' at our disposal. Cultural representations offer forms within which we can choose to narrate ourselves and our lives in order to produce a sense of identity and meaning.

Later chapters take up many of the issues raised here in further detail and in relation to specific topics. For example, the next chapter has a section on gay and lesbian representation, chapter 8 extends the discussion by focusing on the concept of subjectivity and chapter 9 thinks about our identities as consumers. Indeed, issues of identity are central to the study of culture: how we define ourselves, who we want to be and how we are defined by others is inextricably related to the 'production and circulation of meaning' in a particular society at a particular time.

Chapter 3

Representation

Introduction

Stuart Hall, a leading contributor to many of the debates in cultural studies since the 1970s, argues that culture

> is not so much a set of *things* – novels and paintings or TV programmes and comics – as a process, a set of *practices*. Primarily, culture is concerned with the production and the exchange of meanings – 'the giving and taking of meaning' – between the members of a society or group. (Hall, 1997, p. 2)

Representation is one of the key practices by which meanings are produced. By the end of this chapter we hope you will have begun to understand what we mean by 'representation' and something of how it functions. Working through the readings and activities that follow this introduction will enable you to recognize the often complex ways in which meanings are produced through systems of representation – primarily, in this chapter, written language, visual images and objects. We begin by considering what is meant by the term 'representation', and then move on to consider how the links between meanings, representation and culture might be explained.

ACTIVITY 3.1

Spend a few minutes thinking about what is meant by the word 'represent'. You might find it helpful to use a dictionary.

The word 'represent' has many possible meanings. Here we are concerned with just three:

- To stand in for, as in the case of a country's flag, which when flown at a sporting event, for example, signals that country's presence at the event. The flag stands for or symbolizes a nation, distinguishing France from China or Ireland from the USA. In Britain, the Royal Standard represents or symbolizes the royal family and the institution of monarchy.
- To speak or act on behalf of, as in 'A spokesperson representing lesbian mothers voiced the concerns of the group on television.' A person who represents a group in this sense may also serve a symbolic function. An example might be the Pope, who speaks and acts on behalf of the Roman Catholic community but might also stand as a symbol of Roman Catholicism.
- To re-present. In his sense, a biography or historical writing re-presents the events of the past. Equally, a photograph re-presents a moment or event which has already occurred – it presents the occasion again. A photograph or painting can also, of course, represent someone or something in the sense of standing in for. Posters of rock stars, religious paintings and public statues all fulfil this function. Images that function in this way are said to be **iconic**.

In practice the three meanings we have identified frequently overlap and merge. None the less, it is worth spending a few moments thinking about further examples of each meaning from your own experience. In which sense is a photograph of a child's birthday party working? What about road signs? What about the golden arches used by the hamburger chain McDonald's? In what sense is a written autobiography a representation? Is a novel or a TV soap opera a representation and, if so, of what?

Language and Representation

Language is an arbitrary system of **signs** in which we tacitly agree to accept, for example, that the letters/sounds d.o.g. will represent (stand in for) the animal we wish to classify as different from, say, elephant or mouse. It is only at the moment when we agree that the **signifier** d.o.g. equals a mental concept of a certain animal (the **signified**) that an animal known to us as 'dog' and therefore not 'elephant' or 'mouse' exists. Signifier plus signified produce the sign, dog. Furthermore, we understand d.o.g. as dog because it is not the letters or sounds c.a.t. nor l.o.g. rather than because there are physical differ-ences between cats and dogs that fall into naturally pre-existent categories of what constitutes a dog or a cat. Language works through a system of differ-entiation 'readily experienced as natural, given, but in reality constructed by the language itself' (Belsey, 1980, pp. 39–40). Prior to its constitution in lan-guage (the sounds/letters d.o.g.) we do not possess a *shared* conception of dog that can be socially communicated. This does not mean that we are unable to see or think about certain animals with certain characteristics, but that such animals are not known specifically as dogs or cats or elephants or mice that can be talked, thought and spoken about as different, until language consti-tutes them as such. Now read this extract from Catherine Belsey's *Critical Practice*, which expands the ideas that we have just glossed.

Reading 3.1

We use signifiers to mark off areas of a continuum. The [colour] spectrum again illustrates this point. It is not that I cannot distinguish between shades of blue but that the language insists on a difference, which readily comes to seem fundamental, *natural*, between blue and green. The world, which without signification would be experienced as a continuum, is divided up by language into entities which then readily come to be experienced as essentially distinct. The way in which we use signi-fiers to create differences appears in the labelling of otherwise identical toothmugs, 'his' and 'hers' . . .

Only a social group can generate signs. Noises which have no meaning may be purely individual, but meaning intelligibility, cannot by definition be produced in isolation. The sign is in an important sense arbitrary – the sound *dog* has not more necessary or natural connection with the concept *dog* than has *chien* or *Hund*. Even onomatopeic words, which seem to imitate the sounds they signify, are by no means international: French dogs say *ouaoua*; *to splash* in French is *éclabousser*. And it is the arbitrariness of the sign which points to the fact that language is a matter of convention. The linguistic community 'agrees' to attach a specific signified to a specific signifier, though in reality, of course, its agreement is not explicitly sought but merely manifested in the fact that certain linguistic units are used and under-stood. 'The arbitrary nature of the sign explains in turn why the social fact alone can create a linguistic system. The community is necessary if values that owe their existence solely to usage and general acceptance are to be set up' [Saussure, 1974, p. 113]. And conversely, of course, a community needs a signifying system: social organization and social exchange, the ordering of the processes of producing the means of subsistence, is impossible without the existence of a signifying system. Language therefore comes into being at the same time as society . . .

Language is not, of course, the only signifying system. Images, gestures, social behaviour, clothes are all socially invested with meaning, are all elements of the symbolic order: language is simply the most flexible and perhaps the most complex of the signifying systems. Thought, if not exclusively dependent on language, is inconceivable without the symbolic order in general. 'Thought is nothing other than the power to construct representations of things and to operate on these representations. It is in essence symbolic' [Benveniste, 1971, p. 25]. (Belsey, 1980, pp. 39–45)

ACTIVITY 3.2

- Can you think of examples of language marking differences that have social meaning? For example, the forms of address, Miss, Ms, Mr, Dr, Reverend.
- Think about the concept of 'race'. Is this an instance where 'the language insists on a difference, which readily comes to seem fundamental, *natural*'? Is 'race' a form of linguistic differentiation and classification rather than a natural phenomenon?

Communicating Meaning

You should now read the following passage by Stuart Hall.

Reading 3.2

Members of the same culture must share sets of concepts, images and ideas which enable them to think and feel about the world, and thus to interpret the world, in roughly similar ways. They must share, broadly speaking, the same 'cultural codes'. In this sense, thinking and feeling are themselves 'systems of representation', in which our concepts, images and emotions 'stand for' or represent, in our mental life, things which are or may be 'out there' in the world. Similarly, in order to *communicate* these meanings to other people, the participants to any meaningful exchange must also be able to use the same linguistic codes – they must, in a very broad sense, 'speak the same language' . . . They must also be able to read visual images in roughly similar ways. They must be familiar with broadly the same ways of producing sounds to make what they would both recognize as 'music'. They must all interpret body language and facial expressions in broadly similar ways. And they must know how to translate their feelings and ideas into these various languages. Meaning is a dialogue – always only partially understood, always an unequal exchange.

Why do we refer to all these different ways of producing and communicating meaning as 'languages' or as 'working like languages'? How do languages work? The simple answer is that languages work *through representation*. They are 'systems of representations'. Essentially, we can say that all these practices 'work like languages', *not* because they are all written or spoken (they are not), but because they all use some element to stand for or represent what we want to say, to express or communicate a thought, concept, idea or feeling. Spoken language uses sounds, written language uses words, musical language uses notes on a scale, the 'language of the body' uses physical gesture, the fashion industry uses items of clothing, the language of facial expression uses ways of arranging one's features, television uses digitally or electronically produced dots on a screen, traffic lights use red, green and amber to 'say something'. These elements – sounds, words, notes, gestures, expressions, clothes – are part of our natural and material world, but their importance for language is not what they *are* but what they *do*, their function. They construct meaning and transmit it. They signify. They don't have any clear meaning *in themselves*. Rather, they are the vehicles or media which *carry meaning* because they operate as *symbols*, which stand for or represent (i.e. symbolize) the meanings we wish to communicate. To use another metaphor, they function as *signs*. Signs stand for or *represent* our concepts, ideas and feelings in such a way as to enable others to 'read', decode or interpret their meaning in roughly the same way that we do. (Hall, 1997, pp. 4–5)

In order to explore what Hall is saying more fully, let us take a simple example. The word 'star' can mean, among other things, an extra-terrestrial form in the galaxy, a celebrity, an award for good work or behaviour, an architectural formation. It all depends on the meaning attributed to the sign 'star' in a particular context. The letters s.t.a.r. have no intrinsic meaning in themselves – as Hall says, words are important not for what 'they *are* but what they *do*, their function'. They are a symbol or sign to which we tacitly agree to attach certain meanings. Taking the first meaning, until a group or society 'agrees' to use the letters s.t.a.r. to signify the shiny dots that can be seen in the sky at night, the word star has no meaning. The letters s.t.a.r. represent (stand in for) the physical objects we can see in the night sky, and allow us to communicate this meaning to others who use the same language. To use the word 'star' to represent (symbolize) a particular kind of celebrity is to understand 'star' as a metaphor – it suggests a connection or likeness between a star in the firmament and certain 'brilliant' people. Stars are also physical shapes used for buildings, decorations, swimming or dancing formations. Here, they are being used as a visual sign, rather than a verbal one, but one which works through shared ways of seeing: we recognize a particular shape as 'star' because we share the same codes of communication. A star used as a reward can function as both a visual and a verbal symbol – a symbol of, or a way of representing, special achievement. The point to grasp is that the concept 'star' has no fixed or single meaning for all time. What it means will depend upon the context in which it is used, how it is represented and the codes which govern that representation. For example, schoolchildren do not believe that the award of a gold star will mean being presented with a star from the galaxy; they understand the meaning of star within the context of its use and the codes of representation in their education system, which designates stars as symbols of excellence. Again, if asked to form a star in a dance class they would not confuse this with the award for achievement. In summary, meaning is produced via **signifying practices**, in which signs are assembled according to sets of codes in order to represent, in material form (speech, the written word, visual images, music, body language, clothing, the environments we live and work in), the mental conceptualizations shared by a particular grouping of people.

ACTIVITY 3.3	• List as many meanings for the sign 'star' as you can think of. • Collect some visual images of stars (in any of the senses used). Do they connect with the words and stories used about stars? • Can you think of physical gestures that function as signs in the particular body language you recognize? For example, in many cultures a nod of the head signifies assent, but it might signify differently in another culture.

In order to interpret the world we inhabit, we need a framework of meanings that will enable us to place people, objects and events in ways that make sense for us. Think back to chapter 1, where we made the point that it was possible to know what a cathedral was without actually being in or looking at one. We have a mental concept of 'cathedral' that we can access even when we are nowhere near an actual, bricks and mortar cathedral. The same is true of objects like tables, chairs or computers. It is also true of less tangible things, like love, loyalty, justice or cruelty, and even of things that we have never experienced or seen, such as dragons, fairies or prehistoric cavemen. This ability to conceptualize mentally even abstract things allows us to represent the world to ourselves in ways which are meaningful, and to communicate those meanings to others who share broadly similar systems of representation. Try explaining Father Christmas to someone from a culture in which this figure does not exist. In order to understand Father Christmas we need a shared concept and a way of communicating this or, if we belong to a culture which does not have Father Christmas, we will try to relate the concept of Father Christmas to something similar in our own culture in order to classify it as 'similar to'/'different from'. The concepts we use to make sense of the world are arrived at by a process of **categorization** and **classification**. Signs only operate to produce meaning within a system of other signs that signify along chains of similarity and difference. For example, night means not-day, a dark-room means not-night because it is created by artificial means – no electric light, drawn curtains – whereas night signifies a natural state, but a dark-room is like night in that both a dark-room and night are unlike a lighted room or daytime. In this way we are able to form complex meanings that can be communicated to others through systems of representation that are constituted in:

- the signs we use, such as s.t.a.r., a nod of the head;
- the categorization and classification of signs according to similarity or difference, e.g. the sign w.o.m.a.n. signifies in relation to other signs, such as m.a.n. or a.n.i.m.a.l. or h.u.m.a.n.;
- the codes that govern how we assemble the signs to produce meaning, e.g. the context in which 'star' means a heavenly body or a symbol of achievement;
- the signifying practices through which meanings are communicated, e.g. sounds, writing, visual images, musical notation, physical gestures, clothing.

In order to explain how this works in practice I will describe how a specific advertisement can be analysed. A recent advertisement for Jack Daniel's whiskey features men's working overalls and some sheets hung on a line, blowing in the wind. The strap line is 'Paris got fashion. We got whiskey'. The advertisement suggests that this whiskey is not something that will go out of fashion, that it has a long pedigree. It also suggests that Jack Daniel's whiskey comes from a certain part of America and is drunk by a certain kind of people. It does all this without explicitly saying so but by using images that convey particular meanings. What we see is lines of washing, consisting of three pairs of dungarees and some white sheets. The dungarees carry meaning beyond their literal description as clothing. They suggest the southern states of the USA (Tennessee in particular) and they suggest masculinity and hard physical work. They may even have racial connotations, being the standard clothes of working black men in the southern states of America. This is suggested by the highlighting of the dungarees against the white sheet. The dungarees appear to be dancing in the breeze. In order to direct how we read these images the caption tells us 'Paris got fashion. We got whiskey'. Thus Jack Daniel's whiskey is represented as timeless rather than at the whim of fashion. The reference to Paris also works to suggest that this whiskey is not aspiring to sophistication or fashion but is content to be seen as down-to-earth, for ordinary hard-working people. Using words or a caption to ensure the meaning of a visual image is referred to as **anchoring** the meaning. In this advertisement the words 'Paris' and 'fashion' ensure that the meanings discussed above are secured. Without those words we might read the image of the dungarees in ways not intended by the advertisers. The pronoun 'We' attempts to include the reader/viewer who is invited to recognize themselves as the sort of person who would prefer the down-to-earth drink of labouring men to the sophisticated pleasures of Paris. You might care to look back to chapter 2 and Althusser's theory of **interpellation** at this point. The whole advertisement is photographed in black and white. Black and white photographs generally suggest the past and here the intention is to invoke a sense of continuity and tradition in contrast to the ephemeral and transient nature of 'fashion'. Jack Daniel's whiskey thus becomes associated with these values.

The signs used here are **encoded** so as to suggest particular meanings. By encoding we mean using them in certain ways and in particular relations to other signs so as to convey a specific meaning or 'message'. Dungarees, for example, could be encoded in other ways that suggest they are fashion items or the standard wear of radical feminists. Paris can be encoded as a city of romance and sophistication that is desirable rather than rejected as here. The particular assemblage of signs in this advertisement offers a **preferred** meaning that attempts to preclude other meanings that cling to the signs used.

ACTIVITY 3.4

- Search through magazines, brochures and advertisements to find examples of Paris, dungarees, whiskey being used to suggest different meanings and values.
- Select an advertisement and try to analyse it as we have done. Note in particular how the different aspects combine to produce a specific meaning.

By now you may be thinking that it is all very well to encode a meaning by placing signs in particular relation to each other, but how can we know that this encoded meaning will be received (decoded) in precisely the form intended, given the range of possible meanings of even an apparently straightforward sign such as 'star'? In his essay 'Encoding/decoding in television discourse', Hall argues that 'decodings do not follow inevitably from encodings', that there is no natural symmetry between encoders and decoders (Hall, 1990, p. 100). TV news producers, for example, may encode events in ways that point to an intended or preferred meaning, but these encodings may be decoded or 'read' differently. The Jack Daniel's advertisement, for example, encodes a 'preferred' meaning but the producers of the advertisement can only attempt to persuade us into reading the meaning they intend. As 'readers' we bring our own histories, understandings, place in the world to our reading of the advertisement, and therefore possibly produce meanings from it which were not intended by the designers. Hall uses the word **articulation** to suggest the point at which encoding and decoding meet. This is a useful word to convey the process he is attempting to describe. To articulate means two things: to express something and to link two things in a way which retains the independence of each. Think of an articulated lorry in which the cab and the container are interdependent but not permanently joined; each can be articulated to another vehicle if needed. Now read the extract from Jacqueline Bobo's study of black women's readings of the Steven Spielberg film of Alice Walker's book *The Color Purple*.

Reading 3.3

From political sociology, the encoding/decoding model was drawn from the work of Frank Parkin, who developed a theory of meaning systems [Morley, 1989, p. 4]. This theory delineates three potential responses to a media message: dominant, negotiated or oppositional. A dominant (or preferred) reading of a text accepts the content of the cultural product without question. A negotiated reading questions parts of the content of the text but does not question the dominant ideology which underlies the production of the text. An oppositional response to a cultural product is one in which the recipient of the text understands that the system that produced the text is one with which she/he is fundamentally at odds [Grossberg, 1984, p. 403].

A viewer of a film (reader of a text) comes to the moment of engagement with the work with a knowledge of the world and a knowledge of other texts or media products. What this means is that when a person comes to view a film, she/he does not leave her/his histories, whether social, cultural, economic, racial, or sexual at the door. An audience member from a marginalized group (people of colour, women, the poor, and so on) has an oppositional stance as they participate in mainstream media. The motivation for this counter-reception is that we understand that mainstream media has never rendered our segment of the population faithfully. We have as evidence our years of watching films and television programmes and reading plays and books. Out of habit, as readers of mainstream texts, we have learned to ferret out the beneficial and put up blinders against the rest.

From this wary viewing standpoint, a subversive reading of a text can occur. This alternative reading comes from something in the work that strikes the viewer as amiss, that appears 'strange'. Behind the idea of subversion lies a reader-oriented notion of 'making strange' [Gledhill, 1984]. When things appear strange to the viewer, she/he may then bring other viewpoints to bear on the watching of the film and may see things other than what the film-makers intended. The viewer, that is, will read 'against the grain' of the film. (Bobo, 1988, p. 55).

Bobo's interviews with black women who saw *The Color Purple* demonstrate the ways in which these women read the film 'against the grain' of dominant critical readings that condemned the film for its negative representation of black people. She suggests that, rather than finding the portrayal of the black community stereotypical and negative, as argued by numerous critics, these women 'discovered something progressive and useful in the film' (Bobo, 1988, p. 54).

A further example: advertising that uses images of white, young, slim, attractive and healthy females to sell a product is encoding a particular version of femininity. In these adverts femininity equals whiteness, youth, beauty, slenderness and health. A reader who straightforwardly accepts that whiteness, youth, beauty and a slender, healthy body connote femininity can be said to be reading from within the dominant code in which this image is encoded. An unquestioning acceptance of these **dominant** codes of femininity may lead to a continuing quest for youth, beauty and slenderness and, if one is non-white, possible attempts to 'pass as white', A **negotiated** decoding may accept the encoded definition of femininity at the level of the advertisement, possibly as an unattainable ideal or fantasy, but this meaning of femininity may have minimum impact on or bear little relation to everyday experience. A woman who decodes from a negotiated position may enjoy looking at the femininity offered in advertisements and magazines but may, quite happily, spend very little time or money in her daily life attempting to emulate these. Neither, however, is she likely to question the underlying structures that posit femininity in these terms – as Bobo writes, she 'does not question the dominant ideology which underlies the production of the text'. Someone who decodes the images of femininity from an **oppositional** position would read such images as harmful to women, in that they render women of colour, older women, large women, poor women and women with disabilities invisible and promote a dominant ideology of heterosexuality. They might actively seek to change the ways in which advertisements represent women through the politics of feminism and black rights movements (see chapter 2; Betterton, 1987; Bonner *et al.*, 1992; McCracken, 1993; Dines and Humez, 1995).

ACTIVITY 3.5

- Select an advertisement or series of advertisements. Try to work out how the advert might be read from: (a) a dominant decoding position; (b) a negotiated decoding position; and (c) an oppositional position.
- Watch a film with friends, family or fellow students. Try to identify the preferred meanings that are being conveyed. Discuss the film with the other viewers. Does the discussion demonstrate examples of dominant, negotiated or oppositional positionings? Dominant and oppositional will probably be the easiest to identify, but have a go at identifying negotiated decoding positions both in the discussion and in your everyday life.

Representation and Discourse

You may have begun to wonder how and why dominant meanings are sustained, often consistently over a long period, when it is possible for people to produce alternative and oppositional meanings that may be subversive. In order to think about this we need to turn our attention to how meanings 'circulate', and the way we have chosen to explore this is through the concept of discourse developed by Michel Foucault. Discourse moves the focus from an examination of the relation of signs within a signifying system to asking questions about how certain ways of thinking about an area of knowledge acquire authority, how certain meanings attach themselves to certain signs in specific historical periods and how meaning and knowledge produce and sustain power relations. Discourse is a social act, in that it links systems of representation with the real world in which people experience social relations. Foucault argues that how human beings understand themselves in relation to the social world is not fixed or universal, but that this knowledge is produced differently at different historical moments. Such knowledge, he claims, is produced through discourse, and is inextricably linked with the ways in which power operates: that

> power produces knowledge (and not simply by encouraging it because it serves power or by applying it because it is useful); that power and knowledge directly imply one another; that there is no power relation without the correlative constitution of a field of knowledge, nor any knowledge that does not presuppose and constitute at the same time power relations. (Foucault, 1975, p. 27)

Before we go on to think about discourse, let us consider what is meant by 'there is no power relation without the correlative constitution of a field of knowledge'.

ACTIVITY 3.6

Look back to the extract from Said in chapter 1, in which he writes of imperialism's need to differentiate 'us' from 'them' (reading 1.7). What particular knowledges or ways of seeing the world are connected with the power relations of imperialism?

In order for one area of the globe to colonize and rule another it is necessary for the colonizers and colonized to know and represent the world in certain ways. For example, in the nineteenth century, imperialists understood Africa as 'the dark continent', a primitive and unknowable place, to be 'civilized' by Christianity, science and the 'forces of reason'. Such knowledge constructed oppositions in which the West represented enlightenment, reason and civilization, while Africa was the scene of ignorance, irrationality and savagery. This 'knowledge' legitimated the European colonization of Africa and the racism that structured (and continues to structure) social relations in the US. In the eighteenth and nineteenth centuries power relations between black and white people, in which black signified subordination and servitude, while white signified superiority and ownership, were represented as the 'natural' order of things, thus closing off any discussion of these relations. Blacks were 'by nature' lazy, 'primitive' and childish, and this legitimated the subjection of their bodies, as well as their work, homes, leisure and environment, to white authority. This 'knowledge', often validated by scientific findings about the 'true nature' of black Africans, was crucial to the white imperialist project. Once black inferiority was accepted as 'true', certain practices – economic and social – could be carried out in the name of that 'truth' (Mackenzie, 1986; Gates, 1988; hooks, 1992; McClintock, 1995; Hall, 1997). And we might also ask how the colonized saw *themselves* in this system. The next extract is taken from a collection of life stories by Jamaican girls published in 1986, and describes the feelings of a creole woman when she read *Jane Eyre* as a schoolgirl receiving a British education in Kingston, Jamaica.

Reading 3.4

In third form, they gave us *Jane Eyre* to read. It was the only piece of literature in which there was any mention of the Caribbean. It was also the only book by a woman which they had given us to read. We liked the bits about school and then we came upon the mad heiress from Spanish Town locked up in the attic. At first we giggled, knowing that it was Jane we were supposed to identify with and her quest for independence and dignity. Then we got to the part where this masterpiece of English Literature describes Bertha Mason as 'inferior, blue skinned . . . etc.' Someone was reading it out loud in the class as was the custom. Gradually the mumbling and whispering in the class room crescendoed into an open revolt with loud choruses of 'it's not fair, Miss!' Miss admitted it seemed unfair but she went on to do nothing with that insight . . . I couldn't put it down . . . anxiously looking for a chapter, a paragraph or a sentence that might redeem the insane animal inferiority of the Caribbean. It was a women's novel and I had liked so much of the earlier part, but I couldn't stomach the way I had been relegated to the attic. I felt betrayed. (Cited in Duncker, 1992, p. 26)

Novels like *Jane Eyre* are one of the ways in which 'truth' and knowledge are circulated. So 'naturalized' are these 'truths' that we often fail to see the power relations they uphold until someone, like this Jamaican schoolgirl, reading from a different position makes these visible. White European students reading *Jane Eyre* are often shocked and sometimes resistant when they first encounter the passage above.

ACTIVITY 3.7

- Whether or not you have read *Jane Eyre*, what was your reaction to the idea expressed above that this masterpiece of English Literature represented the Caribbean, through the figure of Bertha Mason, as 'insane', 'animal' and inferior. If you were shocked, try to work out why. If you were resistant to the idea that a writer like Charlotte Brontë could express racist sentiments, ask yourself why you find it hard to believe.
- Can you think of other cultural forms (novels, paintings, films, TV programmes etc.) in which the non-white is represented as different, 'abnormal' or 'deviant'? These could be contemporary or from another historical period.

Constructing, sustaining and reproducing 'truths' is essential to the maintenance of power. Until recently, women's 'natural destiny' was seen as motherhood: this was a 'truth' that required no comment (although, of course, in any age, such ideas have been challenged, as the schoolgirl above challenges the norm that allows the Caribbean to be represented as 'other' and inferior). The 'truth', that a woman's 'destiny' was motherhood, validated the exclusion of women from many spheres of public activity, at the same time making it difficult for those excluded to question publicly the knowledge on which their exclusion was based. Thus certain knowledges about women could be maintained and reproduced by those whose interest was best served by such 'truths'.

According to Foucault, knowledge and 'truth' are produced through discourses. There are no pre-existent 'truths' that representations simply reflect. The numerous representations of mother and child in Western art, in advertising, in newspapers, are not a mirror reflection of an already existing 'fact' – that is, that women's highest destiny is motherhood – but are one element of the system of representation that constructs women as primarily mothers. Discourse is the term used to describe the network of statements, images, stories and practices by which certain beliefs or a set of ideas about a particular topic are circulated and sustained in order to **naturalize** these as self-evident or common sense. Thus, we could speak of a patriarchal discourse of gender in which it is perceived as 'natural' that women should exhibit a predisposition to mothering as a result of their biology (see also, in this connection, our references in chapter 2 to essentialism). We could equally refer to a feminist discourse of gender that has contested what were perceived as common-sense beliefs about the 'nature' of women. Now read the extract by John Fiske.

Reading 3.5

Discourse is a language or system of representation that has developed socially in order to make and circulate a coherent set of meanings about an important topic area. These meanings serve the interests of that section of society within which the discourse originates and which works ideologically to naturalize those meanings into common sense. 'Discourses are power relations' [O'Sullivan et al., 1983, p. 74]. Discourse is thus a social act which may promote or oppose the dominant ideology, and is thus often referred to as a 'discursive practice'. Any account of a discourse or a discursive practice must include its topic area, its social origin, and its ideological work: we should not, therefore, think about a discourse of economics, or of gender, but of a capitalist (or socialist) discourse of economics, or the patriarchal (or feminist) discourse of gender. Such discourses frequently become institutionalized, particularly by the media industries in so far as they are structured by a socially produced set of conventions that are tacitly accepted by both industry and consumers.

Discourses function not only in the production and reading of texts, but also in making sense of social experience. A particular discourse of gender, for example, works not only to make sense of a television program . . . but also to make a particular pattern of sense of gender in the family, in the workplace, in school, in social clubs – in fact, in our general social relations. (Fiske, 1987, pp. 14–15)

ACTIVITY 3.8

Try to think of some specific examples of how and where discourses of gender, either feminist or patriarchal, are produced. We have started you off; you carry on and add to our examples.

How	Where
• By making statements	In parliament, in the newspapers, in studies of gender
• Through representations	In novels, advertisements
• By teaching	In schools and in the family
• By social practices	Marriage, parenting, jobs
•	
•	
•	

Looking at your list, select those examples which you think would be most likely to authorize the patriarchal discourse of gender. Why? Are there any examples that might offer a space in which the patriarchal discourse could be challenged?

A discourse operates across a range of diverse practices, texts and the institutions in which these are located. Discourse, as a way of understanding representation, extends the **semiotic** concern with signs and symbols beyond systems of language by linking representation to the ways in which power operates in specific social situations and historical periods. Although Foucault recognizes that language is the medium through which discourses produce knowledge, he is also concerned to stress that since 'all social practices entail meaning, and meanings shape and influence what we do – our conduct – all practices have a discursive aspect' (Hall, 1992, p. 291). Hence, it is not language alone that produces discourse, but also behaviours and practices. For example, the star-shaped piece of gold paper kept in the teacher's desk or stationery cupboard becomes 'a gold star for achievement' not only when it is named as such but also when it is awarded to a pupil. The meaning of 'gold stars' is produced through specific social acts, as well as linguistic naming and visual objects. Gold stars take on a particular meaning within a child-centred discourse of education, which includes, *inter alia*: statements about the value of schooling and the importance of achievement; authorization of the practice of rewards and encouragements by psychologists and other 'experts'; and rules that prescribe when and how such awards will be made.

Let us look at another example. The sixteenth and seventeenth centuries witnessed widespread persecution and punishment of those people, mostly women, 'known' to be witches. If you have seen Arthur Miller's play *The Crucible*, watched the film adaptation or studied American history, you will know that in the seventeenth century, Salem, Massachusetts, experienced a ferocious witch-hunt. In order for this to occur, certain elements had to come together to produce a context in which witchcraft had particular meanings that legitimated the identification and punishment of some people as witches. For example:

1 Statements about the practices and customs of witches, providing the community with certain kinds of knowledge about what constituted witchcraft.
2 Rules which made it possible to say some things but not others about witchcraft. For example, it was not possible in the seventeenth century to understand or talk about so-called witches as wise, rational or moral beings.
3 Actual people – 'subjects' – who, because their behaviour, attributes or habits fitted the period's knowledge of witches, constructed in 1 and 2 above, could be identified as 'witches'.
4 Institutional frameworks which allowed the knowledges produced by 1, 2 and 3 to acquire authority and thus come to constitute the 'truth' at a specific historical moment, for example religious communities, the legal system, schooling and education.

Now read the following extract from Elaine Showalter's *Hystories: Hysterical Epidemics and Modern Culture*.

Reading 3.6

Preconditions of a witch-hunt were consistent, whether the events took place in Scotland or Salem. The community had to know something about the practices of witches and to be convinced of their habits. Lawyers and judges also had to believe in witchcraft, since they controlled the judicial process and could halt the hunts. For successful prosecutions, specific anti-witchcraft legislation and the establishment of jurisdiction were necessary. Witch-hunts were smaller where inquisitional procedures and torture were prohibited, as in seventeenth-century England.

In addition, witch-hunts required an emotional atmosphere stirred up by sermons, discussions and rumors. They often began with individual denunciations stemming from personal grudges. Sometimes malice played a role. Sometimes disturbed individuals confessed. In England, witch-hunts were usually limited to those originally accused. In Switzerland, Germany and Scotland, medium-sized witch-hunts . . .

prevailed: the accused were tortured and implicated a group of accomplices. These panics burned themselves out when the local group of suspicious persons had been exhausted.

Large witch-hunts, 'characterized by a high degree of panic or hysteria' [Levack, 1995, p. 174] took place in France, Sweden, and of course in Salem. These were driven by both the clinical conversion hysteria of the demoniacs and the collective hysteria of the community. (Showalter, 1997, p. 25)

This passage not only suggests how witch-hunts gathered momentum in the past but also makes statements about how they can be understood in the present. Witchcraft in the seventeenth century was understood within the discourses of religion and the law, so that we can speak of the religious discourse of witchcraft or the legal discourse of witchcraft. In the present day, the same events and facts are given meaning by Showalter within the discourses of psychology, sociology and medicine – witch-hunts are now to be

Figure 3.1   Old rose-tinted spectacles/New dark shades, by Posy Simmonds

understood as 'collective hysteria'. It is also possible to construct a feminist discourse of witchcraft in opposition to the patriarchal discourse in which 'a witch' is a specifically gendered identity.

ACTIVITY 3.9

Can you think of any contemporary 'witch-hunts' in which a certain group is characterized as dangerous? Look at the list of elements on page 77 that it is suggested need to come together for this to occur. Can you relate this to the contemporary world? You could usefully look back to the discussion of **heterophobia** in chapter 2.

Let us try another example. Figure 3.1 makes a neat point about the ways in which meanings about children and childhood change over time. Take each of the elements listed above (1 to 4) and apply them to the ways your culture defines children and childhood. Our examples are taken from British culture because that is what we know best, but you should use the culture with which you are most familiar.

ACTIVITY 3.10

Where might you expect to find 'official' statements about children and childhood? 'Official' here means those statements that are generally available, carry authority and/or are ratified by 'expert' knowledge. We have started you off; you carry on.

- Dictionary definitions.
- Legal definitions of childhood, as, for example, in the age of consent for sexual activity.
- Medical textbooks.
- Books about the psychological development of children.
-
-
-
-

Where might you find 'unofficial' statements?

- Conversations between mothers.
-
-
-
-

Where might you find visual and/or imaginative representations of children and childhood?

- TV programmes for children.
-
-
-
-

Do these visual/imaginative representations carry the same meanings as official statements, or do they offer different meanings of children and childhood? Or both? For example, do TV programmes about children adhere to the legal statements about the age of consent for sexual activity?

Are there things it would be unacceptable or unthinkable to say about children and childhood? For example, to suggest that children might work in factories or sweep chimneys, as they did in nineteenth-century Britain and America, would be unacceptable in today's advanced industrial societies, although child labour remains a reality in many less affluent parts of the world. What is it about our understanding of childhood that makes such an idea unacceptable? In this context you might also think about childhood and sexuality.

Who are 'children'? How do we recognize and define certain people as 'children'? Think about physical attributes. What other attributes define someone as a child? (For example, see the extract from Susan Isaacs below.) What do we mean when we say of a grown man, 'He's still such a child'?

Can you identify social practices or instructions in which the statements, visual images and stories that represent children and childhood are acted out? For example, the education system authorizes an ending to childhood, as do social practices such as coming-of-age parties. In relation to this question, think about the part played by the family in constructing the meaning of children and childhood.

If you already have, or think one day you might have, children, where have your ideas come from about how you will bring them up?

As result of working through the above, can you identify some of the meanings that are represented by the words 'children' and 'childhood' in the present day? As you worked through the questions did your answers reveal any contradictory or conflicting meanings?

If you wanted to challenge the generally accepted meaning of children and childhood in your culture, would any of the elements above offer a potential space for doing so? Where would you begin? Try to plan a strategy that would enable new meanings to emerge.

We hope this exercise has demonstrated how the production of meaning is dispersed across a range of sites where representation occurs (statements, visual images, what can and cannot be said, the physical bodies of human beings, institutions and practices). Each element both takes from and contributes to the accepted meanings of children and childhood in a particular historical period. Taken together, the elements constitute a discourse, and each element is meaningful only within the discourse of which it is a part. The readings that follow may suggest to you how the meaning of childhood has changed over time. They offer examples of historically specific discourses of childhood.

Reading 3.7

From a report by a Factory Inspector to the Home Secretary in 1852

In my last report I gave an account of the vast increase of factories during the two preceding years, and there is no cessation, for new mills are going up everywhere. It is not to be wondered at, therefore, that I should hear of a great scarcity of hands, of much machinery standing idle from the want of people to work it, and of a rise of wages. This scarcity of hands has led to a considerable increase in the number of children employed in my district which indeed has been going on, happily, for a long time; I say 'happily' without hesitation, for now that children are restricted to half a day's work and are required to attend school, I know no description of work so advantageous for them as that in a factory . . . (Golby, 1986, p. 9)

From the Second Report (1864) of the Children's Employment Commission

The introduction of the machine has necessitated the employment, on the whole, of older children and girls, the usual age for commencing being about 14, one consequence of which is that in these factories the great majority of the employed being above 13 are either adults or 'young persons' as defined by the Factory Act, and therefore entitled to work full time, thus facilitating the introduction of legislative measures. (Golby, 1986, p. 15).

From a paper given to the British Psychological Society: 'The Mental Hygiene of the Pre-School Child' by Susan Isaacs (1928)

[M]any of the ways of behaviour in a very young child which would at once suggest the possibility or even the certainty of neurosis to the more experienced observer are actually welcomed by the parent and educator as signs of moral development, or chuckled over as evidences of childish quaintness and precocity. A pleasing docility, the absence of open defiance and hostility, particular tidiness, a precise care in folding and arranging the clothes at bed-time, careful effort not to spill water when drinking or washing, anxious dislike of soiled hands or mouth or meticulous kindness and sensitive dislike of cruelty to other children or pet animals, ritual attention to the saying of prayers, frequent endearments and shows of affection, waiting always until one is spoken to before speaking, the offering of gifts to older and stronger children, an ardent desire to be good or clever, an intense ambition not to have to be helped, docility to punishment, drawing-room politeness, the quiet voice and controlled movements – most of these things either please or amuse the parent. Yet any one of them, and particularly several of them found together, may be and often are effects of a deep neurotic guilt and anxiety. (Isaacs, 1948, pp. 3–4)

In summary, meanings are encoded in representations by the assembly of a particular set of signs in a particular context which may be decoded from a number of positions. However, there is no guarantee that the meanings encoded will be directly and unambiguously decoded. In order to communicate there must be some shared meanings that are tacitly accepted by encoder and decoder, but this process is always mediated by the possibility that the decoder will bring alternative or oppositional understandings to the exchange. Furthermore, representations only become meaningful within discourse. Discourse is all those statements, images, practices and institutions which represent a particular body of knowledge. One of the tasks of the cultural analyst is to explore how discourses are formed, how they function to constitute and sustain power relations and how and where dominant discourses have been, and are, challenged.

ACTIVITY 3.11

- We have briefly examined the concept of discourse in relation to witch-hunts and to childhood. In order to extend your understanding of discourse you could explore either of these two examples further or you could look at other discursive formations. Foucault was particularly interested in 'madness', 'punishment' and 'sexuality'. You could usefully read more widely from the suggested list for this chapter.

> • You might select a topic and trace how it is constructed within discourse, drawing on a range of texts, practices and institutions. Examples might be 'home', 'royalty', 'homeopathy', 'motherhood', 'Third World', 'education', 'woman' – but there are many more you could choose.

Representation, Discourse and Resistance

In the previous section we saw how a Jamaican schoolgirl resisted the representation of the Caribbean as 'animal' and 'insane'. Charlotte Brontë's representation of the Caribbean, for this reader, was a misrepresentation not only of her country but also of personal identity. Discourse and representation are profoundly implicated in the construction of personal identities as well as group identities, as you will recall from chapter 2, where we discussed autobiography and personal life narratives. In the previous section we discussed how producing and sustaining 'truths' was crucial to the maintenance and reproduction of power relations. Once something becomes established as 'truth' or 'common sense' it becomes naturalized and difficult to challenge. As the Jamaican woman said, 'Miss admitted it seemed unfair, but she went on to do nothing with that insight.' Our focus in this section is on the ways in which groups who believe themselves to be consistently misrepresented have resisted or challenged the 'truths' embedded in certain discourses. Now read this extract from an article by Richard Dyer, entitled 'Seen to be believed: some problems in the representation of gay people as typical'.

Reading 3.8

'Homosexual' and 'lesbian' have been negative sexual categories, at best to be viewed pathologically, at worst as moral degeneracy, and in either case calling forth images in which such features as skin pallor, hooded eyes, and genital deformity have been used as visual correlatives of sickness and sin. Such views of lesbianism and (male) homosexuality have been challenged above all by those people who found themselves designated by the categories. There have been two predominant forms of challenge.

One has attempted to alter the object of the categories, to change the terms of what they refer to by shifting from persons to acts. The most familiar form that this argument takes is that people who perform homosexual acts are in every other respect just like everyone else: their sexuality does not imply anything else about their personality. This has been a major plank in the arguments of homosexual civil rights and law reform movements, and it is in the logic of this position that all typification is anathema. The problem was and is that the arguments about homosexuality are very hard to make on the terrain of existing definitions, which do inexorably imply categories and types. Thus a statement like 'homosexuals are just like anyone else' already reproduces the notion that there are persons designated homosexuals. Moreover, the development of gay sub-cultures meant that many homosexual people did participate in a lifestyle, a set of tastes, a language and so on that meant that their lives were, in more respects than the sexual, different from that of most heterosexual people.

The sub-cultural activity was itself a form of resistance to the negative implications of the lesbian/homosexual categories, in that it took the categories as a basis for a way of life rather than as something to be overcome or cured. From this sub-culture emerged the politics of the late 1960s gay movement, with its stress on accepting oneself as lesbian/homosexual, identifying oneself with other homosexual people under the term 'gay' and coming out, openly declaring and showing oneself as gay to society as a whole. These strategies of identifying and coming out immediately raise the problem of visibility, of being seen to be gay. Wearing badges, kissing in the streets were means of being visible, but so equally were behaving and dressing in recognizably gay ways – they brought you together in an act of sharing and they made you obvious on the streets. Typification (visually recognizable images and self-presentation) is not just something wished on gay people but produced by them, both in the pre-political gay sub-cultures and in the radical gay movement since 1968. (Dyer, 1993, pp. 20–1)

Dyer is concerned to demonstrate the difficulties involved in attempts by gay people to change the ways in which they represent themselves. Since the 1960s the gay movement has openly resisted and challenged the dominant representations of homosexuality that were produced through the discourses of medicine and religion. Homosexuality, according to these discourses, is either pathological (caused by physical or mental sickness) or a symptom of moral depravity. Both views imply that a solution to the state of homosexuality is necessary. Depending on which view is taken, this will be either cure or punishment. In the article from which the extract is taken, Dyer's focus is on the representation of homosexuality in film, and he is very much concerned with visual typification. However, he argues that, in the case of homosexuality, visual representation is all-important.

A major fact about being gay is that it doesn't show. There is nothing about gay people's physiognomy that declares them gay, no equivalents to the biological markers of sex and race. There are signs of gayness, a repertoire of gestures, expressions, stances, clothing, and even environments that bespeak gayness, but these are cultural forms designed to show what the person's person alone does not show: that he or she is gay. (Dyer, 1993, p. 19)

Within a discourse in which homosexuality is 'sickness or sin', those who are charged with cure or punishment need to be able to recognize homosexuality in order to be able to 'solve' it. Recall from the previous section that one of the elements of a discourse is that there should be people (subjects) who can be recognized as personifying the attributes assigned to them by the particular 'truth' constructed in discourse. The physical bodies of women, black people, those with disabilities and the old declare their categorization. As Dyer points out, this is not the case for gay people. As a result, a repertoire of images emerged (men dressed and acting in a feminine way, women wearing men's suits, women who make no concessions to femininity, among others) that signalled homosexuality in the way skin colour or anatomy signalled 'race' or sex. Dyer argues that there have been two strategies which the gay movement has adopted in order to challenge these visual typifications.

ACTIVITY 3.12

- Can you identify the two strategies to which Dyer is referring?
- What is problematic about each strategy?

Whatever your own views, the point to note is that the gay movement has not simply rejected conventional representations of homosexuality as mis-representations. Instead, it has attempted to rework the coding of those visual typifications that produced negative meanings so as to signify dignity, pride in one's gayness and solidarity with other gay people. In this way gay people have challenged how they are represented, not by producing new representa-tions, but by insisting on the revaluation of previously negative images. Through self-representation they are re-presenting homosexuality as a posi-tive category. In doing so they have attempted to take control of the meanings produced, rather than allowing themselves to remain invisible and/or repre-sented by others. Black people have used the same strategy – the word 'negro' has been appropriated as a positive term by some black people (see reading 8.6, for example).

ACTIVITY 3.13

How far do you think these strategies can counter the negative discourses of homosexuality and the discriminatory treatment of gay people in society?

We end this chapter with an extract from the work of Jo Spence. Jo Spence (1934–92) was a photographer and educator who used her photography to challenge radically, among other things, conventional representations of class, illness and women's bodies. Photography, along with TV and film, is the source of much of the visual imagery we consume now. As a consequence it has enormous power to construct 'truthful' and 'normative' ways of seeing ourselves and the world we inhabit. Photographic journalism, documentary photography, advertising and fashion photography 'make sense' of the world by representing it to us visually. As students of culture you need to remain aware of the ways in which such representations are encoded, the discourses within which they acquire meaning and the possibilities for resistance and challenge.

Reading 3.9

[C]ommercial photography . . . is still dominated by incredibly narrow definitions of photography which are straddled by news and advertising and a multitude of state uses of photography many of which employ the window-on-the-world documentary mode of representation. Often these are a thinly disguised form of surveillance, a way of offering phoney evidence of surface phenomena, or of defining individual or group cultural identities which appear to be grounded in the 'real world' but are in fact total fictions offered up for consumption. We must never forget that all this is the background to any kind of radical professionalism in which we are engaged. Such images as we produce which we feel challenge the dominant ideology, even if they initially attempt to show something which has never been seen before, will soon be sucked up by the industrial machine of the mass media. We must expect this and have strategies for dealing with ways in which work is appropriated.

Equally fictitious are the fantasies (apparently more pleasurable, often engaging with our unconscious desires and traumas) offered to us by advertising. Some of us are also offered images of the fragmented female body, which are often called pornography. These images appear to present men with a kind of pseudo control over women in which they can day-dream of being dominant whilst in fact they continue to occupy a kind of childlike notion of omnipotence. This is often in contradiction to the economic and political impotence of many men. These interconnected spheres of image-making create regimes of desire in which we are always flattered into assuming positions which are difficult to escape in imagination – even if our daily lives totally differ. (Spence, 1995, p. 103)

Spence goes on to suggest that it is 'only by having a theory of what it is possible to speak about or to represent visually that we can began to understand what is absent from all these agendas' (Spence, 1995, p. 104). This connects to our previous discussion about discourse: that which is absent, that which cannot be said, remains outside discourse. Representations have no meaning until they are made sense of through a particular discourse – even where these representations are resisting or challenging dominant knowledge. For example, Spence's photograph of an adult man sucking at a woman's breast (figure 3.2) can only be understood as challenging normative assumptions about breastfeeding, mothering and adult sexuality once we know what those normative assumptions are. And it is within discourse that these assumptions are constructed as 'the norm'.

ACTIVITY 3.14

Try to work out precisely what assumptions about breasts, sexuality and motherhood figure 3.2 is challenging. Where do these assumptions come from? Try to identify the discourses which produce these assumptions. For example:

- Breasts are erotic playthings for men: patriarchal discourse of gender.
-
-

Conclusions

In order to summarize the material covered in this chapter we have chosen to quote from Richard Dyer's introduction to *The Matter of Images: Essays on Representation*, in which he argues that the cultural representation of social groups raises political questions about oppression and dominance. Who represents whom, where and how determines the representations available for us to look at and read, but people do not necessarily make sense of these representations in terms of the preferred or intended meaning. We bring to our

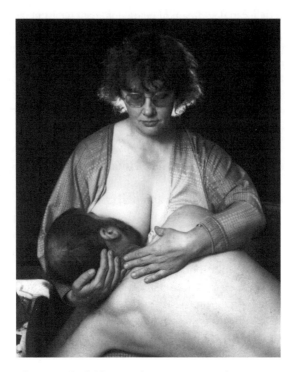

Figure 3.2   *Madonna and Child*, 1982, by Jo Spence and Terry Dennett (from the series The History Lesson)

viewing and reading a range of codes and conventions in order to make sense of the material offered: the codes used will depend upon the position we occupy in the social world and the ways in which we understand that world. However, despite the impossibility of single, predetermined meanings, we are limited as to the range of meanings we can bring to any text – representations do refer to realities at the same time as they affect reality. To understand a picture of a horse as representing a motor car is an error of seeing which could result in being seen as insane or visually impaired. Furthermore, as Dyer points out,

> The prestige of high culture, the centralization of mass cultural production, the literal poverty of marginal cultural production: these are aspects of the power relations of representation that put the weight of control over representation on the side of the rich, the white, the male, the heterosexual. Acknowledging the complexity of viewing/reading practices in relation to representation does not entail the claim that there is equality and freedom in the regime of representation. (Dyer, 1993, p. 2)

The relation of representation to the lives and experiences of people in the real social world is complicated, but representations do 'have real consequences for real people'. Dyer insists that

> how social groups are treated in cultural representation is part and parcel of how they are treated in life, that poverty, harassment, self-hate and discrimination (in housing, jobs, educational opportunity and so on) are shored up and instituted by representation. The resonances of the term 'representation' suggest as much. How a group is represented, presented over again in cultural forms, how an image of a member of a group is taken as representative of that group, how that group is represented in the sense of spoken for and on behalf of (whether they represent, speak for themselves or not), these all have to do with how members of groups see themselves and others like themselves, how they see their place in society, their right to the rights a society claims to ensure its citizens. Equally re-presentation, representativeness, representing have to do also with how others see members of a group and their place and rights, others who have the power to affect that place and those rights. How we are seen determines in part how we are treated; how we treat others is based on how we see them; such seeing comes from representation. (Dyer, 1993, p. 1)

You could usefully link your work on representation with that on identity and difference by rereading Rashid Araeen's account of his meeting with the professor of fine art (reading 2.1) in the light of Dyer's comments about the politics of representation.

Chapter 4

History

Introduction

Although we have referred to history and used material from the past in the previous chapters, we have not, so far, considered what we mean by 'history' and how we might approach the past as students of culture. In chapter 1 we wrote about the 'contemporary turn to culture', and in recent decades the study of history has been influenced, along with literature and sociology, by this 'cultural turn'. It is not necessary to have studied history in order to engage with the material in this chapter. If, up to now, you have not enjoyed historical study you may find that approaching the past through culture offers perspectives that stimulate a new interest. If you have enjoyed history we hope you will find material and ideas in this chapter that provoke fresh insights.

The first definition of 'history' in the *Concise Oxford English Dictionary* reads: 'a continuous, usually chronological, record of important or public events'. However, we tend to use the word 'history' far more broadly than this. We say of a person, 'she has a history', meaning she has an exciting or chequered past; or we say 'anyway, it's all history now', by which we mean that certain events are over and done with – relegated to the past. History as studied in universities or at school tends to follow the dictionary definition: students study 'important or public events'. Professional historians construct the chronological record of important events, and what constitutes an important event is the subject matter of historical debate and research. The point is that history is a human construction, or perhaps more accurately a reconstruction. The past does not present itself 'as it really was': writing history involves the interpretation and selection of elements in the past to produce an account that 'makes sense' to those who read or study it in the present.

Think back to chapter 3, where we introduced you to the concept of 'representation'. History is one of the ways in which we re-present the past in the present, and like all representations it requires a set of shared understandings or a discourse within which it becomes meaningful. For example, from the eighteenth century onwards there was a widespread belief in progress and evolution. Many nineteenth-century historians stressed the ways in which the past had been improved upon or could be learned from. History demonstrated the onward march of civilization and the lessons to be learned from its failures. Yet the writing of history from within a discourse of progress was itself one of the elements of nineteenth-century culture that *produced* a discourse of progress. In the twentieth century, the Holocaust, two world wars, the threat of nuclear war and the continuing existence of poverty, starvation and barbarism exposed the myth of progress. Contemporary accounts of the past are less likely to emphasize history as a continuing triumph of 'civilization' over 'the primitive'. Raymond Williams (1976, p. 147) comments, 'history as a tale of accidents, unforeseen events, frustration of conscious purposes . . . is probably a specific 20th century form of history as general process, though now used, in contrast with the sense of achievement or promise of the earlier and still active versions, to indicate a general pattern of frustration and defeat' (Williams, 1976, p. 147).

Nevertheless, the belief that history is a story of gradual and sustained progress is one that is often implicit in discussions about the past. We all want to believe that the world can become a more humane place. The past could be represented by a catalogue of random, arbitrary events, unconnected with each other or with the present, but this is rarely the case. History is a way of creating order out of the mass of material that is the past's legacy to the present. In chapter 2, when we looked at autobiography, we suggested that life stories were a way in which individuals shaped the random experience of their lives into something with meaning. To represent the past by selecting certain versions of events or certain personages as significant is to create an order that bestows meaning on the events, people and objects of past times. Choosing, as historians do, to represent the past in terms of cause and effect or as less evolved than the present are two of the ways in which specific meanings of the past are produced and circulated. If you recall, in chapter 1 we introduced you to the definition of culture as 'the production and circulation of meanings'. History, in all its forms, and it has many, as we shall see, is therefore a key practice in the processes of culture. In this chapter we shall be exploring history as one aspect of culture and identity. Social groups, nations and communities all have their histories. History is one of the ways in which human beings acquire identities and make sense of the world and their experience of it. Thinking about how the past is represented, and how ideas about it are communicated, in the present can offer insights into the process by which meaning is produced and circulated. So we begin this chapter by posing the question 'what is history?'; we then discuss some recent challenges to orthodox **paradigms** of history, and finally, we want you to think about history as a cultural product, a commodity that is consumed and produced in the present. In order to do this, you will be invited to engage in a discussion about what is often called the 'heritage' industry.

The Past 'As It Really Was'?

In his book *The Nature of History*, the historian Arthur Marwick identifies three senses in which the term 'history' is used. As you read this extract note down the three different meanings Marwick identifies.

Reading 4.1

'History' as commonly used has three levels of meaning. First it can connote the entire human past as it actually happened. Life, doubtless, would be simpler if this usage could be abandoned in favour of the unambiguous locution 'the past'. Language however is a common property, ill-defined, often badly cultivated, but not subject to enclosure by precious academics. Even those scholars who have publicly renounced this usage of the word will be found at some stage to betray themselves, for it is very hard to avoid such plump pronouncements as 'History is not the handwork of hero-figures', or 'Now is the time to take stock of human history'. History, secondly and more usefully, connotes man's [*sic*] attempt to describe and interpret that past: it is, in the words of Professor Barraclough, 'the attempt to discover on the basis of fragmentary evidence the significant things about the past'. This is the history with which we are concerned when we talk of history as a social necessity, of history being an 'industry'; which comes nearest to the original Greek meaning, 'Inquiry'. Some ventures in discovery or inquiry are clearly more successful than others: some ages have regarded as 'significant' matters which we would now relegate to the realms of superstition, myth or polemic. We can enjoy and profit from historical works spread across the entire timespan of human literary activity, such as those of Thucydides, Ssu-ma Chi'en, Bede or Machiavelli: but we must note that the systematic study of history, history as a *discipline* (the third meaning), is a very recent phenomenon, becoming established in West European and North American universities only in the nineteenth century, far in arrears of philosophy, classical languages, mathematics and natural sciences. In this book we shall be specially concerned with the development of modern historical studies; but an important theme will be the difficult, but highly exciting tensions generated between history as an academic and sometimes pedantic discipline, and history as an essential facet of human experience. (Marwick, 1970, p. 15)

The term 'history' is often used as synonymous with 'the past'. However, in its earliest use history meant a narrative of events which had passed. In this sense its meaning was very close to that of story; either history or story might be used to connote imaginative accounts of events or accounts of events which were assumed to have happened. History, meaning an account of past events, also included the idea of inquiry: why did this happen; what caused it to happen? In a third sense history connotes the academic discipline of history, in which scholarly, systematic methods are applied to the source material from which interpretations of past events are constructed and disseminated.

ACTIVITY 4.1

Read the following statements and note against each one which of the three senses of 'history' is being used.

1 I really enjoyed reading the novel *The History of Mr. Polly*.
2 It's all history now!
3 Visiting museums can teach us a lot about history.
4 That film was an excellent piece of history.
5 I hope to go on to study history at university.
6 Many of Shakespeare's plays offer a version of history.
7 Shakespeare used drama to present history.
8 The history of baseball in this country has yet to be written.
9 The history we were taught at school was not very interesting.

Don't worry if you found it difficult to distinguish between history as an academic discipline and history as a less scholarly account of the past, but do ensure you understand the distinction between history as the past and history as the reconstruction, narrating and interpretation of the past (whether academic or not). Points 2, 3 and 6 are using history to mean the past, 5 and 9 are using history to mean the scholarly, academic discipline, 1, 4, 7 and 8 are using history in a more generalized sense, to suggest a narrative account of the past. In the rest of this chapter it is the second and third meanings of the term 'history' with which we are concerned.

Marwick makes a distinction between the disciplined, systematic study of the past undertaken by academic historians and 'history as an essential facet of human experience'. By the latter he means the ways in which the past is made sense of in a variety of ways other than through the scholarly work of professional historians. While he concedes that 'superstition, myth and polemic' have been important as ways of passing on knowledge of the past, his implication is that it is only through the academic discipline of history that we can gain a 'true' understanding of past events. The nineteenth-century historian Leopold von Ranke, who pioneered the modern discipline of history, was concerned that history should be seen as a science, providing facts and objective deductions. For Ranke, history should aim to present the past as 'it actually was'. Marwick, while acknowledging that Ranke may have been somewhat optimistic in believing that history can inevitably yield an 'exact, objective, scientific account of "what actually happened"', writes within the paradigm of history established by Ranke (Marwick, 1986, p. 16). The aim of scholarly history should be to represent as closely as possible the events of the past as 'they really happened'. In order to achieve this, the historian's task is to produce an interpretation of past events from a range of primary sources, the most important of which are written documents produced in the period being studied (manuscript materials). Autobiographies, oral accounts, folklore, novels and ballads, although essential in order 'to understand an age from, as it were, the inside', may not give the historian 'one single piece of concrete information' (Marwick, 1970, p. 139). In order to reconstruct and interpret the past, professional historians require a lengthy training in the analysis of primary source material and the use of footnotes and bibliographies, as well as access to archive materials. According to Marwick these are the 'experts' in interpreting the past: those who write autobiographies or trace their family's genealogy or collect nursery rhymes are 'amateur' historians. The history produced by 'experts' tends to be assigned a privileged place in hierarchies of knowledge, and for this reason, it can be argued, historians play a significant role in the 'production and circulation of meanings'.

You will recall that in chapter 3 we discussed the concept of discourse as a process by which certain forms of knowledge are produced. Marwick offers what was, until the 1960s, an orthodox view of historical **epistemology**; a view which concurs with a specific understanding or discourse of what constitutes valid knowledge more generally. Orthodox historical research is concerned with the systematic production of 'objective' knowledge. It is 'scientific', seeking out facts and proven hypotheses. In pursuit of 'objectivity', myth, anecdote, personal and fictional accounts are relegated to a secondary place, in which the meanings or knowledges offered through subjectivity, polemic and imagination can be categorized as less 'true'.

Now read the following extract from *The Pursuit of History*, by John Tosh.

Reading 4.2

Whereas the individual's sense of his or her past arises spontaneously, historical knowledge has to be produced. Society has a past which extends back far beyond the lives of the individuals who happen to comprise it at any one time, the raw materials out of which a historical consciousness can be fashioned are accordingly almost unlimited. Those elements which find a place in it represent a selection of truths which are deemed worthy of note. Who produces historical knowledge, and who validates it for general consumption, are therefore important questions. How well the job is done has a bearing on the cohesion of society and its capacity for renewal and adaptation in the future. That is why what historians do should matter to everyone else. Their work can be manipulated to promote desired forms of social consciousness; it can remain confined to academic circles, powerless to influence society for good or ill; or it can become the basis for informed and critical discussion of current issues. (Tosh, 1991, p. 2)

Tosh raises some important questions about the social and cultural significance of historical knowledge. Let us explore these further.

ACTIVITY 4.2

- Think back to the history you learned at school. What topics can you recall covering? Which nations' histories did you learn about? Which social groups did you learn about? Following Tosh, can you identify those elements which have found a place in your historical consciousness? Can you think of any period, group, place or idea of which you have little historical knowledge?
- Can you think of examples of history being used as a starting point for informed and critical discussion of current issues?

The point Tosh is making is that the production of historical knowledge is political, by which we mean that researching, writing and disseminating history is one of the means by which power relations can be sustained. For example, in George Orwell's novel *Nineteen Eighty-Four*, the state rewrites the history books in order to construct a version of the past in which the current totalitarian regime is presented as the best and, indeed, the only way of ordering society. Equally, writing and researching history can contest existing power relations. Tosh cites a resolution carried by the International Congress of African Historians in 1965, which stated 'that an African philosophy of history which would serve as a liberation from the colonial experience must be a vital concern of all historians studying in Africa' (Tosh, 1991, p. 5). Making visible those whom the history books have ignored can challenge the apparent 'naturalness' of a historically specific social order. Serious discussions by feminists of the position of women in society gained momentum in the late 1960s and early 1970s. Some, like Carroll Smith-Rosenberg, took the invisibility of women in the historical record as a starting point for the recovery of a history of women (Smith-Rosenberg, 1985).

In 1963, the Marxist historian E. P. Thompson published *The Making of the English Working Class,* in which he argued that the working class did not 'rise like the sun at an appointed time' but 'was present at its own making' (Thompson, 1963, p. 8). By this he means that working-class people in the early nineteenth century were actively involved in the process by which they acquired a consciousness of themselves as working-class. They were not simply born into a pre-given 'class' but, by their own agency, created a set of relations with others whose interests were different from theirs. In terms of our understanding of culture, they were actively engaged in the process of producing certain meanings which contributed to the social phenomenon we understand as 'class'. Now read the following extract from Thompson's preface to *The Making of the English Working Class.*

Reading 4.3

This is a group of studies, on related themes, rather than a consecutive narrative. In selecting these themes I have been conscious, at times, of writing against the weight of prevailing orthodoxies. There is the Fabian orthodoxy, in which the great majority of working people are seen as passive victims of *laisser faire*, with the exception of a handful of far-sighted organizers (notably, Francis Place). There is the orthodoxy of the empirical economic historians, in which working people are seen as a labour force, as migrants, or as the data for statistical series. There is the 'Pilgrim's Progress' orthodoxy, in which the period is ransacked for forerunners – pioneers of the Welfare State, progenitors of a Socialist Commonwealth, or (more recently) early exemplars of rational industrial relations. Each of these orthodoxies has a certain validity. All have added to our knowledge. My quarrel with the first and second is that they tend to obscure the agency of working people, the degree to which they contributed by conscious efforts, to the making of history. My quarrel with the third is that it reads history in the light of subsequent preoccupations, and not as in fact it occurred. Only the successful (in the sense of those whose aspirations anticipated subsequent evolution) are remembered. The blind alleys, the lost causes, and the losers them-selves are forgotten.

I am seeking to rescue the poor stockinger, the Luddite cropper, the 'obsolete' handloom weaver, the 'utopian' artisan, and even the deluded follower of Joanna Southcott, from the enormous condescension of posterity. Their crafts and traditions may have been dying. Their hostility to the new industrialism may have been backward-looking. Their communitarian ideals may have been fantasies. Their insur-rectionary conspiracies may have been foolhardy. But they lived through these times of acute social disturbance, and we did not. Their aspirations were valid in terms of their own experience; and if they were casualties of history, they remain, condemned in their own lives, as casualties. (Thompson, 1963, pp. 11–12)

Don't worry if you don't understand many of the historical references. However, if you are interested, do follow these up in Thompson's book. For now the point to try to grasp is the significance of Thompson's challenge to 'prevailing orthodoxies'.

ACTIVITY 4.3

- Do you think history ('posterity') has represented working people in ways that are condescending? Can you think of any examples from history books, TV programmes, films?
- Why do you think it matters whether working people are represented, for example, as victims of an economic system? Are there consequences for the way in which they are treated? You could remind yourself of the conclusion of chapter 3 if you feel you need help with this question.

Thompson's history has justifiably been highly influential. As an account of the experiences, values and beliefs of 'ordinary' people at a moment of dramatic social change, *The Making of the English Working Class* contested the idea that history was inevitably about the great and good (or bad). Moreover, it demonstrated that 'ordinary' people could act as agents of social change and were not simply at the mercy of historical and economic forces beyond their control. Such a belief is important, as it can enable 'ordinary' people to believe that social change might be possible. This was important in the 1960s, as movements 'from below' challenged the dominance of the most powerful groups in society. In the 1960s, student demonstrations, the civil rights movement, the women's liberation movement, and youth sub-cultures more generally, questioned the right of a small, powerful elite to control access to knowledge and wealth. Writing in the 1960s, Thompson's concern for the 'poor stockinger', like Smith-Rosenberg's for the invisibility of women, is, at least in part, intimately connected to the preoccupations of the present. In the present our dialogue with Thompson and our dialogue with 'the poor stockinger' are equally related to our contemporary concerns. It could be argued that in the present we construct the past we would like: historians like Marwick, Tosh, Thompson and Smith-Rosenberg remain critically alert to the dynamics of this tension, but in less scrupulous hands history can become a powerful weapon in political struggle. None the less, an awareness of a shared history is one of the most powerful ways in which group identities, be they family, national, ethnic or social, are formed and strengthened.

> **ACTIVITY 4.4**
> - Think about your own sense of identity. Are you conscious of sharing a history with others? How would it feel if you had no knowledge of the history of the people with whom you share a sense of belonging? Look back to the discussion on identities in chapter 2 to help with this.
> - Look out for examples of history being used to create bonds between people. The newspapers and TV would be useful sources for this exercise.

When you write, rewrite or read history you should aim for a critical awareness of the relation between past and present and of the part history can play in the shaping of identities. This takes us back to Tosh's point about the ways in which history can become 'the basis for informed and critical discussion of current issues'.

Challenges to Objectivity: Post-structuralist Theories of History

In recent years the Rankean paradigm of history, within which the historians discussed above work, has been radically challenged. Indeed, the work of Smith-Rosenberg and Thompson questions the supposed 'objectivity' of history, revealing the gaps and omissions in the historical record that functioned to hide certain groups from historical scrutiny, and the significance of historical interpretation that, consciously or not, reconstructs in line with present preoccupations. However, recent post-structuralist theories have gone further, questioning the very nature of that reality the historian aims to reconstruct. The German critic Walter Benjamin wrote, 'The true picture of the past flits by. The past can be seized only as an image which flashes up at the instant when it can be recognized and is never seen again . . . For every image of the past that is not recognized by the present as one of its own concerns threatens to disappear irretrievably' (Benjamin, 1973, p. 257). So far we have assumed that the past is a reality that can be accessed and thus faithfully reproduced by the historian in the present. Benjamin problematizes this belief, suggesting instead that the past can never be recognized 'as it really was', but only in the ephemeral and transient form of flashing images which if not immediately grasped by the present are forever lost.

ACTIVITY 4.5

- Think of a historical period of which you have some knowledge, however limited. Could your knowledge of this period be characterized as flashing images? What is missing in your mental picture of the period?
- Think back to your own childhood. How do you know what happened when you were very small?
- If the past can only be known as flashing images, what becomes of the historian's authority to represent the past as it really was?

We want now to introduce you to another way in which orthodox **historiography** has been challenged in recent years. Historiography means the process by which history is written. Read the following extract by Hayden White, an American historiographer, from his book *Metahistory: the Historical Imagination in Nineteenth Century Europe*. White begins by making a distinction between histories and chronicles, where a chronicle is understood to be simply a list of events in chronological order of their occurrence.

Reading 4.4

Historical *stories* trace the sequences of events that lead from inaugurations to (provisional) terminations of social and cultural processes in a way that *chronicles* are not required to do. Chronicles are, strictly speaking, open-ended. In principle they have no inaugurations; they simply 'begin' when the chronicler starts recording events. And they have no culminations or resolutions; they can go on indefinitely. Stories, however, have a discernible form (even when that form is an image of a state of chaos) which marks off the events contained in them from the other events that might appear in a comprehensive chronicle of the years covered in their unfoldings.

It is sometimes said that the aim of the historian is to explain the past by 'finding', 'identifying', or 'uncovering' the 'stories' that lie buried in chronicles; and that the difference between 'history' and 'fiction' resides in the fact that the historian 'finds' his stories, whereas the fiction writer 'invents' his. This conception of the historian's task, however, obscures the extent to which 'invention' also plays a part in the historian's operations. The same event can serve as a different kind of element of many different historical stories, depending on the role it is assigned in a specific motific characterization of the set to which it belongs. The death of the king may be a beginning, an ending, or simply a transitional event in three different stories. In the chronicle, this event is simply 'there' as an element of a series; it does not 'function' as a story element. The historian arranges the events in the chronicle into a hierarchy of significance by assigning events different functions as story elements in such a way as to disclose the formal coherence of a whole set of events considered as a comprehensible process with a discernible beginning, middle and end.

The arrangement of selected events of the chronicle into a story raises the kinds of questions the historian must anticipate and answer in the course of constructing his narrative. These questions are of the sort: 'What happened next' 'How did it all happen?' 'Why did things happen this way rather than that?' 'How did it all come out in the end?' These questions determine the narrative tactics the historian must use in the construction of his story. But such questions about the connections between events which make of them elements in a *followable* story should be distinguished from questions of another sort: 'What does it all add up to?' 'What is the point of it all?' These questions have to do with the structure of the entire set of events considered as a complete story and call for a synoptic judgment of the relationship between a given story and other stories that might be 'found', 'identified', or 'uncovered' in the chronicle. (White, 1973, pp. 7–8)

White's point is that history may be no more objective than any other form of narration: for example, fiction. Because historical narratives are communicated through the medium of language, they cannot escape those features of language that are common to all spoken or written texts. Such features include the structuring of material into a narrative with a beginning, middle and end: that is, making a story out of a series of events. And what is important for White's argument is that historians do not 'discover' or 'find' a pre-existing story; they construct a story as part of the process of communicating through language. In doing so, historians, according to White, produce completed stories by arranging and selecting events in specific ways. As a consequence there are always other ways in which the events might be organized: these remain unspoken and unwritten in the form of gaps, silences and traces. And in structuring their material in certain ways, historians produce a meaning from it: 'what it all adds up to'. Thus, the significance of historical events is produced by the historian; it does not pre-exist her or his reconstruction of the past into a series of meaningful events. For White, historiography is closely linked to the writing of fiction, using similar fictive devices, such as plot and character. White's insistence on blurring the distinction between history and fiction has raised a number of important issues and problems, but it can also prove a fruitful way of approaching both historical and literary texts.

ACTIVITY 4.6

- If we accept White's argument that history is akin to fiction, are there any political consequences? Look back to what Tosh said about the role of historians.
- Does White's proposition have implications for Thompson's wish to rescue working people from the condescension of posterity?
- Does it matter if history is seen as a fiction?

Finally, read the following extract from a paper by the historian Carolyn Steedman, on history and autobiography. Steedman is remembering herself attempting to write history as an eight-year-old. What is your response?

Reading 4.5

It is at this point that I remember most clearly an eight-year-old in a crowded post-War South London classroom, writing a life of Queen Victoria in three volumes (three LCC [London County Council] exercise books): the holly pinned to the little princess's collar to make her sit up straight at meal times, the moment of destiny on the stairs when the men in frock coats fell at her feet. This story I write (dip pen, a good round hand: it's 1955) is me, but also, exactly at the same time, not-me. It will go on operating like that, the historical past will, as acceptance and denial.

I know that there is no 'really how it was' at all. But knowing about all the pretensions of the historical enterprise that seeks to conjure the past before our eyes, as it really was, does not stop me from wanting what all of history's readers want: the thing we cannot have, which is past time; the past 'as it really was'. The child in the 1950s South London classroom knew (she might be able to articulate this, if you asked her the right question) that the point isn't what happened, nor how the young Victoria sat at the table, nor the hurried drive through the dark to announce ascension to the throne; the point is what the child does with that history. (Steedman, 1992, pp. 46–7)

We have suggested above that we require a shared history in order to know ourselves as belonging to certain groups. Steedman seems to be suggesting that there is a deeper individual need for history, an unconscious or subconscious yearning for past time; a past that is always already lost to us and that we can never recapture. Steedman's 'historical enterprise that seeks to conjure the past before our eyes as it really was' is a long way from Ranke's systematic sifting of the evidence. For Steedman, the whole enterprise of history is located in fantasy and desire, memory and loss: our relationship with history and with the past constitutes psychological selfhood, both individually and collectively. In seeking to identify with the past we recognize both our belonging in it and our distance from it: 'acceptance and denial'. We will leave you to think about your own response to this.

The Past and Popular Memory

In this section we want to take up the point made by Steedman about what we do with history. If, as White suggests, history is simply another fiction, another text, then the authority of the historian to make sense of the past is limited. If he or she cannot represent the past to us 'as it really was', what is the role of the historian? How, in Tosh's words, can 'what historians do . . . matter to everyone else'? The following extract comes from the introduction to a book entitled *Narrating the Thirties: a Decade in the Making*.

Reading 4.6

The eminent Tudor historian, Geoffrey Elton, a staunch defender of methodological orthodoxy, described historical method as 'a recognised and tested way of extracting from what the past has left the true facts and events of that past, and so far as possible their true meaning and interrelation'. Even overlooking the obvious questions, 'recognised and tested by whom?' and '*which* facts and events?', and accepting for the sake of argument that historians can tell us fairly unproblematically 'what happened', there are still insurmountable problems with the claim that they can tell us with authority what those events *mean*. And this is a serious matter, because it is meanings, rather than factual accuracy, that the present looks for when it contemplates the past. Events may be part of a fixed past, but their meanings are part of the changing present, and cannot therefore be settled for good by the authority of professional experts. Walter Benjamin reminds us that the meaning of a historical event can be determined, 'posthumously, as it were, through events that can be separated from it by thousands of years. A historian who takes this as his point of departure stops telling the sequence of events like the beads of a rosary. Instead, he grasps the constellation which his own era has formed with a definite earlier one' [Benjamin, 1973, p. 265]. (Baxendale and Pawling, 1996, p. 8)

In the extract above, we have a suggestion that what is important about history is its meanings: history is one aspect of culture, understood as 'the production and circulation of meanings'. You will recall the discussion in chapter 3 of how meanings are produced through representation, and the processes of encoding and decoding involved in this. In their book, Baxendale and Pawling go on to analyse the ways in which a particular decade of British history, the 1930s, has been given certain meaning and significance:

> in particular, how narratives about or including the Thirties have not only been shaped by subsequent history, but also have been used to shape it, to influence subsequent events and give them particular meanings. These meanings, like the meaning of episodes in a novel, arise less from the intrinsic nature of historical events than from their position in the story – in Elton's phrase, 'their interrelations' with other events . . . disagreements about the history of the Thirties have rarely been about factual matters, but more often about the way the elements of the story have been emplotted, and thereby given meaning. (Baxendale and Pawling, 1996, p. 9)

ACTIVITY 4.7

- What meanings do you associate with the period referred to as 'the sixties'? Compile a list of words, images, events, books, films and people that seem to you to connote 'the sixties'. If you can, compare your list with someone else's. Are there common elements?
- What or who were your sources?

This activity can reveal the enormous range of practices and materials from which we construct a sense of the past. You may have listed any of the following: history books, TV documentaries and drama, autobiography and biography, individual memory or the memories of older relatives, photographs, popular music, exhibitions in museums, films of the period, family saga fictions, magazines and comics of the period, local history groups, school or university study, topic work undertaken at school (until recently the last two were less likely for the sixties, as school and university history tended to end round about 1945). This suggests, as Raphael Samuel (1994, p. 8) points out, that 'history is not the prerogative of the historian, nor even, as postmodernism [see reading 4.4 above by Hayden White] contends, a historian's "invention". It is, rather, a social form of knowledge; the work, in any given instance, of a thousand different hands'. History, according to Samuel, is not the work of individuals, but 'the ensemble of activities and practices in which ideas of history are embedded or a dialectic of past–present relations is rehearsed' (Samuel, 1994, p. 8). Our sense of the past is not simply revealed to us by professional historians but produced from a storehouse of popular memory, which may include the works of individual historians, from which we draw the impressions and ideas that together constitute a collective consciousness of a particular historical event or period.

Let us begin to examine what is meant by the term 'popular memory' by thinking about the different ways in which history is encountered in everyday life. For example, as this is being written, the day's viewing on television offers three historical documentaries, two shows about tracing family and individual origins, and an entire satellite channel devoted to history. There are five films made between 1930 and 1950 and two films about the past: one is set in 1950s Los Angeles, the other is a Second World War thriller, The newspaper carries a short article on a newly published book for children about the Holocaust, reviews of the celebrations to mark the 250th anniversary of Mozart's birth, and a number of obituaries. Political analysis of the situation in the Middle East includes references to events in the recent past such as 9/11. The building I work in was founded as a teacher training college for 'Christian gentlemen' in the mid-nineteenth century and overlooks York Minster, erected in the eleventh century. A local café has tables made from the bases of old treadle sewing machines, a cast iron cooking range and sepia photographs of Victorian and Edwardian street scenes. The estate agents across the road are advertising houses with 'period' features, and a trip to the outskirts of the city passes through a council estate built in the 1920s. There are shops offering replica art deco ceramics, Celtic jewellery, William Morris wallpapers, Victorian recipe books and medieval stained glass, as well as greetings cards featuring eighteenth- and nineteenth-century reproductions. Within the region it is possible to visit, for example, Eden camp, a theme museum based on the Second World War, and the Brontë Parsonage Museum, housing a collection of Brontë memorabilia. In the city is the Jorvik Centre, which offers opportunities to 'experience' life in Viking York. The local paper advertises evening classes in local history and tracing your family tree. We are surrounded in our daily lives not only by historical buildings, landscapes and artefacts but by contemporary representations of the past in TV programmes, films, novels, advertisements, shops, furniture and wallpaper. Moreover, we are also invited to use our leisure time to engage in or 'experience' history joining classes or local groups, and by visiting museums and theme parks.

ACTIVITY 4.8

- Choose a week (or a day if you prefer) and keep a diary of all the different ways in which you encounter history during that time. Note, as we have tried to do, everything you come across that has anything to do with history.
- Divide your list into those things that are: (a) legacies or traces left from the past; (b) contemporary representations of the past; (c) practices which involve engagement with the past.
- Are there any periods or themes in history that feature time and again in your list? If so, do they seem to have particular meanings? Do they seem to stand for any particular values? Or do they appear to be offering lessons to be learned? Do certain personages recur again and again?
- Can you discern any patterns of meaning from your analysis so far? Have you noticed any contradictory 'messages' among the apparent jumble of popular memory? For example, the reminders of the grinding poverty in which many people existed, alongside the frequent insistence by those who experienced this that these were 'the good old days'.

Now read this extract from *Theatres of Memory*, by Raphael Samuel. Samuel argued that British culture in the 1990s was steeped in history, much of it visual.

Reading 4.7

The last thirty years have witnessed an extraordinary and, it seems, ever growing enthusiasm for the recovery of the national past – both the real past of recorded history, and the timeless one of tradition. The preservation mania, which first appeared in reference to the railways in the early 1950s, has now penetrated every department of national life. In music it extends from Baroque instruments – a discovery of the early 1960s, when concerts of early music began to be performed for the *cognoscenti* – to pop memorabilia, which bring in six-figure bids when they are auctioned at Christie's or Sotheby's. In numismatics it has given trade tokens the status of Roman coinage. Industrial archaeology, a term coined in 1955, has won the protective mantle of 'historic' for abandoned or salvaged plant. The number of designated ancient monuments (268 in 1882, 12,900 today) also increases by leaps and bounds: among them is that brand-new eighteenth-century industrial village – product of inspired scavengings as well as of Telford New Town's search for a historical identity – Ironbridge. Country houses, on their last legs in the 1940s, and a Gothic horror in British films of the period, attract hundreds of thousands of summer visitors and have helped to make the National Trust (no more than a pressure group for the first seventy years of its existence) into the largest mass-membership organization in Britain. New museums open, it is said, at a rate of one a fortnight and miraculously contrive to flourish in face of repeated cuts in government funding: there are now some seventy-eight of them devoted to railways alone.

One feature of the historicist turn in national life – as of the collecting mania – has been the progressive updating of the notion of period, and a reconstruction of history's grand narrative by reference to the recent rather than the ancient past. Thus in TV documentary, the British Empire is liable to be seen through the lens of 'The Last Days of the Raj', as it is in Paul Scott's trilogy [*The Jewel in the Crown*], or the films of Merchant-Ivory. The year 1940 – replacing 1688, 1649 or 1066 as the central drama in the national past – becomes, according to taste, 'Britain's finest hour' or a privileged vantage point for studying the national decadence. Twentieth anniversaries, these days, seem to excite as much ceremony and rejoicing as for centenaries or diamond jubilees. Very pertinent here is what Fredric Jameson calls 'nostalgia for the present' – the desperate desire to hold on to disappearing worlds. Hence it may be the growth of rock pilgrimages and the creation of pop shrines. Hence too, it may be – memorials to the fragility of the present rather than the past – the multiplication of commemorative occasions, such as 40th and 50th birthdays, and the explosive growth in the production of commemorative wares. The past under threat in many retrieval projects, as in the mass of 'do-it-yourself' museums, and self-made or family shrines, is often the recent past – the day before yesterday rather than as say, in nineteenth century revivalism, that of the Elizabethan sea-dogs, medieval chivalry or Gothic architecture. (Samuel, 1994, pp. 139–40)

Can you see the point that Samuel is making? A profound concern with the past is something that all societies, both now and in the past, share. A sometimes obsessive need to engage with the past has proved common to all cultures; non-literate cultures have orally transmitted stories, legends and myths handed down from generation to generation. You might want to think about this need in the light of the suggestions made by Steedman in the extract with which we ended the previous section. The point Samuel is making is that in our own time this concern with the past has taken a particular form – an emphasis on the recent past – that is different from, for example, the form taken by nineteenth-century historicism. Samuel claims that our concern is not with the distant past but with what he calls 'the day before yesterday'. He goes on to argue that what societies do with the past, which aspects of it are emphasized in popular memory and what forms these take are all themselves historically specific. In the United States, for example, the Holocaust or Shoah, as some prefer to call it, is remembered publicly in the form of a memorial and a museum. There is no equivalent in the United Kingdom. This is, in part, due to the political and economic influence of the Jewish community in the United States. In eighteenth-century England the histories of ancient Greece and Rome were used as models for architecture, literature and intellectual thought. The same civilizations are taught in schools today but used to encourage an interest in how so-called ordinary people lived in the past. The classic 1950s Hollywood Western in which native American Indians were always represented as the enemy to be vanquished by the fearless, ultramasculine cowboys presented a version of American history that has since been replaced in the light of changing ideas about 'race' and gender. Samuel's wider point is that a study of the popular forms in which history is presented can tell us much about the values, aspirations, beliefs and tensions of the present and the relationship of these to the value, aspirations, beliefs and tensions of the past.

ACTIVITY 4.9	Did the exercise you carried out for activity 4.8 confirm Samuel's claim that much of our concern with the past is focused on 'the day before yesterday'? Can you identify any specific period(s) as offering particular values for the present?

Now read the following letter to the *Daily Telegraph*, a UK daily newspaper.

Reading 4.8

Sir – I have recently visited HMS Victory in Portsmouth Dockyard, and was both perplexed and disappointed by the commentary given by the guide.

As a child I remember being fascinated by the description given by the sailor who was then our guide, not only of the function of the ship's equipment and weapons and the duties of all who sailed in her, but of the battle of Trafalgar and its place in our history.

But now Victory is presented simply as an ancient artefact. The guide dwells mainly on the dreadful conditions suffered by the men below deck and the punishments meted out to them by the officers, who enjoyed great comfort on the deck above.

No mention is made of the fact that all these officers, including Nelson, would have gone to sea as midshipmen, aged as young as 10, they would have lived and worked on the same decks as the men, going aloft with them to handle the sails.

There was no purchase of commissions in the Royal Navy, so they would have risen to become officers only if they had mastered the skills of seamanship required to sail and fight.

Nelson's death is now presented as little more than an incident at the battle of Trafalgar. Anyone without historical knowledge might think he died just because he was standing carelessly on deck at the time. There is no explanation of why Nelson and his flagship have been held in such esteem by the nation. No reference is made to his genius, the signalling innovations he used, or his new tactics which enabled him to win his great battle.

This is deplorable today, when so little history is taught in many schools. We need our national heroes as never before. (Jean Gordon, Petersfield, Hants, 'Letters to the Editor', *Daily Telegraph*, 14 March 1994; cited in Samuel, 1994, p. 164)

ACTIVITY 4.10

1   To what does Jean Gordon object in the commentary accompanying her visit to HMS Victory?

2   Why is she concerned about the treatment of Nelson as a historical figure?

3   What is your response to her claim that national heroes are needed 'as never before'?

4   Can you think of other heroes or heroines of popular memory? What are they remembered for? We have started you off; you carry on.

Hero/heroine	Remembered because
• Martin Luther King	Fought for civil rights for black Americans
• Emily Davison	Died for the cause of women's right to the vote
• Joan of Arc	
• Davy Crockett	
•	
•	
•	

Those historical figures who become established in popular memory as heroes or heroines often acquire mythical status. Stories circulate which affirm their lives and actions as especially virtuous, courageous or inspiring and, often despite detailed and painstaking research by historians to reveal them as complex three-dimensional human beings, they remain symbolic figures in the collective consciousness of the group for whom their significance is particularly relevant. For example, while closely argued historical scholarship has attempted to represent a balanced account of the strengths and limitations, as well as the long and chequered career, of Winston Churchill, many people prefer to remember him as the man who, according to the myth, almost single-handedly saved Britain from Nazi invasion. This is not to suggest that the myths which surround a figure such as Churchill offer a completely false representation. Many people who experienced the Second World War accepted that Churchill was one, albeit very important, factor in Britain's victory but were, nevertheless reassured and inspired by the representations and practices that produced his mythical status. He came to represent a belief in the power of the individual against the forces of evil, a belief that, however embattled, 'good' will triumph and that the essence of this 'goodness' was a particular Englishness.

The Churchillian myth offers a particular way of interpreting and narrating history, in which individual figures are seen as responsible for the destinies of whole nations, and conflicts between nations are struggles between the forces of good and evil. **Myths** are another of the signifying practices we introduced you to in chapter 3: their function is to produce meaning by assembling a set of signs that can be read symbolically. In the case of popular memory, certain figures acquire the status of hero or villain, or certain events are invested with particular significance, thereby representing or standing in for a whole nexus of determining factors, motivations and interests. The media, in particular, rely on myth as a way of representing past events. Think, for example, of photo-journalism, which often uses a single image to represent a whole cluster of ideas and meanings. On the 11 September 2001 four planes originating from United States airports were hijacked by Muslim fundamentalists. Two of these planes were flown into the twin towers of the World Trade Centre building in Manhattan, one attempted to do the same at the Pentagon in Washington, and the fourth was brought down in Pittsburgh, Pennsylvania. This was an unprecedented attack on the United States and resulted in the loss of approximately 3000 lives. As a result the president, George Bush, declared a 'war on terrorism', American forces invaded Afghanistan, and Bush instigated a military operation to crush fundamentalist regimes in the Middle East. 9/11, as it came to be called, was seen as a defining moment in contemporary American, and indeed world, history. Interestingly, the focus of attention in the media very quickly became the attack on the twin towers of the World Trade Centre and the mayhem that ensued in lower Manhattan. Images of 9/11 are nearly all of the planes flying into the twin towers. Certain pictures, such as the moment the planes hit the towers, have gained currency as emblematic of the shocking destruction and tragedy of the event. Ground

Zero, the name given to the ground where the twin towers once stood, became a memorial to the many lives lost and to the shock that reverberated around the globe as we watched the destruction on TV of one of the most potent symbols of the United States' power and prosperity. The whole event and its aftermath were captured by world media in the form of TV news, books and reporting. A search on Amazon.com reveals over 1000 books written on the topic. The front covers of these nearly all use images of the twin towers, the American flag or the Statue of Liberty. In May 2002, when I (Judy Giles) visited Ground Zero, street vendors were selling memorabilia and postcards of the twin towers, as well as books of photographs and eyewitness accounts, in the Manhattan streets surrounding Ground Zero. This outpouring of cultural artefacts that attempt to memorialize 9/11 shapes the way in which we are encouraged to collectively remember the event. Individual memories of that day will be varied and may not match the collective memory that is produced by a particular culture. Nor will the meanings attributed to 9/11 by the media and by politicians necessarily be the only ways of understanding the event. Nevertheless, as the specificity of the events fades, certain cultural memories will become emblematic of it. For example, certain motifs and images are foregrounded – the twin towers, Ground Zero, the New York firefighters who, rightly, became heroes overnight. The simultaneous attack on the Pentagon and the bringing down of the plane in Pittsburgh are less photographed and less discussed, and therefore will be less well remembered in the collective consciousness of the world. I want to conclude this discussion by looking at two images.

ACTIVITY 4.11

Look at figures 4.1 and 4.2. The photograph of the New York firefighters was taken on 11 September 2001 as they struggled with the aftermath of the attacks on the twin towers of the World Trade Centre. Figure 4.2 shows the raising of the American flag on the Japanese island of Iwo Jima during the fierce battle that took place there in 1945. Can you suggest what ideas and meanings are encoded in these images?

The image (figure 4.1) captured by the New Jersey newspaper, *The Record*, came to symbolize the spirit of America as it struggled to deal with the shock of 9/11. New York firefighters are shown erecting the United States flag in the rubble and devastation of Ground Zero. The image is intended to represent the bravery, resilience and adherence to American values (represented by the

Figure 4.1   Firefighters raise the American flag on 11 September 2001

Stars and Stripes) shown by the firefighters and, by extension, the American people. This picture has been reproduced and circulated over and over again and has come to be emblematic of America's response to the tragedy (it is possible to buy a poster of this image on the Internet). It acts as both a memorial to the dead and a symbol of hope over tragedy. The attack on 9/11 has frequently been likened to the attack by the Japanese on Pearl Harbor on 7 December 1941, which was also seen as a 'sneak' attack and an 'act of infamy'. The US Naval Historical Center website says of the Pearl Harbor attack that the 'great Japanese successes, achieved without prior diplomatic formalities,

Figure 4.2 Marines raise the American flag on Iwo Jima on 23 February 1945

shocked and enraged the previously divided American people into a level of purposeful unity hardly seen before or since', until, we might add, 9/11 (www.history.navy.mil).

The image of the firefighters works particularly well because it very specifically recalls another important image in America's cultural memory. Figure 4.2 shows US marines raising the American flag on the Japanese island of Iwo Jima, during the fierce battle that took place there from 19 February to 16 March 1945, between Japanese and American forces. The casualties on both sides were enormous but the battle has been immortalized in America as a triumph of heroism for US marines, as well as as a tragic loss of life, because it enabled American B-29 bombers to land on the island, thereby facilitating the end of the conflict in the Pacific. One-third of all marines killed in the Second World War lost their lives at Iwo Jima. The memorial statue to the marines who lost their lives at Iwo Jima, situated in Connecticut, is a huge sculpture that exactly replicates the photograph. Like the 9/11 picture of the firefighters, the Iwo Jima image is intended to symbolize American resilience and heroism. It is readily recognized by people who were not even alive at the time of Iwo Jima and has become highly charged with meaning. The similarities between these two pictures are striking: the image of American males raising the US flag as in these pictures has become an **icon** of American values.

This discussion is intended to get you thinking about how important events in a nation's, country's or group's history are shaped in collective memories by their cultural representations. Such representations, however, almost always simplify the event, making it, as here, a simple celebration of victory or hope. In fact two of the marines raising the flag were killed before the end of the battle, there were huge Japanese casualties, and the atomic bomb was dropped on Hiroshima by the Enola Gay, a Boeing B-29 bomber, only five months later on 6 August 1945.

You might now be asking whether it matters how societies remember events in the past; after all, it is the present that matters. I would argue that it does. Cultural memories, as of Iwo Jima, find their way into contemporary understandings of the world we live in and these can shape a nation's aspirations or the way in which it responds to other nations. The linking of Iwo Jima, Pearl Harbor and 9/11 constructs a particular version of America that is then played out in the political and economic arena of global relations. Equally, cultural memories may change, be adapted, even be fought against, but the past, the way it is remembered in culture, and the part such memorialization plays in shaping the present are inextricably linked.

Roland Barthes, in his highly influential book *Mythologies*, first published in France in 1957, argued that myth is one of the most significant ways in which human beings deal with the complexities of experience.

Reading 4.9

[M]yth is constituted by the loss of the historical quality of things: in it, things lose the memory that they once were made. The world enters language as a dialectical relation between activities, between human actions; it comes out of myth as a harmonious display of essences. A conjuring trick has taken place; it has turned reality inside out, it has emptied it of history and has filled it with nature, it has removed from things their human meaning so as to make them signify a human insignificance. The function of the myth is to empty reality: it is, literally, a ceaseless flowing, a haemorrhage, or perhaps an evaporation, in short a perceptible absence . . .

Myth does not deny things, on the contrary, its function is to talk about them; simply, it purifies them, it makes them innocent, it gives them a natural and eternal justification, it gives them a clarity which is not that of an explanation but that of a statement of fact. If I state the fact of French imperiality without explaining it, I am very near to finding that it is natural and goes without saying: I am reassured. In passing from history to nature, myth acts economically: it abolishes the complexity of human acts, it gives them the simplicity of essences, it does away with all dialectics, with any going back beyond what is immediately visible, it organizes a world which is without contradictions because it is without depth, a world wide open and wallowing in the evident, it establishes a blissful clarity: things appear to mean something by themselves. (Barthes, 1973, pp. 142–3)

The function of myth, according to Barthes, is not so much to falsify events or deeds but to reduce them to essences in order to render them comprehensible and significant. As Barthes says, myth 'abolishes the complexity of human acts, it gives them the simplicity of essences . . . it organizes . . . a world wide open'. This is particularly relevant for our consideration of popular memory, since our collective sense of the past is frequently organized around myth. For example, the story that, on hearing that the Spanish Armada had set sail for England, Sir Francis Drake insisted on finishing his game of bowls has outlasted the historical accuracy of scholars who have demonstrated that, while it is likely that a game of bowls was being played, it is most unlikely that an astute 'sea dog' such as Drake would waste time finishing the game at such a critical moment. The myth that has Drake saying 'Time to finish the game' captures some perceived essence of 'Englishness' which can 'explain' more 'naturally' than detailed historical evidence why the Armada was defeated by the English. The victory over Spain becomes the victory of good over evil, rather than the outcome of a nexus of historical, political and economic factors – complex, fallible, human actions are represented as natural forces or, in Barthes's words, myth 'has turned reality inside out, it has emptied it of history and has filled it with nature'. As Barthes says, myth 'does not deny things': the main elements of the story are true, there was a game of bowls, the Armada was sailing for England, Drake was at Plymouth. What myth does is 'to talk about them . . . it gives them a natural and eternal justification, it gives them a clarity which is not that of an explanation but that of a statement of fact' – and it does so by arranging the elements of the story in certain ways, by creating heroic characters and by reducing the complex interplay of myriad determinations to a statement of fact (in this case victory over Spain). And this statement of fact requires no explanation: it goes without saying, for example, that it was a victory and that it was self-evidently the triumph of good over evil.

ACTIVITY 4.12 Consider figure 4.3, which reproduces the cover picture of a 1942 leaflet designed to stir up hatred for the enemy against whom the Allied Forces were waging war. How does this representation contribute to myths of the Second World War?

To cultural historians the ways in which myths become established at any particular moment are worthy of study: exploring how and why a myth developed can yield insight into the meanings ascribed by popular memory to

Figure 4.3 'The Battle for Civilisation'

historical events. Furthermore, as Angus Calder, the historian, comments, 'Myth may distort what has happened. But it affects what happens' (Calder, 1992, p. 14). In the Second World War, the people of Britain were encouraged to believe that they were making history, that this was Britain's 'finest hour', the moment for which all the years of 'our island's history', a historical mythology that included heroes like Drake and Nelson, had prepared them. Because it is important and inevitable that in wartime people make sense of what is chaotic and frightening by reference to heroic mythologies, many people tried to conduct themselves in accordance with these myths, and in doing so helped to sustain and legitimate the story of Britain's heroic stand against the forces of barbarism. As Calder (1992, p. 14) neatly puts it, 'Heroic mythology fused with everyday life to produce heroism.' We cannot simply dismiss myth as falsehood, lies, fiction. Instead, we need to engage with the discourses (see chapter 3) in which specific myths can be understood and the ways in which myth interacts with everyday life to produce certain behaviours and understandings of the world at a specific moment.

History as 'Heritage'

Finally, we want to introduce you to the contemporary debate around the idea of heritage in England. We have focused upon England here because there is a very specific relationship between Englishness and a sense of the past. Unlike the Scots or Irish, for many of whom there is an intimate and personal connection with the past, the English are both strangely reluctant to celebrate the nation's actual history and very keen to commemorate an imagined past, shorn of most of its historical reality (Paxman, 1998, pp. 234, 264–5; Giles and Middleton, 1995, pp. 3–9). The historical construction of England is important, as it is what the United Kingdom sells to tourists. Americans have crossed the Atlantic to experience English heritage since the nineteenth century, and certain mythical images have come to symbolize 'England' in the imaginations of visitors from other countries as well as in the minds of some British people. Thatched cottages, village greens, beefeaters at the Tower of London, 'olde Englishe pubs' and stately homes are some of the icons that stand for a certain form of 'Englishness'.

Although the term 'heritage' means in its broadest terms that which is inherited, it has increasingly come to mean those material artefacts, places and buildings left by the past which are worthy of preservation. English Heritage and the National Trust, the two major organizations committed to the conservation and preservation of the past's legacy, have large memberships, many of whom are willing to work voluntarily on conservation or restoration projects, as well as contributing to fund-raising along with the general public. Furthermore, such organizations command royal patronage and substantial financial subsidies. On the one hand, 'heritage' has been attacked for shoring up a decaying and beleaguered aristocracy by subsidizing the upkeep of their country homes and a certain level of luxurious living (Hewison, 1987). On the other hand, 'heritage' has been criticized for opening historic monuments and sites to the dangers of mass tourism, as more and more historical sites, bygones and memorabilia are preserved and crowds of people spend their leisure time and holidays visiting country houses, theme parks, living history museums and working farms. Equally attacked is the proliferation of historical replicas for purchase, from Victorian Christmas cards to 'art deco' ceramics, from reproduction fireplaces to replica storage jars. Those who oppose what they see as the commodification of the past for the purposes of a profit-making tourist and leisure industry point to the ways in which the country is being turned into a giant Disneyland-type museum, catering to a 'vulgar English nationalism'.

> Where there were mines and mills, now there is Wigan Pier Heritage Centre, where you can pay to crawl through a model coal mine, watch dummies making nails, and be invited 'in' by actors and actresses dressed as 1900 proletarians. Britain, where these days a new museum opens every fortnight is becoming a museum itself . . . The Total Museum, though it can entertain, is a lie. Pretending to open a window into the past is a technique which weakens imagination much in the way that colour television weakens the intuition, whereas radio – by its incompleteness – so strongly stimulates it. (Ascherson, 1987, cited in Samuel, 1994, p. 262)

The arguments put forward in condemnation of 'heritage' resemble in some ways the debates over mass culture that we encountered in chapter 1. Richard Hoggart railed against 'the candy floss world' of milk bars and juke boxes for its tendency, as he perceived it, to entertain rather than educate. A similar charge is brought against 'heritage'. Visits to living history museums or working farms are a social practice engaged in as a leisure pursuit: as such, it is argued, they encourage the passive consumption of images and impressions rather than the active engagement of reading or study. Equally, to purchase replica 'period' crockery or furniture is to engage in a celebration of the past rather than critical inquiry. The consumption of history in the form of 'heritage', so it is argued, is a popular activity of 'the masses' and, therefore, by its very nature is degraded and degrading. Historians, as well as arbiters of aesthetic taste, have attacked the 'heritage' industry for offering sanitized and sentimentalized versions of the past which avoid confronting the complexities of human motivation and the fragmentary, often contradictory, nature of the historical record. In his book, published in 1985, *On Living in an Old Country*, the cultural critic Patrick Wright argued that the contemporary British obsession with 'heritage' was symptomatic of a wider malaise, in that it represented a pervasive nostalgia for the 'good old days' of British ascendancy. Such nostalgia, he argued, supported a collective mentality that was backward-looking rather than fostering a more dynamic and radical engagement with the present (Wright, 1985). Wright's argument, which is a complex one and has to be placed in the context of mid-1980s Thatcherite Britain, has been critiqued by the historian Raphael Samuel, most memorably in *Theatres of Memory*, in which he mounts a provocative defence of 'heritage' and calls for a reassessment of 'the sources of its energies and strengths' (Samuel, 1994, p. 274). Now read the following extract from *Theatres of Memory*.

Reading 4.10

The hostility of historians to heritage is possibly exacerbated by the fact that they are in some sort competing for the same terrain. Each, after its own fashion, claims to be representing the past 'as it was' . . . Interpretation, the privilege of the archive-based historian, and 're-creation', the ambition of heritage, also share a common conceit; the belief that scrupulous attention to detail will bring the dead to life . . .

Whatever the reasons, history and heritage are typically placed in opposite camps. The first is assigned to the realm of critical inquiry, the second to a merely antiquarian preoccupation, the classification and hoarding of things. The first, so the argument runs, is dynamic and concerned with development and change, the second is static. The first is concerned with explanation, bringing a sceptical intelligence to bear on the complexities and contradictoriness of the record; the second sentimentalizes, and is content merely to celebrate . . .

The perceived opposition between 'education' and 'entertainment' and the unspoken and unargued-for assumption that pleasure is almost by definition mindless, ought not to go unchallenged. There is no reason to think that people are more passive when looking at old photographs or film footage, handling a museum exhibit, following a local history trail, or even buying a historical souvenir, than when reading a book. People do not simply 'consume' images in the way in which, say, they buy a bar of chocolate. As in any reading, they assimilate them as best they can to pre-existing images and narratives. The pleasures of the gaze . . . are different in kind from those of the written word but not necessarily less taxing on historical reflection and thought. (Samuel, 1994, pp. 270–1)

ACTIVITY 4.13

- Think about the various arguments put forward here about heritage: (a) the 'heritage' industry supports the aristocracy in a certain lifestyle which is not appropriate in a democratic society; (b) Britain is becoming one huge museum in which crowds of visitors and tourists spend their leisure time passively and uncritically viewing historic spectacles or buying replicated historical products and gifts; (c) 'heritage' does not simply offer passive spectacle but can provide valuable opportunities for discovering history. Can you put forward evidence and argument for each position?
- What is your own experience of 'heritage'? How do you respond to the different standpoints on it? What do you think?
- Think about the use of 'living history' and themed museums in schools. Do you think these offer a valuable experience of history or not? Give reasons for your answer.

Conclusions

This discussion of 'heritage' has brought us back to Tosh's point that history 'can become the basis for informed and critical discussion of current issues'. Wright and Samuel are both concerned with the relationship between the current political climate and the ways in which the past is represented and used in the present. In relation to this you might think about the histories of other cultures or the histories of so-called ordinary people and consider how much or how little you know of these. Do your musings lead you to see any connection to wider political issues both nationally and globally?

Many of the ideas raised in this chapter will be taken up again in different ways later, notably in the case study in chapter 6, where you will find discussion of 'heritage' as part of the tourist industry. As students of culture you will frequently find yourselves having to engage with the historical past, whether it be in the form of popular memory and myth, archival research, fiction, politics and identities or 'heritage'. Remind yourself when you encounter any form of history to ask questions about the paradigms of knowledge within which it is located and the purposes it serves in the present.

Chapter 5

Location, Location, Location
Cultural Geographies

Early on in James Joyce's novel *A Portrait of the Artist as a Young Man* (1916) we find the central character, Stephen Dedalus, daydreaming during a geography lesson:

> He turned to the flyleaf of the geography and read what he had written there: himself, his name and where he was.
>
> Stephen Dedalus
> Class of Elements
> Clongowes Wood College
> Sallins
> County Kildare
> Ireland
> Europe
> The World
> The Universe
> (Joyce, 1993, p. 255)

Stephen's sense of identity ('himself') is closely linked to his name ('Stephen Dedalus') and, importantly for our purposes, a listing of ever larger geographical spaces. Just as they affirm his own identity, the places in which he locates himself also shape our response to him, because we take into account the connotations of the places he mentions. How would your view of him alter if the address were Tokyo, Japan, or Cape Town, South Africa, or even Eton, Berkshire, England? As we saw in chapter 2, a sense of identity is derived from a number of sources, one of which will be the connotations which a given locale or region has for an individual. What cultural geography does is to focus on the context from which such connotations arise. It is concerned with teasing out the ways in which places and spaces are shaped by and can themselves come to shape the beliefs and values of those who inhabit them. As Peter Jackson (1994, p. 23) argues, 'cultural geography . . . focuses on the way cultures are produced and reproduced through actual social practices that take place in historically contingent and geographically specific contexts.'

In this chapter we will be discussing some of the ways in which an awareness of the role and meanings of place in shaping individual and group identities can help you to study both represented and actual environments.

ACTIVITY 5.1

Work with someone else if you can, preferably somebody from a different part of the world or country to you. Jot down a list of places or locations which have particular meaning for you (and your community), and then get your partner to write down his or her views of the same places. We have started you off with an example.

Place/locale	Your view	Partner's view
• Florida	Holiday place	Place of employment
• Blackpool	A great lads' night out	The epitome of vulgarity
•		
•		

Take an example on which you had particularly divergent opinions and discuss what differences emerged. What caused these?

What we imagine this simple exercise points up is that you have different views about a particular place: For a Christian the local church might be a location with associations of communal support, a place of particular significance as a space in which one's beliefs and values can be nourished. For an atheist, the church might be an architecturally interesting old building but is unlikely to be seen to have any bearing upon her or his behaviour in and around it. Another perspective on this emerges if you talk to people from different generations: your grandmother, for example, may well have very different ideas about the meaning and purpose of a church to the ones that you may hold.

Place and Identity: a Brief Introduction

A sense of identity is derived from a number of sources (see chapter 2), one of which will be the connotations that a given locale or region has for an individual. What cultural geography does is to focus on the context from which such connotations arise (Jackson, 1994, p. 23). By focusing upon the competing and changing meanings of places for different individuals, cultural geography focuses upon the contingent nature of identity. The problem of identity as either complicit with or subversive of the ideologies that shape a given locale is, at root, based on the logic of **binary opposition**; a logic which much postmodern theory is sceptical of. What might be needed, then, is a way of thinking that doesn't stop at 'either/or' but allows many more shades of opinion, for example hot *and* cold, rather than hot *or* cold. It is exactly this kind of non-binary-based logic that can be identified in the postmodern Marxism of Laclau:

> Any articulation of identity . . . is only momentarily complete, it is always in part constituted by the forces that oppose it (the constitutive outside), always contingent upon surviving the contradictions that it subsumes (forces of dislocation) . . .
>
> Consequently, identities and their conditions of existence are inseparable. There is no identity outside of its context: Identity depends on conditions of existence which are contingent, its relationship with them is absolutely necessary. (Laclau, 1990, p. 21)

Simplifying somewhat, we can understand the term 'constitutive outside' as a way of talking about the varied factors informing our identity, not least of which would be the places we inhabit and move through. As we move into different arenas of activity, the shifting meanings attached to these locations inform the ways in which we operate and thus help to shape our experience of a given place. For Laclau, we operate across different settings and, in doing so, actually present different identities: by accepting postmodernist notions regarding the multiplicity of identities an individual can inhabit, however, we must not lose sight of the ways in which location informs a subject's identity (Keith and Pile, 1993, p. 30).

Cultural critic Raymond Williams promoted an approach to the analysis of culture which included everyday and ordinary experiences (see chapter 1). Williams warned against any single approach in the analysis of culture and argued for multiple ways of reading (Williams, 1965, pp. 59–60); for him the study of culture is

> the study of relationships between elements in a whole way of life. The analysis of culture is the attempt to discover the nature of the organisation which is the complex of those relationships . . . [I]t is with the discovery of patterns of a

characteristic kind that any useful cultural analysis begins, and it is with the relationships between these patterns, which sometimes reveal unexpected identities and correspondences in hitherto separately considered activities, sometimes again reveal discontinuities of an unexpected kind, that general cultural analysis is concerned. (Williams, 1965, p. 63)

It is Williams's interest in recovering – as far as is possible – the lived experience of a particular culture which has been taken up by human geographers looking for new ways of examining the experience of living in a particular place. As the geographer Peter Jackson notes (1994, pp. 35–6), it is Williams's interest in the 'specific and indissoluble real processes' (Williams, 1977, p. 82) that paved the way for a cultural geography which was alert to the dynamics of social interaction. With his concern to trace the ways in which language, operating as discourse, shaped cultural meanings at specific historical junctures, the French cultural theorist Michel Foucault has also been influential in providing a key foundation for cultural geography (Smith and Katz, 1993, pp. 72 –4). Foucault has argued (1986, p. 23) that 'we do not live in a kind of void . . . we live inside of a set of relations that delineates sites which are irreducible to one another and absolutely not super-imposable on one another.' Given the complex relationship between location and an individual or social group's use of it Foucault conceives a given representation of place (i.e., ideological space) as a 'heterotopia' (Foucault, 1986, pp. 25, 27; Lefebvre, 1991, pp. 163–4). A heterotopia is a social space whose meanings are constructed through their articulation/definition within the discourses of a culture. Thus the meanings which adhere to a heterotopic space mutate over time or according to who is using it:

> The heterotopia is capable of juxtaposing in a single real place several spaces, several sites that are in themselves incompatible . . . [T]hey have a function in relation to all the space that remains. This function unfolds between two extreme poles. Either their role is to create a space of illusion that exposes every real space, all the sites inside of which human life is partitioned, as still more illusory . . . or else, on the contrary, their role is to create a space that is other, another real space, as perfect, as meticulous, as well arranged as ours is messy, ill constructed, and jumbled. The latter type would be the heterotopia, not of illusion, but of compensation, and I wonder if certain colonies have not functioned somewhat in this manner. (Foucault, 1986, pp. 25, 27)

Here is cultural geographer Edward Soja's explanation of Foucault's ideas:

Foucault outlined his notion of 'heterotopias' as the characteristic spaces of the modern world, superseding the hierarchic 'ensemble of places' of the Middle Ages . . . [He] focused our attention on another spatiality of social life, an 'external space', the actually lived (and socially produced) space of sites and relations between them . . . Foucault's heterotopias . . . are constituted in every society but take quite varied forms and change over time, as 'history unfolds' in its adherent spatiality. He identifies many such sites: the cemetery and the church, the theatre and the garden, the museum and the library, the fairground and the 'vacation village', the barracks and the prison, the Moslem hammam and the Scandinavian sauna, the brothel and the colony. Foucault contrasts these 'real places' with the 'fundamentally unreal spaces' of utopias, which present society in either a perfected form or else 'turned upside down'. (Soja, 1989, p. 17)

For Foucault, and the postmodern geographers who have worked with his ideas, space and place are not simply either physical forms or mental constructs, but rather concrete and abstract at the same time. As Foucault argued (1993, p. 169), 'what is interesting is always interconnection.' Foucault's work foregrounds the contingent aspect of subjectivity; in the analysis of culture, it is essential that one follows through the logic of an argument which suggests that identities do not get formed in a vacuum and accepts that identity isn't simply linguistic or discourse-based but is the product of interaction with the 'relations of power and discipline [which] are inscribed into the apparently innocent spatiality of social life' (Soja, 1989, p. 6).

ACTIVITY 5.2

- Thinking about your role as university student, outline some of the forces which make up the 'constitutive outside' of your academic life. Then jot down some of the 'forces of dislocation' which disrupt your academic life. Where do these emanate from? Is there a particular location? We imagine that when you are located in the university the 'forces of dislocation' are going to be from outside: your part-time job, your family or friends elsewhere in the country, and so on.
- Can you identify any of the locations you are familiar with as heterotopias in Foucault's sense? What makes your experience of them fit his descriptor?

A cultural geography approach is just one of many which the cultural analyst can utilize, but it is one which is particularly useful in the exploration of patterns of behaviour and interaction in specific locales, and as such can bring into sharper relief the 'structure of feeling' which arises from such patterns (Williams, 1965, p. 64). Far from being an irrelevance or a mere 'back-drop', the places in which the micro-episodes of our lives occur are part and parcel of the structure of feeling of a particular locale and therefore central to any reading of the constructions of identity. Places are overlaid with meaning since they are incorporated into or produced by a culture which codes and classifies in competing and often mutually contradictory ways. Thus a war memorial might be a place of painful memory for ex-soldiers who served in the Second World War, but for local teenagers it might be the place they congregate with skateboards. This phenomenon suggests that we need a nuanced way of reading place, alert to its different meanings for different social groups. As Agnew suggests:

> In order to explain human behaviour one must deal with the 'micro-episodes'
> of everyday life and their embeddedness in concrete milieux or con-texts . . . [P]eople do not experience life in the abstract context of 'mass society'.
> Their knowledge is acquired, and they live their lives, in the context of 'social
> worlds' dominated by the perspectives of different 'reference groups', in which
> meaning is attributed to acts and events through communication and interac-tion with limited numbers of people. (Agnew, 1993, pp. 261–2)

Look back at your responses to the first part of Activity 5.2. Your notes from this exercise will be indicative of the ways in which your experience of university overlaps and interacts with your experience of other contexts and locations in your life. These 'concrete milieux', however transitory and intermittent, are part of the complex patterns of interaction that inform your engagement with contemporary culture. In reflecting on this, you can begin to see the complexity of ideas of place. Agnew goes on to argue that,

> Interwoven in the concept of place suggested here, therefore, are three major
> elements: locale, the settings in which social relations are constituted (these can
> be informal or institutional); location, the effects upon locales of social and
> economic processes operating at wider scales; and sense of place, the local
> 'structure of feeling' . . . Place, therefore, refers to discrete if elastic areas in
> which settings for the constitution of social relations are located and with which
> people can identify. (Agnew, 1993, p. 263)

Locales are those concrete contexts within which the micro-episodes of your life occur. Locations, in the sense that Agnew intended here, are the consequences for our locales of wider social and economic forces: the complex issues that inform the range of employment options, leisure facilities, health-care and education provision within a specific geographic area. Put these two factors together – the particular and local experience of places, overlaid by an understanding of the wider social and economic factors informing them – and you begin to map a sense of place which can be the foundation for a cultural analysis. A place is thus encountered and experienced as always already constructed through the practices of signification which are employed to read it: in reading a place we make use of a repertoire of ways of seeing or – more accurately – discourses which help us decode, but are also means of encoding an experience or place according to a particular set of beliefs. These ways of seeing may have nothing to do with the culture we are examining and can, in fact, distort our analysis.

While cultural geography has been informed by Williams's legacy of a focus on the ordinary and everyday it has also been shaped by a response to debates around 'the new spatial disorientation in postmodern society, where the inability of subjects to map urban space . . . is a manifestation of a larger and more serious problem of their inability to position themselves individually and collectively within the new decentred communication networks of capitalism' (Best and Kellner, 1991, p. 188). The insistence upon the individual and the local at the expense of the global and the national in our summary of Agnew's position may, at first, appear to be naive, but commentators are increasingly arguing that a sharper sense of who one is and where one comes from becomes the starting point for a resistance to the discourses of capital which seek to shape individuals as consuming subjects (Jameson, 1984; Soja and Hooper, 1993). Care must be taken, however, not to focus on the individual alone; as Bondi argues in a useful essay on this issue, cultural geography can help us examine the ways in which place, position and location are created and produced precisely because it promotes a reconception not just of place but also of the identities of the subjects which inhabit and interact within a given place: 'It seems to me that the emphasis on where – on position, on location – is allowing questions of identity to be thought in different ways . . . encouraging a concern with the relationship between different kinds of identities and therefore with the development of a politics grounded in affinities and coalitions' (Bondi, 1993, p. 98).

Reclaiming the local and individual as starting points for a contemporary cultural studies may actually be a means of getting closer to an era's structure of feeling and can, perhaps, provide a means of counterbalancing the views promoted by the selective tradition (on this see our discussion of ethnography in chapter 10). A cultural studies alert to the politics and poetics of place is one that can explore the ways in which locations are shaped and experienced via culturally determined meanings. We can examine this further by thinking about the relationship between maps and the places which they represent.

Mapping Realities?

Representations of spaces, whether in our minds or in the material form of a map or plan (on this distinction see Lefebvre, 1991, pp. 33–46), are abstractions which emerge from a particular cultural context. For example, what we may have imagined the location 'university' to be like will depend upon our experience of 'universities' and the experiences (and beliefs and values) of our immediate networks of family, friends and social contacts. Once we have been attending a university for some time we can quickly read its maps not just in terms of guiding us around the campus but also in terms of their encoding of issues of power inherent in the location. Figure 5.1 is a map of Bath Spa University's Newton Park Campus. The Main House houses the University's Senior Management suite, the Registry, the Finance Department, the Academic Office (responsible for the systems whereby the university monitors and enhances the quality of its courses) and the Marketing Department. The Cultural Studies department is in the Stable Block (you can draw your own conclusion about this).

Real or imagined, places are products of specific cultural conditions and, as such, not simply arenas for action but always already a part of the action and its meanings. Over time a place becomes part of what Raymond Williams calls the documentary record of a society. Thus the Newton Park Campus is an historic parkland, originally shaped for purposes far removed from higher education by the eighteenth-century landscape gardener Capability Brown at the behest of a rich patron. The site includes the remnants of a fourteenth-century castle and its gatehouse (figure 5.1, GH); within the gatehouse is a wall on which are preserved graffiti ranging from seventeenth-century soldiers' names to 1950s football scores. (At this point you might look again at Raymond Williams's description of his bus journey in reading 1.5.)

In conducting a cultural study of place and location one is often rereading other people's representations, in the form of maps, reflections, paintings, photographs and so on, in the hope of producing a fuller sense of the complex processes by which a given culture can be characterized; in effect, the cultural geographer makes a cognitive map of the cultural phenomenon being investigated.

Such maps do not, it must be stressed, claim to be complete or direct reflections of a location's 'reality'. As Smith and Katz (1993, p. 70) explain,

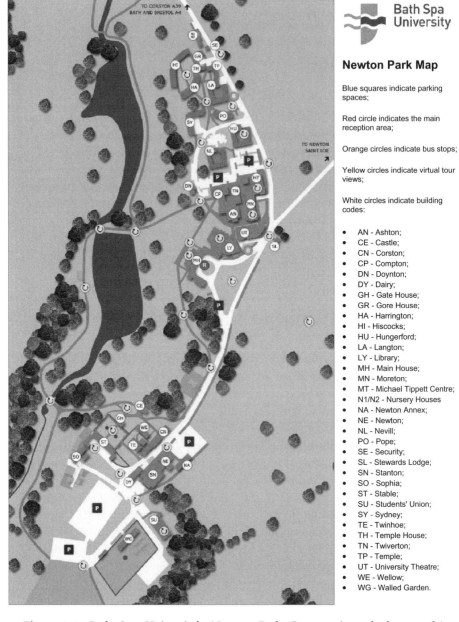

Figure 5.1 Bath Spa University's Newton Park Campus (www.bathspa.ac.uk/contact/map-newton-park.asp)

Although geographers and cartographers habitually give lip service to the selectiveness involved in mapping and to the realisation that maps are strategic social constructions, they more often proceed in practice from traditionally realist assumptions. Only recently have a few geographers and cartographers begun a . . . critique of cartographic conventions of positioning, framing, scale, absence and presence on the map, and, a critique of the absent if omniscient cartographer.

ACTIVITY 5.3

- Look at a map of your own university and develop your own critique of its use of 'cartographic conventions of positioning, framing, scale, absence and presence'. Think about such things as the location of senior management, where the library is, which academic departments are in the shiny new buildings that everyone can see and which are tucked away from the main public thoroughfares.
- Draw from memory a map of your home town, highlighting the five places that are most important to you. Now compare your map to, say, the town's write-up in a tourist guide or other public document. What is left out of this discursive description of the place that is included in your map? Can you explain any omissions and overlaps?

Now read the following extract from an influential book on spatial politics by the French social theorist Henri Lefebvre.

Reading 5.1

To compare different maps of a region or country . . . is to be struck by the remarkable diversity among them. Some, such as maps that show 'beauty spots' and historical sites and monuments to the accompaniment of an appropriate rhetoric, aim to mystify in fairly obvious ways. This kind of map designates places where a ravenous consumption picks over the last remains of nature and of the past in search of whatever nourishment may be obtained from the *signs* of anything historical or original. If the maps and guides are to be believed, a veritable feast of authenticity awaits the tourist. The conventional signs used in these documents constitute a code even more deceptive than the things themselves, for they are at one more remove from reality. Next, consider an ordinary map of roads and other communications . . . What such a map reveals, its meaning – not, perhaps, to the most ingenious inspection, but certainly to an intelligent perusal with even minimal preparation – is at once clear and hard to decipher . . .

These spaces are *produced*. The 'raw material' from which they are produced is nature. They are products of an activity which involves the economic and technical realms but which extends well beyond them, for these are also political products, and strategic spaces. (Lefebvre, 1991, p. 84)

- What would you say was the main point of Lefebvre's argument?
- Lefebvre was writing in France in the 1970s: to what extent can his remarks about the relation to the past here be applied to contemporary culture's attitudes towards national monuments and other 'historic' places? (On this you might like to refer back to chapter 4.)
- In what ways can a space be a strategic or political product? You might like to think about, say, the development of housing on green-belt land in relation to this issue. Other examples to think about would be the Rock of Gibraltar at the western entrance to the Mediterranean, or Ascension Island in the South Atlantic.

Lefebvre's approach to maps seeks to unpack the ways in which what may appear to be a fixed, stable locale is in fact overlaid and shaped by ideology. As Peter Vujakovic notes (1995, pp. 129–30), 'All maps can be regarded as "propagandist" in the widest sense of the word . . . [and] national atlases can be seen as important ideological devices, telling the story of a nation and locating the national identity in both time and space.' As you will see in the case study at the end of this chapter, this is as true of the Rand McNally map of Los Angeles (figure 5.2) as it is of the *Concise Atlas of the Republic of Croatia*, which Vujakovic analyses.

Real spaces are no less constructed or shaped by powerful ideologies than are maps. In the next section we examine the phenomenon of supermarket shopping from a cultural geography point of view.

Going Shopping

The great expansion of retail parks and out-of-town shopping centres may, in the UK, have slowed, but many people still spend a great deal of time shopping and an increasing number of people shop at these centres. Out-of-town shopping centres offer a constructed locale and a site of consumption (see chapter 9) which can tell us much about contemporary culture, not least because they are sites which are often utilized in ways that subvert the intentions of their planners and owners. Much recent work on shopping centres has focused upon them as a specific phenomenon of contemporary culture in industrialized societies (Kowinski, 1985; Morris, 1988). In particular, shopping centres have been studied as spaces in which individuals interact with powerful, often global, commercial forces at a local level. As John Fiske comments in an essay on the culture of everyday life, 'The supermarket is an arena full of the goods and information produced by the political economy of capitalism, but within it, shoppers construct for the period and purposes of shopping their own settings' (Fiske, 1992, p. 160). Fiske examines the ways in which individuals redefine the space of a supermarket in their own terms. He distinguishes between setting and arena – settings are defined as 'repeatedly experienced, personally ordered and edited versions of the arena' (Lave, 1988, p. 151, cited in Fiske, 1992, p. 160) – and links these ideas to the distinction between place and space found in the work of Michel de Certeau (1984). Fiske's summary can help us think through the ways in which individuals can use space in a subversive or, at least, unintended way.

Reading 5.2

For . . . [de Certeau] place is an ordered structure provided by the dominant order through which its power to organise and control is exerted. It is often physical. So cities are places built to organise and control the lives and movements of the 'city subjects' in the interests of the dominant. So, too, supermarkets, apartment blocks, and universities are places. But within and against them, the various formations of the people construct their spaces by the practices of living. So renters make the apartment, the place of the landlord, into their space by the practices of living; the textures of objects, relationships, and behaviors with which they occupy and possess it for the period of the renting. Space is practiced place, and space is produced by the creativity of the people using the resources of the other. De Certeau stresses the political conflict involved, the confrontation of opposing social interests that is central to the construction of space out of place. Lave focuses more on the functional creativity of the activities involved in constructing a setting out of an arena. But her argument shows that a setting is a material and cognitive space where the inhabitant or shopper is in control, is able to cope successfully. (Fiske, 1992, p. 160)

ACTIVITY 5.5

- Can you think of any ways in which Fiske's claims about the freedom of the shopper might be challenged?
- Fiske suggests that renters can make a place their own space: can you think of some constraints on their ability to do this?
- Think about a place which you habitually utilize: are there ways in which you use it which suggest that you are creating your own space? Are there any constraints on your ability to do this?
- As Meaghan Morris notes, individual stores often work to create settings in the wider arena of a shopping centre (Morris, 1988, p. 316). Can you think of some examples from your own experience of shopping and perhaps suggest some reasons for why they might do this?

We need to strike a judicious balance between seemingly optimistic claims that we are free agents who can boldly remake in our own image the places we inhabit and move through, and apparently pessimistic claims that we are all the pawns of a capitalist system (for further discussion of these issues see chapters 8 and 9).

In the act of going shopping in the kind of setting we have been discussing individuals are fundamentally implicated in the processes of contemporary Western consumer culture. Not only does what we buy have meanings through which we signal identity and are identified by others; in going shopping we are actors in a corporate space which stages encounters. The various people who work in a supermarket are carefully constructed by their employers through particular uniforms or specific activities. Susan Willis writes about this in an American context.

Reading 5.3

The current practice in many supermarkets is to put a theatrical form of production on display, while the real work that goes in to maintaining the store and serving the customers is either hidden from view or made to appear trivial because of deskilling. The work of pricing the merchandise, stocking the shelves, cleaning the store, and preparing the meat and produce for sale is accomplished by a largely invisible work-force, whose members labor behind the scene in a backroom warehouse, or at night after the store is closed. The work of managing, which includes decisions over purchases and personnel, is conducted by a number of upper-level employees whose photos sometimes decorate the store's service counter, but who are seldom seen by shoppers. The work of checking, which in a bygone era would have anchored the customer's apprehension of work in the supermarket, has today been greatly undermined by the installation of computerized scanners that weigh and price the commodities and often speak to the customer. The supermarket checker has been deskilled to the point of becoming a human robotoid extension of the checkout system.

As if to compensate for the marginalization and in some cases the erasure, of productive labor, the supermarket offers an array of theatrical labors, whose importance has more to do with the spectacle they create than the actual services they render. Most supermarkets today offer in-store bakeries, deli-counters, florist shops, and gourmet food sections. These are staffed by a corps of store-personnel whose uniforms are more theatrical than practical. Often, the employees' pert hats and aprons mimic the colors and patterns of the store's interior decor, making the supermarket something of a stage for sales and the costumed employees the actors enacting service. If we take the supermarket as the place where we most commonly come into contact with the festishized commodities of daily life, then all the strategies developed by a supermarket to render service personal, to make it visible, rebound in a theatricality whose effect is to create the appearance of use value in the commodities we buy. (Willis, 1991, p. 17)

- Think about the organization of supermarkets you have visited. Can you identify any of the features Willis discusses?
- Do you agree that the labour on show is purely theatrical? How does buying bread from a section of a store labelled Bakery or meat from a section labelled Butchers give a different set of meanings to the transaction and the product from the ones they would have if we simply picked the items out of a chill cabinet or off a shelf? Note down some of the meanings which are 'added' by the kind of theatrical organization Willis describes.

Willis offers a Marxist reading of capitalism (for more on this see chapter 9) which seems to suggest that everyone is positioned and defined by the vast impersonal forces of economics. Meaghan Morris has argued: 'Shopping centres illustrate very well, I think, the argument that you can't treat a public at a cultural event as directly expressive of social groups and classes, or their supposed sensibility. Publics aren't stable, homogenous entities' (Morris, 1988, p. 304). This is because when we shop we do so in our own terms, and central to our experience of shopping centres is the construction of our own mental map of the place determined by our habitual needs (Fiske, 1992, p. 160). That this map is never simply of our own making underlines the ways in which our experience of culture is very much built upon processes and interactions.

As we move into different arenas of activity the shifting meanings attached to these locations inform the ways in which we operate and so help to shape our experience of a given place. For Laclau, the ethical dilemma we may experience over whether or not to buy imported fresh vegetables produced as a cash crop in a country whose need for foreign currency outweighs the needs of its people for food staples is an important factor of our identity. That we can both buy the mange-touts and be opposed to the extension of airport runways is part of the way in which we can operate across different settings and actually present different identities (for more on this see chapter 8). As Keith and Pile argue (1993, p. 30), by accepting the multiplicity of identities an individual can inhabit we must not lose sight of the ways in which location informs a subject's identity.

The act of leaving your home to go shopping does not seem a very huge shift in location, and so may appear unlikely to occasion any great change in identity. In fact, as Michel de Certeau has argued (cited in During, 1993, pp. 157–8), to trace an individual's actions – glancing in store windows, stopping to look at an item, reading an advertising hoarding, asking a sales assistant for information, interacting with other shoppers – and their impact upon identity is almost impossible. If, as we suggested in chapter 3, everything signifies, then all the actions and interactions of an individual shopper become part of the shifting arena in which his or her identity ought to be read. At a simplified level, you can trace the larger shifts by thinking through the ways in which who you are subtly changes as you move through a set of locations.

ACTIVITY 5.7

Think about the different ways in which you see yourself and are seen by others in the following settings. Identify as many factors as possible that inform the way in which a given setting informs your identity.

1   Waiting for a bus
2   Queuing in the university library to return textbooks
3   Queuing in a shop
4   Discussing a film in a seminar group
5   Discussing the same film with friends in a coffee shop
6   Visiting a foreign country for a holiday
7   Working or studying in a foreign country

The differences you are able to identify may be slight but we should not neglect these micro details of daily life as part of the 'structure of feeling' of our culture. Sometimes historical distance or a shift in context may allow the ways in which place impacts upon identity to become much more visible for analysis. In this area we would direct you to the extensive work which has been done on colonialism and on travel and exploration as occasions when we are often actively mapping (literally and metaphorically) a new terrain, but often at a loss to make sense of our experiences because the relationship which exists between context and identity has become so removed that we struggle to bring the two together. (For an introduction see Boehmer, 1995. For more detailed work see, among others, Bhabha, 1994 and Ryan, 1994.) Even in our daily lives we can experience something of this dislocation: when we first start school, university or a job there is a short period when the strangeness of our environment has an impact on how we feel and interact with others.

Now read the extract from an article by the cultural geographer, Doreen Massey.

Reading 5.4

This is an era – it is often said – when things are speeding up, and spreading out. Capital is going through a new phase of internationalization, especially in its financial parts. More people travel more frequently and for longer distances. Your clothes have probably been made in a range of countries from Latin America to South East Asia. Dinner consists of food shipped in from all over the world. And if you have a screen in your office, instead of opening a letter which – care of Her Majesty's Post Office – has taken some days to wend its way across the country, you now get interrupted by e-mail.

. . . It is a phenomenon which has been called 'time-space compression'. And the general acceptance that something of the sort is going on is marked by the almost obligatory use in the literature of terms and phrases such as speed-up, global village, overcoming spatial barriers, the disruption of horizons, and so forth . . .

To begin with, there are some questions to be asked about time-space compression itself. Who is it that experiences it, and how? Do we all benefit and suffer from it in the same way?

. . . [W]e also need to ask about its causes: what is it that determines our degrees of mobility, that influences the sense we have of space and place? Time-space compression refers to movement and communication across space, to the geographical stretching-out of social relations, and to our experience of all this. The usual interpretation is that it results overwhelmingly from the actions of capital, and from its currently increasing internationalization. On this interpretation, then, it is time space and money which make the world go round, and us go round (or not) the world. It is capitalism and its developments which are argued to determine our understanding and our experience of space.

But surely this is insufficient. Among the many other things which clearly influence that experience, there are for instance, race and gender. The degree to which we can move between countries, or walk about the streets at night, or venture out of hotels in foreign cities, is not just influenced by 'capital'. Survey after survey has shown how women's mobility, for instance, is restricted – in a thousand different ways, from physical violence to being ogled at or made to feel quite simply 'out of place' – not by 'capital' but by men. (Massey, 1991, pp. 232–3)

ACTIVITY 5.8

- Can you suggest which social groups from which parts of the world are more likely to be mobile in the sense described in the first paragraph of the reading?
- Can you think of groups who move from one region in the world to another but are less in charge of their mobility? Who or what does control the mobility of such groups?
- Massey mentions race and gender as things that influence our experience of time-space compression. Can you think of an example of how race might determine this? Can you think of other social factors that might influence the experience of time-space compression?

Your answers to these questions are likely to have suggested that the ways in which people experience time-space compression are varied and complex. It is not enough to say that it is caused solely by the effects of global capitalism, of, for example, global corporations such as Mars, Coca-Cola or McDonald's or of global networks of communication like the Internet, MTV and Hollywood. Those who control, organize and distribute international currency, international markets or international media are often those who have access to electronic technology, long-haul flights, and worldwide contacts through fax, e-mail and conference calling. These groups are the ones who see the benefits of time-space compression and whose power and influence is increased by the growth of global economies and global media. However, there are other groups, such as refugees, whose mobility is enforced not by the movements of international 'capital' but by tribal war and fears of genocide. Moreover, even where the movement of a group from one place to another is the result of economic forces, as in the case of migrant workers from Mexico who attempt to enter the USA in search of work, the people 'on the move' may not be in control of this mobility or its outcomes. Their movements are as likely to be controlled by immigration laws and racial prejudices as by capitalism. Massey also notes another group: those on the receiving end of time-space compression. She cites as an example the pensioner trapped in an inner-city bedsit by fear of what lurks outside, who eats British fish and chips from a Chinese takeaway and watches an American film on a television made in Japan. The cosmopolitanization of culture has done little to improve the lives of people like this.

We touched on the issues around globalization in chapter 2 and will return to these in chapter 9 in the context of consumerism and chapter 10 in relation to electronic technology. For now, you could think about the ways in which the world appears to becoming a 'smaller' space or, as some commentators call it, a 'global village'. Do you think this is true for you or the people you know? Do you see it as a positive or negative thing? Can you see any evidence that people are trying, in the face of this, to retain or imagine a sense of local, individual place in which they can counter the supposedly homogenizing effects of global cultures? For example, might the popularity of soap operas like *EastEnders* and *Coronation Street* be to do with the fictional 'communities' they create? How important is place to these 'communities' and do they represent homogeneity or diversity or what? What about the place you live? Where are the meeting places? What connections do you make with this place and the rest of the world by phone, by letter, through your memories and in your imagination?

An obvious occasion when our lack of familiarity with a location can cause disorientation and confusion is a visit to an unfamiliar city. For the remainder of this chapter we will be providing materials that enable you to undertake a short case study of Los Angeles from a cultural geography perspective.

Case Study: Mapping Los Angeles

In this case study we will be asking you to do some detailed project work on the cultural geography of the city of Los Angeles. We ask you to explore some of the issues that arise from its development from a small village to today's mega-city, with the second largest metropolitan area population in the USA after New York and the tenth largest of any city in the world.

Reading 5.5

Los Angeles is now profoundly, irremediably ethnic. The issue confronting the region is whether this new polyglot metropolis can work. And that is not a question for the region alone. In L.A., late twentieth century America finds a mirror to itself. Los Angeles, after all, is not an old, decaying inner city. Instead, it is America's quintessential suburb, the dynamic product of post-war U.S. capitalism at its most robust, and for that reason, as the writer David Reid noted, 'the American city the world watches for signs and portents' . . .

The region's pattern of ethnic specialization . . . constitutes a system of inequality. Even the most fortunate of the new Angelinos are some distance from the top of the hierarchy, as can be seen from a comparison with native born Russians/Jews, the one persistently ethnic European-origin group . . . Chinese and Japanese Americans have moved into advantageous specializations where they find ample opportunity to work in white collar jobs and do better in industries of lower ethnic density. Other groups – African- and Mexican-American, as well as Korean, Filipino, and

Vietnamese immigrants, for example – occupy the middle ranges of the continuum, sometimes doing better in industries of high ethnic density, sometimes doing worse. Mexican, Salvadoran, and Guatemalan immigrants – the most concentrated of all – do the very worst, crowding into menial employments where the wage ceiling is extremely low. (Waldinger and Bozorgmehr, 1996, pp. 447, 449)

Today, the legacy of the rapid and brutal development of the early twentieth century is a city that is constantly failing to live up to its own vision. Without a coherent centre, held together with roadways that link what were once separate towns, Los Angeles has become less a place of 'equali[zed] . . . spatiality' within which all people can live the suburban dream than an atomized, segregated, 'surreal[ly] polariz[ed]' place, 'a site of despair, brutalization, balkanization and Hobbesian individualization' in which the vision of private spaces of freedom has given way to predominantly white 'carceral, gated communities' on the one hand, and predominantly non-white 'homelessness and poverty' on the other (Keil, 1998, p. xxv). But it is also a haunted city that bears the traces of a past almost, but not quite, under erasure. It is a city in which 'creaky Victorian cottages' stand 'stranded along streets just south of Sunset, cut short by a roaring freeway . . . , in which steps lead to empty spaces, in which tunnels exist that have no hills above them, as if a large bird has flown away with [the city]' (Klein, 1997, p. 1). It is a city then, that constantly reminds itself of its past and of its failure to become a 'paradise metropolis' (Klein, 1997, p. 45).

Until the 1960s, Los Angeles promoted itself to mainly white immigrants – the population of the city and the five-county greater metropolitan area was 80 per cent Anglo – but in the later twentieth and early twenty-first centuries demographers have seen a marked decline in the city's non-Hispanic white and African-American populations and a notable increase in its Latino population. In the late twentieth century something like 20 per cent of all immigrants in the USA lived in the Los Angeles metropolitan area (Soja, 2000, p. 283), with large numbers of people from Asia and the Pacific as well as a significant Latino population. By 1990 Anglos made up 49.8 per cent of the population of 14.5 million and Latinos 33 per cent: between 1990 and 2000 the African-American population fell by 14 per cent while the Latino population grew by 40 per cent. In 2000 the Hispanic population of Los Angeles and Los Angeles County was over 6.5 million in a total population of some 16.3 million – 39.8 per cent of the whole and 'the largest ethnic group' (Soja, 2000, p. 286). Anglos have moved from the city to surrounding counties – an exodus of 1.3 million in the 30 years between 1960 and 1990 – in a phenomenon dubbed 'white flight' (ibid.). In parts of south-east Los Angeles, what in the

1960s were white working-class suburbs – places like Huntington Park, Downey, Lynwood and Cudahy – have seen populations transformed from '80 percent white in 1965 to, in many areas, over 90 percent Latino today' (Soja, 2000, p. 292). Soja notes that

> A distinctively Central American barrio has developed immediately west of downtown in the communities of Westlake and Pico-Union. Located in what many local observers expected to be the major zone of expansion for the city center of Los Angeles, this still low-rise and intensely overcrowded area now reportedly contains population densities comparable to Manhattan or Calcutta. Refugees from war-torn El Salvador, post-revolutionary Nicaragua, and the repressive regimes of Guatemala have given the area a more rebellious political flavor than most other immigrant enclaves. (ibid.)

Drawing upon the detailed study of ethnicities in Waldinger and Bozorgmehr (1996) and Allen and Turner (1997), Soja provides the statistical data on the metropolitan area's ethnic populations in 1990 given in table 5.1. There are notable income differences between ethnic groups here, though Soja's analysis also comments on some polarities within ethnic groups that include the most recent waves of immigrants as well as more established groups.

The racial diversity and related disparity of opportunity has created what Soja calls an 'exceedingly volatile cityspace' (2000, p. 299), a city which for one influential commentator is now shaped by an ecology of fear (Davis,

Table 5.1 Population, median income and country of birth for Los Angeles in 1990 (adapted from Soja, 2000, p. 286)

Population by country of origin	Population in 1990	Median household income ($)	Percent foreign born over age 25
Mexican	3,751,278	29,160	62.7
African	1,229,809	26,350	7.5
English	993,735	43,000	7.4
Chinese	304,588	39,600	90
Filipino	291,618	48,000	92
Salvadoran	274,788	22,200	99
Russian	196,467	51,000	13.3
Korean	194,437	32,000	97.9
Japanese	173,370	46,000	37.1
Vietnamese	148,217	34,700	99
Guatemalan	139,650	22,650	98.1
Armenian	111,138	30,300	81.4

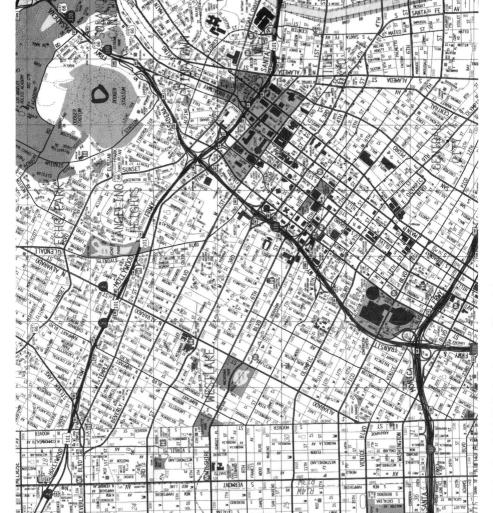

Figure 5.2 Rand McNally local map of Westlake

1999). The dominance of this ecology has meant that the utopian boosterism of Los Angeles' early years has been replaced by a pervasive dystopian vision of what Davis has called 'Fortress LA' (1998, p. 223). But what is the reality of this view of the city? To help you begin to explore this topic we have put together some material on the Westlake area of the city, but we hope that you will use Web and library resources to explore this subject in more detail than we can here. This activity is one that you might want to undertake with a small group of people so that the work can be shared out and more material covered in a shorter period of time.

We want you to develop your own sense of place for Westlake. To do this, you will need to reflect on issues relating to the location's socio-economic status (look back to the beginning of this chapter and our discussion of Agnew for more on this). You might like to look back at the statistical data from Soja and from Waldinger and Bozorgmehr as well.

Using the extract from the Rand McNally map (figure 5.2) of the Westlake district, we would like you to do some work to research this area in more depth. We have provided material from the online encyclopaedia Wikipedia and from weblogs and interviews to get you started. All of these sources are generated by individuals with an interest in the region and, while they are subjective and often biased, this, in fact, is what makes them useful in building a sense of what Agnew calls locale, of the embeddedness of people's experience of this district in concrete milieux.

Reading 5.6

Westlake, Los Angeles, California

Geography and transportation

Westlake is bordered by Downtown Los Angeles on the southeast, Pico-Union on the south, Korea town on the west, and Echo Park on the north and northeast. Its boundaries are roughly the Hollywood Freeway on the northeast, the Harbor Freeway on the southeast, Olympic Boulevard on the south, and Hoover Street on the west. Major sub districts include Filipino town, Rampart, and Lafayette Park Square.

Principal thoroughfares include Beverly, Wilshire, and Rampart Boulevards and Alvarado, Temple, Hoover, and Third Streets. The district is served by the Hollywood and Harbor Freeways. The Metro Red Line subway runs through the district on its way to Hollywood and Korea town, with a stop at Alvarado Street.

History

One of the first areas of Los Angeles west of Figueroa Street to see residential development, by the 1920s Westlake resembled the Upper East Side of Manhattan (complete with a large Jewish population). Wealthy businessmen commuted to downtown, Wilshire Center (now Korea town), Hollywood, and the Miracle Mile from the district's Spanish Revival and Art Deco mansions. The district's less affluent north-eastern blocks also became the home of Los Angeles' Filipino population, much of which remains in Westlake and nearby neighborhoods to this day.

Westlake suffered greatly from the closure of the Pacific Electric streetcar line and the construction of Los Angeles' network of freeways in the 1950s. By the 1960s, virtually all of its white population had decamped to the West Side or the suburbs, replaced with transients who had been pushed out of Bunker Hill by 'urban renewal' in the 1950s. Most of Westlake's elegant mansions were subdivided into apartments at this time, and many of its Beaux-Arts apartment buildings became residential hotels. Meanwhile, MacArthur Park became notorious for its narcotics dealers, heroin addicts, and prostitutes.

In the 1980s Westlake became the home of Los Angeles' vibrant but severely impoverished Salvadoran community, which was drawn to the area's cheap housing. The concurrent development of adjacent Bunker Hill as a major commercial district provided many of the newcomers with employment as custodians and restaurant kitchen staff . . .

The Neighborhood Today

Westlake is now the most densely populated neighborhood in the United States outside of New York City, with a population density of 36,095 persons/mile . . . (Given that the Westlake Community Plan Area also includes Pico-Union, which is considerably less dense, it is likely that Westlake's population density exceeds 45,000 persons/mile . . .) As a surprisingly large number of these residents own cars, the district has severe traffic congestion that was only partially relieved by the late-'90s addition of the Red Line. Much of its school-age population must be bussed to schools in the San Fernando Valley and Glendale, owing to delays in the construction of the troubled Belmont Learning Center (just west of the Harbor Freeway at 1st and Beaudry) and overcrowding at the area's other schools. MacArthur Park, while somewhat less dangerous than at its nadir in the 1980s, is still notoriously unsafe. It has become a popular destination for illegal immigrants, playing host to numerous vendors of phony driver's licenses, work permits, and Social Security cards. Westlake gained greater notoriety in the late 1990s from the Rampart Division scandal that rocked the Los Angeles Police Department.

The California real estate boom that began in the early 2000s has brought some gentrification to Westlake. Korean immigrants, priced out of increasingly expensive

Korea town, have begun to establish themselves in the district. Several major residential developments, most notably The Medici (an apartment complex notably popular among students at the University of Southern California), have been built in the district, and a large, currently vacant 1987 office tower at 1100 Wilshire is currently undergoing conversion into a high-end condominium development. The district's economic revitalization remains slow and fitful, however, with crime remaining a major concern. (http://en.wikipedia.org/wiki/Westlake,_Los_Angeles,_California, accessed 10 June 2007)

ACTIVITY 5.9

Thinking back to Waldinger and Bozorgmehr's commentary and Soja's data on income and ethnicity (see pages 137–9 above), comment on the ethnic mix in the district as described in this Wikipedia entry.

Fortress LA? Policing Westlake

The Los Angeles Police Department (LAPD) division for Westlake is Rampart, a branch of the force notorious for being at the heart of a scandal that rocked LAPD in 2000 and 2001 as it dealt with a history of corruption and police brutality stretching back to 1997.

Reading 5.7

LAPD Rampart Division

The Rampart Division of the Los Angeles Police Department serves the districts to the west and northwest of Downtown Los Angeles, including Echo Park, Pico-Union and Westlake. Its name is derived from Rampart Boulevard, one of the principal thoroughfares in its patrol area. The station house is located at 2710 W. Temple Street in Westlake.

The 'Rampart Scandal'

The Community Resources Against Street Hoodlums (CRASH) anti-gang program initiated under the direction of LAPD Chief Daryl F. Gates had encountered some success in the Rampart Division. However, in 1998–99, graphic allegations emerged of extreme police misconduct among Rampart's CRASH squad. The result-

ing scandal – exacerbated by what is widely viewed as inept public relations management by then-chief Bernard Parks – severely compromised the credibility of the
LAPD, and the Rampart Division in particular, during a time when the department
had only just begun to recover from the public relations fiasco of the Los Angeles
Riots.

The most prominent casualty of the scandal was Parks, who was not rehired by
newly elected Mayor James K. Hahn in 2001. While Parks's termination was hailed
by outside observers and the LAPD's rank and file, Hahn's indelicate handling of the
matter cost him the support of South Los Angeles's black community, leading to his
crushing defeat by Antonio Villaraigosa in the 2005 election.

The pullback in Rampart Division CRASH operations following the scandal is
widely believed to have enabled Mara Salvatrucha (MS-13), a notoriously violent
gang, to establish a firm base of power in Westlake's huge Salvadoran population.
(http://en.wikipedia.org/wiki/LAPD_Rampart_Division, accessed 10 June 2007)

Sergeant Brian Liddy: interview comments

I think there was an impact on the quality of life in Rampart Division, in the level
of violence and the level of crime that the gangs were participating in . . . In 1990,
I believe Rampart had right around 150 murders in the division. In 1997, it was
down to about 33. When I left Rampart, in the afternoon, people would take their
kids to the park and play at Rampart. When I had first went to Rampart, nobody
took their kids to the park. So the quality of life in those eight years had changed
drastically in Rampart. Crime was down. The gangs were nowhere near as bold as
they had been. They had taken to staying in the back of the buildings and not
showing their face, because they could expect to get visited by the CRASH officers . . . (From an interview with Sergeant Brian Liddy, a former CRASH officer
implicated but then cleared in the Rampart Scandal: www.pbs.org/wgbh/pages/
frontline/shows/lapd/scandal/crashculture.html.)

Outdoor chess in MacArthur Park, Westlake

Macarthur Park: Yes, there is a real park named 'Macarthur Park' in Los Angeles, a
32-acre park in the Pico-Union area of Los Angeles (from downtown Los Angeles,
take Wilshire Boulevard west for a couple of miles and you can't miss it, although
that's not necessarily a good thing), and yes it has an area for chess players. In the
old days this was a popular chess spot frequented at one time or the other by most
of the strong players in Southern California. These days, Macarthur Park falls smack
in the middle of the 18th Street Gang's territory (the 18th Street Gang being the
largest gang in LA) and is, to put in mildly, in a high crime area. It's still possible to
play chess there during the day if you are brave of heart (or foolish of mind) and
don't mind witnessing the occasional drug deal or knifing, and being propositioned

by prostitutes of various persuasions and levels of aggression. But please don't go looking for a chess game there at any time approaching dusk because, despite recent police efforts to 'clean up' the park, it is not a place you want to be in after dark. In fact, it is one of the places you least want to be in except in the clear, bright light of day and preferably with a noticeable police presence (think of an area a small fraction of the size of Central Park in New York City but with more total crime). If you are particularly bold you can certainly find a game for money there (you can find almost anything you can imagine in Macarthur Park for enough money), but don't necessarily plan to get paid if you win or even to leave the park with your wallet if you show any green. Chiefly of historical interest these days, or a place to visit with a large group of friends (or perhaps a small group of large friends). I don't know of any strong players who frequent Macarthur Park anymore, although admittedly it's been a couple of years since I went there looking. (Blog posting by Geof Strayer at November 8, 2004 11:58; www.chessninja.com/dailydirt/2004/11/places_to_play_chess.htm, accessed 10 June 2007)

Westlake/the Rampart Inquiry: further research

There is further material on the Rampart Inquiry at www.pbs.org/wgbh/pages/frontline/shows/lapd/scandal/. The full text of the Rampart Board of Inquiry is available at www.lapdonline.org. There is also a digest of press reports at www.streetgangs.com/topics/rampart/, a site devoted to street gang culture maintained by a graduate student working on the topic for a PhD at the University of Southern California.

The incidents and related negative view of the LAPD have informed a number of films, including *Training Day* (2001) and *Crash* (2005), whose title is a knowing allusion to the notorious CRASH units (Community Resources Against Street Hoodlums) at the heart of Rampart scandal: if you have time you may like to watch these films as part of your research on the city.

Further accounts of Westlake include Mike Davis's brief discussion of the reception its Salvadoran and Guatemalan inhabitants gave to the Pope during his 1987 visit to the city (Davis, 1998, p. 325), and his account of a fatal tenement fire in 1993 and the efforts of local councillors to deal with the underlying causes of the problem (Davis, 1999, pp. 122–4, 136–9). Davis included a graphic that shows the long history of fatal fires in the district (p. 116). For a wide-ranging overview of recent trends in Los Angeles's development as a mega-city see Soja (2000), especially chapter 5, 'An introduction to the conurbation of Greater Los Angeles', pp. 117–44. On policing in Los Angeles, see Davis's somewhat polemical account (1998, pp. 223–63), Herbert (1997) and Domanick (1994).

ACTIVITY 5.10

- What sparked the Rampart Inquiry? What was the outcome of its deliberations? You will need to have read beyond the material in this chapter to answer these questions.
- The views of Macarthur Park offered by the police officer and the chess player in the extracts reproduced above paint very different pictures. The Los Angeles Police Department website contains detailed reports on crime data for the city as a whole (see www.lapdonline.org). The LAPD's Statistical Digest 2004 provides detailed statistical analysis of crimes within the city. These data can be used to test the subjective views of Liddy and the chess player and will help you to deepen your understanding of this locale. Table 5.2 shows some headline figures for 2004 – the last year for which, at the time of writing, the LAPD had produced detailed data.

ACTIVITY 5.11

- After reading the data in table 5.2, comment on the nature of the reported crimes. How do these shape your view of the locale? If you have time, look at the most recent statistics on the LAPD website and see if you can note any changes in the area's fortunes since 2004.
- Reflecting on the Wikipedia entry and other reading material, offer some speculations about any underlying factors that may have a bearing on the district's crime statistics.
- Using the map we have excerpted as a template, work to create your own map of Westlake, complete with tourist FAQs, safety tips on locations to avoid and other information specific to this district.

Conclusions

Throughout this chapter we have focused upon the relationship between place and identity, and have drawn upon the work of social theorists and cultural geographers to tease out the often complex ways in which people interact with their physical environment. We have concentrated upon contemporary examples relevant to Europe or North America but many of the sources listed in the recommended further reading will help you to work on the intersection of place and identity in other cultures.

Our survey has not made much use of approaches to the geography of culture in terms of landscape studies. We have, however, tried to strike a balance between an engagement with the materiality of cultural experience and more abstract approaches to the processes at work in shaping individual

Table 5.2 LAPD crime statistics for 2004, for stations in the Central Division, including Rampart

Homicides

Community police station	Number of crimes	
	No.	Percent of city total
CENTRAL	11	2.1
RAMPART	27	5.2
HOLLENBECK	30	5.8
NORTHEAST	16	3.5
NEWTON	48	9.3

Forcible Rape

Community police station	Number of crimes	
	No.	Percent of city total
CENTRAL	59	5.4
RAMPART	94	8.6
HOLLENBECK	43	4.0
NORTHEAST	43	4.0
NEWTON	56	5.1

Aggravated Assault

Community police station	Number of crimes	
	No.	Percent of city total
CENTRAL	929	3.6
RAMPART	1660	6.4
HOLLENBECK	1308	5.0
NORTHEAST	1225	4.7
NEWTON	1906	7.3

Robbery

Community police station	Number of crimes	
	No.	Percent of city total
CENTRAL	857	6.1
RAMPART	1228	8.8
HOLLENBECK	454	3.2
NORTHEAST	534	3.8
NEWTON	1082	7.7

Source: *LAPD Statistical Digest 2004:* www.lapdonline.org/crime_maps_and_compstat (accessed 3 September 2007).

identities in specific locations. In this chapter we have tackled one of the central problems for cultural studies: how to describe and analyse what is often fleeting, ephemeral and prosaic but none the less fundamental to the ways in which human subjects make sense of themselves and the world they inhabit. The importance of cultural geography to cultural studies is that it forcibly reminds us that a culture cannot be reduced to a set of discourses, but has to take account of the physical places in which those discourses operate. In order to explore some of these ideas further, you could reflect upon your own experience and understanding of a range of places and spaces: those you have lived in, those you have visited, those you have worked in, those you have imagined, those you have seen represented in pictures, films or TV, those you have read about, those you would like to visit, those you wouldn't, those that produce goods and services for you to purchase, those that are in the news. Think about the ways in which these places and spaces are linked in your consciousness: is it through memory or imagination, through relatives, by international media, or through what you buy? Think about the social relations that certain spaces produce (classrooms, for example), but also think about the ways in which a particular place or space could be produced as a result of a set of social relations (two friends sharing a house might produce a different 'place' to a married couple sharing a house). Some of the ideas in this chapter feed into discussions in chapters 6, 8 and 9, and there are suggestions for further reading in the bibliography if you are interested in pursuing this topic.

Chapter 6

Case Study
Global Tourism

This chapter comprises a case study in which you can see applied the concepts introduced in the previous five chapters: culture, identity, representation, history and cultural geography. We have chosen to focus on global tourism for a number of reasons. First, it is one of the fastest-growing industries in the world today and is part of the everyday lives of people in post-industrial societies. Those who live in Europe, North America and Japan may either be tourists, travelling the globe for business and holidays, or act as hosts to tourists from other parts of the world. Secondly, a consideration of global tourism does not only mean thinking about the economics of a worldwide industry, but also involves us in issues of identity and difference, representation, 'heritage' and history, and the transformation of geographical spaces into meaningful places. Finally, exploring tourism as a worldwide cultural phenomenon is a way of introducing you to a concept that we have not yet discussed: globalization. This is a much-contested and hotly debated term, with battle lines drawn between those who see globalizing tendencies as a positive thing and those who see them as a manifestation of United States imperialism or as entirely destructive to less wealthy communities. Hence, our exploration will take us into debates about ethics, about power geometries, and about tourism as a significant element of what is meant by the word globalization. This chapter will therefore start with tourism, but the later sections will integrate this discussion into a wider exploration of globalization. Before we start to make sense of all this, let us begin by trying to define what we mean by tourism.

- List all the places you have visited for pleasure in the last two years or so.
- Why did you choose to go there?
- What did you do while there and how long did you stay?
- Would you go back? Give reasons for your answer.
- Having done this, can you begin to define the characteristics of tourism and holidays?

Answers to the above will undoubtedly vary enormously, but there will be some common ground. For example, although you may have said that your reason for a visit was to see relatives or friends, you may also have said something about 'getting away' to an unknown place, and indeed the two are not mutually exclusive. You may have said you travelled in order to have a holiday from work and to see or do something that is in distinct contrast to your everyday life. Your stay will almost certainly have been short. That is, there was every intention of returning 'home' within a relatively short time. In answer to the question about whether you would go back and why, there will have been a variety of answers. You may have answered 'no' because there are so many other places to visit. If you said 'yes', you may want to return because you feel you haven't seen or done everything there was to do there, or because the place was 'perfect' and provided intense pleasures that are not encountered at 'home'.

We can list the characteristics of tourism and holidaymaking as follows:

- Tourism is a leisure activity that is distinguishable from and in direct contrast to the world of organized work, whether paid or unpaid.
- Tourism involves a movement from 'home' to 'away'. It involves journeys to places that are then stayed in rather than lived in.
- The stay is temporary and is undertaken with a clear intention to return to home and work.
- The places visited are different from those in which work and everyday life are carried out. Indeed, it is their difference that makes them holiday destinations.
- The activities undertaken while away are different either in scale or intensity. As tourists we look more keenly at the environment than we probably do in our daily life, or we enjoy sensory experiences such as swimming, sunbathing, eating, drinking, walking and cycling at a more intense level than at 'home', or we engage in reading and thinking that we do not have time for when rushing to and from work.

- The point about holidaymaking is that the tourist experience is entirely different from that of our everyday life in terms of at least one of the following: location, activities, landscape, sensory experience.

ACTIVITY 6.2

Find an advertisement for holidays or a picture in a travel brochure. What meanings about tourism and holidays are encoded in your chosen image? If you are unsure how to do this, refer back to the discussion of encoding and decoding in chapter 3. We have given you some headings to help you with this exercise.

Subject matter What does the picture depict?
Connotations List the ideas that you associate with the images in this picture.
Narrative Can you make up a story around this picture? What happened before and what might happen next?
Written text How do the words anchor the images? What connotations attach to the words used?
Style Can you say anything about the way it is photographed? Look, for example, at the use of light, shade, perspective, shapes and colour.

We cannot know what you have found in your particular picture but it is likely that some of the following meanings will have come up: exotic, far away, getting away, relaxing, luxury, doing something different, new experiences, pampering, meeting different people, discovering a different culture.

Completing this exercise should enable you to see how the meanings of tourism and holidays are encoded in the holiday brochures provided by tourism professionals. Do we see holidays as intense experiences in distinctive locations because we are encouraged to do so by the advertising of those selling us tourism, or does the advertising simply tap into our existing ideas about holidays? There is no right or wrong answer to this question. Indeed, it is not possible to say for sure how or where precisely our ideas about holidays come from. What is clear is that while there are historical and sociological variations of what constitutes tourism, there are some common features of those social practices we describe as 'tourism' in the twenty-first century. These features are commonly understood at least among those who live in industrialized economies where societies are structured around a clear demarcation between work and leisure. As John Urry says, tourism is a leisure activity which presupposes its opposite, namely regulated and organised work. It is one manifestation of how work and leisure are organised as separate and regulated spheres of social practice in 'modern' societies. Indeed acting as a tourist is one of the defining characteristics of being 'modern' and is bound up with major transformations in paid work. This has come to be organised within particular places and to occur for regularised periods of time. (Urry, 2002, p. 2)

You were able to make sense of the brochure image and the discussion that preceded this because we have a shared understanding of what is meant by the terms 'tourism' and 'holidays'. It is unlikely that you found much, if anything, to disagree with in the bullet list above. Indeed, you may have found it a rather obvious exercise. This is because we are rarely called upon to define what we mean by 'tourism'. We don't need to explain what is meant by the term because 'everyone knows what it means': the meaning of tourism is a deeply embedded part of our generally unexamined 'common-sense' knowledge of the world we inhabit. Think back to chapter 1 and our discussion of culture. The shared understandings, the 'everybody knows, it's obvious' feeling that enables those of us familiar with the culture of 'modern' societies to define tourism, are culture in Williams's sense of 'structure of feeling' and in du Gay's sense of meanings that are produced and circulated within society. The term 'tourism' is understood within a network of meanings about work, leisure, home and away that is cultural. This network of meanings is produced from a range of discourses that enable us to understand and communicate ideas about, among other things, work, leisure, the exotic, everyday, home, far away, pleasure, freedom, obligation and responsibility. In a society where people do not 'go away' either because of poverty, lack of knowledge of other places, political danger, the demands of work or lack of transport (or indeed all of these), there will be little understanding of tourism in the way discussed above. However, there may be understandings based on being on the receiving end of mass tourist incursions into societies previously isolated from the rest of the world (for example, some African societies). We shall look at this in more detail later in this chapter.

The Story of Tourism

Mass tourism in which millions of people go on holiday, visit places and travel for leisure is a characteristic of 'modern' life. Indeed, 'going away' has become a marker of status in contemporary societies. Not to go on holiday is perceived as equivalent to not having a nice house, nice clothes or a car. Being unable to afford a holiday may be seen as a marker of deprivation and poverty. Charities and social groups often organize holidays for groups of people who normally would be unable to go away, because 'going away' is thought to be beneficial for people's well-being. Where I (Judy Giles) live, elderly people are encouraged to go on organized visits to historic sites, the seaside and landscapes of natural beauty. Those with physical and mental disabilities are offered trips that include activities suitable for them as a group. This was not always the case: it is only in the last two hundred years that mass tourism has become widespread, particularly in North America and Europe but, increasingly, across the globe.

The idea of visiting other cultures in order to encounter an intense or different experience is not a new one. Urry cites imperial Rome, observing that a travel infrastructure made it possible for some people to travel for business and pleasure. Feifer (1985, p. 9) quotes Seneca, who said, 'men travel widely to different sorts of places seeing different distractions because they are fickle, tired of soft living, and always seek after something which eludes them.' The search for intense religious experience or simply distraction was behind the phenomenon of pilgrimage that was a feature of the Middle Ages. If you know Chaucer's *Canterbury Tales*, you might think about the reasons given by the various characters for undertaking the pilgrimage to Canterbury. In thirteenth- and fourteenth-century Europe, people made lengthy pilgrimages to religious shrines, staying on their way at charitable hospices and monasteries, and by the fifteenth century it was possible to visit the Holy Land from Venice (Urry, 2002, pp. 4–5).

By the eighteenth century the Grand Tour was established as a high cultural education for the sons of the British aristocracy. To begin with, the purpose of this tour was to visit the classical sites of ancient Greece and Italy, and to record and discuss the galleries, museums and cultural artefacts seen. By the nineteenth century, it had been extended to the sons of the professional middle classes and involved the more sensory and aesthetic experience of gazing upon the sublime and the beautiful, usually in the form of scenery and landscape. In the nineteenth century, wealthy Americans began to travel to Europe to experience its historical, cultural and scenic sites. The novels of Henry James written in the latter part of the nineteenth century are full of Americans who come to Europe and are forever marked by the experience, as are those whom they encounter. However, before the twentieth century, all these examples of travel for pleasure and culture were accessible only to the wealthy and elite. Most people rarely travelled anywhere unless it was connected to work or business. It was in the twentieth century that the social practices were established by which 40 per cent of people's leisure time is occupied by travel (Urry, 2002, p. 5). Holidays have become an essential element in people's lifestyle. We believe that a holiday will restore us physically and mentally, hence the statement doubtless uttered by most of us at one time or another, 'I need a holiday'.

The World Tourism Organization (WTO) collates data on the flows of people who travel abroad for short periods either on holiday or on business. 'International tourists' are defined by the Organization as those who stay in a country for at least 24 hours. According to the statistics of the WTO, international tourism grew from just over one million tourists in 1950 to more than 600 million in the year 2000. This huge increase in what the WTO calls international tourist arrivals (that is the number arriving for a short stay in any country in the world) has generated a dramatic growth in global earnings. For example, from 1995 to 1996 there was a 7.6 per cent increase, with international travellers generating around $423 billion in 1996 (Cohen and Kennedy, 2000, p. 213). Between 1995 and 2003, for example, international tourist arrivals in the Americas (North America, the Caribbean, Central and South America) grew from 108,994,000 to 112,987,000. There are very few other industries that can sustain these rates of growth and some observers believe that during the 1990s tourism became the largest industry in the global economy, outstripping even oil and vehicle production (Cohen and Kennedy, 2000, p. 213). However, this growth is unevenly distributed with some areas of the world benefiting more than others.

<table>
<tr><td>ACTIVITY 6.3</td><td>

• Using table 6.1, answer the following questions:
  1 Did anything surprise you in the figures shown in the table?
  2 Which countries have the largest number of tourist arrivals?
  3 Why do you think this is?
  4 Which countries have the smallest number of tourist arrivals?
  5 Why do you think this is?
  6 Which country's figures for tourist arrivals have grown the most?
  7 Which have been the steadiest?
• Group the countries into regions as follows:
  Africa: South Africa, Kenya, Sierra Leone
  the Americas: United States, Mexico, Cuba, Brazil
  Asia: China, Japan, Thailand, India
  Europe: United Kingdom, Spain, France
  the Middle East: Iraq
</td></tr>
</table>

> 1 Which *region* has the largest number of tourist arrivals?
> 2 Which has the smallest number?
> 3 Which has grown the most?
> 4 Is there any evidence of a region remaining static or declining?
> • Summarize this information in a short paragraph, emphasizing what you
>   think are the main points of interest in these figures.

When I first looked at these figures, I was surprised to see that France had the most international tourist arrivals between 1995 and 2003. I expected other Mediterranean countries and the USA to score as highly as France. I was unsurprised that Sierra Leone and Iraq showed very little tourist activity: both countries have been the subject of political conflict and war during the last ten years. It is interesting to note that in Cuba tourism has increased enormously since 1995. Tourism is one of the ways in which a poor country can generate income for itself. Opening up to international visitors brings money and jobs to a poor country, and the developing economies of East Asia

Table 6.1 International tourist arrivals 1995–2003, in thousands

	1995	2000	2001	2002	2003
South Africa	4,684	6,001	5,908	6,550	6,640
Kenya	896	899	841	838	927
Sierra Leone	38	16	24	28	37
Brazil	1,991	5,313	4,773	3,783	4,091
Cuba	742	1,741	1,736	1,656	1,847
United States	43,490	51,219	46,907	43,525	41,212
Mexico	20,241	20,641	19,810	19,667	18,665
China	20,304	31,229	33,167	36,803	32,970
Thailand	6,952	9,579	10,133	10,873	10,082
Australia	3,726	4,530	4,435	4,420	4,354
Japan	3,345	4,757	4,772	5,239	5,212
India	2,124	2,649	2,537	2,384	2,726
United Kingdom	23,537	25,209	22,835	24,180	24,715
France	60,033	77,190	75,202	77,012	75,048
Spain	34,920	47,898	50,094	52,327	51,830
Iraq	61	78	127	No figures	No figures
Czech Republic	3,381	4,666	5,194	4,579	5,076

Source: World Tourism Organization (data as collected by WTO December 2004), Annex 4–8.

(Thailand, Malaysia and Singapore) have been particularly adept at attracting overseas visitors. It is also noteworthy that countries like the Czech Republic, which was able to develop tourism after the fall of communism in 1989, have grown steadily. There are many Eastern European countries which have found this much harder to do. The wealthier countries continue to dominate the market for international travellers. France, Spain, the United States and the United Kingdom retain their positions at the top of the list. However, in recent years their position as the dominant destinations for visitors has been threatened by the growth of tourism in South East Asia. Moreover, China has emerged as a major player on the global stage and the figures for tourist arrivals reflect this. Its figures outstrip those of the United Kingdom, though not those of France, Spain and the United States. One of the reasons for the growth of tourism in Asia is the growth of the Asian economies. People living in Singapore, Korea, Japan, Australia and, more recently, China visit Indonesia, Malaysia, Thailand, and the Philippines for their holidays, often in preference to destinations in the United States or Europe. At the same time, visitors from Europe seeking more exotic and 'faraway' locations than France or Spain are travelling to the countries of South East Asia. The result has been the development of a thriving tourist industry in the Asian region. However, as we shall see later in this chapter, there is a price to pay for this. Despite this growth in Asia, the United States and Europe continue to hold their position as front-runners in the tourist industry, though this position is less undisputed than perhaps it once was. As tourism is an enormously lucrative industry, there is no doubt that the United States and Europe will seek to shore up tourism in their countries and will develop new ways of attracting visitors in what is becoming an increasingly competitive and complex industry.

This is a long way from the pilgrims who visited shrines in the Middle Ages, or is it? In the next section we will explore some of the ways in which tourism has been understood as a social and cultural phenomenon.

Tourism as Social Practice

Reading 6.1

'Modern man' and 'modern woman' become tourists in two senses: quite literally they become sightseers but, in addition, they are tourists in a spiritual sense, searching for authenticity and value whilst beset by continuous change and uncertainty. Through tourism in the latter sense, modernity is provided with its dominating ideology and tourist attractions take on the functional significance previously held by religious symbols. The tourist is thus a modern pilgrim and tourist attractions, be they objects, places or even entire communities or societies are shrines at which authenticity is worshipped albeit in vain: in discovering new sources of authenticity, tourists inevitably pollute that which they seek to preserve. (Harrison, 1995, p. 240)

Emile Durkheim, one of the earliest sociologists, argued that in all societies a distinction is made between what he called the sacred and the profane. His study of religious life, published in 1915 as *The Elementary Forms of Religious Life*, argues that religious rituals, objects and beliefs (the sacred) are separated from the objects and practices of everyday life (the profane). Places of worship and the objects used in the rituals of religion – books, vestments, altars – are treated with respect, awe and veneration, in distinction to the books, clothes and furnishings that are used in daily life. The function of the sacred is to bring communities together to affirm shared beliefs through the practice of ritualistic and ceremonial activities. The profane is not marked by this special treatment and is understood through common sense and everyday experience. To know the sacred, it is necessary to leave ordinary life and experience the extraordinary. In pre-modern societies, religion functioned as the sphere of the extraordinary, and, while some people experienced the extraordinary through becoming pilgrims, most people tasted the sacred in the form of local religious festivals, saints' days, and the rituals of holy days ('holidays'). In the twenty-first century in industrialized societies, religion is far less likely to structure the distinction between sacred and profane. Instead, Harrison argues, holidays and travel are the ways in which we now seek to experience the extraordinary (the sacred). We visit tourist attractions in order to gaze with 'awe and veneration'. We hope that holidays will transport us from the daily grind of work and routine to an extraordinary realm of pleasure in which our senses will be heightened and from which we will return renewed and restored. Indeed, as Cohen and Kennedy point out (2000, pp. 216–17), intensive preparations are made for the holiday experience: brochures are perused, travel guides read, clothing is bought. When we return we display souvenirs and photographs and share our memories with other 'pilgrims' who have visited the same 'shrines'. Holidays and tourism are deeply embedded social practices that have a particular function and meaning in modern societies. This function can be explained using Durkheim's concepts of the sacred and the profane. In this way tourism accrues certain cultural meanings that are shared and circulated among the members of industrialized societies.

- List places that are tourist 'shrines', either in your own country or elsewhere.
- What are your hopes and expectations when setting out on holiday? How are these met by the actual experiences you encounter?
- Do you find Durkheim's idea of the sacred and the profane useful as a way of thinking about tourism?

Durkheim's ideas are suggestive when applied to the phenomenon of tourism and holidays. Tourists, however, do not 'worship' at one specific 'shrine'. They collect experiences which may range from gazing on the beauties of natural landscapes (the Grand Canyon, the French Alps) to experiencing life in an artificially re-created historical period, for example in New Salem, USA, or in the Beamish museum in north-east England. Equally, tourists may choose to look at the culture of indigenous groups such as Maoris in New Zealand or American Indians in the United States. And how would we explain the attractions of Disneyworld Florida in Durkheim's terms? It is difficult to see how awe and veneration might operate here, though it is possible to understand the carnivalesque nature of Disneyworld as one in which the normal conventions of everyday life are suspended as people indulge in pleasurable and playful 'non-serious' behaviour. The Walt Disney World Resort website homepage uses the word 'magical' four times, inviting people to enter a world of 'enchantment' that is entirely unlike anything else they know. Disneyland has been created by the vast Disney corporation as a 'magical' place in which the 'vacation of your dreams is closer than your imagination', thus tapping into people's need to find 'enchantment' in a secular world in which religion no longer promises to transport people to the realm of the extraordinary.

However, not all tourists seek 'magic'. Many are looking for the 'authentic', whether it be a reconstruction of the past, an indigenous culture, or a workplace. For example, the Tokyo stock exchange can be visited by tourists who are allowed, at certain times, to watch the trading from platforms erected for their exclusive use. And the hard labour of a nineteenth-century domestic servant or the excitement of a Wild West rodeo can become the object of the tourist gaze through 'authentic' reconstructions. Tourism in the twenty-first century increasingly involves 'gazing' on someone else's reconstructed 'real life', whether in the past or present. As Urry observes, '[t]he tourist is a kind of contemporary pilgrim, seeking authenticity in other "times" and other "places" away from that person's everyday life' (Urry, 2002, p. 9).

Tourist Places

In the section above, we noted how the Walt Disney World Resort in Florida is packaged as a place of 'enchantment' and 'magic'. All tourist sights become places that acquire significant meanings as a result of their inclusion in tourist itineraries. This picks up the discussion in chapter 5 about spaces and places, in particular reading 5.1 from the work of Lefebvre, in which he says that 'spaces are produced' and the 'raw material from which they are produced is nature'. The spaces produced, he goes on to say, 'are products of an activity which involves the economic and technical realms'. The advertising blurb for a book called *The World's Must-See Places* states: 'Stonehenge, the Taj Mahal, the Great Pyramid . . . There are certain places that demand to be seen' (QPD, 2005, p. 12). Places are constructed in travel guides and books like this as 'shrines' to be visited. Photography, digital technology and TV bring images of these tourist 'shrines' into our homes. The organization English Heritage, for example, has produced a CD-ROM guide to all the historical sites that it is involved in preserving and conserving. The CD-ROM provides the following:

- Comprehensive information about every English Heritage location
- Interactive iPIX 360° × 360° photographs
- Fully illustrated with stunning photographs
- Detailed location maps
- Search facility to help you locate each site
- Comprehensive histories and descriptions
- Key additional historical features to compliment [*sic*] selected sites
- Unique timelines to help you understand the development of selected sites
- Descriptions and examples of a selection of art or archaeological collections
- Site plans for selected sites
- Detailed information on English Heritage and its ongoing work
- Comprehensive information about membership of English Heritage (English Heritage Interactive Visitors' CD-ROM Guide)

This kind of publishing ensures that we know what we are going to see before we go, what we are expected to see when we get there and how we should understand the attraction, and encourages us to become collectors, ticking each place off as we visit. Status accrues to those who have collected the most visits, as well as the widest range of souvenirs, photographs and information. Certain places are **represented** in specific ways that distinguish them from other places. For example, Paris is represented as the city of romance, Spain as the land of passion and flamenco, the Seychelles as a tropical paradise, India as the exotic Orient. To complement this discussion you might look back at the discussion of cathedrals in chapter 1.

ACTIVITY 6.5

Collect a range of travel books and travel brochures. How are certain places represented, and what means are used to produce these representations? Revisit chapter 3 if you are unsure how to do this exercise.

Let us look now at an example of how a specific place can generate a number of meanings. Niagara Falls in North America is one of the continent's most popular and famous tourist sites. Straddling the boundary between Canada and the United States, the Falls are a site of great natural beauty that have called forth strong emotional responses from those who come to see them. However, as Urry and others have pointed out, Niagara, as an object upon which tourists come to gaze, has undergone a series of transformations, so that its meaning as a tourist site is now layered and complex. In the eighteenth century, it was understood as a sublime landscape that generated 'awe and veneration'. In the nineteenth century it became the favoured haunt of honeymooners and those seeking romance. As Urry observes (2002, p. 55), '[t]ravellers expected the Falls to be exceptional, a place where the limits of ordinary experience were transcended' and the conventions of everyday life could be left behind, a liminal space in which to experience the heightened emotions so often outlawed by the daily strictures of bourgeois life. In the present day this aspect of the Falls has been translated into a commercial spectacle with a wide range of artificially created entertainments such as 'luv tubs' and wedding packages that offer, for example, a 'Bliss by the Falls Wedding Service', with jewellery hire if required. There are numerous entertainment attractions such as casinos, an Imax theatre, a Whirlpool Jet Boat, Marineland and a Butterfly Conservatory, with tailored holiday packages to experience these. Niagara has become emptied of meaning: it is simply a conglomeration of commercial props and stage sets in which the Falls, as such, have disappeared. They can no longer be experienced directly as a natural wonder but can only be seen filtered and mediated by the commercial spectacle and kitsch that surrounds Niagara. This is apparent in its marketing to tourists, where the advertising mixes older understandings of Niagara with its contemporary commercial appeal. For example, 'there is something about

Niagara Falls, Canada that appeals to the lover, daredevil and poet in everyone'; 'with Niagara's stunning scenery, and the breath-taking power of the Falls, having your wedding celebration here is an unbeatable experience'; 'stunning Niagara Falls is known as the Honeymoon Capital of the World. Combine your special day of exchanging vows and expressing your love for each other with a romantic getaway by the roaring Falls at Niagara'. In Lefebvre's terms, Niagara today is a place transformed by economics (the profit-making activities of the numerous commercial entrepreneurs) and by technology (boats, helicopters, whirlpools, casinos, cinemas) from its original raw state as a natural phenomenon. It is thus no longer possible to understand it in any simple, 'original' way. Niagara Falls is not simply a geographical entity: it is a place that has meant different things to different people at different times, and the responses of all who visit, whether to engage in the proffered commercial entertainment or to view the sublime landscape, are shaped by these meanings. Thus, we can say that Niagara Falls is a heavily **mediated** place: there is no longer direct access to one definitive way of understanding this amazing geographical phenomenon. As Urry observes (2002, p. 59), with regard to Niagara, what 'we experience is structured by pre-existing cultural images in which the physical object is barely "seen" at all'.

ACTIVITY 6.6

Consider Niagara Falls or choose another tourist attraction that you know. How might different interest groups see this place? Here are some ideas to get you started.

- The various economic interests: the directors of hotel chains, transport providers, entertainment complexes, and those with land to sell for development.
- The planners and officials who were and are involved in decisions about the regulation of building and the provision of services.
- The people for whom the development of your chosen place meant employment opportunities.
- The people who continue to live and work there.
- Those who have been displaced as a result of the developments.
- The tourists who visit your chosen place.
-
-

What possible conflicts of interest might arise from the development of a place as a tourist attraction?

All of these groups will understand the tourist development of a place from different perspectives, but they will also have drawn on shared meanings about what constitutes 'an attraction' to rationalize decisions made and to make sense of their experience. Those for whom tourist development means employment may welcome the changes for the ways in which it benefits them economically. Those who do not benefit directly but continue to live in the area may take pride in showing 'their' place off to visitors. Those who have been displaced or do not benefit financially, however, may view visitors as unwelcome despoilers of 'their' beautiful place. Those who stand to make vast profits from developing the area will understand it differently from those to whom it offers employment. The regulators and planners may share common perspectives with those who fear the area may be spoilt, but may also welcome the income that tourism will bring. The visitors may demand certain standards of accommodation and service, and this may cause resentment in their 'hosts'. Those who live there may welcome the opportunity to see how other people live and to learn about other cultures from visitors. This nexus of shared understandings, conflicting interests, individual experience, economic interest, policy decisions and the actual geographical place produces the **created environment** known as, for example, Niagara Falls.

Tourism and Identities

There are two ways in which to approach the issue of tourism and identities. First, tourism appears to offer a homogeneous identity, that of 'tourist'. Secondly, within this umbrella identity there are variations that are very important in terms of social status. Looking at identity from the first point of view requires engaging with the relationship between tourists and those who receive or service tourists in their countries or attractions. The second approach involves ideas about the ways in which different kinds of tourist 'gaze' on the attractions and places visited.

We will begin then with the generic identity 'tourist'. This identity exists in direct relation to those who are 'natives' or 'hosts', who welcome, service and tolerate the influx of tourists to 'their' places. It is not possible to be simultaneously 'tourist' and 'native' because, at its simplest, being a tourist involves being away from one's home or 'native' place. The identity 'tourist' is a very good example of the point made in chapter 2 that identities are relational and contingent. Identities are constructed in terms of what they are not as much as what they are: they exist only in relation to what they are defined against. To be a 'tourist' in any situation is to not be a 'native' or 'host'. In chapter 2 we discussed how certain things act as symbolic markers of identity; for example, skin colour marked Africans in the eighteenth and nineteenth centuries as inferior in the imagination of white Europeans. Objects as well as biological characteristics can operate as markers of identity: for example, in northern Europe and North America carrying a handbag can be a marker of femininity. Equally important are the spatial markers that construct identities. For example, in the nineteenth century, men moved freely around the public spaces of the city and the workplace, while women, or at least bourgeois women, were confined to the home. Servants occupied certain spaces in the bourgeois home while their employers occupied others – 'below and above stairs'. To be a servant or a woman was to occupy certain circumscribed spaces that defined social identity.

ACTIVITY 6.7

Can you think of any markers that construct the identity 'tourist'?

The following are some possible symbolic and spatial markers that structure the differences between those visiting places for short periods and those who offer hospitality to the visitors. You will be able to think of others.

- Tourists are accommodated in hotels, complexes, guesthouses or holiday cottages.
- Tourists may not speak the language of the country visited.
- Tourists wear different clothes to their hosts.
- Tourists do not travel on local transport.
- Tourists frequent different shops.
- Tourists may carry cameras.
- Tourists occupy certain spaces in restaurants and bars: those providing hospitality occupy other spaces.
-
-

Perhaps an extreme example is the all-inclusive holiday resort often found in the Caribbean where accommodation, entertainment, food and drink, sport and leisure facilities are all under one roof and included in a package price. The tourist is confined to a specific area and rarely comes into contact with the local people unless they work in the tourist compound. In this example, the marking of the differences between the two identities (tourist/'native') is clear and unambiguous.

Tourist identities are constructed by the economic structures of the tourist industry. Huge international industries have developed to service the needs of tourists. These include transport, retailing, catering, hotels and leisure. Indeed part of the experience of visiting a particular site or place is the opportunity to consume food and drink in surroundings unlike those of home, to shop for local products or gifts and to participate in leisure or entertainment opportunities. All these services require employees who will provide the kind of 'hospitality' expected by tourists. However, employment in the hospitality industries tends to be low-paid and low-status, with little or no opportunity for promotion or development. In these circumstances it is not unusual for resentments to develop between visitors who demand highly personalized and quality service and local service personnel who resent the demands made upon them by both employers and consumers to carry out the demanding emotional work of hospitality (Urry, 2002, p. 62). On the other hand the establishment of a tourist industry in, for example, a poor country or region can bring employment and greater affluence to the local population, who in addition see and learn about cultures that are very distanced from them.

So far we have concentrated on 'tourist' as a homogeneous identity constructed by the mass tourist industry. Numerous commentators have challenged such a formulation, arguing that there is no single tourist 'type' but a variety of ways in which people see themselves when travelling (Apostolopoulos, Leivadi and Yiannakis, 1996). Indeed, one distinction often made is between 'tourists' and 'travellers'. 'Travellers' visit places in search of the authentic, whether it is to view a natural landscape through a semi-spiritual experience or to participate in local culture. 'Tourists', on the other hand, seek recreation and diversion in the company of other people with similar desires. In this construction 'tourists' are often despised as shallow pleasure-seekers who are duped by the trivial, superficial, inauthentic experience provided by the mass tourism industry, while 'travellers' are more akin to the pilgrims of old, seeking to understand and participate in the cultures they visit. The created distinction between tourists and travellers results, as theorists have noted, in 'a long-standing touristic attitude, a pronounced dislike . . . for other tourists, an attitude that turns man against man [*sic*] in a they-are-the-tourists-I-am-not equation' (Cohen, 1996, p. 90).

Central to the idea of tourism is the experience of looking. Tourists 'gaze' on the unfamiliar world in which they find themselves. Urry has identified two modes of looking which can be aligned with the distinctions made between 'travellers' and 'tourists'. These are the 'romantic' and the 'collective' tourist gaze. The romantic gaze demands solitude, privacy and a personal relationship with the object being looked at; solitude, for example, is a key aspect for many who enjoy rambling or mountain-walking. The collective gaze requires other people; the presence of other people is necessary to the carnivalesque atmosphere of Disneyland Florida, for example (Urry, 2002, pp. 43–4). As Urry observes, such distinctions link to class: the romantic gaze 'demonstrates unambiguous good taste', and the arbiters of taste have long been the bourgeoisie or middle classes (Urry, 2002, p. 43; see Bourdieu, 1984, and chapter 9). Erik Cohen (1996, p. 94) has broken these distinctions down further as follows:

1 The Recreational Mode
2 The Diversionary Mode
3 The Experiential Mode
4 The Experimental Mode
5 The Existential Mode

He says of this typology that these 'modes are ranked here so that they span the spectrum between the experience of the tourist as the traveller in pursuit of "mere" pleasure in the strange and the novel, to that of the modern pilgrim in quest of meaning at somebody else's centre' (Cohen, 1996, p. 94).

ACTIVITY 6.8

Using Cohen's typology, map the following forms of tourist motivation onto the modes listed above.

1 Those people for whom 'work will always be emotionally uncommitting and therefore unrewarding . . . they are condemned to seek in their leisure temporary oblivion and comfort for abraded nerve endings' (Glasser, 1975, p. 21).
2 'The person who encounters in his [sic] visit to an Israeli kibbutz a full realization of his quest for human communion [or the person] who finds in a remote Pacific atoll the fulfilment of his cravings for simplicity and closeness to nature' (Cohen, 1996, p. 101).
3 Those who desire to experience the strangeness and novelty of other landscapes, life-ways and cultures, perhaps because of a feeling that everyday life back home is shallow and meaningless and that 'someplace, in another country, in another life-style, in another social class, perhaps, there is *genuine* society' (MacCannell, 1976, p. 159). Such people are content to observe and derive enjoyment from the fact that other cultures operate differently.
4 Those people who sample and participate in other cultures but may not commit to any particular lifestyle. One year they may visit a kibbutz, the next an Indian community, and so on.
5 Those who do not mind the artificiality of the place they are visiting, whose aim is rest and recuperation and who, to this end, are quite happy to accept that the place they are visiting is make-believe. The motivation for travel is not the 'pull' of any particular place but the 'push' of their own everyday life, from which they need temporarily to escape.

Our suggestions are offered at the end of the chapter. However, there are no right and wrong answers to this exercise. The purpose is to get you thinking about the range of motivations that people may have for travelling and show that to characterize tourists as a homogeneous group can be misleading. Indeed, the same person may adopt more than one of the above identities over a lifetime, working in an African village at one point, taking a package holiday in Florida at another. You might also want to consider how other social identities, such as age, gender and ethnicity, cross-cut that of 'tourist'.

It is not simply in the realm of individuals and the relations between them that tourism generates identities but also, and perhaps most importantly, in the area of cultural identities.

Reading 6.2

One of the most interesting examples is the case of the Toraja people living in the central highland of the island of Sulawesi, part of Indonesia . . .

The Toraja people number around 300000. Over the centuries they have been exposed, like most of the other peoples in Indonesia, to Hindu, Islamic and Christian influences among others [Volkman, 1984, p. 153]. Nevertheless, until recently the Toraja retained their ancient religious beliefs based on ancestor worship . . . The arrival of Dutch missionaries from 1906 onwards meant that many of the funeral rituals [associated with their religious beliefs] continued to be performed but they were increasingly relegated to the status of customs and lost much of their earlier deep, religious content [Volkman, 1984, pp. 156–7] . . .

In 1975 roughly 2500 tourists visited the Toraja region, but by 1985 this had risen to approximately 40000. In 1986, the Toraja district was second only to Bali as Indonesia's most important tourist development region. By the mid-1980s a small airport had been opened, while bus services, hotels and restaurants mushroomed all across the island and tour operators were ferrying in visitors from across the world and other parts of Indonesia. (Cohen and Kennedy, 2000, p. 225)

ACTIVITY 6.9

- Find out more about Toraja using the articles cited in the References and Further Reading or by consulting a geographical encyclopaedia.
- Can you suggest any ways in which the development of a tourist industry in the Toraja region of Indonesia might have beneficial effects for the region?
- Can you suggest any ways in which tourism might have a negative impact on the region?

The advent of tourism has meant that Toraja's ancient culture and belief systems have become more widely known, stimulating interest among not only the tourist visitors who come to Toraja, but also historians, archaeologists and curators who write pamphlets, mount exhibitions and publish books. This in turn helps to sustain the religious rituals that were in danger of becoming simply customs with no deeper meaning. The arrival of tourists has engendered an interest in watching religious rituals and in visiting ancient burial sites. These ancient burial sites are now being protected and attempts are being made to seek out lost funeral chants. This has resulted in the people of Toraja taking a pride in their ancient customs and, as Volkman puts it, reviving their ancient religious identity as 'an image through which the outside world can perceive and come to know [the] Toraja' (Volkman, 1984, p. 164; Cohen and Kennedy, 2000). Along with this older cultural identity, traditional crafts such as wood-carving and basket-making have been revived to provide 'authentic' crafts for sale to tourist visitors. This has produced additional wealth for the local population. Cohen and Kennedy comment that 'the wealth that has flowed into the Toraja economy has helped to strengthen the wider political influence of this previously neglected region within Indonesia' (2000, p. 226). You might note that not only economic prosperity has resulted from tourism in Toraja but, equally and as importantly, a political and cultural strengthening of the region.

There are also, of course, negative impacts from tourism. In Toraja, the seduction of instant affluence from tourism has resulted, in some cases, in the stealing of family heirlooms, presumably to sell to tourists keen to purchase local objects. Burial sites have been desecrated, again in order to sell trinkets and religious objects to wealthy tourists. Those who work to preserve ancient religious beliefs and the poor, less educated people who participate in Toraja's traditional cultures are not always those who benefit from the prosperity generated by tourism (Cohen and Kennedy, 2000, pp. 225–6). It is likely too that the transport systems and the development of resort areas have produced environmental damage and pollution in the area.

Thus, while international tourism may help to revive or preserve cultural identities that are threatened by modernization projects or political marginalization, these benefits may come at a price. Cohen and Kennedy suggest some cases where this has happened: Bali in Indonesia (McKean, 1989; Picard, 1995); the Ainu people in northern Japan (Friedman, 1990, pp. 319–23); and the Spanish people living on the island of Ibiza in the Mediterranean (Rozenberg, 1995). We should beware of being overly utopian about tourism's potential: it can also bring with it less favourable changes: crime, drug-dealing, exploitation of labour and, of course, damage to the environment. In a study of tourism and modernity in Swaziland in Africa, it was noted that older

Swazis viewed 'foreign' influences as having a corrupting effect on their young people. In particular they were concerned about drinking, and the wearing of trousers by young women. However, tourism alone does not account for the problems with modernity expressed by older Swazis. It is not only tourists who bring Western ideas to Swaziland. European and North American media are accessible to young people in Swaziland and provide seductive images of Western fashion and lifestyles which they may try to emulate. Nor should we take up a position in which traditional cultures are seen as frozen in time, to be maintained as good-in-themselves at all costs, a position in which the traditional is always positive and the modern always negative. Younger Swazis will learn about Western lifestyles from TV and films and from tourism. Some of these fashions and ideas will be incorporated into their own local cultures and these cultures thereby changed. There will be losses and gains but a perspective that sees such trends simply as a threat is 'to say the least . . . somewhat contentious if not downright patronising' (Harrison, 1992, p. 156). Cultures, and the cultural identities that go with them, are constantly evolving. This can involve integrating or adapting elements from other cultures to create something that is neither 'traditional' culture nor entirely 'modern'; that is, for example, neither entirely North American nor entirely Swazi.

> **ACTIVITY 6.10**
> - Why might a perspective that deplores change to traditional cultures be 'downright patronising'?
> - Can you think of any examples from your own experience of travelling of elements from other cultures being adapted or integrated to create something new?

Tourism and Heritage

One of the most profitable branches of the tourist industry has been that of heritage, that is, the creation of historical sites and historical lifestyles as visitor attractions. Bella Dicks defines the production of heritage as 'both salvaging the past and staging it as a visitable experience' (Dicks, 2003, p. 119). Visitor attractions that feature the past or a historical site have possibly conflicting aims. On the one hand there is a wish to engage people in their own or another culture's past and to preserve that past. On the other hand there is a commercial aspect. This can create paradoxes in which the reconstructed heritage site may be more profitable than the original:

Heritage is a mode of cultural production in the present that has recourse to the past. Heritage thus defined depends on display to give dying economies and dead sites a second life as exhibitions of themselves. A place such as Salem, Massachusetts, may be even more profitable as an exhibition of a mercantile center than it was as a mercantile center. (Kirshenblatt-Gimblett, 1998, p. 7)

It is estimated that in any one year in the United Kingdom, for example, a greater proportion of the population visits a historical building, a museum, a historic park, a cathedral or an ancient monument than attends a football match or the opera (Urry, 2002, p. 96). In the USA the number of places listed on the US National Register of Historic Places rose from 1,200 in 1968 to 37,000 in 1985. At the end of chapter 4 we briefly reviewed some of the debates that have taken place around heritage; you might want to remind yourself of the points made there before attempting the next exercise.

ACTIVITY 6.11

- List any heritage sites that you have visited, either in your own country or elsewhere.
- What reasons would you give for your visits?
- Were there any similarities between what was offered?
- Why do you think people visit heritage sites?

Museums, historic buildings, ancient monuments and even cathedrals have a café or restaurant attached, and it is equally obligatory to provide a shop that sells memorabilia, books and gifts. A visit to a historical site almost always includes purchasing a souvenir, or enjoying a meal or snack in the pleasant surroundings of the café. Read the following extract from Bella Dicks's *Culture on Display*, where she attempts to explain the current enthusiasm for heritage tourism.

Reading 6.3

[H]eritage stages the desire to halt a 'runaway world'. It seems to offer an imaginary space of resistance to 'turbo-capitalism', the destruction of traditional environments and the vanishing of communities. By recreating past environments in material form, it seems to make time stand still; we can walk down an ostensibly medieval street and find all its people, noise, sights and smells still there. Outside, redevelopment marches relentlessly on; inside, we can stroll, literally at our leisure, through spaces of non-development. The voraciously destructive drives behind the seemingly solid edifice of capitalism have been memorably narrated by Marshall Berman in his 1982 book *All That Is Solid Melts Into Air*. Here he describes the coming of the 1960s "expressway world" in which the Bronx of his childhood was literally carved up and smashed to pieces by the tank-like onslaught of arch-modern development. Architects, planners and designers throughout the twentieth century, but increasingly after the Second World War, developed the straight lines, clean vistas, overarching freeways and functional buildings of modernity as an explicit rejection of what they took to be the atrophied traditional living patterns and stubborn group identities of old-fashioned neighbourhoods [Mugerauer, 2001, p. 92]. Heritage can be seen, in its turn, as a material form of rejection of this rejection.

Yet herein too lies the fuel for heritage's fiercest critics. Resistance to these transformations has often been seen as a manifestation of that same stubbornness – a failure to move on, an atrophied clinging to the old ways and a 'yearning for yesterday' [Davis 1979]. Heritage, likewise, has been seen as the same nostalgic turning away from the present [e.g. Wright, 1985; Hewison, 1987, 1989]. (Dicks, 2003, pp. 129–30)

ACTIVITY 6.12 How do you respond to Dicks's points? Do you think the contemporary enthusiasm for heritage tourism expresses a refusal to engage with the modern? Do you think the current preoccupation with the past is emblematic of societies that insist on looking backwards rather than forwards?

I want now to look at a specific example of heritage production in the United Kingdom. The aim of the National Trust is 'to preserve and protect the coastline, countryside and buildings of England, Wales and Northern Ireland . . . in a range of ways, through practical caring and conservation, through learning and discovery, and through encouraging millions of people to visit and enjoy their national heritage' (www.nationaltrust.org.uk). In 1990, it acquired 7 Blyth Grove, Worksop, Nottinghamshire. This house is one of a pair of Edwardian semi-detached villas built in 1905–7 on the outskirts of the town for professional people. Now read the introduction to the souvenir booklet for 7 Blyth Grove.

Reading 6.4

No. 7 Blyth Grove, Worksop, the home of the Straw family from 1923, is, from the outside at least, a typical example of a well-to-do tradesman's house in a provincial town at the beginning of [the twentieth] century. But because the family which lived here were so averse to change, it has remained almost entirely unaltered since the early 1930s. Down to the 1932 calendar on the wall of the Dining Room, there is hardly a trace of the last 60 years.

It was in 1932 that William Straw, a grocer and seeds merchant and father of two sons, William and Walter, died suddenly whilst gardening. The blow was so devastating to the family that they allowed nothing to be changed in the house from that day forward. Father's pipes and tobacco pouch still hang beside the fireplace, his hats and coats on the pegs in the Hall.

Seven years later Florence Straw, the boys' mother, also died and the embalming was complete. The curtains were always kept drawn in her Sitting Room with its piano, small low chairs in their faded case covers, and china and glass ornaments. From this time on, her two sons lived on the surface of the house, existing, it seems entirely in the past. While Walter, the younger son, continued to run the family business, William gave up his teaching job in London and returned to look after the house. The brothers had no telephone, radio, television or central heating, and entering the house today, one steps back three-quarters of a century.

When William, the last of the Straw family, died in 1990 at the age of 92, he left the contents of 7 Blyth Grove, other property in Worksop, and the bulk of his estate to the National Trust, although he had never been a member . . . The National Trust was able to buy the freehold of both Nos 5 and 7 Blyth Grove, which had been left elsewhere, and has made every effort to preserve the house exactly as it was found. (National Trust, 1993, p. 3)

ACTIVITY 6.13

- What does the National Trust see as the particular significance of this house?
- What is the Trust's aim with regard to the house?

The National Trust sees the house as 'a typical example of a well-to-do tradesman's house'. The commentary accompanying the video presentation shown to visitors speaks of a whole way of life 'locked in time' and 'captured' for posterity. You may think there is a tension between the stress on typicality and the 'locked-in-timeness' of 7 Blyth Grove. This particular house is unusual

Figure 6.1   'Junk room', Mr Straw's house, Nottinghamshire

because it has remained unaltered since the 1930s: a more typical house might show signs of change and alteration as well as traces of its past. Moreover, as the National Trust makes clear, it intends to 'preserve the house exactly as it was found'. In order to achieve this aim it is necessary to charge visitors an entrance fee and sell associated souvenirs. Yet, in order to protect the stair carpet, for example, from wear occasioned by visitors' feet, it has been necessary to take it up and replace it with something similar. In order to preserve Mr Straw's house 'as it was found', it is necessary to remove and alter things. And the very act of preserving it, of course, makes it no longer, if it ever was, typical. The history of the house and its inhabitants is unique and unusual – hence its fascination.

Look at figure 6.1. This photograph is on the back cover of the souvenir booklet and shows the Lumber Room at the top of the house, a room that would once have been used to house servants, but was used by the Straws, who dispensed with domestic help after the deaths of their parents, as a junk room.

What strikes you as interesting in this picture, and why?

When we first scrutinized the picture we noticed the air-raid warden's helmet, the 'Baby Daisy' vacuum cleaner, the brown paper bag from the family firm, the bottled fruit, the hatbox and the jug and bowl, all of which suggest a private and a public history (family activities alongside the Second World War). This junk room was, we can assume, a place where objects were continually added and stored, and very possibly some were removed. The 'Baby Daisy' vacuum cleaner may have been put there earlier than the air-raid warden's helmet or the bottled fruit. And it is likely that the whole display has been arranged to show certain items to contemporary visitors. Yet the impression given by the picture is static and fixed: the past, represented by the various objects, has been frozen and captured. It is presented to posterity as a spectacle upon which we may focus our tourist 'gaze', exclaiming at its oddities and its 'authenticity' compared to our modern existence.

Can you suggest what meanings the National Trust is conveying about the past and history in its statements about 7 Blyth Grove and in this picture from the souvenir booklet?

It would be possible to argue that the National Trust represents history as a static, frozen body of knowledge, separated from the present, and only available to us as spectacle. The past is 'captured as it was'. This version of history does not encourage us to engage in critical dialogue with the past or to see it as a process of reconstruction. On the contrary, it invites us to look with wonder and nostalgia at a supposedly fixed and unchanging moment.

However, when I (Judy Giles) visited Mr Straw's house I was as fascinated by the story of the Straw family as by the house and its objects. I was not the only one: the stewards who showed us round told different anecdotes about the Straws, and the other visitors asked numerous questions about William and

Walter. For example, after the death of their mother, William and Walter lived as bachelors and dismissed the maidservant. No women were allowed in the house thereafter. Was this misogyny, or was it connected to the period's ideas of respectability and morality? What did it mean then and how do we understand it now? William took over the domestic management of the house after his mother's death. How was this viewed by others? Was it seen as odd? Were the brothers respected in the town despite their eccentricities, or even because of them, or were they avoided? These questions involved all of us who were there, engaging with the past in terms of our understandings of gender, morality and sexuality in the present. We were actively and critically involved in making sense of and reconstructing the past, rather than simply consuming it as a finished product. In doing so we, the consumers of heritage, were not the passive 'dupes' suggested by some critics of heritage (see chapter 4). Not only were we able to engage critically with what seemed to us pertinent issues, we were also involved in negotiating and adapting the view of history offered by the National Trust.

ACTIVITY 6.16

To complete this section you could visit a heritage site or museum with these questions in mind.

- What view of history is represented?
- How is the past marketed and sold?
- What are the pleasures of 'gazing' at the past?
- Who visits museums and heritage sites, in terms of race and class?

Attempting to answer these questions will not only clarify the discussion above but will help you to think about a question raised by Jim McGuigan, namely, 'whether the museum visitor is conceived of as a customer to be persuaded or as a citizen with a voice in the representation of the past'. As McGuigan points out, 'public museums are now required increasingly to perform like private businesses, adopting a "pro-active" visitor strategy, selectively charging for admission, marketing their wares and selling sundry commodities in gift shops' (McGuigan, 1996, pp. 131–2).

Cultural Imperialism or Cultural Globalization?

In the final section of this chapter we want to think beyond tourism and heritage to the wider question of a global culture of which they are part. There are two ways of understanding the accelerated flow of cultural products, people and goods around the world that is often called **globalization** (see also chapter 2). First, the cultural imperialism thesis has as its basic tenet the idea that, rather than cultural artefacts and products flowing freely around the globe, one culture comes to dominate everywhere in the world. So, for example, rather than seeing the global tourism we have discussed as an equalizing and democratic process, or one in which the benefits are simply unequally spread around the world, this view perceives the process as one in which a particular culture and economic system becomes globally dominant. The cultural imperialism thesis argues, among other things, that the process of cultural globalization which includes the accelerated movement of tourists around the globe means, in reality, American penetration into and domination of all world cultures. As Jim McGuigan observes, 'the export of American popular culture to the rest of the world has frequently been cited as the main contemporary form of cultural imperialism' (McGuigan, 1996, p. 130). The siting of Disney theme parks near Paris and Tokyo (EuroDisney and Tokyo Disneyland) are often seen as examples of American cultural imperialism. It is argued that American cultural exports, originally to Europe, but increasingly to other parts of the world, have a deleterious effect on indigenous and local cultures, destroying traditional values and ways of life (see also the discussion above on cultural identities). Culture is becoming increasingly standardized as American culture – what is sometimes called the 'Americanization' of world culture. Anxieties about Americanization can take a number of forms: for example, concern about the economic power of the US, concern that other cultures are being swamped by American products, and a more generalized conservative stance against the supposed dangers of mass culture.

There is a tendency for the cultural imperialism thesis to oversimplify what actually happens and it is important to consider the consequences of any instance of apparent Americanization in their specific cultural and political contexts. For example, EuroDisney has not achieved the same success as its counterpart in Florida, USA, which, as McGuigan suggests, perhaps illustrates 'the limits to American cultural imperialism'. And in Tokyo Disneyland the name 'the World Bazaar' was adopted instead of 'Mainstreet USA' in order to please Japanese nationalism, suggesting a refusal to be co-opted into American culture quite as easily as the cultural imperialism thesis would have it (McGuigan, 1996, p. 130).

The rapid economic growth of China and the success of the so-called 'Asian Tigers' (Singapore, Hong Kong, South Korea, Taiwan) challenge the idea that economic power flows only from the Western industrialized powers. In future it may be that East and West will be equally dependent on each other economically. A buoyant consumer market in China and Japan provides a market for American goods. Equally, a prosperous East sends tourists to all parts of Europe and America, generating wealth for those regions. Instead of the image of the world conjured up by the perspective of cultural imperialism, in which information, culture, power and wealth flow in one direction from a central source (the West or, more precisely, the USA), a more adequate image may be that of a **decentred network** of shifting and multi-directional flows. We have to be careful here. The idea of decentring is not to suggest that inequalities and disparities are being levelled: extreme poverty remains in areas of Africa, Asia and Latin America, and North America, Europe, Japan and Australia continue to sustain a high quality of life. What the idea of a decentred network does raise is the contingent and shifting nature of wealth and power: it raises the prospect that there is no inherent logic in capitalism that ties it permanently to the West or to the USA. It raises the possibility that, rather than a continuing project of dominance by America, the complexities of global interconnections may shift dominance away from the West towards, for example, East Asia. Of course, we also need to remember that those areas that have enjoyed dominance in the past may struggle to maintain power; we have seen evidence of this in the interventions of the United States in Middle Eastern politics. Nevertheless, the idea of decentring challenges the assumptions of those who argue, following the cultural imperialism thesis, that a certain form (American) of capitalism is increasingly spreading to and dominating all areas of the globe.

International tourism is a significant globalizing force in the contemporary world. The rapid rise in the number of tourists travelling around the globe can bring wealth and prosperity to a region but it can also bring exploitation and environmental damage. Some tourists, particularly from rich, powerful nations, simply attempt to impose their culture and traditions on others. Or they use tourism as a way of escaping the laws and regulations of their own countries. In Thailand and Cambodia, for example, the influx of tourists from Japan, Europe and America has spawned a lucrative trade in 'sex tourism', exploiting women and children in a situation where there are few regulatory mechanisms to prevent this. Again, other tourists may act with reverence and respect towards the culture they visit and some may enhance cultural understanding among different peoples. Tourism, as we saw with Toraja, can revive local cultures but it can also destroy them. The marketing of national heritage can result in the reinvention of traditions or customs that were in the process of dying out. But, as Cohen and Kennedy observe, 'the traditions that survive are ones that have been re-invented. They are not the same as the original prototype' (Cohen and Kennedy, 2000, p. 228). It is also important to note that an increasingly globalized media is as important as tourism for the global spread of cultural products, but that is another story.

The following reading by Amartya Sen nicely highlights some of the points we have been making in this chapter and provides a fitting conclusion.

Reading 6.5

The contemporary world is dominated by the West, and even though the imperial authority of the erstwhile rulers of the world has declined, the dominance of the West remains as strong as ever – in some ways stronger than before, especially in cultural matters. The sun does not set on the empire of Coca-Cola or MTV . . .

The threat to native cultures in the globalizing world of today is, to a considerable extent, inescapable . . .

This is a problem, but not just a problem, since global trade and commerce can bring with it . . . greater economic prosperity for each nation. But there can be losers as well as gainers, even if in the net the aggregate figures move up rather than down.

In the case of culture, however, lost traditions may be greatly missed. The demise of old ways of living can cause anguish, and a deep sense of loss . . . The elimination of old species in favor of 'fitter' species that are 'better' able to cope and multiply can be a source of regret . . .

This is an issue of some seriousness, but it is up to the society to determine what, if anything, it wants to do to preserve old forms of living, perhaps even at significant economic cost. Ways of life can be preserved if the society decides to do just that and it is a question of balancing the costs of such preservation with the value that the society attaches to the objects and the lifestyles preserved . . . There is no compulsion to preserve every departing lifestyle even at heavy cost, but there is a real need – for social justice – for people to be able to take part in these social decisions, if they so choose. This gives further reason for attaching importance to such elementary capabilities as reading and writing (through basic education), being well informed and well briefed (through free media), and having realistic chances of participating freely (through elections, referendums and the general use of civil rights). (Sen, 2004, pp. 624–5)

Conclusions

We hope this chapter has shown you how the ideas introduced in the first five chapters of this book can be applied to a particular cultural formation, in this case tourism. Much more could be said on the subject, and we hope you may be stimulated to carry out your own projects on this topic or related areas. You will find plenty of interesting and relevant material in the suggestions for further reading.

Suggested answers for activity 6.8

1   Diversionary
2   Existential
3   Experiential
4   Experimental
5   Recreational

Chapter 7

Cultural Value
High Culture and Popular Culture

As we have seen, culture can be viewed as a contested field of interaction within which people make and encounter meanings. We have often found that, while many introductory works deal with popular fiction and equip students to tackle such texts (Fiske, 1991, pp. 103–27; Storey, 1996, pp. 29–53), less space is given to exploring the ways in which so-called 'high' culture and its texts are also a part of the process whereby meanings are produced and circulated within a society. As a way of analysing the diversity of meanings circulating within a culture, while avoiding the hierarchical thinking that so affects debates about high culture, we will be introducing the reader to the work of cultural theorist Mikhail Bakhtin. We will examine what is often seen as a tension between popular and so-called 'high' culture via work on everyday life, and also through discussion of two perspectives, from Britain and the United States, on the place of literature in the education system. We conclude the chapter with a rereading of Kenneth Grahame's classic children's novel *The Wind in the Willows*, in which we draw upon a number of recent approaches to the culturally grounded study of literary texts.

Our approach cannot neglect questions of popular culture but, by focusing on 'high' culture, we want to address – in this chapter at least – the apparent overemphasis on popular culture in many introductory works (for another perspective on the focus on popular culture in contemporary British cultural studies see Storey, 1993, pp. 181–202; also see McGuigan, 1992). Before you begin to work on the material in this chapter you might find it useful to read or reread chapter 1 in this volume.

Defining Culture

For Raymond Williams, 'culture has two aspects: the known meanings and directions, which its members are trained to; the new observations and meanings, which are offered and tested' (Williams, 1993, p. 6). There is a tension here which arises from the idea that while cultures can train or shape individuals, these same individuals retain the ability to test and otherwise discriminate between forms of culture and meaning. Williams devoted a major study, *Culture and Society: 1780–1950* (1963), to the examination of this issue, and his work remains essential reading for anyone interested in the development of the link between the older sense of culture as 'the tending of natural growth', and the early nineteenth-century idea of culture in which

> It came to mean, first, 'the general state or habit of a mind, having close relations with the idea of human perfection'. Second, it came to mean 'the general state of intellectual development, in a society as a whole'. Third, it came to mean 'the general body of the arts'. Fourth, later in the century, it came to mean 'a whole way of life, material, intellectual and spiritual'. It came also, as we know, to be a word which often provoked, either hostility or embarrassment. (Williams, 1963, p. 16)

What is useful in this assertion is the idea of historically competing definitions of the concept of culture. Today, one dominant version of cultural studies takes as its object of study everyday life and its related material culture. In consequence, the role of 'high' culture, its artefacts and practices, and the socio-political effects of these are, perhaps, less frequently addressed in many introductory works on the subject. It should, of course, be noted that there are a number of different versions of cultural studies currently operating and, often, competing for dominance: cultural studies in the USA has a very different, and some would argue a less politicized, agenda to cultural studies in South Asia, for example (Lal, 1996).

In this chapter we want to concentrate upon aspects of 'high' culture, not because we think this is a more important area than any of the other aspects of culture which we have been addressing in this book, but rather because to forget so-called 'high' culture in any analysis of a given epoch or society means offering a distorted picture of its cultural sphere.

Discriminations

In many ways, studying culture is inevitably going to be about making plain the discriminations and hierarchies of value through which a given culture operates at a given historical juncture. For example, you may recall that in his definition of culture Williams suggests a view which appears to leave out many areas of activity and formations. According to Williams, 'culture' refers to:

i.   the general process of intellectual, spiritual and aesthetic development
ii. a particular way of life, whether of a people, a period or a group.
iii. the works and practices of intellectual and especially artistic activity. (Williams, 1976, pp. 87–93)

In his short commentary on Williams's definition John Storey (1993, p. 2) argues that:

- Williams's category i is unrelated to popular culture.
- Williams's category ii covers what Storey calls 'lived cultures' or cultural practices (i.e., ways in which everyday activities and events can be seen as specific to a particular group, and thus partake of the beliefs and values of that group): here Storey includes activities like Christmas or seaside holidays.
- Williams's category iii includes 'signifying practices' (i.e., ways of encoding and/or communicating a set of meanings/ideas/values): for Storey these include soap operas, pop music, comics, novels, ballets, fine art, etc.

This view of culture as continually in process is evident elsewhere in Williams's own work, in which he refines his original position and argues that cultural formations can be grouped under three broad headings: *dominant, residual* and *emergent* (Williams, 1981, p. 204).

Reading 7.1

Cultural reproduction, in its simplest sense, occurs essentially at the (changing) level of the dominant, . . . The residual, by contrast, though its immediate processes are reproductive, is often a form of cultural alternative to the dominant in its most recent . . . forms . . . At the opposite end of the range, the emergent is related to but not identical with the innovatory. Some kinds of innovation . . . are movements and adjustments within the dominant, and become its new forms. But there is usually tension and struggle in this area. Some innovations – kinds of art and thought which emerge and persist as disturbing – would tend to destroy the dominant in any of its forms, just as some new social forces would tend to destroy the social order rather than reproduce or modify it.

No analysis is more difficult than that which, faced by new forms, has to try to determine whether these are new forms of the dominant or are genuinely emergent. In historical analysis the issue gets settled: the emergent becomes the emerged . . . and then often the dominant. But in contemporary analysis, just because of the complex relations between innovation and reproduction, the problem is at a different level. (Williams, 1981, pp. 204–5)

As Williams suggests, art is a good area of cultural activity in which to observe this phenomenon in action. In the nineteenth century, as today, some forms of conceptual and abstract art, by not fitting the period's dominant notion of what constituted art, were mocked as 'daubings that a child could do', or simply dismissed with, 'that's not art!' Yet the Impressionist and post-Impressionist art of the later nineteenth and early twentieth centuries, once condemned by some sections of the art establishment, is now one of the dominant forms of art, in the sense that it is a form which is widely consumed and through which major art galleries ensure revenues. Using Williams's three concepts (residual, dominant, emergent) we could argue that nineteenth-century Impressionism began as an emergent form, became a dominant form and may now, within the art world if not in the popular imagination, be seen as a highly influential but residual form. Indeed, reproductions of Impressionist paintings are now endlessly recycled on shopping bags, greetings cards and posters on sale in the high street – an example of a high cultural form impinging on aspects of mass culture (you can explore some of these debates further via Flint, 1984; Bullen, 1988; Harrison and Wood, 1992).

ACTIVITY 7.1

Think about the following in terms of whether they seem to be residual, dominant or emergent forms of culture. We have started you off with an example.

- Indie music: Began as independent, alternative to mainstream popular music; has now become mainstream. Therefore an emergent form which is becoming dominant?
- Karaoke.
- The art of Damien Hirst.
- J. R. R. Tolkien's *The Lord of the Rings*.
- The Beatles

When we examine the ways in which we understand the cultural practices and associated signifying systems of contemporary societies, there are clearly no right or wrong answers: what we are looking at is the way in which we read cultural practices and the judgements we might make about people who express themselves through or in relation to different cultural formations. Cultures invest value in specific formations, and to become part of a culture we are expected to share these values. This operates at all levels, from a national government's determination of the cultural knowledge required of those foreign nationals who wish to become citizens, to the 'rules' you have to observe to be part of a peer group of fans of a particular style of music. In all of these cases it is interesting to reflect upon how far you feel able to state your own viewpoint (your 'individual' meanings), and how far you feel constrained by your awareness of what you are expected to think about a topic (the 'common-sense' meanings).

If you are a foreign national applying for British citizenship you are currently required to pass a government- run test on life in the UK which is based on a particular view of British culture: in its introduction to the test the British Citizenship website states that 'What brings British people together is that they listen to different points of view, they have respect for equal rights and they believe that community is important (www.lifeintheuktest.gov.uk/htmlsite/test_intro_20.html).

If you are a migrant Portuguese agricultural worker living in the isolated Lincolnshire town of Boston you may well have experienced a Britain rather different from this (http://society.guardian.co.uk/ruralcommunities/story/0,,2038541,00.html), but will have little capacity to dissent from this official line. Yet, if you think about it carefully, what capacity do you have to dissent from the cultural values of your peers? If you want to hang out with the Green Day fans you'd better not tell them about your extensive New Jack Soul collection.

ACTIVITY 7.2

- Group five or so of the following aspects of British culture according to whether you believe them to be facets of 'high', mass or popular culture. If you are not familiar with British culture you might like to take this opportunity to do some web-searching on the various stores and media organizations we cite. Alternatively, you could draw up a list that works for your own country: you will need a mixture of mass-market and more 'high-end' stores: the US equivalent of Marks & Spencer might be Sears while that of Harvey Nichols might be Saks Fifth Avenue. You might also like to think about the perspective you are working from; would your parents and your grandparents share your views? Would someone from a different ethnic group to yourself share your views? Would someone from a different part of the world to you share your views?

Shopping at Marks & Spencer

Shopping at The Gap

Shopping at Harvey Nichols in Leeds

Shopping at Harvey Nichols in Knightsbridge

Buying a copy of Jane Austen's *Pride and Prejudice* from a Borders bookstore

Buying a copy of Jane Austen's *Pride and Prejudice* from Amazon.com online bookstore

Shopping for make-up at Boots

Shopping for make-up at John Lewis

Shopping for food at Kwik Save

Shopping for food at Sainsbury's

Eating at McDonald's

Eating at Pret A Manger

Watching *EastEnders*

Watching *The O.C.*

Watching BBC News

Watching CNN News

Poster of one of Monet's paintings of water lilies purchased from Athena

Poster of one of Monet's paintings of water lilies purchased from the Tate Gallery

Looking at Monet's paintings in an art gallery

Reading *The Times*

Reading the *Guardian*

Reading the *Sun*

Reading *Hello!* magazine

Reading *Vogue*

Reading *NME*

Listening to Green Day

Listening to Mozart

Listening to U2

- How did you know which category to put each practice into?
- Try to decide if the cultural practice is dominant, residual or emergent.

Given Williams's insistence that dominant cultural forms are always integral to the social structures of a society, in the sense that they interact with economic factors, family structures and the education system to produce, reinforce and sustain that society's social relations and stratifications, you might want to consider the extent to which popular culture could ever be said to be in a dominant position in contemporary society. How far does the perspective which you, and perhaps your circle of friends, have on aspects of contemporary culture suggest that beliefs about the value of cultural forms and practices are shared by people of, say, the same age, class, region, gender or ethnic group? To what extent does cultural value get decided by you and how far might it be imposed by, for example, the mass media, family practices or peer pressures? You might like to follow up this activity by reading the work of the French sociologist Pierre Bourdieu on this area (Bourdieu, 1986, pp. 187–90; see also Storey, 1993, and Frow, 1995, pp. 27–47).

The divisive nature of culture may well have been foregrounded by activity 7.2, in which you attempted to classify various aspects of culture and society in contemporary Britain. Culture is shaped by patterns of social power, and its divisiveness is part and parcel of the social milieu in which we find ourselves, one in which difference carries with it social meanings that can shape our interaction with our world. Now read the following by John Fiske.

Reading 7.2

Bourdieu's work is valuable because in his account of proletarian culture he reveals cultural practices that are typical of subordinate allegiances. So women, regardless of their class, can and do participate in soap operas in a way that parallels what Bourdieu has identified as a mark of proletarian culture, but that can be generalised out to refer to the culture of the subordinate, or popular culture. Similarly, . . . [a study] in Germany has shown how women's tastes in news are functional (another characteristic of proletarian taste identified by Bourdieu): women prefer the local news to the national because they can use its accounts of burglary and assaults in the local streets, or road accidents, and of missing children as part of their maternal function of preparing their children to face their immediate social world. Women's tastes and proletarian tastes are similar not because women are proletarian or because the proletariat are feminine, but because both are disempowered classes and thus can easily align themselves with the practices of popular culture, for the people are formed by social allegiances among the subordinate.

Everyday life is constituted by the practices of popular culture, and is characterised by the creativity of the weak in using the resources provided by the disempowering system while refusing finally to submit to that power. (Fiske, 1991, p. 47)

- What was your reaction to the passage by Fiske? How would you describe the image of women and of the working class which emerges from this extract?
- Would you want to counter Fiske's assertions? What arguments would you use?
- Can you think of any examples of the ways in which people creatively use the resources of a disempowering system? You could consider, for example, the ways in which gay culture has recycled a mainstream film like *The Wizard of Oz*, or the ways in which different forms of popular music are consumed by different audiences.

Fiske's summary of some of Bourdieu's ideas suggests that popular culture is the arena in which the disempowered and subordinate operate. In *Understanding Popular Culture* (1991), he attempts to celebrate the potential of forms of culture (like soap operas) which do not have the sanction of state or semi-state organizations such as the education system. Fiske goes on to explore how people can relate creatively to mass forms of entertainment in ways that allow them to resist categorization and classification by those who are better positioned to produce dominant forms of knowledge (you might at this point remind yourself of the discussion on discourse and power in chapter 3). Fiske's outline of popular culture as a contested and dynamic terrain draws upon the work of Michel de Certeau. You might want to look again at the discussion of issues of location in chapter 5.

Reading 7.3

The everyday life of the people is where the contradictory interests of capitalist societies are continually negotiated and contested. De Certeau (1984) is one of the most sophisticated theorists of the culture and practices of everyday life, and running through his work is a series of metaphors of conflict – particularly ones of strategy and tactics, of guerrilla warfare, of poaching, of guileful ruses and tricks. Underlying all of them is the assumption that the powerful are cumbersome, unimaginative, and over organized, whereas the weak are creative, nimble and flexible. So the weak use guerrilla tactics against the strategies of the powerful, making poaching raids upon their texts or structures, and play constant tricks upon the system.

The powerful construct places where they can exercise their power – cities, shopping malls, schools, workplaces and houses, to name only some of the material ones. The weak make their own spaces within those places; they make the places temporarily theirs as they move through them, occupying them for as long as they need or have to. A place is where strategy operates; the guerrillas, who move into it, turn it into their space; space is practiced place. (Fiske, 1991, pp. 32–3)

If, as Fiske suggests, popular culture is the product of a sequence of skir-mishes with a dominant and official 'high' culture, it would seem important to know what it is that the popular is defining itself against. The postmodern-ist idea that hierarchies have been abolished in the contemporary cultural sphere seems to have little impact on, for example, the position of Shakespeare in the official culture of Britain. His work is validated by its central position in the school curriculum and regularly featured in the media as a marker of high cultural value. The Shakespeare Birthplace Trust website, while promot-ing what it calls 'the complete Shakespeare experience', reflects this with its emphasis on 'rare and exquisite items of period furniture' and 'centuries of English and Shakespeare History' (www.shakespeare.org.uk/). Popular cul-ture's raids on 'Shakespeare' include the production of such artefacts as fridge magnets of swear words, websites that generate Bardic insults (pangloss.com/seidel/Shaker/index.html), cigars, T-shirts, and even dolls. While, for some, these guerrilla tactics function to make 'Shakespeare' part of a more contem-porary and familiar world, such devices fail to engage productively with what it is that makes his works an essential component of the school curriculum: wearing a 'Big on the Bard' sweatshirt to your English class is hardly an act of guerrilla expropriation.

Not 'either/or' – 'and/but': Bakhtinian approaches to culture

A helpful way of describing the processes of cultural interaction and negotia-tion, which can, perhaps, avoid some of the pitfalls of the popular = good, 'high' = bad, or indeed the popular = bad, 'high' = good, approach can be found in the work of the influential Russian thinker Mikhail Bakhtin.

For Bakhtin, the individual consciousness is the product of a multiplicity of interactions within a social context in which meanings are contested. We have seen already the ways in which we can be aware of a difference between those values held by society in general and those which we might use individu-ally when it comes to such things as shopping or listening to music. We may personally not own any recording of work by Mozart but we are likely to be aware that his work has a status within our culture which is very different to that afforded to Green Day or U2. This diversity of positions – the fact that in the early twenty-first century there are people who are passionate about Mozart and would not consider Green Day to be music, and people who are passionate about Green Day and would not consider Mozart music, as well as those who consider both to be music – at a given moment in history is conceptualized by Bakhtin as heteroglossia – a 'diversity of languages' (Todorov, 1984, p. 56). The multiple interactions an individual has with the discourses which operate within her or his social milieu are described as a process of **dialogism**. Dialogism, which is engendered by the interaction of a range of perspectives on the same subject, makes it possible to continually subvert any claims on the part of a particular ideology for the existence of its single, or **monological**, value system. For example, if you have just left home to attend university your parents may urge you to spend your evenings doing your coursework; your friends may urge you to join them in the student union; your tutor may urge you to read more feminist theory; your landlord may urge you to clean up your kitchen, and your bank manager may urge you to get a part-time job. All these competing claims could be part of your experience of being at university and, as such, will tend to challenge the idea that being at university is only about study, or sorting out your own finances, or drinking in the union bar.

However, some of the discourses which seek to shape your activities as a student have more power than others. For Bakhtin the dominance of certain discourses within a specific cultural or social space can be seen as an actualization, at the micro-level, of the socio-economic divisions within the society that produces them. Thus you may find that your parents or schoolteachers warned you away from studying a subject like cultural studies at university, perhaps urging you to do a 'proper' degree in a 'traditional' subject like history or a 'useful' degree in an area like business management or leisure sciences. You may find that your landlord has similar views to your parents about what a degree ought to be and, on reflection, you can probably see that these perspectives stem from ideas that assume a link between higher education and employment prospects. These ideas may clash with the values expressed, implicitly or explicitly, by your tutors, whose idea of a university may focus on its role as a place in which knowledge can be pursued for its own sake. Your friends, in opposition to these ideas of what it means to be at university, may assert that university is about mixing with your peer group in the pub, the student union or a club. Dominant discursive positions (represented here by the beliefs and values espoused by your landlord, parents and tutors) seek to suppress opposition because more is at stake than a communication system: a group's identity and status (as parents, as tutors) is maintained by the wide acceptance of the validity of its set of values. The positions represented by parents and tutors in this example are **hegemonic** in so far as they are able to secure a measure of consent from you, and this is true of the education system as a whole. Hence, it is constantly reasserted that working hard and preparing for employment are 'in your best interests'. Opposition to these ideas constitutes a way of subverting and resisting these dominant or hegemonic meanings. And, of course, in practice it is likely that your perspective as well as that of your parents and tutors will include, to greater or lesser extents, possibly warring elements of all the foregoing ideas. Thus, as Bakhtin argued, individual consciousness is itself produced from the interaction of multiple voices within a particular social context.

Let us link these ideas of cultural value and consider how competing claims for status can be linked to a particular group's way of seeing the world. A useful illustration of this is the persistence of Arnoldian views regarding the place of literary culture in the education system.

Versions of Literary Culture

One of the early definitions of culture which we looked at in chapter 1 of this book was that of Matthew Arnold, who defined culture as the best that has been thought and read. We want now to look at ways in which the education system has sought to define what constitutes 'the best'.

Reading 7.4

From The Newbolt Report on the Teaching of English in England (1921), introduction

We believe that . . . an education based upon the English language and literature would have important social, as well as personal, results; it would have a unifying tendency. Two causes, both accidental and conventional rather than national, at present distinguish and divide one class from another in England. The first of these is a marked difference in their modes of speech. If the teaching of the language were properly and universally provided for, the difference between educated and uneducated speech, . . . which at present causes so much prejudice and difficulty of intercourse on both sides, would gradually disappear. Good speech and great literature would not be regarded as too fine for use by the majority, nor, on the other hand, would natural gifts for self-expression be rendered ineffective by embarrassing faults of diction or composition. The second cause of division amongst us is the undue narrowness of the ground on which we meet for the true purposes of social life. The associations of sport and games are widely shared by all classes in England, but with mental pleasures and mental exercises the case is very different. The old education was not similar for all, but diverse. It went far to make of us not one nation, but two, neither of which shared the associations or tastes of the other. An education fundamentally English would, we believe, at any rate bridge, if not close, this chasm of separation. The English people might learn as a whole to regard their own language, first with respect, and then with a genuine feeling of pride and affection. More than any mere symbol it is actually a part of England: to maltreat it or deliberately to debase it would be seen to be an outrage; to become sensible of its significance and splendour would be to step upon a higher level. In France, we are told, this pride in the national language is strong and universal; the French artisan will often use his right to object that an expression is not French. Such a feeling for our own native language would be a bond of union between classes, and would beget the right kind of national pride. Even more certainly would pride and joy in the national literature serve as such a bond. This feeling, if fostered in all our schools without exception, would disclose itself far more often and furnish common meeting ground for great numbers of men and women who might otherwise never come into touch with one another. We know from the evidence of those who are familiar with schools of every type that the love of fine style and the appreciation of what is great in human thought and feeling is already no monopoly of a single class in England, that it is a natural and not an exceptional gift, and that though easily discouraged by unfavourable circumstances it can also, by sympathetic treatment, be easily drawn out and developed. Within the school itself all scholars, though specialising perhaps on different lines, will be able to find a common interest in the literature class and the debating or dramatic society. And this common interest will be likely to persist when other less vital things have been abandoned. The purely technical or aesthetic appeal of any art will, perhaps, always be limited to a smaller number but, as experience of life, literature will influence all who are capable of finding recreation in something beyond mere sensation. These it will unite by a common interest in life at its best, and by the perpetual reminder that through all social differences human nature and its strongest affections are fundamentally the same.

ACTIVITY 7.4

- What, for the authors of this report, is the function of the study of English literature and language?
- Draw up a list of the positive terms which the report uses in connection with the kind of education it seeks to promote: to what extent can you begin to make judgements about the political beliefs and values of the report from this listing?

Reading 7.5

From *The Newbolt Report*, chapter VIII, Literature and Adult Education: Literature and the Nation

We were told that the working classes, especially those belonging to organised labour movements, were antagonistic to, and contemptuous of, literature, that they regarded it merely as an ornament, a polite accomplishment, a subject to be despised by really virile men. Literature, in fact, seems to be classed by a large number of thinking working men with antimacassars, fish knives and other unintelligible and futile trivialities of middle-class culture, and, as a subject of instruction, is suspect as an attempt to side-track the working-class movement. We regard the prevalence of such opinions as a serious matter, not merely because it means the alienation of an important section of the population from the *confort and mirthe* of literature, but chiefly because it points to a morbid condition of the body politic which if not taken in hand may be followed by lamentable consequences. For if literature be, as we believe, an embodiment of the best thoughts of the best minds, the most direct and lasting communication of experience by man to men, a fellowship which binds together by passion and knowledge the vast empire of human society, as it is spread over the whole earth, and over all time, then the nation of which a considerable portion rejects this means of grace, and despises this great spiritual influence, must assuredly be heading to disaster . . .

At the same time we are unable to subscribe to the dictum that literature, as generally interpreted, is a part of middle-class culture. We sincerely wish it were. We find, on the contrary, an indifference among middle-class persons to the claims of literature, even more disheartening than the open hostility which we are told exists among certain circles of working-class opinion. Here, quite as much as there, is to be found a striking contrast with mediaeval conditions . . . Does poetry play anything like the same part in the domestic economy of the average well-to-do household to-day? The question answers itself. Children at the Secondary or Public School learn to pay a certain lip-service to literature, but it is safe to say that more than 90 per cent. of middle-class people have ceased to read poetry in adult life. Why is this? We can find no more satisfactory answer than that already given in dealing with the attitude of the working man, namely, that poetry is not recognised as having any vital connection with a workaday world.

It is natural for man to delight in poetry; the history of mediaeval society, to say nothing of all primitive societies, proves this. Further, we claim that no personality can be complete, see life steadily and see it whole, without that unifying influence, that purifying of the emotions, which art and literature can alone bestow. It follows from what we have said above that the bulk of our people, of whatever class, are unconsciously living starved existences, that one of the richest fields of our spiritual being is left uncultivated – not indeed barren, for the weeds of literature have never been so prolific as in our day. It is easy to blame Education for this, but Education cannot proceed far in advance of the general outlook of its age. The true cause lies deeper, is rooted among the very foundations of our civilisation. Yet we believe that it belongs to a transitory phase of human development and will, therefore, in course of time cease to operate . . .

The interim, we feel, belongs chiefly to the professors of English literature. The rise of modern Universities has accredited an ambassador of poetry to every important capital of industrialism in the country, and upon his shoulders rests a responsibility greater we think than is as yet generally recognised. The Professor of Literature in a University should be – and sometimes is, as we gladly recognise – a missionary in a more real and active sense than any of his colleagues. He has obligations not merely to the students who come to him to read for a degree, but still more towards the teeming population outside the University walls, most of whom have not so much as heard whether there be any Holy Ghost. The fulfilmnt [*sic*] of these obligations means propaganda work, organisation and the building up of a staff of assistant missionaries. But first, and above all, it means a right attitude of mind, a conviction that literature and life are in fact inseparable, that literature is not just a subject for academic study, but one of the chief temples of the human spirit, in which all should worship. We say all, for there is a tendency to suppose that literature is the preserve of the cultured, a tendency from which Matthew Arnold, the apostle of culture, was himself not entirely free. The great men of culture, he wrote, are those who have had a passion for diffusing, for making prevail. for carrying from one end of society to the other, the best knowledge, the best ideas of their time; who have laboured to divest knowledge of all that was harsh, uncouth, difficult, abstract, professional, exclusive; to humanise it, to make it efficient outside the clique of the cultivated and learned, yet still remaining the best knowledge and thought of the time, and a true source, therefore, of sweetness and light. A noble ideal, yet one that is incomplete without Henry Sidgwick's comment upon it: If any culture really has what Mr. Arnold in his finest mood calls its noblest element, the passion for propagating itself, for making itself prevail, then let it learn to call nothing common or unclean. It can only propagate itself by shedding the light of its sympathy liberally; by learning to love common people and common things, to feel common interests. Make people feel that their own poor life is ever so little beautiful and poetical; then they will begin to turn and seek after the treasures of beauty and poetry outside and above it. Culture, like all spiritual gifts, can only be propagated by enthusiasm; and by enthusiasm that has got rid of asperity, that has become sympathetic; that has got rid of Pharisaism, and become humble. The ambassadors of poetry must be humble, they must learn to call nothing common or unclean, not even the local dialect, the clatter of the factory, or the smoky pall of our industrial centres.

ACTIVITY 7.5

- Comment on the extract's views of the working and middle classes and the attitudes towards literature attributed to these groups.
- Why does the report value poetry so highly?
- What problems can you envisage facing a professor attempting to take up the challenge to missionary action set out in the report? Would the situation in the 1920s be any different from that which exists today? What, if any, are the relations between your higher education institution and its nearby towns or surrounding city?

Here is what one US School District prescribes for its younger High School pupils (equivalent to the GCSE level in the UK).

Reading 7.6

High School English Department: Literature Titles: June 2000

The following works of literature will be used in the High School English Curriculum in the grades indicated. Titles from one grade level may not be used by any other grade level.

Grade 9
Romeo and Juliet
The Odyssey
Lord of the Flies
Great Expectations
A Separate Peace
My Antonia
Julius Caesar
Ethan Frome
Medea

High School English Department: Optional Titles Reserved for Specific Grade Levels: June 2000

The following works of literature will be assigned as supplemental reading in the grades indicated. Titles listed for each grade level are reserved for that grade level and may not be used as part of the language arts curriculum in another grade level.

Grade 9
Silas Marner
The Disappearance
The Wave
Twelve Angry Men
Hoops
Kaffir Boy
The Accident
The Yearling
The Miracle Worker
The Pearl
(www.nksd.net/admin/curriculum/Standards/E–LA/ELAhscurr9.htm#Literature% 20Titles, accessed 10 June 2007)

For information on North Kingstown High School, including links to sites that details its demographics, see http://en.wikipedia.org/wiki/North_ Kingstown_High_School.

By way of comparison, here is a list of texts from which teachers in the UK could draw upon in 1994 when devising English classes for pupils of a similar age.

Reading 7.7

5.1 Pupils should be introduced to literature of 'high' quality, including works written in previous centuries, those from earlier in the twentieth century and contemporary writing. Pupils should be encouraged to appreciate the distinctive qualities of such works through activities which emphasise the interest and pleasure of reading them rather than necessitating a detailed, line-by-line study. Pupils working at Levels 1, 2 and 3 should be introduced to these significant authors and works in the English literary heritage by means appropriate to the pupils' maturity and reading abilities.

5.2 During each of Key Stages 3 and 4, pupils should read:

- a range of drama, including a play by Shakespeare;
- a range of fiction, including
  - i.   one work published before 1900 by an author listed in 5.3;
  - ii.   one work published since 1900 by an author listed in 5.4;
- a range of poetry, including
  - i.   poems by two significant poets whose works were published before 1900, listed in 5.5;
  - ii.   poems by three significant poets whose works were published since 1900, listed in 5.6;
- a range of non-literary and non-fiction texts

5.3 Authors whose fiction works were published before 1900:
Jane Austen, Charlotte Brontë, Emily Brontë, John Bunyan, Wilkie Collins, Arthur Conan Doyle, Stephen Crane, Daniel Defoe, Charles Dickens, George Eliot, Henry Fielding, Elizabeth Gaskell, Thomas Hardy, Nathaniel Hawthorne, Henry James, Edgar Allan Poe, R. L. Stevenson, Jonathan Swift, Anthony Trollope, Mark Twain, H. G. Wells.

5.4 Authors whose fiction works were published since 1900:
Stan Barstow, H. E. Bates, Nina Bawden, Arnold Bennett, Ray Bradbury, Joseph Conrad, Marjorie Darke, Berlie Doherty, Gerald Durrell, Ford Madox Ford, E. M. Forster, Leon Garfield, Alan Garner, William Golding, Graham Greene, Rosa Guy, L. P. Hartley, Ernest Hemingway, Susan Hill, Ann Holm, Janni Howker, Richard Hughes, Aldous Huxley, Ruth Prawer Jhabvala, James Joyce, D. H. Lawrence, Harper Lee, Laurie Lee, Rosamond Lehmann, Ursula Le Guin, Doris Lessing, Joan Lingard, Penelope Lively, Michelle Magorian, Olivia Manning, Katherine Mansfield, Jan Mark, Somerset Maugham, Iris Murdoch, Beverley Naidoo, V. S. Naipaul, Edna O'Brien,

George Orwell, Philippa Pearce, Jean Rhys, Rukshana Smith, Muriel Spark, John Steinbeck, Mildred Taylor, Gwyn Thomas, J. R. R. Tolkien, Evelyn Waugh, H. G. Wells, Virginia Woolf, John Wyndham.

5.5. Poets whose works were published before 1900:
Matthew Arnold, Elizabeth Barrett Browning, William Blake, Robert Bridges, Robert Browning, Robert Burns, Lord Byron, Geoffrey Chaucer, John Clare, S. T. Coleridge, Emily Dickinson, John Donne, John Dryden, Thomas Gray, George Herbert, Robert Herrick, G. M. Hopkins, John Keats, Christopher Marlowe, Andrew Marvell, John Milton, Alexander Pope, Christina Rossetti, Shakespeare (sonnets), Percy Bysshe Shelley, Edmund Spenser, Alfred Lord Tennyson. William Wordsworth, Sir Thomas Wyatt.

5.6 Poets whose works were published since 1900:
Dannie Abse, Fleur Adcock, W. H. Auden, James Berry, John Betjeman, Charles Causley, Gillian Clarke, Wendy Cope, Douglas Dunn, T. S. Eliot, U. A. Fanthorpe, Robert Frost, Robert Graves, Thom Gunn, Thomas Hardy, Seamus Heaney, Ted Hughes, Elizabeth Jennings, Jenny Joseph, Philip Larkin, D. H. Lawrence, Liz Lochhead, Norman MacCaig, Louis MacNeice, Edwin Muir, Grace Nichols, Leslie Norris, Wilfred Owen, Brian Patten, Sylvia Plath, Siegfried Sassoon, Vernon Scannell, Stephen Spender, Anne Stevenson, Dylan Thomas, Edward Thomas, R. S. Thomas, Derek Walcott, W. B. Yeats.
(HMSO, 1994, pp. 17–18)

ACTIVITY 7.6

- Using a reference work like *The Oxford Companion to English Literature* or *The Oxford Companion to American Literature*, examine the authors listed in any one section. Compare the US school's curriculum to the UK curriculum: are there any significant differences that strike you? How would you account for these? Consider the ratio of men to women, the number of non-white authors, and any other issues that strike you about the writers or texts cited for inclusion.

- Look at a best-seller list (usually to be found in a broadsheet Sunday newspaper or via the website of the *Bookseller*): do any of the authors listed in the curriculum appear? What reasons can you suggest for their presence or absence?

- Draw up a list of the books you have read in the past six months; try to categorize them by genre, e.g., literary fiction, horror, thriller, romance. Can you also distinguish between books read for pleasure and those read as part of course requirements? Do any of the authors whose works you have read for pleasure appear on the lists above?

- How important do you think it is that school pupils study the range of literary works outlined? What role do you think the study of literature has in today's society? Now look back at your comments on the material from the Newbolt Report. Can you identify points of difference and points of similarity between the ideas you have generated and those of the Report?

We have spent some time thinking about these various statements regarding the place of literature in the education system, as they point up the ways in which the official ideas of the state and its organizations have retained a remarkable degree of coherence over a long period of time. Both curriculum lists foreground the ways in which the state legitimates and promotes a particular set of texts. Indeed, so powerful is this process that when students begin to study culture at university it is very often assumed that 'high' culture will be the focus of their studies. The *Newbolt Report* and *English in the National Curriculum* promote a set of values which suggest that there is only one version of literary history, and that there is no real argument about what constitutes literary studies or, indeed, the purpose of a literary education. In fact, within university literature departments, fierce debates have raged about the nature and relevance of literature to contemporary culture and anyone who has followed the sometimes acrimonious deliberations of the Man Booker Prize judges knows that literary worth is not always easily agreed upon. Moreover, teachers who are charged with implementing the curriculum may not always agree fully either as individuals or as an organized body with the version of literary study represented in the state's official curriculum.

In all three documents, there is at least an implicit assumption that the inculcation of a literary culture is part of the state's duty; a duty which for the Newbolt Committee and, it would appear, for today's curriculum advisers, still seems to rest on Arnoldian notions of the benefits of encountering cultivated minds. We are not suggesting that schoolchildren should not study and benefit from the writings of Shakespeare or other authors from previous epochs, but we are drawing attention to the ways in which the debate is framed and to the assumptions that underpin it. As we have pointed out, the official version is not the only version but it may well be the most powerful, partly because it can draw on notions of history and tradition which many cultures valorize, and partly because it is legitimated through the power of government.

Within the culture of the education system, then, there appears to be an idea that although the system operates in a disparate and heterogeneous social sphere, shared values remain which can be disseminated through exposure to cultural artefacts like literary texts.

Rereading Literature

As we have seen, Raymond Williams's work on cultural history foregrounded 'high' culture, especially literary culture, as a means of opening up the workings of hegemony (Williams, 1963). The contemporary version of Williams's approach might be found in **new historicist** and **cultural materialist** rereadings of literary works, which examine texts as embedded in and produced by specific cultural contexts (on these terms see Barry, 2002). In between and alongside these positions exists a range of other approaches that treat texts which are just as likely to be sold in a supermarket as in a bookshop, work on romance, comics or thrillers, and so forth (for example, McCracken, 1998). A characteristic of these approaches is that the text comes to be seen as a commodity or material object, produced at a particular time, in a particular place, under particular social and economic conditions, as opposed to being studied solely for its aesthetic value.

Among the most influential of the new approaches to texts which have been adopted by those engaged in looking at literary works are new historicism and its variant cultural materialism (for accessible overviews of these approaches, see Knowles, 1996, and Barry, 2002). Alongside these approaches, there has been a great deal of interest in postcolonial theory and queer theory (see Barry, 2002). We conclude our consideration of 'high' culture with discussion of the ways in which contemporary cultural-studies approaches to literary texts can lead to a rereading of a classic work of the kind promoted by the school curriculum: rereadings that can re-engage the work in question with the particular culture in which it was produced. We have chosen to work with the Edwardian children's classic, *The Wind in the Willows* (1908), which tells the story of Mole, Rat, Badger and Toad and their adventures along the River Bank. Locating this text in relation to the wider culture of its era can suggest alternative ways of reading it that can contribute to a greater understanding of the interrelation between text and context. Such an approach can go some way to blurring the high/popular divide because it insists upon the interpenetration of text and wider society.

Rereading Texts: *The Wind in the Willows* (1908) and English Masculinity

This section draws upon a **new historicist** approach to develop a contextualized reading of Grahame's novel. It also makes use of ideas from **queer theory** to illuminate the bonds of male friendship at the centre of the novel; if you are unfamiliar with this approach we suggest you read the introductory guide in Barry (2002). In what follows we provide signposts for a rereading of Grahame's novel that draws upon these critical approaches to texts and suggests something of their power to challenge dominant readings. For some commentators the kind of dialogic reading this section develops is a fundamental part of a cultural studies reading strategy (Johnson et al., 2004, chapter 10). To get the most out of this section we recommend that you read the whole of *The Wind in the Willows* before you work through the remainder of this chapter. We begin with a short introductory overview of the topic, which is designed to help you work with the material in the various activity sections.

A crisis of English masculinity?

The novel's central characters are all male, and their relationships can be read in the light of the ongoing debates in the 1900s about the nature of English masculinity. At this time there was considerable anxiety about the stability of gender roles, and several books and articles were written on the subject, including Edward Carpenter's *The Intermediate Sex: a Study of Some Transitional Types of Men and Women*, one of the first English studies of homosexuality, which appeared in the same year as Grahame's novel. The anxiety about the changing nature of gendered identity was particular acute in Britain in the later nineteenth century, as it was given impetus by events like the passing of the Labouchère Amendment of 1885 (which made male homosexual acts criminal), and the trial and imprisonment of Oscar Wilde in 1895. In the later 1890s there was something of a backlash against certain kinds of 'decadent' behaviour – a decadence which was closely related to the beliefs and attitudes expressed in work featured in the magazine *The Yellow Book* – a literary and artistic periodical for which Grahame was writing in the 1890s (for further information on the cultural background to this see Ledger, 1997, pp. 94–121).

In Britain, this backlash against decadence and degeneration was given added impetus by anxieties about Empire; Britain's imperial holdings were increasingly seen as threatened by the expansionist activities of other powers, notably Germany. The idea of national degeneracy as a threat to Britain's imperial mission informs the period's fears about the fate of the Englishman, especially after the drawn-out events of the second Boer War (1899–1902), when officers regularly wrote home and to the press to lament the poor physical condition of their troops. Related to this was a growing perception that modern urban living was morally and physically damaging. This middle-class anxiety fed a sense of a growing gulf between the classes which is evident throughout the later nineteenth century and the early Edwardian period (Marriott, 1996; Schwarz, 1996); something of this fear is manifested in Grahame's novel in the portrayal of the Wild Wooders.

Fears of national decline in the face of what were seen as growing internal and external threats led to increased emphasis on normality, on being a proper English man or woman. Signs of deviance from these social codes were mocked: the free-thinking New Women of the 1880s and 1890s were consistently satirized because they were seen as a threat to traditions of femininity (Ledger, 1997). These largely middle-class women, by acting autonomously and resisting traditional patterns of feminine respectability, were often seen as setting a bad example to the 'lower orders' and as failing in their duty as 'mothers of the nation'. With the rise of so-called new women there came to be perceived a breed of new men: henpecked and downtrodden at best, or actively camp and effeminate (the urban middle-class dandy) at worst, these masculine roles were seen as just as much of a threat to the future of the nation (Ledger, 1997, pp. 94–121).

It is in this context that, during the later nineteenth century, the concept of 'the gentleman' becomes more inclusive. It was extended to cover public-school-educated middle-class men (as opposed to members, however minor, of the hereditary aristocracy) and, from 1880 onwards, the public-school gentleman became the dominant stereotype of English masculinity. Educated to a limited level, instilled with a version of muscular Christianity, the late nineteenth-century English gentleman came to be perceived as the backbone of the administrative class at home and abroad, and an environment was created in which male solidarity was valorized:

> masculine privilege was sustained by male friendships within institutions like the public schools, the older universities, the [gentlemen's] clubs and the professions. Because, however, the continuing dominance of bourgeois males also required that they marry and produce offspring, the intensity and sufficiency of male bonding needed to be strictly controlled by homophobic mechanisms.
> (Dellamora, 1996, p. 83)

The Wind in the Willows focuses upon a small clique of privileged males, living a leisured existence in a rural Arcadia. This world is threatened by the irrational pursuit of pleasure of the spendthrift Toad, which encourages the encroachment of the underprivileged masses, represented by the Wild Wooders. The novel ends with order restored through the 'heroic' activity of the central males, acting together to re-establish the status quo. What this tale of the fruits of male bonding appears to overlook is any sense that the male middle-class values of comradeship and solidarity were, in some quarters, being recast as part of the wider problem of gender identity.

The Edwardian homosexual

Edward Carpenter's ground-breaking study of lesbians and gay men, *The Intermediate Sex: a Study of Some Transitional Types of Men and Women* (1908), can provide us with contextualizing material from the period which addresses itself to the nature of gender identity. Just as Grahame's novel evokes a rural Arcadia confidently able to resist the threats of the wider world and the Wild Wood, so Carpenter's work evokes a lost era of sexual freedom when queerness was not marginalized: both implicitly critique modern social conditions, albeit from different perspectives and for different ends (Mason, 1994, p. 12). Carpenter's work was taken up in left-wing circles but was especially influential with members of the Bloomsbury group a little later (Weeks, 1981, p. 174). In the extract that follows, Carpenter offers his views on the gender crisis of the early twentieth century.

Reading 7.8

If the modern woman is a little more masculine in some ways than her predecessor, the modern man (it is to be hoped), while by no means effeminate, is a little more sensitive in temperament and artistic in feeling than the original John Bull. It is beginning to be recognised that the sexes do not or should not normally form two groups hopelessly isolated in habit and feeling from each other, but that they rather represent the two poles of one group – which is the human race; so that while certainly the extreme specimens at either pole are vastly divergent, there are great numbers in the middle region who (though differing corporeally as men and women) are by emotion and temperament very near to each other . . .

More than thirty years ago, however, an Austrian writer, K. H. Ulrichs, drew attention in a series of pamphlets . . . to the existence of a class of people who strongly illustrate the above remarks, and with whom specially this paper is concerned. He pointed out that there were people born in such a position – as it were on the dividing line between the sexes – that while belonging distinctly to one sex as far as their bodies are concerned they may be said to belong mentally and emotionally to the other; that there were men, for instance, who might be described as of feminine soul enclosed in a male body . . ., or in other cases, women whose definition would be just the reverse. And he maintained that this doubleness of nature was to a great extent proved by the special direction of their love-sentiment. For in such cases, as indeed might be expected, the (apparently) masculine person instead of forming a love-union with a female tended to contract romantic friendships with one of his own sex; while the apparently feminine would, instead of marrying in the usual way, devote herself to the love of another feminine.

People of this kind (i.e., having this special variation of the love-sentiment) he called Urnings;[1] and though we are not obliged to accept his theory about the crosswise connexion between 'soul' and 'body,' since at best these words are somewhat vague and indefinite; yet his work was important because it was one of the first attempts, in modern times, to recognise the existence of what might be called an Intermediate sex, and to give at any rate some explanation of it.

Since that time the subject has been widely studied and written about by scientific men and others, especially on the Continent (though in England it is still comparatively unknown), and by means of an extended observation of present-day cases, as well as the indirect testimony of the history and literature of past times, quite a body of general conclusions has been arrived at – of which I propose in the following pages to give some slight account . . .

It is partly for these reasons, and to throw a little light where it may be needed, that I have thought it might be advisable in this paper simply to give a few general characteristics of the Intermediate types.

As indicated then already, in bodily structure there is, as a rule, nothing to distinguish the subjects of our discussion from ordinary men and women; but if we take the general mental characteristics it appears from almost universal testimony that the male tends to be of a rather gentle, emotional disposition – with defects, if such exist, in the direction of subtlety, evasiveness, timidity, vanity, etc.; while the female is just the opposite, fiery, active, bold and truthful, with defects running to brusqueness and coarseness. Moreover, the mind of the former is generally intuitive and instinctive in its perceptions, with more or less of artistic feeling; while the mind of the latter is more logical, scientific, and precise than usual with the normal woman. So marked indeed are these general characteristics that sometimes by means of them (though not an infallible guide) the nature of the boy or girl can be detected in childhood, before full development has taken place; and needless to say it may often be very important to be able to do this . . .

We have so far limited ourselves to some very general characteristics of the Intermediate race. It may help to clear and fix our ideas if we now describe in more detail, first, what may be called the extreme and exaggerated types of the race, and then the more normal and perfect types. By doing so we shall get a more definite and concrete view of our subject.

In the first place, then, the extreme specimens – as in most cases of extremes – are not particularly attractive, sometimes quite the reverse. In the male of this kind we have a distinctly effeminate type, sentimental, lackadaisical, mincing in gait and manners, something of a chatterbox, skilful at the needle and in woman's work, sometimes taking pleasure in dressing in woman's clothes; his figure not unfrequently betraying a tendency towards the feminine, large at the hips, supple, not muscular, the face wanting in hair, the voice inclining to be 'high'-pitched, etc.; while his dwelling-room is orderly in the extreme, even natty, and choice of decoration

---

[1] Note: From Uranos, heaven; his idea being that the Uranian love was of a higher order than the ordinary attachment ... [original note].

and perfume. His affection, too, is often feminine in character, clinging, dependent and jealous, as of one desiring to be loved almost more than to love . . .

These are types which, on account of their salience, everyone will recognise more or less. Naturally, when they occur they excite a good deal of attention, and it is not an uncommon impression that most persons of the homogenic nature belong to either one or other of these classes. But in reality, of course, these extreme developments are rare, and for the most part the temperament in question is embodied in men and women of quite normal and unsensational exterior. Speaking of this subject and the connection between effeminateness and the homogenic nature in men, Dr. Moll says: 'It is, however, as well to point out at the outset that effeminacy does not by any means show itself in all Urnings. Though one may find this or that indication in a great number of cases, yet it cannot be denied that a very large percentage, perhaps by far the majority of them, do not exhibit pronounced Effeminacy.' And it may be supposed that we may draw the same conclusion with regard to women of this class – namely, that the majority of them do not exhibit pronounced masculine habits. In fact, while these extreme cases are of the greatest value from a scientific point of view as marking tendencies and limits of development in certain directions, it would be a serious mistake to look upon them as representative cases of the whole phases of human evolution concerned.

If now we come to what may be called the more normal type of the Uranian man, we find a man who, while possessing thoroughly masculine powers of mind and body, combines with them the tenderer and more emotional soul-nature of the woman – and sometimes to a remarkable degree. Such men, as said, are often muscular and well-built, and not distinguishable in exterior structure and the carriage of body from others of their own sex; but emotionally they are extremely complex, tender, sensitive, pitiful and loving, 'full of storm and stress, of ferment and fluctuation' of the heart; the logical faculty may or may not, in their case, be well-developed, but intuition is always strong; like women they read characters at a glance, and know, without knowing how, what is passing in the minds of others; for nursing and waiting on the needs of others they have often a peculiar gift; at the bottom lies the artist-nature, with the artist's sensibility and perception. Such an one is often a dreamer, of brooding, reserved habits, often a musician, or a man of culture, courted in society, which nevertheless does not understand him – though sometimes a child of the people, without any culture, but almost always with a peculiar inborn refinement . . .

That men of this kind despise women, though a not uncommon belief, is one which hardly appears to be justified. Indeed, though naturally not inclined to 'fall in love' in this direction, such men are by their nature drawn rather near to women, and it would seem that they often feel a singular appreciation and understanding of the emotional needs and destinies of the other sex, leading in many cases to a genuine though what is called 'Platonic' friendship. There is little doubt that they are often instinctively sought after by women, who, without suspecting the real cause, are conscious of a sympathetic chord in the homogenic which they miss in the normal man . . .

I have now sketched – very briefly and inadequately it is true – both the extreme types and the more healthy types of the 'Intermediate' man . . . : types which can be verified from history and literature, though more certainly and satisfactorily perhaps from actual life around us. And unfamiliar though the subject is, it begins to appear that it is one which modern thought and science will have to face. Of the latter and more normal types it may be said that they exist, and have always existed, in considerable abundance, and from that circumstance alone there is a strong probability that they have their place and purpose. (Carpenter, 1908, pp. 17–37)

ACTIVITY 7.7

Create a checklist of the characteristics of the male Urning. You may find it helpful to do this in two categories (e.g., 'extreme' and 'normal') but may need a third (intermediate) category.

You will refer to your notes on Carpenter in further work on Grahame's novel.

The English gentleman

Carpenter seeks to identify the characteristics of what, for the period, might be imagined as the antithesis of the English gentleman. He is careful to stress the 'normality' of the average Urning and, while this might be intended to reassure, in the climate of anxiety which existed in Edwardian Britain, this capacity to appear normal while being different may well have occasioned concern. In order to take further our work on the male roles of *The Wind in the Willows* we will spend a little time considering the extent to which the values and behaviour of the novel's central characters can be related to some definition of the English gentleman. While reading the following extracts, note what each writer suggests are the main characteristics of this type.

Reading 7.9

The idea of the gentleman is not a class idea . . . it is an idea which has had its mutations. In the eighteenth century a gentleman knew his tenants, his fields, and his foxes: he helped to govern his country, and might sit in parliament at Westminster; he might even be interested in architecture and painting, and indulge himself in music. He was an amateur furnished with ability – the apotheosis of the amateur. But the essence was a code of conduct – good form: the not doing of the things which are not done: reserve: a habit of understatement. The code became disengaged, and explicit, with the spread of boarding or 'public' schools during the nineteenth century. It was in many ways a curious code. It was hardly based on religion, though it might be instilled in sermons: it was a mixture of stoicism with mediaeval lay chivalry, and of both with unconscious national ideals half Puritan and half secular. Yet if it contained such national ideals, it was not a national code, in the sense that it embraced the nation: it was the code of an elite (from whatever classes the elite was drawn) rather than a code of the nation at large. On the other hand elites will always count; and 'social idealism', or snobbery at its best, made the code of the gentleman pervasive. It is impossible to think of the character of England without thinking also of the character of the gentleman. But it is also impossible to think of the character of the gentleman clearly. It has an English haze. The gentleman is shy, yet also self confident. He is the refinement of manliness; but the manliness is sometimes more obvious than the refinement. (Barker, 1947, reprinted in Giles and Middleton, 1995, p. 59)

The Englishman feels very deeply and reasons very little. It might be argued, superficially, that because he has done little to remedy the state of things on the Congo, that he is lacking in feeling. But, as a matter of fact, it is really because he is aware – subconsciously if you will – of the depth of his capacity to feel, that the Englishman takes refuge in his particular official optimism. He hides from himself the fact that there are in the world greed, poverty, hunger, lust or evil passions, simply because he knows that if he comes to think of them at all they will move him beyond bearing. He prefers, therefore, to say – and to hypnotise himself into believing – that the world is a very good – an all-good-place. He would prefer to believe that such people as the officials of the Congo Free State do not really exist in the modern world. People, he will say, do not do such things . . . the especial province of the English nation is the evolution of a standard of manners. For that is what it comes to when one says that the province of the English is to solve the problem of how men may live together . . . It is true that in repressing its emotions this people, so adventurous and so restless, has discovered the secret of living . . . this people which has so 'high' a mission in the world has invented a saving phrase which, upon all occasions, unuttered and perhaps unthought, dominates the situation. For, if in England we seldom think it and still more seldom say it, we nevertheless feel very intimately as a set rule of conduct, whenever we meet a man, whenever we talk with a woman: 'You will play the game.' (Ford Madox Ford, 1907, reprinted in Giles and Middleton, 1995, pp. 46–52)

ACTIVITY 7.8

These passages from Barker and Ford can serve us as a checklist of English masculinity in the early twentieth century, and so give a context for understanding the representation of masculinity in *The Wind in the Willows*. The Englishman is shy but self-confident, manly rather than refined and, while capable of feeling deeply, is unreflective about his emotions; indeed, rather than face contradictions he will take refuge in what Ford calls official optimism.

- How far do these traits relate to the characteristics of the main characters in Grahame's novel? Make a list of the characteristics of each character; we have started you off.

Rat	Mole	Badger	Toad
Poet and warlike	Domestic	Free spirit	Shows off

- In your analysis, how far did the characters fit Barker and Ford's definitions of the English gentleman?
- What features do the characters have that are not part of the listing provided by your notes on the extracts? How do you explain apparent contradictions like the fact that Rat is both a dreamy poet and, when the occasion calls for it, very warlike?
- Look back at your notes on Carpenter: how far are the characteristics he identifies visible in the novel? Can you, for example, make a case for Rat as a type of Urning? Which scenes and sequences would you refer to in order to make your case? What material might you use to refute such a reading?

Homosociality in The Wind in the Willows

When juxtaposing material on 'the gentleman' with Carpenter's work on queerness, it is important to recall Dellamora's point about protecting and controlling homosexuality via homophobia. What your notes may reveal is that the masculinity of a character like Rat is far less fixed and stable than might at first appear. At this stage it is helpful to step back from the text and reflect briefly upon some of the approaches associated with queer theory, before turning once more to Grahame's novel. Eve Sedgwick, an influential critic working in this field, has argued that patriarchal society requires homophobia – a fear of homosexuality – and that this phobia is inevitable in a male-dominated culture. Sedgwick uses the term 'homosocial' when talking about male-dominated cultural milieux:

> Homosocial is a word which is today gaining a wider currency; it is used in history and the social sciences to describe social bonds between persons of the same sex: it is a neologism, obviously formed by analogy with homosexual, and just as obviously meant to be distinguished from homosexual. In fact, it is applied to such activities as male bonding, which may . . . be characterised by intense homophobia, fear and hatred of homosexuality. (Sedgwick, 1985, p. 1)

Given that society is often organized by men promoting the interests of other men, homosociality has been constructed as especially antagonistic towards the idea of men loving men (homosexuality) (Sedgwick, 1985, pp. 4–5). By focusing upon the ways in which heterosexual male dominance requires the marginalization of the queerness that threatens its social dominance, critics like Sedgwick and other queer theorists have facilitated a rereading of masculinity which is alert to the role's contradictions and complicity in the status quo. As Koestenbaum has argued, queer theory 'questions heterosexuality's privileges and forces masculine writing to take seriously the threat of queerness . . . within male texts of all varieties lurks a homosexual desire [often disguised as homosociality] which, far from reinforcing patriarchy, undermines it, and offers a way out' (Koestenbaum, 1989, p. 5). Bearing in mind Koestenbaum's argument about the ways in which homosexuality can 'lurk' within homosociality, read the following argument and then consider the questions that follow it.

Reading 7.10

Mole comes out of the closet

If we trace the movement of Mole in this novel we see him travel from a position where he is associated with private domesticity to one in which he has become a respected member of the River Bank world. The story first places Mole with Rat as his companion but it is through his liaison with the more uncomplicatedly masculine Badger that he achieves his mature status. Mole is an interesting figure in the contexts afforded by the debates about masculinity in the period. His terror in the Wild Wood, his irrationality whilst Rat deduces the location of Badger's home and his readiness to adopt helper-type roles all mark him off as somewhat short of the period's masculine ideal. Mole's house is a further register of this slippage. Perhaps the most striking feature of this house is its statuary:

> In the middle was a small round pond containing goldfish and surrounded by a cockle shell border. Out of the centre of the pond rose a fanciful erection clothed in more cockle shells and topped by a large silvered glass ball that reflected everything all wrong and had a very pleasing effect. (Grahame, 1983, p. 52)

Mole's tastes are indicative of his (repressed?) sensuality (sexuality) and a privileging of the aesthetic over the practical. His cockle-shell erection is in a style that today might be called kitsch and, given the wider Edwardian context (partially reflected in the novel) in which threatened hierarchies are to be maintained, his delight in an artefact which 'reflected everything all wrong' and in consequence had a 'very pleasing effect' is, at least, suggestive.

Our first meeting with Mole sees him running from this domestic locale, casting aside his 'feminine' duties to embrace the bachelor life of the river; a locale which is associated with a loss of maturity and of the related need for adult responsibility: 'By the side of the river he trotted as one trots, *when very small, by the side of a man, who holds one spellbound by exciting stories*' (Grahame, 1983, p. 2; emphasis added).

Mole meets Rat who offers to show him more of the river and to take him on a picnic. The river world of Rat is one of freedom and leisure, recalling (perhaps) the world of middle-class coteries which were often the circles in which gay men met in the later nineteenth century (on this see Weeks, 1989, p. 260). In one sense the book clearly diverges from the idealized homosexual world of the *fin de siècle* in that the working-class body is not the focus of middle-class interest as it certainly was in, say, Oscar Wilde's circle (Weeks, 1989, p. 262). In E. M. Forster's novel of homosexual awakening, *Maurice*, written a few years after Grahame's novel, it is the rural working-class male who is the physical lover that Maurice has sought – a lover whose closeness to nature allows Maurice to express his animal lusts (as they are seen in the text) in the specifically rural, idealized setting of the Greenwood. In Grahame's text, however, Mole and Rat set up their bachelor existence in a seemingly sexless Arcadia.

Yet what is noticeable in these early chapters are the ways in which Mole takes up the domestic and 'feminine' role: he is the one who is strongly emotional – little ecstasies over unpacking the picnic hamper, tears of remorse; his ineptness at rowing – and his repeated flights of emotion are repeatedly framed in the text as signs of a failure of manly self-restraint. Rat, on the other hand, is both the man of action and the poet – the very type of masculinity promoted by the public school and made flesh for many a few years after this novel was written in the person of the warrior-poet Rupert Brooke. We see Rat taking charge of situations and frequently laden with phallic weaponry (guns, pistols etc.) whilst the Mole is left to deal with the dishes.

In Chapter 2 the friends go caravanning with Toad and amongst everything else that happens during this trip we have an illustration of the way in which homosociality (i.e. male bonding) might be read as homosexual. Fed up with Toad's demands and the effort of life on the road, the two chums hold hands in the dark and plan to escape to their dear old hole by the river (Grahame, 1983, p. 18). This scene evokes both a public school experience of isolation and male friendship and also hints at the kind of escapist turn evident in E. M. Forster's turn to the Greenwood in *Maurice*; both texts establish the rural as the location in which the middle-class male can do as he pleases.

In Mole and Rat we have, then, what Sedgwick might term a homosocial couple and their relationship cannot stand apart from the widespread gender panic of the early twentieth century. This is not to say that Grahame was latently gay nor that this text is 'about' homosexuality: it is to suggest that by placing the novel in the wider context afforded by the culture of the period and Grahame's own biography we can start to read its account of homosociality in ways that he may not have intended but which are certainly relevant to an account of the shifting perceptions of English masculinity in the period. The richness and ambiguity of a text like *The Wind in the Willows* allows for a diversity of decodings, some of which, like the reading above, may run counter to its intended meaning, but nevertheless offer insights into the discourses that produced certain understandings of masculinity at a particular historical moment. (From an unpublished lecture by Tim Middleton)

ACTIVITY 7.9

- What was your reaction to this extract? If you thought it was misguided (or even stupid), can you think about why you reacted in this way?
- How far does it support the findings of your own work on the version of Grahame's novel which emerges after its central characters' traits have been set alongside those described by Barker, Carpenter and Ford?

The persistence of high culture

Did your response to the lecture extract have anything to do with your sense of the status of the novel? The edition published by the Oxford University Press in its World's Classics series (a title which in itself seems to guarantee the text's prestige and global importance) offers the potential buyer the following back-cover blurb:

> *The Wind in the Willows* (1908) is a book for those 'who keep the spirit of youth alive in them; of life, sunshine, running water, woodlands, dusty roads, winter firesides'.
>
> So wrote Kenneth Grahame of his timeless tale of Toad, Mole, Badger, and Rat in their beautiful and benevolently ordered world. But it is also a world under siege, threatened by dark and unnamed forces – 'the Terror of the Wild Wood' with its 'wicked little faces' and 'glances of malice and hatred' – and defended by the mysterious Piper at the Gates of Dawn. *The Wind in the Willows* has achieved an enduring place in our literature: it succeeds at once in arousing our anxieties and in calming them by giving perfect shape to our desire for peace and escape. (Grahame, 1983)

This firmly (and unsurprisingly) suggests that *The Wind in the Willows* is a 'classic' children's book, and this status may well shape the ways in which we respond to readings of it.

ACTIVITY 7.10

Notice how the blurb sets up oppositions as a means of describing the text's content: we have started you off, but you can add oppositions you identified in your own reading to create a more detailed account.

Favoured – River Bank	Not favoured – non-River Bank
beautiful	dark
benevolent	wicked

The novel organizes itself around what were, and by and large remain, oppositions fostered by the dominant culture. As a text written for a middle-class child (and, in fact, a particularly difficult and unhappy child), the preaching of peace and happiness through adherence to River Bank values is clearly part of an overtly ideological message. Any reading of the novel has to take on board the fact that the River Bank world is threatened, but what the kind of reading we have been investigating here can do is to shift attention away from the obvious sources of trouble (Toad's selfishness, the 'working-class' Wild Wooders) to a more deep-seated threat (as the dominant discourse of the period might have perceived it) to the middle-class males who dominate the River Bank milieu – a threat which, ironically, is actually inherent in the very nature of the all-male milieu they fight to preserve. The fact that the kind of reading sketched here may (at first) appear to be 'unthinkable' can be seen as a register of the lengths to which the dominant culture of patriarchy goes in order to bury any hint of homosexuality in its celebration of homosociality.

Conclusions

In this discussion of the homosocial in *The Wind in the Willows* we have, of course, only begun to explore the ways in which a text changes when situated in its original cultural context. To take the reading we have been considering further you will need to find out more about the period and the debates about gendered identity which were current at the time. It will also help if you learn more about Grahame's own life: the suggested reading and other resources listed below can help you to make a start on this.

This chapter has examined some of the ways in which cultural studies has approached a divided and disparate cultural sphere. In this chapter we have tended to concentrate upon literary culture, but other areas of 'high' culture, like classical music, opera, painting or dance, can all provide rich sites for your own investigations. An approach to literary, as well as popular, texts that involves seeing both as inextricably linked aspects of the production and circulation of meanings at a specific historical moment can identify not only the ways in which dominant discourses manifest themselves but also those latent trends, nuances and tendencies that run counter to the dominant.

Suggested further reading

This covers suggestions for further reading on new historicism, queer theory and approaches to gender and literature in the period. For works cited in the chapter as a whole please see the references near the end of this book.

Peter Barry (2002) *Beginning Theory: an Introduction to Literary and Cultural Theory.* Manchester: Manchester University Press. Has a good discussion of new historicism and its UK variant cultural materialism, and a chapter on what he terms Lesbian and Gay Criticism; a good starting point.
Peter Green (1959) *Kenneth Grahame: a Study of his Life, Work and Times.* London: John Murray. The standard biography.
Philip Holden and Richard J. Ruppel (eds) (2003) *Imperial Desire: Dissident Sexualities and Colonial Literature.* Minneapolis: University of Minnesota Press. Explores the intersection of colonialism and homosexuality in fiction and travel writing from Robinson Crusoe to the present.
Steve Humphries and Pamela Gordon (1996) *A Man's World: from Boyhood to Manhood, 1900–1960.* London: BBC Books. Based on oral history work for a TV series, this book offers a wide range of recollections about aspects of masculinity in the period, including discussion of homosexuality.
Scott McCracken (1998) *Pulp: Reading Popular Fiction.* Manchester: Manchester University Press. A good one-volume introduction to the critical analysis of popular fiction, with chapters on best-sellers, detective fiction, romance, science fiction and gothic horror fiction.
Lyn Pykett (1995) *Engendering Fictions: the English Novel in the Early Twentieth Century.* London: Arnold. A very readable account of the debates about gender as they manifested themselves in the fiction of the era; contains an appendix of quotations from a range of period sources on the topic which can be productively juxtaposed with material on Grahame and the extracts from Barker, Carpenter and Ford provided here.
Eve Kosofsky Sedgwick (1994) *Epistemology of the Closet.* London: Penguin. Not an easy read but worth persevering with; this book is a landmark in queer theory.
Martin Taylor (1989) *Lads: Love Poetry of the Trenches.* London: Constable. Offers an example of another approach to the kind of rereading we sketch here. Examines homosocial poetry from the First World War and teases out its homosexual aspects.

Websites

Queer theory resources are provided as part of David Gauntlett's very accessible Theory.org.uk website www.theory.org.uk/ctr-quee.htm.

Queer Resources Directory has links to a range of queer theory/culture sites at www. qrd.org/qrd/culture/.

People with a History: an Online Guide to Lesbian, Gay, Bisexual and Transsexual History is a wonderfully rich site, with masses of material and links to hundreds of other sites: www.fordham.edu/halsall/pwh/index.html.

Chapter 8

Subjects, Bodies, Selves

Introduction

You will recall that in chapter 2 we separated identity and subjectivity, promising to return to subjectivity later. We hope that the ideas introduced in this chapter will not simply be added on to your understanding of identity but will also cause you to reflect back on and rethink your ideas about identity in the light of this discussion. Although the terms identity and subjectivity are sometimes used interchangeably, they are not quite synonymous but neither are they entirely separated concepts. Indeed, thinking about the different ways in which the terms are used and the nuances of meaning, which may defy definition, will focus your mind on what is at stake when cultural and social theorists write about these issues. This chapter refers to some of the most influential theorists of the self in the twentieth century: Sigmund Freud, Jacques Lacan, Michel Foucault, Louis Althusser. However, it is not our intention to offer comprehensive accounts of complex theories or areas of knowledge. These are readily available elsewhere and should be the subject of in-depth study as your interests dictate. Our aim, in this chapter, is to flag up important areas for your further consideration, to introduce you to the possibilities in such areas and to stimulate your thinking based on your own experience.

In chapter 2 we introduced you to humanist ideas of the self, which hold that individual consciousness is the centre from which meaning, identity and language originate. We went on to problematize this idea by suggesting that identities are not simply a matter of individual choice; nor are we born with a core self. Instead, we argued, identity is socially and historically formed. In doing so we adopted an **anti-humanist** position that challenges common-sense beliefs about the nature of selfhood and identity: 'the concept of subjectivity decentres the individual by problematizing the simplistic relationship between language and the individual which common sense presumes' (Easthope and McGowan, 1992, p. 67). Now read the following definition.

Reading 8.1

'Subjectivity' can be defined as that combination of conscious and unconscious thoughts and emotions that make up our sense of ourselves, our relation to the world and our ability to act in that world. Unlike the individualist notion of people as rational, self-motivated individuals in pursuit of their own clear and stable self-interest, the concept of subjectivity can capture both the notion of people as intentional subjects – actors in the world – and at the same time as subject to forces beyond their conscious control. For that reason, it has proved very useful to feminist theory, which has recognized that as women we behave in ways which we do not intend and are not always in our own interests. Such 'irrational' behaviour has been experienced by women as their own failure to make personal and emotional changes that politically and intellectually seem desirable. A need to understand why this happens, or how what is called a contradictory subjectivity is produced, led feminists to examine, among other accounts, psychoanalytic theories of the unconscious . . .

Even though our subjectivity is, by definition, what we experience as most personal and most individual, our desires and expectations are acquired in a social context. (Crowley and Himmelweit, 992, p. 7)

There are two points we can make here, which will be discussed further in later sections. First, you may have noted that Crowley and Himmelweit point to a significant meaning of the term 'subject', that is the sense of being 'subject to'. As they suggest, people are 'subject to forces beyond their conscious control'. When we act 'irrationally' or apparently against our best interests, either as women or as men, we are not the coherent, centred selves presupposed by humanism, but may experience a lack of control, a fragmentation of who we think we are and a sense of confusion – 'a contradictory subjectivity'. We will look at the psychoanalytic theories of Jacques Lacan, which have been used to examine how this sense of a fractured self is produced.

Second, the extract refers to the idea we met in chapter 2 that, while consciousness is experienced at a personal and individual level, our desires, needs and hopes are produced within the parameters of the social and historical context in which we are situated. Thus, apparently 'irrational' behaviours can be examined from a social as well as a psychoanalytic perspective. This is important. If 'irrational' motivations are a product of unconscious impulses that can only be interpreted by the analyst in the process of psychoanalysis, we may find ourselves locked into unchangeable behaviours that could be as determining as those ascribed to biological imperatives. Thinking about the relation between social and unconscious processes in the production of subjectivities allows for the possibility of change. In order to examine how subjectivity is constituted by the structures of society, we shall consider Foucault's theories of the **discursive** construction of subjectivity. You will remember that we introduced you to Foucault's theory of discourse in chapter 3. It would be useful to remind yourself of this. You might also find it helpful to reread the brief discussion of Althusser's theory of the subject in chapter 2.

Before we continue, here is a summary of the main ideas of anti-humanist conceptions of **decentred** subjectivity. We shall be extending our discussion of these in the sections that follow.

- The subject 'I' is not a unified, coherent identity but a sometimes contradictory set of multiple or fragmented selves.
- Individual subjectivities do not precede language but are themselves constituted in language.
- Subjects are both able to act in the world and subject to forces outside their control.
- The constitution of a particular subjectivity involves a relationship between unconscious motivations and social structures.
- Subjectivity is also constituted in relation to our physical bodies.

Bullet points one and two could usefully be considered alongside reading 2.4 by Trinh T. Minh-ha.

One other important point we want to raise here is that, while we have adopted an anti-humanist position with regard to subjectivity, we are aware of the possible difficulties of such a position for political movements concerned with combating oppression and the subordination that accompanies this. Feminism, for example, has argued that women have always experienced a sense of fragmentation and find it difficult, in a male-dominated culture, to express an authentic sense of self. One aspect of feminist endeavour has been to create spaces in which women could construct representations of women that were more valid than the images frequently reproduced in literature and the media. Women, like other oppressed groups, may need to validate themselves as coherent beings with a voice of their own in order to counter the misrepresentations of dominant culture. There has been considerable debate within feminism about the advantages and disadvantages of adopting an anti-humanist stance towards subjectivity, but whatever the difficulties, many feminists now recognize the impossibility of speaking or writing in a single voice – that of 'woman'. Instead there is an awareness that 'I' may encompass a diversity of intersecting subjectivities: for example, those of generation, 'race', ethnicity, sexual orientation, class (Fuss, 1989; Butler, 1990; hooks, 1991; Hill Collins, 2000).

> **ACTIVITY 8.1**
>
> You may have noted that in this paragraph we have moved from writing about 'fragmentation' to writing about 'diversity'. Does 'diversity' suggest a more positive way of seeing subjectivities? If so, how?

Fragmented or Multiple Selves?

Because individual subjectivity is formed from the unconscious and the social, any apparently coherent conscious selfhood remains precarious and fragile, relying, as it does, on the repression of the unconscious. Most of us have behaved at some time or another in ways that took us by surprise or threatened our sense of the kind of the person we believe ourselves to be. Have you ever found yourself thinking or saying, 'Why did I do that – it's not like me at all'?

> **ACTIVITY 8.2**
>
> Can you think of examples in your own life when your sense of self might be **destabilized** in this way? We have suggested some possibilities. Try to add to these.
>
> - At an interview for a job that you really want you 'find' yourself saying something that you know will lessen your chances of getting the job.
> - Catching sight of your reflection in a shop window or mirror, you think for a moment that it is someone else.
> - Knowing that you are very short of money this month you 'find' yourself buying an expensive item of clothing.
> -
> -

In any of the situations above we 'find' ourselves behaving as if we were a different person – someone we don't 'know', a stranger – and we appear to have no control over this. We just 'find' ourselves acting or looking in ways that appear to contradict what we know about ourselves at the level of conscious thinking. The point to grasp is that this is not a matter of moving between different aspects of a fixed, pre-given personality or adopting certain roles in specific situations. Instead, subjectivity is constantly in flux, constantly in process and only ever briefly stabilized. Equally, following Althusser's concept of interpellation, situations offer us or 'recruit' us to socially appropriate modes of subjectivity. For example, a woman who has just had a baby is invited to take up the socially appropriate subject position that constitutes being a mother in contemporary Western societies, and she may 'recognize' herself in this invitation (see the section on language and subjectivity below). However, she may experience, simultaneously, intense feelings of hostility towards her newborn baby that threaten this subject position. She may feel unaccountably guilty: 'Why, when I've got a beautiful baby, do I feel so unhappy and depressed? What's wrong with me? I must be a bad mother.' The subject position 'mother' into which she has been interpellated and where she has located herself cannot contain or incorporate these contradictory feelings and impulses, and the result for the woman may be a sense of splitting or fragmentation, what is sometimes described as a sense of 'falling apart'. She does not experience herself as the coherent individual of humanist thought but in multiple ways: as subject to uncontrollable forces; as the subject of society's narratives about mothers and motherhood; and as the subject of her own actions and feelings (she physically cares for the baby, she loves the baby).

The point to grasp is that the concept of subjectivity always implies an unconscious dimension. It is not synonymous with personality or selfhood but offers a way of connecting conscious and unconscious dimensions of the self with the social world in which these are formed and acted out. Certain forms of mental illness are characterized by extreme manifestations of 'split personality' in which the sufferer may be partially or totally unaware of extreme shifts in persona. Close relatives can be devastated by the loss of the person they once knew and find it difficult to accept that 'he's not the man I married' or 'she's not my mother any longer'. We also say similar things about changes in people we know, changes brought about as a result of illness, social mobility, political commitment and even excess alcohol. To summarize:

- subjectivities may be assumed temporarily;
- a particular subjectivity may be more dominant in specific contexts but may remain as traces in other situations;
- the positions in which we locate ourself at any one moment may be fragile, open to disruption from other subject positions and from those desires, impulses and needs that form the unconscious;
- we may be invited to assume certain subject positions and this will involve issues of power and dominance (we shall discuss this later in the chapter).

Now read the following poem, *Recognition*, by Carol Ann Duffy.

Reading 8.2

Recognition

Things get away from one.
I've let myself go, I know.
Children? I've had three
and don't even know them.

I strain to remember a time
when my body felt lighter.
Years. My face is swollen
with regrets. I put powder on,

but it flakes off. I love him,
through habit, but the proof
has evaporated. He gets upset.
I tried to do all the essentials

on one trip. Foolish, yes,
but I was weepy all morning.
Quiche. A blond boy swung me up
in his arms and promised the earth.

You see, this came back to me
as I stood on the scales.
I wept. Shallots. In the window,
creamy ladies held a pose

which left me clogged and old.
The waste. I'd forgotten my purse,
fumbled; the shopgirl gaped at me,
compassionless. Claret. I blushed.

Cheese. Kleenex. *It did happen.*
I lay in my slip on wet grass,
laughing. Years. I had to rush out,
blind in a hot flush, and bumped

into an anxious, dowdy matron
who touched the cold mirror
and stared at me. Stared
and said I'm sorry sorry sorry.
(Duffy, 1994, pp. 40–1)

What contradictory selves are experienced by the speaker of the poem? Is she able to reconcile these in the poem? What are the speaker's feelings about these conflicting selves? What contradictions are there between her sense of herself and the ways in which she is seen by others? What subject positions are offered to her in the social world she inhabits?

The speaker of the poem tries to hold on to memories of herself as a young girl in love with, presumably, her husband. She remembers herself as slim and attractive – a sexually desirable woman. In the present, however, she knows herself to be 'an anxious, dowdy matron', menopausal and overweight, for whom sex has become 'habit'. She experiences these two senses of herself as in conflict. Note how the structure of the poem constantly juxtaposes past and present realities by using the items of her shopping list to trigger off memories and make connections, 'Claret. I blushed. Cheese. Kleenex. *It did happen.*' She experiences herself as both joined to her younger self and cut off from it; a sense of fragmentation which causes her sadness and guilt. Looking in the mirror, her older self apologizes to her younger self, thus reinforcing the sense of irreconcilable split with which the poem ends. The shopgirl sees her simply as a silly middle-aged lady who has forgotten her purse, or that is how the speaker believes she is perceived. Her husband 'gets upset' – by her indifference to sex, by the fact she is no longer the youthful girl he courted? And her children have grown up and gone away. Other people's perceptions of who she is shape her own view of herself but do not constitute it totally. The subject positions available to her are wife, mother and middle-aged woman, but she cannot fit herself neatly into these, nor can she any longer see herself or be seen as a young, sexually desirable woman.

You might note that the speaker/poet does not suggest anywhere that one of these selves is the 'real' self. Instead the poem expresses a powerful sense of dislocation and fragmentation. And, something we shall return to, she experiences this sense of dislocation through her body: she weeps, she blushes, she wears make-up to hide her feelings, she is saddened by her thickening body, she experiences a hot flush and remembers her body being swung in his arms. The memories and traces of her different selves are marked bodily as well as known cognitively. How did you respond to this? Did you feel saddened by the speaker's confusion and loss of selfhood? Is it possible to see conflicting selves in a more positive way? Now read the following extract by Gloria Anzaldúa, a Chicano and lesbian-feminist poet and writer who works in the United States. Anzaldúa mixes a range of dialects and languages in her work, including North Mexican, Castilian Spanish and English, in order to draw attention to the relationship between subjectivity and language. Anzaldúa suggests a new subject, neither woman, nor lesbian, nor American, nor Chicano, that 'has to shift out of habitual formations' of rational thinking and move towards a mode of 'divergent thinking . . . one that includes rather than excludes'. She calls this new consciousness *la mestiza*.

Reading 8.3

The new *mestiza* copes by developing a tolerance for contradictions, a tolerance for ambiguity. She learns to be an Indian in Mexican culture, to be Mexican from an Anglo point of view. She learns to juggle cultures. She has a plural personality, she operates in a pluralistic model – nothing is thrust out, the good, the bad and the ugly, nothing rejected, nothing abandoned. Not only does she sustain contradictions, she turns the ambivalence into something else.

She can be jarred out of ambivalence by an intense, and often painful, emotional event which inverts or resolves the ambivalence. I'm not sure exactly how. The work takes place underground – subconsciously. It is work the soul performs. The focal point of fulcrum, that juncture where the mestiza stands, is where phenomena tend to collide. It is where the possibility of uniting all that is separate occurs. This assembly is not one where severed or separated pieces merely come together. Nor is it a balancing of opposing powers. In attempting to work out a synthesis, the self has added a third element which is greater than the sum of its severed parts. The third element is a new consciousness – a mestiza consciousness – and though it is a source of intense pain, its energy comes from continual creative motion that keeps breaking down the unitary aspect of each new paradigm. (Anzaldúa, 1987, pp. 79–80)

ACTIVITY 8.4

- This reading offers a more positive and radical way of seeing the conflicts and tensions of subjectivity. Can you identify words and phrases which suggest this?
- How do you respond to this?
- Does this passage have anything in common with Carol Ann Duffy's poem?

You may have noted the emphasis on movement and creativity: 'performs', 'creative motion'. There is an energy in this piece which contrasts with the static, trapped sense of Duffy's poem. Yet both speakers desire or seek some kind of unity or synthesis. For Anzaldúa it is this quest for synthesis that offers creative and dynamic opportunities; for Duffy's speaker the experience leads to despair. You might also note that in both there is an awareness of a split between an outer, 'public' self and an inner, 'private' self. Remind yourself of what we said earlier about the relationship between social and unconscious processes in the construction of subjectivity. Recognition that individual subjectivity is split and fractured need not be cause for despair, as Anzaldúa demonstrates. Instead it can offer opportunities for new ways of thinking – we can, according to Anzaldúa, 'learn to juggle cultures' and, albeit painfully, create new forms of consciousness that embrace ambivalence and contradiction rather than seeking to resolve these.

In your reading you will encounter examples of subjectivity represented as fragmentation and atomization, and subjectivity represented as fluid, flexible and plural. Although the distinction between optimism and pessimism may not always be as stark as we have made it here, it is worth pausing to think carefully about where on the continuum (optimistic–pessimistic) the writer/ speaker positions herself or himself.

ACTIVITY 8.5

Can you think of images or motifs that are used in writing, films and the media in attempts to capture this sense of the self as something constructed but fluid and potentially fragile? We have started you off. Try to find examples of the motifs we have listed in novels, advertisements, autobiographies, TV drama, poems, films, photographs and paintings and think about whether they suggest pleasure in multiplicity or whether they suggest a negative fragmentation, or something between. Make notes of your responses and ideas. You could add to this list as you come across other images and motifs.

- Mirrors (see Duffy's poem above)
- Clothes
- Body parts
- Borders (see Anzaldúa above)
- Masks
- Twins/doubles
- Child in an adult body/adult in a child's body
- Metamorphoses – animal to human, human to animal, for example
- Robots, machines, technology

Language and Subjectivity

We said earlier in this chapter that 'individual subjectivities do not precede language but are themselves constituted in language'. At this point it would be useful to remind yourself of the discussion about language and representation in chapter 3. The theories of the French psychoanalyst Jacques Lacan (1901–83) give language a far more prominent place in the construction of the psyche than did Freud. Freud suggested that the newborn baby has no sense of itself as a separate entity, that it lives in a symbiotic relationship with the mother (or mother surrogate) in which there are no boundaries between the self and another. Not only does the baby experience itself in this amorphous way, it also has no sense of being male or female. For Lacan, the acquisition of a gender identity occurs, significantly, at the same time as the baby is acquiring language.

At what point and how does the baby recognize itself as a bodily form, separate from the mother? According to Lacan this occurs around the age of six months when the child sees its reflection in a mirror and identifies with an imaginary image of itself as a 'self' with boundaries. Lacan uses the mirror as a metaphor to suggest how this moment of awareness is both recognition and misrecognition. The baby, who has up until now experienced itself as fluid and unbounded, sees, in the mirror, an image of a bounded entity. This image is experienced as seductive and pleasurable, but also as false – the baby still *feels* undefined and unbounded. The mirror image is both the baby and not the baby, both subject (myself) and object (image of myself). Think of the sentence 'I see myself'. The 'I' who is doing the looking cannot at the same time be the object (myself) that is being looked at. The mirror reflection gives the baby a coherent image of itself with which it can identify; yet, at the same time that this mirror image offers a sense of a separated, bounded self, it also occasions a split between the desired image/illusion (object) and the experiencing subject (the 'I' who looks). We 'misrecognize' the mirror reflection as an authentic identity when, in fact, it gives us only *an imaginary sense* of self. Throughout our lives, according to Lacan, we seek authenticity and identity in illusions of selfhood that depend upon the ways in which other people (mirrors) offer us reflections of ourselves or are seen as images of who we think we are. The primary reflector is, of course, the mother (or surrogate mother). As Rosalind Minsky explains. 'this taking of an identity from outside will form the basis of all [the baby's] other identifications. The baby narcissistically arrives at some kind of sense of "I" only by finding an "I" reflected back by something outside itself and external – its (m)other' (Minsky, 1992, p. 189).

The use of the mirror as a metaphor for the way in which the small child comes to perceive itself as 'I', separate from its mother and others, is one of Lacan's most accessible ideas. However, it is in Lacan's highly original reworking of Freud's Oedipal moment (which occurs later than the mirror phase) that the significance of language is introduced. We want to turn to this now.

Reading 8.4

To go back to the mirror phase in the imaginary pre-Oedipal period for a moment, the child contemplating itself in the mirror can be seen as something that bestows meaning – a kind of 'signifier' – and the image in the mirror as a kind of 'signified' . . . The image of the child in the mirror is for the child apparently the meaning of itself – when it *felt* it had only a very chaotic, unbounded meaning before this moment. We can also see what Lacan calls 'the mirror phase' as a kind of metaphor: one item, the child, discovers a likeness of itself in something else, an 'other' (the reflection). This is really for Lacan how he sees everything that happens in the imaginary: objects repeatedly reflect themselves in a kind of sealed unit where there are no apparent differences or divisions, where everything is fluid. The mirror images in the 'Imaginary' are ones of fullness, wholeness, totality, complete identity. There is no separation or gap between the experience of the child and the world it inhabits. For Lacan this is the imaginary world of 'demand' where, through identification with the other, the self is actually annihilated while imagining itself complete and full because it is *completely* dependent on the mother. It is also the world where satisfaction is never entirely complete: the baby never feels that the mother's response to its demand is ever quite enough; there is always an element of dissatisfaction.

With the entry of the father onto the scene [at the Oedipal moment], the child is precipitated into a crisis. It has to recognize that identities can only come into being, as Saussure argued, as a result of the perception of *difference*. One term or subject only has meaning because it is different from other terms and other subjects, and excludes them. At the time when the small child is first discovering sexual difference it is also, highly significantly, acquiring language. And in the discovery of language the child unconsciously learns that a sign (in this case a word) only has meaning because it is different from other signs (words) and that signs always stand for, or represent, the absence of what they signify. The words in language stand in for objects, and in this sense operate like metaphors . . . And here we get to perhaps the central point in Lacan's theory. As the child learns about language standing in for objects in the world, it is also unconsciously learning about them in the psychic world of sexuality – in the discovery of sexual difference. The father, symbolized by the phallus, legislates to the child that it must take its place within a family which is defined by sexual difference, by exclusion (it cannot be its parents' lover) and by absence (it must give up its relationship with its mother). Its identity as a human subject capable of operating viably within the family and in society depends on its recognition that it is different from some people and the same as others. In its recognition of this pre-determined social fact, the child is enabled to move from a world of fantasy, into the world of language and the symbolic. The intrusion of the third term into the child's world turns out to be not only the father – the possessor of the phallus – but also, in Lacan's theory, the law of how we *perceive* the world, that is language and culture. In this way Lacan links the sexual psychic world with the social world – the dimension of language. The child recognizes the meaning of the phallus as a signifier (as something which bestows meaning although empty in itself) – as crucially the signifier of *difference* and at the same time the signifier of the *power* to break into the child's world with the mother and shatter it. Only this allows the child to enter into the rest of the chain of empty signifiers which bestow meaning – language.

The small child becomes a human subject capable of identifying with, seeing itself reflected in, the 'I' of language by means of this joint entry into language and at the same time sexual ordering and identity ('he', 'him', 'she', 'her' are positions which preexist and lie in wait to receive the child when it 'steps into' language). The child finds the idea of its gendered self awaiting it in language and can then identify with the sense of coherence and self it bestows, just as it did with the image in the mirror. (Minsky, 1992, pp. 191–3)

ACTIVITY 8.6

This extract has a lot of complex ideas in it so take time to reread and think about it. Go through it once and make notes of what you see as the three or four main points. Then reread it, but this time try to fill in some detail for each of your main points. Finally, reread the extract again and note down your response to it. Does it make sense to you? Do Lacan's theories help to explain the acquisition of identity? What specifically do you find difficult to accept, if anything? Why? Does it help to remind yourself that Lacan is using the mirror and the phallus metaphorically? He is not referring to an actual, visible penis.

Lacan's theories have been taken up by feminist theorists who see, in the focus on language, potential for disrupting the negative representation of femininity posited in Freud's accounts of sexual difference. Julia Kristeva, for example, has focused attention on the way in which the language of the pre-Oedipal Imaginary – a language of babble and fluidity, which she has termed 'semiotic' – can disrupt and transgress the laws of the symbolic order. Kristeva links the 'semiotic' with the feminine and the symbolic with the masculine, but not in ways which fix these positions to biological sex. Men as well as women can seek to rediscover the language of the Imaginary that is lost at the moment when the child 'steps into' language and the symbolic order. If this interests you, we suggest you look at the titles cited in the References and Further Reading for this chapter, which will introduce you to the ideas of

Kristeva and other influential French feminists, Luce Irigaray and Hélène Cixous.

Reading 8.5

What I call 'the semiotic' takes us back to the translinguistic states of childhood where the child babbles the sounds s/he hears, or where s/he articulates rhythms, alliterations, or stresses, trying to imitate her/his surroundings. In this state the child doesn't yet possess the necessary linguistic signs and thus there is no meaning in the strict sense of the term. It is only after the mirror phase or the experience of castration in the Oedipus complex that the individual becomes subjectively capable of taking on the signs of language, of articulation as it has been prescribed – and I call that 'the symbolic' . . .

What I call 'the semiotic' is a state of disintegration in which patterns appear but which do not have any stable identity: they are blurred and fluctuating. The processes which are at work here are those which Freud calls 'primary': processes of transfer. We have an example of this if we refer once again to the melodies and babblings of infants which are a sound image of their bodily instability. Babies' and children's bodies are made up erotogenic zones which are extremely excitable, or, on the contrary, indifferent, in a state of constant change, of excitation, or extinction, without there being any fixed identity.

A 'fixed identity': it's perhaps a fiction, an illusion – who amongst us has a 'fixed' identity? It's a phantasm; we do nevertheless arrive at a certain type of stability. There are several steps which lead to this stability and one step which has been accentuated by the French psychoanalyst Jacques Lacan is the specular identification which he calls 'the mirror phase'. In this phase one recognizes one's image in a mirror as one's self-image. It is a first identification of the chaotic, fragmented body, and is both violent and jubilatory. The identification comes about under the domination of the maternal image, which is the one nearest to the child and which allows the child both to remain close and to distance itself.

I see a face. A first differentiation takes place, and thus a first self-identity. This identity is still unstable because sometimes I take myself to be me, sometimes I confuse myself with my mother. This narcissistic instability, this doubt persists and makes me ask 'who am I?', 'is it me or is it the other?' The confusion with the maternal images as first other remains.

In order for us to be able to get out of this confusion, the classical pattern of development leads us to a confrontation inside the Oedipal triangle between our desire for the mother and the process of loss which is the result of paternal authority. In the ideal case, this finishes by stabilising the subject, rendering her/him capable both of pronouncing sentences which conform to the rules, to the law, and of telling her/his own story – of giving her/his account. (Kristeva, 1986, in Eagleton, 1996, pp. 352–3)

ACTIVITY 8.7

- Go back to the list of motifs you began to compile in the previous section. Can these motifs be explained with reference to the ideas discussed above?
- Select a film, advertisement, novel etc. Try to 'read' it using ideas and concepts from Lacan and/or Kristeva.

Discourse and the Subject

So far we have looked at theories of the constitution of subjectivity that focus on the individual psyche and on language. We suggested earlier in this chapter that 'we may be invited to assume certain subject positions and this will involve issues of power and dominance.' Althusser drew on Lacan's theory of the mirror stage in order to explain how and why people invest in those specific social relationships that enable the perpetuation of the capitalist mode of production, and that may not be in their best interests. According to Althusser, we 'recognize' ourselves in the subject positions we are invited to occupy and may experience an (illusory) sense of security and belonging in the process of interpellation into a specific subject position (Althusser, 1971). Equally, however, we may experience our 'self' as oscillating between contradictory subject positions as we are 'hailed' or interpellated by competing subject positions, or we may attempt to resist a particular address because it invites us to take up a position of powerlessness.

Foucault's theories of discourse hold that the individual subject is produced in and through the specific discourses that circulate in any society at any given moment. Thus, for example, according to Foucault, subject categories, such as 'lunatic' or 'criminal', do not pre-exist their construction in language and discourse. People differentiated as lunatics' only begin to know themselves as such and are known as such in and through the discourses of science and medicine that construct bodies of knowledge about a subject named as 'the lunatic' or 'the criminal' (Foucault, 1967, 1975).

Let us illustrate this with an example. Before the late nineteenth century there were, of course, people who engaged in same-sex sexual practices, but there was not a specific identity 'homosexual' that described and circumscribed certain individuals on the basis of their sexual behaviour. The late nineteenth and early twentieth centuries, however, witnessed the emergence of a category of person, named homosexual, in the vocabularies of medical and psychological knowledge and in legal practices. It was this homosexual person or 'subject', rather than the sexual practices, that became the focus of concern for medicine, psychology and the law. Thus, a new subject, 'the homosexual', emerged and, having been named, could be observed and regulated by the medical profession and the law. The furore surrounding the trials of Oscar Wilde in 1895 in Britain produced a public image of the newly emerging identity 'homosexual', an image that was to be used as a scapegoat during outbursts of moral panic. Yet, at the same time, the production of 'the homosexual' in the medical, psychological and legal discourses of sexuality opened up possibilities for homosexuals themselves, who adopted the term 'homosexual' in order to assert their own sense of identity and right to name themselves. The subject position 'homosexual' classified, and thereby had the power to survey and circumscribe, individual behaviours, while at the same time offering a subject position from which to assert the dignity of a homosexual subjectivity. By the end of the nineteenth century the outline of a ' "modem" male homosexual identity was beginning to emerge', offering possibilities for self-expression as well as producing an intensely oppressive definition that legitimated punitive moral regulation (Weeks, 1989, pp. 96–122; 2003).

Foucault was concerned with what he called disciplinary power and the means by which this is exercised. His focus is on the emergence in the nineteenth and twentieth centuries of new large-scale institutions that regulate, govern, discipline and 'police' modern populations: schools, prisons, clinics, hospitals, factories. This disciplinary power is asserted through administrative systems, professional expertise and the knowledge provided by 'disciplines' such as psychology. Unlike Althusser's concept of interpellation, which 'recruits' subjects through and in ideology, constructed in language, Foucault's discourse has a materiality in that it is about language *and* practice. Discourse is not, as you will remember from chapter 3, simply at the level of address and representation: it involves social practices and institutions. Discourse, according to Foucault, not only addresses us as subjects in language, as 'woman', 'man', 'homosexual', 'lunatic', 'criminal', 'witch', 'immigrant' and so forth, but functions to position us materially as embodied subjects. Its aim is to produce human beings who can be treated as 'docile bodies' to be labelled, measured, trained, cured, punished, imprisoned, exiled, tortured (Foucault, 1967, 1973, 1975). It is not necessary to accept all the details of Foucault's theories of power and discourse to accept the usefulness of these for understanding some of the paradoxes and complexities of power relations in modern societies. Now read the next extract, in which Stuart Hall draws upon his own experience in order to think about the ways in which 'a particular complex of discourses' generates certain sets of power relations around the concepts of 'race' and colour.

Reading 8.6

At different times in my 30 years in England, I have been 'hailed' or interpellated as 'coloured', 'West Indian', 'Negro', 'black', 'immigrant'. Sometimes in the street; sometimes at street corners; sometimes abusively; sometimes in a friendly manner; sometimes ambiguously. (A black friend of mine was disciplined by his political organization for 'racism' because, in order to scandalize the white neighbourhood in which we both lived as students, he would ride up to my window late at night and, from the middle of the street, shout 'Negro!' very loudly to attract my attention!) All of them inscribe me 'in place' in a signifying chain which constructs identity through the categories of colour; ethnicity, race.

In Jamaica where I spent my youth and adolescence, I was constantly hailed as 'coloured'. The way that term was articulated with other terms in the syntaxes of race and ethnicity was such as to produce the meaning, in effect, 'not black'. The 'blacks' were the rest – the vast majority of the people, the ordinary folk. To be 'coloured' was to belong to the 'mixed' ranks of the brown middle class, a cut above the rest – in aspiration if not in reality. My family attached great weight to these finely-graded classificatory distinctions and because of what it signified in terms of distinctions of class, status, race, colour insisted on the inscription. Indeed, they clung to it through thick and thin, like the ultimate ideological lifeline it was. You can imagine how mortified they were to discover that, when I came to England, I was hailed as 'coloured' by the natives there precisely because, as far as they could see, I *was* 'black', for all practical purposes . . . It is the position within the different signifying chains which 'means' not the literal, fixed correspondence between an isolated term and some denotated position in the colour spectrum . . .

As a concrete lived individual, am I indeed any one of these interpellations? Does any one of them exhaust me? In fact, I 'am' not one or another of these ways of representing me, though I have been positioned as all of them at different times and still am some of them to some degree. But, there is no essential, unitary 'I' – only the fragmentary contradictory subject I become. Long after, I encountered 'coloured' again, now as it were from the other side, beyond it. I tried to teach my son he was 'black' at the same time as he was learning the colours of the spectrum and he kept saying to me that he was 'brown'. Of course, he was *both*.

Certainly I am from the West Indies – though I've lived my adult life in England. Actually, the relationship between 'West Indian' and 'immigrant' is very complex for me. In the 1950s, the two terms were equivalents. Now, the term 'West Indian' is very romantic. It connotes reggae, rum and coke, shades, mangoes, and all that canned tropical fruit salad falling out of the coconut trees. This is an idealized 'I'. (I wish I felt more like that more of the time.) 'Immigrant' I also know well. There is nothing remotely romantic about that. It places one so equivocally as *really belonging somewhere else*. 'And when are you going back home.' Part of Mrs. Thatcher's 'alien wedge'. Actually I only understood the way this term positioned me relatively late in life – and the 'hailing' on that occasion came from an unexpected direction. It was when my mother said to me, on a brief visit home: 'I hope they don't mistake you over there for one of those immigrants!' The shock of recognition. I was also on many occasions 'spoken' by that other, absent, unspoken term, the one that is never there, the 'American' one, undignified even by a capital 'N'. The 'silence' around this term was probably the most eloquent of them all. (Hall, 1996, pp. 27–9)

ACTIVITY 8.8

- What do you think Hall means when he says of the term 'black' that it 'is the position within the different signifying chains which "means" not the literal, fixed correspondence between an isolated term and some denotated position in the colour spectrum'?
- What do you make of Hall's point that the silence around the term 'nigger' was 'the most eloquent of them all'? Can you suggest how and in what ways a silence can be 'eloquent'?
- Can you suggest ways in which 'the fragmentary, contradictory subject [Hall] become[s]' is positioned materially as well as linguistically?

Embodied Selves

Let us look now at another, very different, example of how narratives of the self may have social effects. The following extract, from a paper by Emily Martin, is concerned with the social implications of scientific and popular images of biological reproduction in humans. As well as scientific textbooks and journal articles, Martin has studied a range of biology teaching materials and films that have been produced in order to educate the public about reproductive physiology. She argues that this material consistently uses stereotypes in which egg and sperm are represented in terms of the human characteristics conventionally attributed to femininity and masculinity. Thus, the egg is represented as passive, a Sleeping Beauty who 'once released from the supportive environment of the ovary . . . will die within hours unless rescued by a sperm' (cited in Martin, 1992, p. 413). Martin also shows how this imagery is used in a popular film, *Look Who's Talking*.

Reading 8.7

Other popular materials also do their part: the recent film *Look Who's Talking* begins with a simulation of a hugely magnified egg floating, drifting, gently bouncing along the fallopian tube of a woman who is in the midst of making love with a man. The soundtrack is 'I Love You So' by the Chantals. Then we see, also hugely magnified, the man's sperm barreling down the tunnel of her vagina to the tune of 'I Get Around' by the Beach Boys. The sperm are shouting and calling to each other like a gang of boys: 'Come on, follow me, I know where I am, keep up, come on you kids, I've got the map'. Then as the egg hoves into view, they shout, 'This is it, yeah, this is definitely it, this is the place, Jackpot, right here, come on, dig in you kids'. And when one sperm finally pushes hard enough to open a slit in the egg (a slit that looks remarkably like a vulva), that sperm (as his whole self is swallowed up) cries out, 'Oh, oh, oh, I'm in!'

When I got to this point in my research, I was already wondering what social effects such vivid imagery might be having. I thought perhaps this imagery might encourage us to imagine that what results from the interaction of egg and sperm – a fertilized egg – is the result of intentional 'human' action *at the cellular level*. In other words, whatever the intentions of the human couple in this microscopic 'culture', a cellular 'bride' (or *femme fatale*) and a cellular 'groom' (or her victim) make a cellular baby . . . Endowing egg and sperm with intentional action, a key aspect of personhood in our culture, lays the foundation for the point of viability [of life in abortion debates] being pushed back to the moment of fertilization.

Why would this matter? Because endowing cells with personhood may play a part in the breaking down of boundaries between self and the world, and a pushing back of the boundary of what constitutes the inviolable self. In other words, whereas at an earlier time, the skin might have been regarded as the border of the individual self, now these microscopic cells are seen as tiny individual selves. This means that the 'environment' of the egg and sperm, namely the human body, is fair game for invasion by medical scrutiny and intervention. It is not, of course, that the interior of our bodies was not the object of study and treatment until now. But we may be experiencing an intensification of those activities (made more potent by state support) which are understood as protecting the 'rights', viability, or integrity of cellular entities. It would not be that endowing cells with personhood by means of imagery in biology automatically *causes* intensification of initiatives in the legislature and elsewhere that enable protection of these new *'persons'*. Rather, I am suggesting that this imagery may have a part in creating a general predisposition to think of the world in a certain way that can play an important role whenever legal and other initiatives do take place.

It is possible that in the 1990s what was the patient (or person) has itself begun to become *an environment* for a new core self, which exists at the cellular level. This change may be adding to our willingness to focus ever more attention on the internal structures of this tiny cellular self, namely its genes. In turn, such a shift in attention may encourage us to permit dramatic changes in the 'environment' of the genes in the name of maintaining their welfare. (Martin, 1992, pp. 414–15)

Martin's analysis demonstrates how a particular way of talking about the world becomes naturalized. We are so used to the language used to describe the functions and actions of cells in our bodies that we barely notice its metaphoric function. In making visible the images and metaphors used to describe human reproduction, Martin stops us taking these for granted and requires us to think about the social implications of seeing our bodies as the home of cellular 'persons'. In doing so she also raises questions about what characterizes personhood and individuality. But she does so from a very different perspective than that of Lacan: her concern is with the human body rather than the human psyche.

The previous sections have considered how subjectivity is produced through the unconscious and through the ways we are positioned in relation to social formations. In this section we want to extend our discussion by looking at the relationship between the bodies we inhabit and the social context in which these are experienced. In chapter 2 we introduced you to the idea of biological essentialism and suggested, via the reading from Linda Birke (reading 2.7), the possibilities involved in challenging orthodox conceptions of the dualistic relationship of mind to body. Recent sociological thinking has begun to theorize how our bodies not only sustain physical life, but also shape identity and a sense of self. Such theorizing attempts to explore how the body as a material object is shaped by social processes as well as biology, and how social processes and practices are, in turn, shaped by the materiality of actual physical bodies. In recent years the human body has been more and more intensely scrutinized, reconstructed and investigated by scientists, educationalists, the state, consumer culture and individuals. In Foucault's terms, we could say the human body has become the subject of disciplinary power – it is regulated, surveilled, 'policed' by medical expertise, scientific knowledge and bureaucratic systems.

ACTIVITY 8.9

Spend a few minutes compiling examples of the ways in which science and technology can have an impact on physical bodies and biological functions. We have started you off with two examples.

- Organ transplants
- Fitness regimes via aerobic classes, gyms, sport etc.

Recent technological and medical advances have begun to threaten the previously stable boundaries between human and machine, between nature and technology. The day may not be far off when computer chip brain implants will be available, while medical science has already made it possible for us to change our bodies over our lifetimes by exchanging diseased organs for donated organs or by replacing worn-out limbs with new, artificial ones. Genetic engineering, thrown into prominence by the cloning of a sheep, threatens traditional ideas of individual uniqueness, and *in vitro* fertilization has already removed the need for heterosexual intercourse in human reproduction. Many of these advances have the potential to benefit humanity, and many remain in the future and may never happen. Nevertheless, the rapid development of these technologies has thrown into uncertainty our knowledge of the body as a natural entity. Science and technology have replaced religious belief as the means by which we know the world, but rather than providing new certainties they have destabilized our understanding of what constitutes a bodily self (Shilling, 1997, pp. 67–9; Howson, 2003; Shilling, 2004). As a result, as Shilling points out, 'we potentially have the means to exert an *unprecedented degree of control* over bodies, [but] we are also living in an age which has *thrown into radical doubt* our knowledge of the consequences of this control, and of *how we should control* our bodily selves' (1997, p. 67, original emphasis).

Scientific interventions into bodies raise complex moral issues which will require extensive debate legally and politically. Questions about responsibility for the actions of a body which is not biologically 'owned' but made up of artificial parts or parts from the bodies of others will produce moral and legal dilemmas about issues of individual responsibility and ownership (Turner, 1992). Recent developments not only create new moral and legal dilemmas around the concept of the individual, but can also permit radical changes to what have traditionally been seen as 'natural' functions. Martin cites an example of a patented method by which a man's sperm can be 'washed' to remove those sperm that carry a gene complex which may predispose the individuals thus reproduced to certain diseases. She comments that this method 'profoundly affects and fragments the act of sexual intercourse for both men and women, replacing it with masturbation followed by chemical operations on the sperm and then artificial insemination' (Martin, 1992, p. 419). Equally, scientific advances can have far-reaching implications for social practices. Genetic testing for predisposition to certain diseases could be extended to the workplace, with employers including genetic assessment as part of the selection process for new appointments.

The ability to change one's body is neither new nor limited to science and medicine. Individuals have, from choice or coercion, frequently altered their bodies in a variety of ways. For example, the binding of women's feet in China to reshape the foot, the wearing of corsets to alter a woman's bodily shape in nineteenth-century Western societies, body piercing and tattooing, weight training to develop muscles, male and female circumcision and cosmetic surgery are all ways in which the body is altered for social rather than medical reasons. Such practices have consequences for self-identity. A nineteenth-century middle-class Western woman bound tightly into a corset (fashionable waist sizes in the 1880s were thirteen to sixteen inches) experiences her body as confined, a bodily experience that is reinforced by social conventions that require her to undertake little physical activity. The physical discomfort and even illness caused by overtight lacing is understood as emanating from her general fragility and predisposition to sickness rather than from the effects of excessive corsetry. If she has to sit down and rest frequently this is understood in terms of her 'natural' femininity rather than as a consequence of the artificial manipulation of her body. Thus, being a Western woman in the nineteenth century may come to mean feeling confined and often unwell.

The following letter to the agony column of a broadsheet newspaper suggests how closely body image is associated with self-identity.

> You'll think this a trivial problem, but last week I had beautiful long hair and I went to the hairdresser asking for a trim and he persuaded me to have it all cut off in a new, short style. Since then I have been beside myself with unhappiness. I cry every time I look in the mirror. People will say it will grow again, but it could take months or even years. I can't bear the idea of wearing a wig. I just don't look like me any more. But I can't understand why I am so depressed. I have even felt suicidal though I would never go ahead with it. (The *Independent*, 6 November 1997)

ACTIVITY 8.10

- Do you think the writer of the letter above is male or female? Give reasons for your answer.
- How would you respond to the writer's problem? Write a reply. If you are able, compare your response to that of other people. What assumptions about body image do these responses reveal?
- Try to imagine the effect on self-identity if you had never seen yourself in a mirror (or photograph). How might you experience your body? Would it be different?

In affluent contemporary Western societies the body has become a site for asserting or transforming identity. Like our homes, the body can be reconstructed in order to convey messages about who we are and how we want to be seen. Consumer culture encourages us to see our bodies as projects to be worked on through fitness regimes, diet, nutrition, clothing, make-up, body building and general self-care of our bodies (Rosen, 1983; Shilling, 1993).

These projects are not only about protecting our bodies from disease but also intimately connected with self-confidence and self-image. While there are undoubted advantages in the increased focus on our bodies, we should not forget that there is a lot of money to be made from selling body projects; nor, as yet, can we halt the inevitability of ageing. The modern concern with bodily perfection has implications for how we see ourselves as we get older and for how old age, physical disability and ageing are perceived and represented.

ACTIVITY 8.11

- Are fitness clinics, gyms and beauty clinics more accessible to certain groups of people than others?
- What consequences might there be for the way in which we see older people as a result of modern concerns with fitness, 'the body beautiful' and health?
- Are there implications for how older people might be treated (legally, medically, politically, socially) as a result of the ways in which ageing is constructed and represented?

Finally, we want to consider how the body functions as what Mary Douglas calls 'a symbol of society' (Douglas, 1966, p. 115).

Reading 8.8

In advanced consumer capitalism, as Robert Crawford has elegantly argued, an unstable agonistic construction of personality is produced by the contradictory structure of economic life [Crawford, 1985]. On the one hand, as producers of goods and services we must sublimate, delay, repress desires for immediate gratification; we must cultivate the work ethic. On the other hand, as consumers we must display a boundless capacity to capitulate to desire and indulge in impulse; we must hunger for constant and immediate satisfaction. The regulation of desire thus becomes an ongoing problem, as we find ourselves continually besieged by temptation, while socially condemned for overindulgence. (Of course, those who cannot afford to indulge their desires as consumers, teased and frustrated by the culture, face a much harsher dilemma.)

Food and diet are central arenas for the expression of these contradictions. On television and in popular magazines, with a flip of the page or barely a pause between commercials, images of luscious foods and the rhetoric of craving and desire are replaced by advertisements for grapefruit diets, low-calorie recipes, and exercise equipment. Even more disquieting than these manifest oppositions, however, are the constant attempts by advertisers to mystify them, suggesting that the contradiction doesn't really exist, that one can 'have it all'. Diets and exercise programs are accordingly presented with the imagery of instant gratification ('From Fat to Fabulous in 21 Days', 'Size 22 to Size 10 in No Time Flat', 'Six Minutes to an Oympic-Class Stomach') and effortlessness ('3,000 Sit-Ups Without Moving an Inch . . . 10 Miles of Jogging Lying Flat on Your Back' . . . '85 Pounds Without Dieting', and even, shamelessly, 'Exercise Without Exercise'). In reality, however, the opposition is not so easily reconciled. Rather, it presents a classic double bind, in which the self is torn in two mutually incompatible directions. The contradiction is not an abstract one but stems from the specific historical construction of a 'consuming passion' from which all inclinations toward balance, moderation, rationality, and foresight have been excluded.

Conditioned to lose control at the mere sight of desirable products, we can master our desires only by creating rigid defenses against them. The slender body codes the tantalizing ideal of well-managed self in which all is kept in order despite the contradictions of consumer-culture. Thus, whether or not the struggle is played out in terms of food and diet, many of us may find our lives vacillating between a daytime rigidly ruled by the 'performance principle' and nights and weekends that capitulate to unconscious 'letting go' (food, shopping, liquor, television, and other addictive drugs). In this way, the central contradiction of the system inscribes itself on our bodies, and bulimia emerges as a characteristic modern personality construction. For bulimia precisely and explicitly expresses the extreme development of the hunger for unrestrained consumption (exhibited in the bulimic's uncontrollable food binges) existing in unstable tension alongside the requirement that we sober up, 'clean up our act', get back in firm control on Monday morning (the necessity for purge – exhibited in the bulimic's vomiting, compulsive exercising, and laxative purges). (Bordo, 1990, pp. 96–7)

ACTIVITY 8.12

- Collect examples of exhortations to (a) let go, (b) restrain ourselves, (c) have it all in advertisements, on TV, in magazines and newspapers. Do you find these messages contradictory?
- Can you find examples in your own experience of patterns of binge and purge?
- Can you suggest ways in which the ideal of the slender body regulates or disciplines human populations? Consider figure 8.1.

Bordo suggests that 'the self is torn in two mutually incompatible directions'. This connects with the discussions of fragmented selves with which we began this chapter. However, can you see how Bordo's fragmented self is experienced through the physical body as well as known cognitively and patterned unconsciously? Subjectivity here is manifested in bodily practices – eating, drinking, exercise, purging – which are also social practices – enjoying

Figure 8.1   An illustration from *Fit Body*, number 16

leisure and going to work. Our bodies, what we do to them and how we use them are subject to social as well as biological processes. Thus, it becomes possible to speak of human beings as **embodied subjects**. Not only are we invited to locate ourselves linguistically, psychologically and cognitively in certain subject positions, but the body is 'directly involved in a political field; power relations have an immediate hold upon it; they invest it, mark it, train it, torture it, force it to carry out tasks, to perform ceremonies, to emit signs' (Foucault, 1975, p. 25).

Bordo cites Crawford's claim that the structures of economic capitalism produce an unstable personality formation, oscillating between 'immediate gratification' and self-discipline. Does this focus on a specific economic structure as the determining factor in the formation of a collective personality negate Lacan's theory of a mirror stage, the Imaginary and the self constituted in language? Is it possible to construct links between Lacan's theories and the points made here about embodied subjects? Can thinking about a particular form of economic life at a certain moment in history counteract the universalizing, ahistorical tendency of Lacan's theories of identity acquisition? These are not easy questions and, although we will leave you to think about them, we hope you will return to them by extending your reading in what is a complex but rewarding area. Refer to the suggestions for further reading for this chapter.

Conclusions

In conclusion we offer you a summary of the main points we have covered here.

- Subjectivity means our sense of ourself as separate from others, with the ability to act in the world we inhabit. It also, at the same time, involves a sense of being subject to, under the control of, something external to ourself, and at the mercy of desires, fantasies, impulses that are lodged deep in the unconscious and inaccessible to the conscious thinking mind of the subject (the unconscious is accessible only through the interpretations of the analyst in the process of psychoanalysis). In this way the subject does not create the social world he or she inhabits but is produced by it, through language and culture.
- Post-structuralist theories focus on the precariousness and unfinished nature of subjectivity. The idea of multiple and fragile subjectivities can be understood as cause for despair or the source of new forms of subjectivity which could challenge existing oppressions.
- Lacan's theories of how subjectivity is acquired rework Freudian ideas of the unconscious by focusing on the way language acts to constitute the subject. He also stresses the illusory and utopian nature of our desire for coherence and wholeness, represented by the mirror image.
- Subjectivity is not only acquired at the level of the unconscious. According to Althusser, ideology invites us, through language, to take up and 'recognize' ourselves in subject positions that are socially appropriate for specific situations. Foucault's concept of disciplinary power asserts that we also 'know' ourselves through our relations with others as constituted in the discourses that produce the material practices of 'race', sexuality, gender, nationality, class etc. It should be noted here that Foucault does not

himself deal directly with 'race', gender or nationality, but other theorists have drawn upon his ideas in order to offer analyses and challenges in these areas.

- We do not only experience ourselves through our minds and feelings but equally through our bodies. The body is not separated from thought and feeling but is a material entity on which struggles over identity and self-hood may be inscribed. For example, those who have undergone sex change operations often testify that they could not 'really' claim male or female identity, despite feeling themselves to be a woman or man, until their bodies were marked as female or male.
- The body can act as a 'symbol of society', representing society's anxieties and preoccupations. In this sense the body is not simply a biological entity but a social body structured by the formations of a particular social and economic system.

Chapter 9

Consumption

Introduction

In chapter 8 we ended our discussion with the argument that 'the contradictory structure of economic life' produces a 'preoccupation with the "internal" management of the body' (Bordo, 1990, p. 96). As Bordo explains, 'On the one hand, as 'producer-selves", we must be capable of sublimating, delaying, repressing desires for immediate gratification; we must cultivate the work ethic. On the other hand, as "consumer-selves" we serve the system through a boundless capacity to capitulate to desire and indulge in impulse.'

This chapter focuses on 'consumer-selves': that is, our role as purchasers of commodities and services, audiences for films and TV, and readers of visual and written texts such as advertisements. Bordo's point about the tension between 'producer-selves', bound by the work ethic, and 'consumer-selves', able to 'indulge in impulse', raises two important points which we are going to ask you to think about in this chapter. First, the two processes, production and consumption, are intimately and inextricably connected. Second, our willingness and capacity to consume is linked to deeply felt desires and impulses. Although much of our discussion is focused on the consumption of commodities, we are also consumers of a diversity of cultural forms, such as TV programmes, films, books, leisure activities and, as we discussed in chapters 4 and 6, history in the form of museums, artefacts and other 'heritage' products. Throughout this chapter we shall be asking you to consider how far, in our roles as consumers, we are able to appropriate such products as symbols of a desired identity, and how far choices about use and meaning are shaped by the concerns of producers.

If you keep these questions in mind as you work through the material it may help you to make sense of the arguments we are presenting. A final point: the recent focus on practices of consumption in sociology and cultural studies has led to the use of qualitative, ethnographic methods of research in which people are invited to talk about their own practices or are observed in everyday situations that involve consumption, such as shopping or watching television. Such approaches have proved valuable in complementing research methods that employ quantitative data or focus on textual analysis. The following studies are stimulating analyses that use qualitative, ethnographic research methods: Radway (1987), Gillespie (1989), Gullestad (1992) and Morley (1986, 1992).

What is a Consumer?

The ninth edition of the *Concise Oxford Dictionary* (1995) offers the following definitions of the word 'consumption':

1   the act or an instance of consuming; the process of being consumed.
2   any disease causing wasting of tissue, esp. pulmonary tuberculosis.
3   an amount consumed.
4   the purchase and use of goods etc.
5   use by a particular person or group.

As you can see, there is a rather negative set of ideas being associated with the process of consumption. Raymond Williams's outline of the shifting meanings of the word 'consumer' can help us to think about the processes involved in a little more detail.

Reading 9.1

In modern English *consumer* and *consumption* are the predominant descriptive nouns of all kinds of use of goods and services. The predominance is significant in that it relates to a particular version of economic activity, derived from the character of a particular economic system, as the history of the world shows. *Consume* has been in English since C14 . . . In almost all its early uses, *consume* had an unfavourable sense, it meant to destroy, to use up, to waste, to exhaust. This sense is still present in 'consumed by fire' and in the popular description of pulmonary phthisis as *consumption*. Early users of *consumer*, from C16, had the same general sense of destruction or waste.

> It was from [the mid] . . . C18 that *consumer* began to emerge in a neutral sense in the description of bourgeois political economy. In the new predominance of an organised market, the acts of making and of using goods and services were newly defined in the increasingly abstract pairings of *producer* and *consumer, production* and *consumption*. (Williams, 1976, pp. 78–9)

In a capitalist economy consumption is the necessary obverse of production. Goods are produced by using the (exploited, in Marxist terms) labour of people and the wealth of capitalist entrepreneurs. These goods are bought and used (consumed), thereby creating profit for those who own the means of production. Following Marx, production – the economic base – was seen as determining the ways in which commodities and cultural forms were received and used. As we saw in chapter 1, the emergence of mass media and mass production gave rise to concerns that people were being manipulated into forms of consumption that were not necessarily in their best interests, but simply served to maintain and reproduce capitalist and materialistic societies at the expense of any real morality or individual autonomy. A good example of this approach is Vance Packard's *The Hidden Persuaders*, published in 1957, in which the advertising industry is represented as a dangerous force that conditions and manipulates the responses of a passive populace. More recently studies have focused on the role of the consumer and debates about the degree of autonomy and choice, as well as the potential available in practices of consumption to resist and negotiate the power relation between producer and consumer. We shall look at some of these arguments later in the chapter but for now the point to think about is how production and consumption, rather than being in a relationship of direct cause and effect (production determines consumption) are constantly engaged in a process of negotiation. For example, in the 1980s when Coca-Cola tried to introduce a 'new' taste Coke in response to competition from Pepsi, this was commercially unsuccessful and they were forced by consumer resistance to return to the taste of 'classic Coke' (Miller, 1998, p. 171).

Buying a Newspaper

To help us think through an act of consumer choice and its place in the wider processes of cultural life, let us look at the act of buying a newspaper.

ACTIVITY 9.1

- If you regularly buy or read a newspaper, can you identify the different kinds of information you expect to be offered?
- Are there other places where you could, as easily, gain this information?
- What do you turn to first when you read a newspaper? Are there things you never read?
- Which newspapers do you read, and why?

While we may buy a paper to read about a major news event, we also use it to find out what's on the television, to read commentary and analysis of a sporting event, to read articles of general interest, to read gossip about celebrities, to find out the weather forecast, to enjoy cartoons, to peruse advertisements for goods and travel, to do the crossword or other puzzles, to read reviews of books, films, music, exhibitions, to find out what's on and where. Yet we can get much of the information we find in newspapers from other sources, so why do we bother to buy them? One answer might be that they provide us with a particular interpretation of events and activities: they offer a particular slant on a topic in the way in which they tell a story. The merely functional aspect of a newspaper is not, in the main, why people buy one; there is an element of choice as regards which paper you purchase and in exercising that choice you make a symbolic statement about who you are. You will already have a mental image of the kind of person who might read a particular kind of paper. Very often this image may be a crude stereotype, but it nevertheless indicates the way in which meanings are invested in the artefacts we purchase and consume during our daily lives. The producers of newspapers (owner, editor, journalists) attempt to shape the symbolic meanings that will be consumed by those who buy the papers by using language and codes which evoke the beliefs and values of its audience (Hartley, 1982, p. 96). In the next activity you can examine some of the ways in which this is apparent via a comparative study of two daily papers.

ACTIVITY 9.2

Buy a mass-circulation, popular newspaper and a quality newspaper. If you wish, you could use a local or regional daily paper instead of one of the nationals.

- Compare the front pages: what is the ratio of stories to pictures? Which stories are foregrounded?
- What kind of products are advertised? Is there a difference in the kinds of product advertised in the two papers you are comparing?

- Can you find any apparent contradictions in terms of opinion, belief, values etc., both within an individual paper and between the two? For example, does the tabloid celebrate the sporting achievements of a black player while containing an argument hostile to other sectors of the black community? Does the broadsheet include images of women on its fashion pages which contradict arguments on its editorial pages?
- Can you summarize the differences and similarities between the two papers' approach to news? What percentage of their stories are about political events? How many deal with elements of popular culture (the lives of soap, film or other celebrities; the stories of 'ordinary' people)?

By working through your chosen newspapers you should begin to build up a sense of the ways in which a given paper presented 'the news' on a particular day. While buying the paper on that day does not automatically mean that you subscribe wholeheartedly to the full spectrum of its views (you may, for example, have purchased a paper for this activity which you wouldn't normally read), the newspaper corporations themselves, and the advertisers who buy space in newspapers, clearly do believe that certain groups of people read certain kinds of papers. When we buy a newspaper we are involved in an act of consumer choice that is also about expressing a sense of or desire for a particular self-identity. For example, advertisers who buy space in newspapers increasingly use **psychographic** variables, such as the ones listed below, in order to classify and target specific consumers.

Trendies	Those who crave the admiration of their peers
Egoists	Those who seek pleasure
Puritans	Those who wish to feel virtuous
Innovators	Those who wish to make their mark
Rebels	Those who wish to remake the world in their image
Groupies	Those who just want to be accepted
Drifters	Those who are not sure what they want
Drop outs	Those who shun commitments of any kind
Traditionalists	Those who want things to stay as they are
Utopians	Those who want the world to be a better place
Cynics	Those who have to have something to complain about
Cowboys	Those who want easy money

(Selby and Cowdery, 1995, p. 25)

ACTIVITY 9.3 Can you identify ways in which your chosen newspapers from activity 9.2 target any of these groups?

You may have noted that buying and reading a newspaper is a good example of consumption as 'using up' and often 'waste'. Think about what happens to your daily newspaper when you have finished with it. Newspapers are a particular example of a disposable commodity: they are not meant to be durable or lasting. This applies literally – the material object can be thrown away or used to wrap rubbish in – and metaphorically – the items of news, gossip and information are ephemeral and quickly replaced by new stories and information. Environmentalists have advocated the recycling of used paper, including newspapers, and many people, concerned with the ethics of a 'throw-away' society, now actively choose this option rather than simply disposing of newspapers as rubbish. Choices about buying and reading a specific newspaper are not the only ones available to us: we are also invited to assert certain ethical values in the ways in which we choose to dispose of the paper.

My High Street and Your High Street

Figure 9.1 is a schematic diagram of a suburban shopping area. This area is less than a kilometre from the centre of the city which has a much greater range of shops, and is over a kilometre from a large supermarket by car or bus. The area around the shops includes Victorian and Edwardian terraced housing, 1930s and 1940s semi-detached homes with gardens, and more modern developments, ranging from an estate of semi-detached properties, immediately behind the shopping area, to low-rise flats and sheltered accommodation.

In the past week, I (Tim Middleton) have gone into properties 2, 5, 18 and 23. Over the past year, I have been into all properties bar numbers 3, 6, 7, 8, 11, 19, 20, 22, 27, 28, 30 and 32. I have lived in this area for over five years and in that time I have visited all the properties bar 6, 7, 20, 22, 30 and 32. In this shopping area I have purchased items ranging from stamps through to a house, but in the main I use the shops for convenience: buying items I have run out of; buying takeaway food when I can't be bothered to cook. The bulk of my shopping is done on a weekly basis in a large supermarket on the

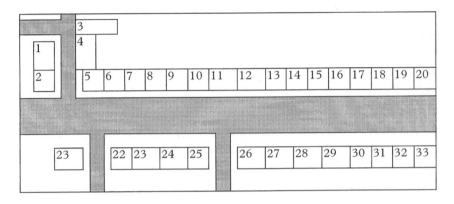

Key

1 Delicatessen.
2 Small supermarket.
3 Carpet and bed shop.
4 Hairdresser.
5 Newsagent and Post Office.
6 Optician.
7 Card shop.
8 Solicitor.
9 Video rental shop.
10 Chinese restaurant.
11 Charity shop.
12 Freezer shop.
13 Indian restaurant.
14 Greengrocer.
15 Pizza takeaway.
16 Ironmonger.
17 Café.

18 Bicycle shop.
19 Estate agent
20 Bookmaker.
21 Antique shop.
22 Italian takeaway.
23 Newsagent.
24 Pharmacy.
25 Fish and chip shop.
26 Small supermarket.
27 Pet shop.
28 Butcher.
29 Greengrocer.
30 Beer and wine making supplies.
31 Chinese takeaway.
32 Launderette.
33 Antique shop.

Figure 9.1 A suburban shopping area

edge of town, and many other purchases, including products for sale near to my home, are also made elsewhere.

ACTIVITY 9.4

- Using the map in figure 9.1 track the journeys you would make if you were reliant upon this range of shops alone for your purchasing over a month. What things can't you buy? What would you normally buy elsewhere?
- All the businesses featured (apart from the Post Office) are local. What would be the difference if the businesses were national chains or international chains?

- By changing the type of shop, tailor the high street to the kind of things you want to buy. What is the difference in terms of the businesses present? How far have you replaced premises supplying basic needs (food, medicines etc.) with those selling less essential lifestyle commodities, e.g. TV, musical instruments, designer clothes, sports gear?

The link between consumption and consumer choice raises a number of issues. When we shape a complex of shops in our own image we are very likely to deny the needs of others: at a basic level you can examine this by exploring the difference between your responses to the exercise above and those of a friend or colleague. In the example above, replacing the small supermarkets with a department store, turning the charity shop into a Gap and the Chinese into a Michelin three-star restaurant might suit us if we are used to an affluent lifestyle in New York or London but is unlikely to be of much use if our income is restricted to meeting basic needs as cheaply as possible.

What makes a large designer fashion store a different place to buy clothes from a charity shop, in the end, comes down to economic factors, but these cannot be easily separated from issues of ideology and identity. And, while consumers can create identities for themselves and for social groups from the range of material objects and cultural products available, such as theatres, football and cinema, the consumer is not always, nor inevitably, in complete control of either the meanings of products or their availability. The example of a suburban shopping zone points up the varied needs of a consuming public by suggesting that acts of consumption can be occasions when we do make meanings out of the world around us. However, these take place through a process of negotiation between the requirement to service our needs and desires and the demands of producers to ensure profitability.

ACTIVITY 9.5

If you have access to newspapers on the web you could search for articles on the setting up of a department store or designer fashion shop in a town or area that you are familiar with. Think about the various interests being catered for. Look back to activity 6.6 for suggestions on how to do this. This could be the start of a longer research project on department stores. (See, for example, du Gay, 1997, for an analysis of the fashion store Benetton)

Having introduced you to the idea of consumer choice and its connection to production and identity, let us begin to explore some of the critical perspectives that explain the relationship between consumption and production.

Theories of Consumption

Broadly speaking, thinking about consumption can focus upon:

- the economic and global impact of consumer activity, positioning consumers as the passive victims of capitalism;
- the ways in which acts of consumption are a creative and active way in which individuals articulate their own identity;
- the ways in which economic and global structures of production are inextricably linked with individual acts of consumer choice.

It is unlikely in contemporary cultural or sociological studies that you will encounter the first position extremely stated. Between these three positions there are a wide range of intermediate positions, and in this chapter we are interested in how far consumption can be an active practice through which people are able to influence what is produced, as well as using 'taste', artefacts and products to construct and express certain identities.

As Williams observed (reading 9.1), the emergence of the consumer as a distinct social role has been a major factor in the shift to a capitalist mode of production, and one approach to the study of consumption has been derived from Marxist thinking about the relationship between individuals and society under capitalism. This approach to the study of consumption, which derives from Marx's ideas about political economy, is one which stresses individuals as trapped within a system of exchange over which ultimately they have little control. John Storey offers the following summary of Marxist ideas regarding consumption.

Reading 9.2

The cultural analysis of consumption begins in the political concerns of Marxism. In order to understand the classical Marxist account of consumption, we must know something about how it conceives the difference between capitalist and pre-capitalist social formations. Pre-capitalist societies (feudalism in Britain, for example) were not consumer societies in that goods were made mostly for immediate consumption or use or to be exchanged for other goods. It is only after the collapse of feudalism and the emergence of capitalism, a system based on the market, on money and on profit, that consumption becomes detached from simple needs and emerges as a significant aspect of human activity.

For Karl Marx and Frederick Engels, the transition from feudalism to capitalism was a transition from production driven by need to production driven by profit. Moreover, in capitalist societies, workers make goods in return for wages. They do not own the goods; the goods are sold on the market at a profit. Therefore to get goods, workers have to buy them with money. Thus: workers become 'consumers', and we have the emergence of 'consumer society'. To ensure the making of profits, people must consume. Therefore consumption is artificially stimulated by advertising. One consequence of this is 'alienation'. According to Marx . . . alienation results from 'the fact that labour is external to the worker . . . the worker feels himself only when he is not working . . . His labour is therefore . . . not the satisfaction of a need but a mere means to satisfy needs outside itself' . . .

In other words, men and women are denied identity in (uncreative) production, and are therefore forced to seek identity in (creative) consumption. But this is always little more than a hollow substitute (a fetish). Moreover, the process is encouraged by the so-called ideology of consumerism – the suggestion that the meaning of our lives is to be found in what we consume, rather than in what we produce. Thus the ideology legitimates and encourages the profit-making concerns of capitalism (a system demanding an ever increasing consumption of goods). (Storey, 1996, pp. 113–14).

Marx's ideas may seem a little abstract and, certainly, seem to suggest that as consumers we are merely powerless functionaries of a grand capitalist master plan. There seems to be little space for what many people might see (perhaps hedonistically) as the enjoyable dimension to consumption. People actually do enjoy consuming and do believe that consumption has significant meaning in terms of their identity. Slavenka Drakulic quotes a frequent complaint from women in Eastern Europe: 'Look at us – we don't even look like women. There are no deodorants, perfumes, sometimes even no soap or toothpaste. There is no fine underwear, no pantyhose, no nice lingerie. Worst of all, there are no sanitary napkins. What can one say except that it is humiliating' (Drakulic, 1992, p. 31).

ACTIVITY 9.6

Drakulic writes about conditions prior to the collapse of communism in Eastern Europe. Do you think that the desire of Eastern European women for consumer goods is a hollow substitute for a real identity that has been lost with the advent of capitalism? How do you respond to their feeling that the lack of consumer products is humiliating?

The first serious attempt to study the role of consumers was by Thorstein Veblen, who studied the consumption patterns of the newly affluent North American bourgeois in the late nineteenth century (Veblen, 1899). Veblen's studies demonstrated that, rather than being at the mercy of capitalist production, people were able to assert their social status, not only through the wealth they accumulated, but also via a display of the products and services they purchased – what he termed 'conspicuous consumption'. Commodities and services acted as symbolic markers of affluence and status in addition to or regardless of their functional necessity. An example will serve to illustrate this. In Britain in the late nineteenth and early twentieth centuries, owning a piano was a sign of status and respectability, as well as having use-value as a form of leisure. Even families with little spare money aspired to owning a piano, which was often displayed in the 'parlour' or best room, Possessing a piano was a form of 'conspicuous consumption' and some people were prepared to spend beyond their means in order to be able to demonstrate their identity as respectable, piano-owning members of society. You might remind yourself of the case study in chapter 6, where we discussed the ways in which purchasing a holiday functioned as a means of asserting distance from some social groups and allegiance with others. It could be argued that people did not 'need' pianos any more than people in contemporary societies 'need' stereo systems or exotic holidays. The cultural theorist Herbert Marcuse claimed that these are 'false needs' orchestrated by advertisers and the manufacturers of pianos or stereo systems in order to lure us into a cycle of consumer desire and gratification (Marcuse, 1964). For example, the argument runs, we buy convenience foods because the demands of paid work leave little time to cook, but the money we earn is spent on expensive foods that could be made more cheaply at home if we were not 'forced' to spend so much time at work earning the money to pay for these expensive foods, as well as other consumer items we have been manipulated by producers and advertisers into believing we 'need'. In this way consumption is seen as determined by the overriding logic of capitalist production: put crudely, we only consume because manufacturers require us to. Now read the following extract from an essay by Theodor Adorno and Max Horkheimer which argues that the cultures we consume, in the same ways as material commodities, are equally determined by the mechanisms of consumer capitalism.

Reading 9.3

The sociological theory that the loss of the support of objectively established religion, the dissolution of the last remnants of precapitalism, together with technological and social differentiation or specialization, have led to cultural chaos is disproved every day; for culture now impresses the same stamp on everything. Films, radio and magazines make up a system which is uniform as a whole and in every part. Even the aesthetic activities of political opposites are one in their enthusiastic obedience to the rhythm of the iron system . . . Under monopoly all mass culture is identical, and the lines of its artificial framework begin to show through. The people at the top are no longer so interested in concealing monopoly: as its violence becomes more open, so its power grows. Movies and radio need no longer pretend to be art. The truth that they are just business is made into an ideology in order to justify the rubbish they deliberately produce. They call themselves industries; and when their directors' incomes are published, any doubt about the social utility of the finished products is removed . . .

[T]he basis on which technology acquires power over society is the power of those whose economic hold over society is greatest. A technological rationale is the rationale of domination itself . . . It has made the technology of the culture industry no more than the achievement of standardization and mass production, sacrificing whatever involved a distance between the logic of the work and that of the social system. This is the result not of a law of movement in technology as such but of its function in today's economy. The need which might resist central control has already been suppressed by the control of the individual consciousness. The step from the telephone to the radio has clearly distinguished the roles. The former still allowed the subscriber to play the role of subject, and was liberal. The latter is democratic: it turns all participants into listeners and authoritatively subjects them to broadcast programmes which are all exactly the same. (Adorno and Horkheimer, 1947, extracted in During, 1993, pp. 30–1)

ACTIVITY 9.7

- Consider the significance of the phrase 'culture industry'. Remind yourself of our discussions in chapter 1 about Arnold and about mass culture. Why do you think Adorno and Horkheimer, writing in the mid-1940s, chose this phrase? Is it purely descriptive?
- Adorno and Horkheimer were living in the United States when they wrote this essay. They were refugees from Hitler's Germany and had experienced state control of cultural production. Can you think of any ways (or examples) in which US cultural production in the 1940s might have led them to their conclusions about the determining force of capitalist production? In order to answer this you may need to consult further reading. The following are suggestions: Gomery (1976), Schatz (1981), Bordwell et al. (1985), Turner (1993, pp. 14–18).

There are a number of points to note in what has been called 'the production of consumption' perspective (du Gay et al., 1997, p. 86). First, as we have seen, this perspective treats consumption as *an effect* of production, thus denying the possibility of human agency. As consumers, it is argued, we have 'needs' that are created and then satisfied by the producers of goods, services and media, and as such are 'false' or inauthentic. Second, consumption has been perceived as less serious than the work of producing goods, services and culture. As well as being seen as a passive activity, consumption is linked to hedonism, pleasure, frivolity – it is less important than the serious work of industry, or finance, or commercial administration. Furthermore, consumption is seen as something that takes place in the private sphere of home and family, whether it be buying a house, watching a TV programme, reading a book, purchasing a piano or replacing a car. As such, it is less authentic as a way of creating a sense of identity than the world of paid work, where a 'real' sense of self can be established. You may have begun to notice an implied gender dimension: consumption appears to be allied to conventional feminine attributes, such as passivity and domesticity, and production to masculine attributes, such as paid labour and activity. The 'production of consumption' perspective relies on a set of oppositional terms in which one term of the opposition is always more dominant or highly valued: production/consumption; true needs/false needs; work/pleasure; active/passive; public/private; art/mass culture; male/female.

Extending the work of Veblen, two recent theorists have contested the 'production of consumption' approach, offering ways in which consumption can be seen, more positively, as linked to culture and identity, rather than as simply the effect of economic phenomena. Jean Baudrillard contested Marcuse's typology of 'false' and 'natural' needs, arguing that while producers do attempt to create markets and therefore a 'need' for a certain product, particularly through advertising, consumers are able to resist the precise blandishments and injunctions of advertising and instead 'play with "needs" on a keyboard of objects' (Baudrillard, 1988, p. 45). As Baudrillard argues, 'We know that advertising is not omnipotent and at times produces opposite reactions: and we know that in relation to a single 'need', objects can be substituted for one another.' Consumption, rather than being simply an economic practice, is also a system of signs that produce meaning in ways similar to language (see chapter 3). Indeed, Baudrillard suggests that 'marketing, purchasing, sales, the acquisition of differentiated commodities and object/signs – all of these presently constitute our language, a code with which our entire society communicates and speaks of and to itself' (ibid.).

As you read the next extract, from a piece by the journalist Suzanne Moore, try to formulate responses to the following questions:

- Is her discussion of these adverts about the product ostensibly being marketed? Is it about something else? If so, why does she focus on advertisements for Lee jeans, Nissan cars and Wallis clothes shop?
- Can you connect Baudrillard's point that commodities and objects, advertising and purchasing constitute a language in which we speak of and to ourselves with the point Moore is making about the three adverts she describes?

Reading 9.4

What Girl Power Means

I am as concerned as the next woman about adverts which show women being violent towards men. I don't think there are anything like enough of them. The three ads that have been singled out by the Advertising Standards Authority – for Lee Jeans, showing a woman's stiletto-heeled boot resting on the buttock of a naked man, with the slogan 'Put the Boot in', the Nissan ad with a man clutching his crotch and the line 'Ask Before You Borrow It' and the Dress to Kill campaign for Wallis which shows men in danger of being killed because they are distracted by beautiful women – have attracted almost 100 complaints. The complaints were not upheld, but the ASA has warned advertising agencies that they should think twice about using such 'Girl Power' imagery . . .

It is fitting that Girl Power should be a concept picked up by the ad industry. For Girl Power is, in essence, a kind of re-branding [of feminism] . . .

The fragility of contemporary masculinity is wondrous to behold. Is it such a delicate thing, that it must be protected at all times by bodies such as the Advertising Standards Authority? Women, I suppose, are simply hardened by being bombarded by imagery about what women should be, so they take it all rather lightly – unless of course they acquire an eating disorder and kill themselves. (Moore, 1997)

Moore uses advertisements as a way of discussing gender relations more widely. In doing so she is assuming a shared understanding on the part of her readership about how advertisements work. Part of this shared understanding is the recognition that advertisements play on our preoccupations, our fantasies and our desires – we all 'know' that advertising is trying to manipulate us. At the same time, we 'know' that advertisements use puns, storylines and imagery that offer visual and other pleasures. We also 'know' how to resist advertisers' exhortations to take up the positions offered in advertisements. Watching the Nissan advertisement, in which it is suggested that a man has been subjected to violence for borrowing his girlfriend's car, is unlikely to result in widescale attacks on males by young women. Yet, as Moore points out, it speaks to unconscious desires around domination and submission and is expressing something about the relations between the sexes in the late 1990s. If you doubt this think about whether this advertisement would have been possible or comprehensible ten or twenty years earlier. We are able to 'read' the advertisements Moore refers to because we understand the visual and graphic languages in which the ideas are inscribed. The advertisements constitute a language or a code with which we communicate just as much as the language or codes of political institutions or medical science. Moore engages with this language in order to explore how society in the 1990s 'speaks of and to itself' on the subject of gender relations. At the same time, the advertisements themselves invite us to buy not only the product but also the desires that they encode. When we buy cars, jeans or fashion clothes we are not able to do so from outside this communicative exchange. It would be very difficult to be entirely neutral or ignorant of the marketing and advertising of the products we purchase. This does not mean we are unable to resist these strategies: we can and do, buying products for other purposes than advertised, appropriating them for our own use and needs, but whenever we do so we cannot but remain aware of what it is we are resisting or adapting. For example, I (Judy Giles) might buy a pair of Lee jeans because they are comfortable and hardwearing, not because advertising tells me they are the fashionable attire of a young, modern *femme fatale*. Nevertheless, at some level I am aware of these coded meanings in order to resist them and insist to myself that middle-aged women can also buy Lee jeans, that they are not only for the young nor is their function purely a sexual one. In doing so, I am saying something about the world I live in and who I am, and I am doing so using the language of material objects, in this case a pair of jeans.

We want to turn now to the ideas of the French sociologist Pierre Bourdieu. So far we have talked about the consumption of objects such as cars or jeans without considering how people are situated differently with regard to their consumption of such products. Obviously, the richer people are, the more choice they have about what, where and when they purchase material objects. This is also true of cultural products: the price of a ticket for the opera may prohibit many people from enjoying this form of culture. Bourdieu developed Veblen's theory of 'conspicuous consumption' by linking consumption more tightly to social class in a study of patterns of consumption in France in the

1960s and 1970s. In order to introduce you to Bourdieu's ideas, we have chosen an extract from his study of the consumption of what he calls 'sports products' in France. However, before you read this we offer a brief introduction to some of his key ideas in order to help you to get the most out of the reading.

Bourdieu argues that any individual's capacity to consume is determined by variations in economic capital (the amount of money for disposal) and cultural capital (what we learn from the family and education). We develop 'tastes' for certain objects as a result of what he calls **habitus**. Habitus refers to a web of knowledge that we gain from the family, our understanding of classification systems such as class and the 'common-sense', taken-for-granted assumptions we operate with, which together predispose us to see objects in terms of whether or not they are appropriate for us as particular kinds of persons. For example, it could be argued that the habitus of some people predisposes them to develop a 'taste' for books, which are then consumed in terms of how much money is available but also in terms of the symbolic value of possessing books and the knowledge therein – what Bourdieu calls 'cultural capital'. Bourdieu shows how French working-class people preferred food that expressed abundance and solidity – red meat, bread and cheese and 'rough' red wine – while middle-class food tastes were for a healthy diet, aesthetic presentation and 'correct' preparation. The point to grasp is that Bourdieu is not suggesting that consumption is a direct reflection of class, but that class differences are constructed through people's ideas about the 'appropriate' products for consumption. A final note: when Bourdieu writes of 'fractions of the dominant class' he has in mind a distinction between those whose social position results from economic capital – wealth and affluence – and those whose social position is derived from cultural capital – education and learning.

Reading 9.5

I think that, without doing too much violence to reality, it is possible to consider the whole range of sporting activities and entertainments offered to social agents . . . as a *supply* intended to meet a *social demand*. If such a model is adopted, two sets of questions arise. First, is there an area of production, endowed with its own logic and its own history, in which 'sports products' are generated . . . Secondly, what are the social conditions of possibility of the appropriation of the various 'sports products' that are thus produced . . . In other words, how is the demand for 'sports products' produced, how do people acquire the 'taste' for sport, and for one sport rather than another, whether as an activity or as a spectacle? . . .

Thus, most of the team sports – basketball, handball, rugby, football – which are most common among office workers, technicians and shopkeepers, and also no doubt the most typically working-class individual sports, such as boxing or wrestling, combine all the reasons to repel the upper classes. These include the social composition of their public which reinforces the vulgarity implied by their popularization, the values and virtues demanded (strength, endurance, the propensity to violence, the spirit of 'sacrifice', docility and submission to collective discipline, the absolute antithesis of the 'rôle distance' implied in bourgeois rôles, etc.), the exaltation of competition and the contest, etc. To understand how the most distinctive sports, such as golf, riding, skiing or tennis, or even some less recherché ones, like gymnastics or mountaineering, are distributed among the social classes and especially among the fractions of the dominant class, it is even more difficult to appeal solely to variations in economic and cultural capital or in spare time. This is firstly because it would be to forget that, no less than the economic obstacles, it is the hidden entry requirements, such as family tradition and early training, and also the obligatory clothing, bearing and techniques of sociability which keep these sports closed to the working classes and to individuals rising from the lower-middle and even upper-middle classes; and secondly because economic constraints define the field of possibilities and impossibilities without determining within it an agent's positive orientation towards this or that particular form of practice. In reality, even apart from any search for distinction, it is the relation to one's own body, a fundamental aspect of the habitus, which distinguishes the working classes from the privileged classes, just as, within the latter, it distinguishes fractions that are separated by the whole universe of a life-style. On one side, there is the instrumental relation to the body which the working classes express in all the practices centred on the body, whether in dieting or beauty care, relation to illness or medication, and which is also manifested in the choice of sports requiring a considerable investment of effort, sometimes of pain and suffering (e.g. boxing) and sometimes a gambling with the body itself (as in motor-cycling, parachute-jumping, all forms of acrobatics, and, to some extent, all sports involving fighting, among which we may include rugby). On the other side, there is the tendency of the privileged classes to treat the body as an *end in itself,* with variants according to whether the emphasis is placed on the intrinsic functioning of the body as an organism, which leads to the macrobiotic cult of health, or on the appearance of the body as a perceptible configuration, the 'physique', i.e. the body-for-others. Everything seems to suggest that the concern to cultivate the body appears, in its most elementary form, i.e. as the cult of health, often implying an ascetic exaltation of sobriety and dietetic rigour, among the lower-middle classes, i.e. among junior executives, clerical workers in the medical services and especially primary-school teachers, who indulge particularly intensively in gymnastics, the ascetic sport *par excellence* since it amounts to a sort of training (*askesis*) for training's sake . . .

It is doubtless among the professions and the well-established business bourgeoisie that the health-giving and aesthetic functions are combined with social functions;

there, sports take their place, along with parlour games and social exchanges (receptions, dinners, etc.), among the 'gratuitous' and 'disinterested' activities which enable the accumulation of social capital. This is seen in the fact that, in the extreme form it assumes in golf, shooting, and polo in smart clubs, sporting activity is a mere pretext for select encounters or, to put it another way, a technique of sociability, like bridge or dancing. (Bourdieu, 1978, reprinted in During, 1993, pp. 340, 353–5)

- Look for examples in magazines, on TV and in the newspapers of the distinctions between 'sports products' that Bourdieu identifies.
- Think about the sports that you, and those you know, engage in either as a spectator or as a participant. Are Bourdieu's assertions about the relationship between class and different sports borne out in your experience?
- Can you suggest ways in which gender, disability, ethnicity or age cut across the class distinctions that are, according to Bourdieu, constructed through the consumption of sports?
- Remind yourself of the discussion of identity and the body in chapter 8. Can you make connections between what was said there and what Bourdieu is saying?

We would suggest that while Bourdieu draws attention to the ways in which practices of consumption are simultaneously economic *and* symbolic acts, thus avoiding the pessimism of theorists like Adorno and Horkheimer, he none the less remains constrained by his focus on the structural forces of class. He is therefore unable to explain the variety of ways in which people actively use the products they consume, be it a particular sport, a TV programme, a pair of jeans or a car, in creating meaningful identities for *themselves*. For example, the engagement in football, as spectators, by upwardly mobile young men, as part of the construction of a 'laddish' identity, involves the appropriation of a sport traditionally associated with the working classes. And this new identity can be seen as a response to changing gender relations rather than a need for young men to ally themselves with the working classes or to reproduce distinctions between classes.

Bourdieu's approach, which used questionnaires, is not dissimilar to that used by market research companies and the media in order to profile social stereotypes for the purposes of monitoring consumer behaviour and identifying lifestyles. Look carefully at figure 9.2, which represents a typology of male lifestyles. Notice how much of the profiling is linked to what each stereotype supposedly consumes. You may not recognize all the references in this article but you can get the gist of what it is saying.

9/NEW MEN

Happy? No, they're just drinking to forget the angst and confusion brought on by the existential ills facing the modern male ...

Nineties Man is angst-ridden, confused and selfish. According to marketing experts, "New Man" is a figment of female imagination, while "New Lad" is a cop-out. Kathy Marks charts a dismal diagnosis of the existential ills of the modern male.

It was so simple a few decades ago. Men were men, and the world was constructed in such a way that they never doubted it. The institutions of static, family and work combined to create and nurture their masculine identity.

Massive social and economic changes since the 1960s have played havoc with the old certainties, shattering men's confidence and leaving them floundering, unsure of self.

This is the dire picture painted by Chad Wollen, an analyst at the Henley Centre for Forecasting. Men are doomed, Mr Wollen told a conference organised by Channel 4, unless they emulate women and learn to cope with an insecure and volatile world. In earlier times, men knew exactly why they existed: to impregnate their wives, bring home the money and protect their families. But all three functions have been profoundly undermined.

Today Nineties Man, who derives self-esteem from being the breadwinner. Nearly 70 per cent of women aged 20 to 59 now work. In their procreational capacity, too, men are far from indispensable, given the latest advances in reproductive science (not to mention falling sperm counts). As for the strong figure procuring his family from danger – research

by the Henley Centre shows that men are increasingly fearful about their own safety.

The institutions which reinforced the classic male image have disintegrated, Mr Wollen argued. The job for life, the traditional family and the paternalistic state no longer exist. In their place are far more fluid and unpredictable structures.

How, then, does modern man handle his identity crisis? Does he rise to the challenge, seek fresh roles, adapt to a shifting society? No, he buries his head, ostrich-like, and pretends that it will all go away.

Day to day, he relies on Nineties Woman to pick up the pieces. Women are now looking after families, jobs, and – most importantly for men – men," said Mr Wollen.

Alternatively, the contemporary male buys his way out of responsibilities. If his wife is not around to cook, he orders in a pizza. If there is housework or childcare to be dealt with, he engages domestic help and nannies.

More and more, he seeks relief from stress through drink and drugs. "Nineties Man is trying to pretend that the world hasn't changed," Mr Wollen said. "When all else fails, he goes out for a beer."

He dismissed New Man – the caring, sharing, nappy-changing 1980s male – as a product of wishful female thinking, and poured scorn on New Lad – the football, sex and booze-obsessed Irish man – as a puerile backlash.

"Men are regressing to a time when the old stereotypes still held true. The Lad is an incredible powerful image, but it's not an adult response. Men have to learn about flexibility and uncertainty. They have to understand that they can't be masters of the universe."

Keeping up appearances: For all his bravado, experts believe that Nineties Man may be suffering a unprecedented identity crisis stemming from the demise of traditional certainties

WHICH TYPE OF NINETIES MAN ARE YOU?

Sean Kelleher, business development manager at Channel 4, has identified five "social stereotypes".

Nathan:
Aged 15-34, mainly from ABC1 class. Appearance is important to Nathan: he enjoys spending money on clothes and skin-care products. He goes out to clubs and wine bars, and is athletic and sporty. Nathan's body is a temple. He regards cooking as a chore, likes eating out in ethnic restaurants and drinks strong beers and lagers such as Lowenbrau. He loves hi-tech gadgets and computers, makes a lot of money, and is bad at managing money.

Dave:
Mainly 15-34, with a C2DE bias. Dave is more settled. He likes his home comforts and spends a lot of time on the sofa, particular when there is football or wrestling on the television. He wears designer labels, shops at Sainsbury's and avoids health foods. Dave enjoys a night out in the pub, drinks lagers such as Labatts and believes that real men should down numerous pints at one sitting. He goes to dog races and plans to buy a satellite dish next year.

Mark:
Mainly 35-54, with an ABC1 bias. Mark is self-assured and confident, a top earner and a National Lottery enthusiast. He knows what he wants out of life and works hard to achieve it. He has staid tastes in fashion, plays squash or badminton once a week and drives a family saloon car. Mark enjoys food, over-indulgence to the point of over-indulgence, and drinks French imported beers. He watches The Grille and probably has a pension.

Brian:
Mainly aged 35-54, C2DE class. Brian has "downmarket" cultural tastes. He watches a lot of television, particularly Sky football, and reads newspapers to keep up with showbusiness gossip rather than world affairs. He likes expensive aftershaves, takeaway meals and gadgets. Brian goes on package holidays and when abroad, wants only to eat, drink and lie in the sun. He despises vegetarians and real ales, and bottled lager is not a man's drink.

Philip:
Aged 55 plus, mainly ABC1. Philip wants to be a Nineties Man, but has deeply-rooted traditional male values. He loves fine wines and gardening, and reads the financial pages to keep tabs on his investments. He takes holidays in Europe, buys organic produce and may be a vegetarian. He exercises by taking long walks, is not obsessed with his appearance and is financially sophisticated. He is a connoisseur who drinks beers such as Theakstons.

Figure 9.2 'New Men'

ACTIVITY 9.9

List the different forms of consumption that are identified in this typology. We have started you off.

- Drinks
- Holidays
-
-
-
-
-

Is there any evidence in these profiles of the taste for different sports identified by Bourdieu?

Selling Identities

Let us pursue the relationship between acts of consumption and individual identity further via a reading from travel writer Jonathan Raban's account of the modern city as an 'emporium of styles'.

Reading 9.6

In the city, we are barraged with images of the people we might become. Identity is presented as plastic, a matter of possessions and appearances; and a very large proportion of the urban landscape is taken up by slogans, advertisements, flatly photographed images of folk heroes – the man who turned into a sophisticated dandy overnight by drinking a particular brand of vodka, the girl who transformed herself into a latter day Mata Hari with a squirt of cheap scent. The tone of the wording of these advertisements is usually pert and facetious, comically drowning in its own hyperbole. But the photographs . . . are brutally exact: they reproduce every detail of a style of life, down to the brand of cigarette lighter, the stone in the ring, and the economic row of books on the shelf . . .

For the new arrival, this disordered abundance is the city's most evident and alarming quality. He feels as if he has parachuted into a funfair of contradictory imperatives. There are so many people he might become, and a suit of clothes, a make of car, a brand of cigarettes, will go some way towards turning him into a personage even before he has discovered who that personage is. Personal identity has always been deeply rooted in property, but hitherto the relationship has been a simple one – a question of buying what you could afford, and leaving your wealth to announce your status. In the modern city, there are so many things to buy, such a quantity of different kinds of status, that the choice and its attendant anxieties have created a new pornography of taste. The leisure pages of the Sunday newspapers, fashion maga-zines, TV plays, popular novels, cook books, window displays all nag at the nerve of our uncertainty and snobbery . . . The piece of furniture, the pair of shoes, the book, the film, are important not so much in themselves but for what they communicate about their owners; and ownership is stretched to include what one likes or believes in as well as what one can buy. (Raban, 1974, pp. 64, 66)

Raban may have been writing over thirty years ago, but his account of the relationship between consumption and identity still seems to ring true today. Sunday newspapers, for example, often carry style sections which include regular reports on what is currently fashionable, with information about where the products featured can be purchased. Such columns also inform their readers about what is no longer considered stylish or fashionable. While most readers will not immediately rush out to buy the goods featured, it is obvious that this kind of column works by linking a certain kind of identity both with the products and with the newspaper itself. What this suggests is that the stereotypes and profiles used by the media are not simply figments of a journalist's or advertiser's imagination. They frequently do have some basis in the world outside marketing; otherwise, how would we recognize aspects of ourselves or people we know in them? Stereotypes work by selecting certain characteristics from the multitude of ways in which people are con-stituted, and asserting these as all there is to be known about a person. In doing so they reduce complicated and fluid identities to one or two 'typical' features, which then come to represent the whole person. Thus, while stereo-types are not direct reflections of real people, they are connected to the exter-nal world in complex ways.

ACTIVITY 9.10

- Look back at the profiles of 'nineties man' in figure 9.2. Do you recognize parts of yourself or anyone you know in these descriptions?
- Try to produce your own profiles of 'twenty-first-century man' or 'twenty-first-century woman'. This would work best if done with other people. Identify the problems you encounter in doing this and try to analyse why you encountered the particular problems you did.
- Look through magazines, advertisements and newspapers. Do you find yourself identifying, at least in part, with any of the stereotypes you encounter?
- Look at the Saturday edition of a range of daily papers. What columns and sections appear only at the weekend? What does this suggest about the projected readership in terms of leisure pursuits etc?

- Look at the review sections of daily papers or monthly magazines. Compare, for example, the *New York Times* book section with the books section of *Marie Claire* magazine. Are any of the same texts reviewed? What are the differences between the reviews? How does the range of works covered construct the idea of a typical reader? You can do the same kind of activity comparing style or cookery pages.
- Look at the style supplements of a range of newspapers. What items emerge as 'must have' products for the 'style slave'? Can you find any of these in the homes of yourself or people you know?

Look now at the advertisement for Tilda's Madhur Jaffrey range of Indian sauces (figure 9.3). Even if you do not know who Madhur Jaffrey is, the photograph shows an Asian woman placing a herb on the side of a dish of curry: this works to suggest the idea of 'home cooking'. While most readers, if they stop to think, will realize that it is unlikely that Madhur Jaffrey has anything to do with the actual manufacture of the product, this advert seeks to reassure us of the authenticity of the sauce. The advert allows for at least two answers to its opening question, 'Who makes yours?': 'I do' or 'The takeaway down the road does.'

This advert wants to sell us authenticity and the idea of quality. It also has behind it the idea of convenience, but cannot readily address this because of the potentially negative association of that idea as well as the contradictions between convenience and quality. 'Quality' and 'authenticity' are attributes to be worked for – they suggest in this context 'home cooking' and 'real ingredients' – while 'convenience' suggests the possibility of compromising on 'quality'. The text of the advert stresses the status of the cook – 'the World's leading authority on Indian cuisine' – and the product – 'greeted enthusiastically by lovers of authentic Indian food' – and then works to stress quality and taste – 'exquisite', 'outstanding', 'sheer mouth-watering opulence [*sic*]'. The image plays an important role as well: the sauces are grouped with a number of fresh ingredients in order to imply some kind of link between them; the cutting-board contains a number of items which have been cut up alone with a knife, all of which reinforces the idea of Madhur Jaffrey making the curry. The freshness of the products, along with the cleanliness of the environment featured, is emphasized by the glass and gleaming steel shelving behind her, the water beads on the tomatoes and peppers, the gloss of the seemingly just cut lime. Having Madhur Jaffrey in the picture also works for the authenticity of the product, partly because it shows her making it, but also because we have a picture of an Asian woman dressed in a sari (think how the meaning would change if she were pictured in chef's whites or in the coverall clothing used in

Figure 9.3   Advertisement for Tilda sauces

the factory which actually produces the sauce). Tilda is selling an idea about a product. Buying the product doesn't necessarily mean you subscribe to that idea, but a cursory examination of a range of store magazines does seem to suggest that ideas about quality and authenticity are very much to the fore in contemporary food retailing. Can you think of other areas of contemporary life in which 'quality' and 'authenticity' are promulgated as important values? For example, the business corporation Mars lists 'quality' as one of the five guiding principles that underpin every aspect of its business operations:

'quality, responsibility, mutuality, efficiency and freedom' (Mars promotion booklet for Graduate Management Training Programme, 1997).

ACTIVITY 9.11

- Examine a range of magazines, including store magazines and popular women's magazines. Examine the ways in which food is being advertised – noting in particular the stress placed on authenticity and quality and any contradictions arising from this.
- Take another type of product and compare and contrast the ways in which it is advertised. It might be best to work on a range, to include both practical items like toilet paper or sanitary towels and luxury products like exotic cars or designer clothes. Are certain values given particular significance?
- Remind yourself of the discussion on Bourdieu's idea of habitus and 'taste'. Can you identify ways in which any of the advertisements construct differentiated (according to social groups) 'tastes'?

Agency, Appropriation and Ethics

As we have seen, the contemporary consumer has a bewildering array of products with which to interact. We want now to return to the work of Jean Baudrillard, from whom we quoted earlier. In the following extract the cultural historian Roy Porter provides an introductory overview of some key points in Baudrillard's ideas about consumption.

Reading 9.7

The modern consumer society . . . [is] a system in which analysis of the laws of production has become obsolete. Consumption is all important, and consumption has to be understood in a novel manner. Thanks to the twentieth century revolutionization of consciousness – through mass communications, hi-tech media, the advertising and publicity industries, the empire of images throughout the global village – modern human beings now inhabit an artificial, hermetically sealed pleasure dome . . . nothing any longer possesses intrinsic value, in and for itself. Meaning is produced by endless, symbolic exchanges within a dominant code, whose rhetoric is entirely self-referential; a sexy woman is used to sell a car; a car sells cigarettes, cigarettes sell machismo; machismo is used to sell jeans; and so the symbolic magic circle is sealed. (Porter, 1993, pp. 1–2)

ACTIVITY 9.12 How far do you think that the world of advertising is purely self-referential? Are there ways in which adverts actually relate to 'the real world'? How would advert-like posters for campaigns like the promotion of slower speeds in built-up areas, the promotion of safe-sex practices or anti-drink-driving campaigns be purely self-referential?

Baudrillard's ideas seem to work more readily when we look at consumer products as opposed to campaigns. Many car advertisements feature a picture of the car in isolation, whereas the reality of driving in the twenty-first century is crowded roads and traffic queues. Designer clothing is often advertised in ways which are reminiscent of the photo-shoot images used by glossy magazines in their reporting on a fashion line. Both these examples can be said to be self-referential in that the world of car sales does not want to remind its audience of the problems of car ownership in the 'real' world, and the fashion industry has a very symbiotic relationship with the fashion press (Braham, 1997).

Baudrillard wrote, as we have seen, that consumption functions like a language, with its own self-referential codes and signs. Bourdieu argued that as consumers we play an important part in creating the meaning of products, be they football or jeans, and are thus active agents in determining who buys what and for what purpose, even if we do so within his rather static version of social class. Both theorists were concerned to assert that the producers of, for example, football or jeans do not have complete control over the ways in which their products are thought about, spoken about and used. Daniel Miller offers an interesting example of how a localized community can appropriate (consume) an object – the steel drum of Trinidadian steel bands – and in doing so invest it with meanings that assert a specific identity in resistance to the meanings conventionally associated with the steel drum, which is used to transport oil. Trinidad depends economically on the exportation of oil and, as a result, has been at the mercy of the fluctuating price of oil in the world economy. The steel oil drum can be seen as a symbol of Trinidad's economic dependency, but by using these drums as musical instruments to create a musical form known internationally, Trinidadians have appropriated the symbol of their dependence as a symbol of local identity. Trinidadians have reused an object associated with their everyday work and their economic poverty to produce a particular style of music that has allowed them to acquire a dignity and status in the global as well as local community. As Miller points out, Trinidadians guard jealously their status as the originators of the steel band (Miller, 1997, p. 32). The manufacturers of the steel oil drums appropriated by Trinidadian steel bands could hardly have envisaged their products being used in this way. Indeed, as we know, business corporations spend enormous sums of money on marketing and advertising in attempts to 'persuade' consumers to see their products in specific ways. If consumers were simply passive dupes manipulated by the forces of economic capitalism, producers would not have to spend such vast sums of money on marketing their products.

One strand of thinking that has developed from the work of Bourdieu and Baudrillard has been to see consumption as a source of pleasure, as a way in which, particularly, young people are enabled to assemble identities creatively from a diversity of styles, products and appropriation of cultural forms – fashion, popular music, sport and material objects. This appropriation and reworking of self-selected cultural forms and commodities is referred to as **bricolage** and is offered as a strategy by which people are able to resist, subvert and negotiate consumer capitalism. An influential proponent of this view is John Fiske, who argues that

> consumer choice between similar commodities is often not between competing use-values, despite the efforts of consumer advice groups, but between cultural values: and the selection of one particular commodity over others becomes the selection of meanings, pleasure and social identity for the consumer . . . Meanings and pleasures circulate . . . without any real distinction between producers and consumers. (Fiske, 1987, pp. 311, 312)

Fiske is discussing TV rather than shopping for commodities. However, if we focus for a moment on shopping, it is fairly obvious that this is not a simple matter of pleasure, with producers and consumers equally aligned. As we saw in the section on the high street, most of our shopping is routinely done to meet food and household needs rather than selecting a lifestyle. Shopping frequently involves frustration, exhaustion and anxiety. A single mother may experience considerable anxiety, both on behalf of her children and in terms of her identity as a parent, if she is unable to afford the latest toy fashion or the particular brand of trainers perceived as *de rigueur* among her children's peer group. Parents frequently experience difficult tensions around the desire to 'treat' their children and the equally strong need to teach non-materialistic values. Anxieties about debt and overspending, about the consumer excess that currently constitutes Christmas in the West, and about affording a holiday are common experiences. Equally, parents may worry, if they cannot afford the school skiing trip or the theatre visit, that they are depriving their children of valuable 'cultural capital' (to use Bourdieu's term). The dominance of the motor car in industrialized countries as a symbol of identity and independence, despite the reality of owning and maintaining a car, has repercussions not only for those for whom cars are an inaccessible luxury, but also for the health, safety and environmental resources of the world.

Finally, we need to think about consumption in terms of the global economy. Most people are not consumer hedonists engaged in a constant cycle of purchasing; nor are most people completely free to consume whatever, whenever and wherever they wish. When people shop they are frequently motivated by thrift and the need to get value for money. Increasingly, it could be argued, there is a concern among 'First World' consumers to be responsible 'global' citizens and not to waste the world's resources or pollute the environment. Daniel Miller has suggested that 'what we see is a desire on the part of consumers to reconstruct small moral worlds that tame [the] vast forces [of modern capitalism]' (Miller, 1997, p. 47). Nevertheless, this focus on 'small moral worlds' – that is, local dilemmas and identities – may impact, in ways which remain unknown to most of us, on other localized groupings in the less industrialized areas of the world. The concern of multinational corporations to provide consumer choice in the form of low prices for a range of different commodities in the 'First World' relies on supporting the cheapest producer. Producing cheap goods is most easily achieved by paying low wages, and the most likely places where this can happen are in developing countries. Mars, for example, developed manufacturing businesses in the former Eastern Bloc countries Russia, Poland and Hungary. Hence, the thriftiness of the 'First World' consumer may impact upon those who work in less affluent countries.

ACTIVITY 9.13

- Next time you go shopping, notice, if you can, where the goods you buy have come from. From which countries do high street shops buy the commodities they sell?
- Do you think we should be willing to pay more for the commodities we consume in order to generate higher wages for those in developing countries? If we did agree to this, how would we know where the extra money we paid went? How could you find out the profit margins of those who sell many of the commodities we buy? How easy would it be to shop ethically? Should there be monitoring and regulation of exploitation by governments or by a global body? How could this be achieved?
- Can you think of other forms of 'ethical consumerism', for example, recycling newspapers?
- Can you think of examples of business corporations that promote themselves as 'ethical producers'?

Conclusions

Rather than summarizing the material we have covered, we want to leave you with a number of questions to think about and research further.

- Corporations like Coca-Cola, McDonald's and Sony are global enterprises. Do they tailor their products to specific, local consumers in different countries or do they simply offer a homogeneous product worldwide? You could usefully look at *No Logo* (Klein, 2000).
- Do you think that most of us tend to think about and respond to the issues of a 'small, moral world' – that is family, neighbourhood, friendship group, workplace, nation – rather than global concerns? If your answer is 'yes', why do you think this is? If you answered 'no', can you give reasons for your answer?
- People who work in marketing, media and advertising, producing TV programmes, magazines, advertisements and branded consumer products are also consumers of the products they produce. For example, according to Mars publicity material, Damian Guha, who graduated in Philosophy, Politics and Economics from Oxford, now works as a brand manager for Pedigree Petfoods, a subsidiary of Mars. He describes the business culture he is part of as one that 'offers a world of opportunities for high energy people who thrive on interaction and challenge and like to set and achieve demanding personal goals'. He is part of a team producing and marketing branded petfood but he is also, presumably, a consumer who buys a range of branded products, many of which may have been targeted at young people like himself: young people who are highly skilled at reading and manipulating the language of consumerism. Is it, therefore, more accurate to see the relationship between production and consumption as circular rather than one of cause and effect? An interesting article which discusses this in relation to magazines for young women is '*More!* New sexualities in girls' and women's magazines' (McRobbie, 1996).

The subject of consumption is a complex one and we have been able to offer you here only a taste of the debates and issues it raises. If the subject interests you, and we hope it will, look at the suggestions for further reading. However, as well as reading further in the area, you could do worse than reflect upon your own experience as a consumer of both material objects and cultural forms. The questions posed above may help you to begin this process.

Chapter 10

Technology

In this book we have been working with a definition of culture that stresses the practices and processes of daily life. Today, the electronic culture of the Web and of personal portable technology like cellphones or computer-linked music players like iPods is so pervasive that our culture's use of technology has become a major source for analysts interested in social and cultural trends. Our daily lives are caught up in electronic technology, whether in the form of credit-card transactions, loyalty-card data, library swipe-cards, or the apparently simpler form of watching a DVD movie, heating a meal in a microwave, or listening to a CD. In the present day, many aspects of life in industrialized countries are reliant upon technology to an extent that even twenty years ago might have seemed surprising. While TV culture has been a mainstay of cultural studies in Britain, Australia and America, the digital culture of the Internet and the Web and the rapid development of cellphones and other personal network technology have only recently become the subject of analysis and debate. In this final chapter we will be looking at contemporary culture's use of technology and providing discussion material, activities and further reading to help you develop your own study of its pervasive reach. We want to begin our discussion with some assertions – in tabular form – from Derrick de Kerckhove, director of the McLuhan Program in Culture and Technology at the University of Toronto, a man hailed by some as today's version of 1960s media commentator Marshall McLuhan. These make broad claims about the trends in late twentieth-century culture and provide us with a starting point for your reflections on the emerging trends of the twenty-first century.

Reading 10.1

	Social Trends	
1960s–70s	**1980s**	
Producerism	Consumerism	
Self-centredness (me decade)	Environmentalism	
Relationships	Fitness	
Hippies	Yuppies	
Feminism	DINKS (double income, no kids)	
Social (and not so social) drugs	Non smokers	
Ideological drive	Bottom line	

Television and computers conquered the industrial world, carrying and shaping corporate psychology according to their own highly distinctive criteria which, in turn, formed and informed distinctive policies within the culture that helped to develop others . . .

	Psychological Trends	
	Television (saturation during 70s)	**Computer** (penetration during 80s)
Dominant concepts	Mass culture	Speed culture
	Mass production	Instant communication
	Being everywhere at once	Being here and now where it counts
Main patterns of communication	Broadcasting (one way) (*Give people what they want*)	Networking (two way) (*Find out what people want*)
Dominant marketing attitudes	Seduction	Precision
Dominant business strategy	Promoting	Accounting
Main source of metaphors	Body – senses – touch (Touch me, feel me)	Brain/central nervous system (*The Soul of the New Machine*)
Favourite buzzwords	Myths, icons, images	Logic, AI, expert systems
Popular mythological representation	Superman (X Ray vision, flying)	2001's HAL (command and control)

If you replace the category headings in the first . . . [table] by Television on the left and Computer on the right, you will be surprised that the new headings actually yield more information. They make even more sense than the classification by periods. TV turned us into inveterate consumers, by bringing the outside world inside our homes, inside the self. We developed a kind of voracious appetite for images and goods. But computers, by projecting outwards from our central nervous systems, giving us access and power over any point in the environment, at any time, for any purpose, made producers of us. The younger generation of men and women got high on small business and new ventures instead of drugs. The computerization of the economy is also key to all the other changes, being the nerve centre of the present body politic. (De Kerckhove, 1995, pp. 131–2)

De Kerckhove is an optimist about technology and might be criticized for having a rather loose sense of the actual history of the periods he identifies. Wasn't there a recession in the late 1980s? Didn't yuppies symbolize excess, including excessive drug taking? How can a computer from a 1970s film be the dominant mythological figure for the 1990s? (How many people reading this book have seen Kubrick's film?) We agree with him that these two technological media are central to any understanding of the cultures of the decade he identifies, but would hesitate over some of his claims.

ACTIVITY 10.1

- What do you think of de Kerckhove's claims? Can you begin to extend his ideas by drawing up your own tables for the dominant social trends of the early twenty-first century? (Some of the earlier sections in this book may help you with this.)
- Who would be the current zeitgeist social group? What is the drug that defines our era? What (if anything) has replaced consumerism? If you don't feel ready to tackle the broad questions raised by de Kerckhove's claims at this stage, then we hope that by the end of the chapter you will be more able to debate and discuss the claims made by him and commentators in this area.
- By thinking about the social trends of the last decade or so, you will have begun to work towards your own view of the interface between the technological and the social in contemporary culture (for some general discussion of this see, for example, Castells, 2004; Batelle, 2005; Friedman, 2005). For a very clear overview of the development of multimedia see chapters 3 and 4 of Richard Wise's *Multimedia: a Critical Introduction* (2000). It is this interface which the activities and discussion offered in this chapter let you begin to explore.

The Place of the Personal: Ethnography and the Practice of Cultural Studies

In this chapter we ask you to look at the impact of technology on contemporary culture in general and in relation to your own experiences of it in particular. The methodology underlying many of the activities in this chapter draws upon concepts and approaches we have introduced earlier, notably the questions of subjectivity that we addressed in chapter 8 and aspects of the work on consumption in chapter 9. The work in this chapter is informed by your own experience of contemporary culture and that of other people in your wider social circle. Here we draw upon a way of working that has become increasingly influential in cultural studies in recent decades.

> All sorts of objects-in-use, including clothes and domestic appliances, and their social and symbolic functions have been analysed in the context of consumer cultures and social identity . . . [but] 'person research' . . . [can ensure] that political and ethical issues are brought out particularly clearly. (Johnson et al., 2004, p. 205)

At the centre of our approach to technology and culture in this chapter is a focus on 'meaning making . . . via the use of objects' (Johnson et al., 2004, p. 205): Johnson and his colleagues make a powerful argument for the centrality of person-based research in contemporary cultural studies; before we move on to look at your uses of technology we need to establish the wider implications of this way of working and to rehearse some of its strengths and pitfalls.

Reading 10.2

When we start out on a project of cultural research, our first resource is our own lived relationship with our topic area. Where we choose to work on topics close to home . . . , an explicit dialogue can begin between past experiences and selves that have been marginalized in the past by dominant definitions and our own strategies of defiance or defence. Researching such a topic may sometimes confirm or validate our previous experience, sometimes challenge and extend it . . .

. . . As we encounter new situations in the process of research, our own foreknowledge and horizons will be changed and this process will have to be 'digested' internally . . . The reconfiguration of the self is both an effect of research and, if reflected on, a continuing resource within it . . .

Another way in which to see this process is to view research as constructing relationships between our present and future selves and our past selves ... – a process that involves a whole politics of remembering (and forgetting) ...

Yet, although our cultural experiences may be intense, they remain partial, so that reaching out to others' worlds is also necessary. Indeed, such worlds will impinge, often forcibly, on our own. Research becomes a way of extending our horizon even when a cultural practice is very close to us. Being a fan or a practitioner of a particular kind of music or dance and remembering particular episodes of collective enjoyment or exclusion, for instance, will itself yield many clues to the nature of such fascinations and pleasures. Our experience, systematically recollected and represented, can be a primary source, but it will still be necessary to check out these insights with new others who are similarly or differently placed to ourselves ...

The move from auto/biography to ethnography is a specialized and, in some ways, heightened instance of a more general process: the analogical recognition of the equal reality of another body, identity and cultural world ... The sense of self is, therefore, necessarily involved in understanding the other; ethnography presupposes auto/biography. Self-possession or self-knowledge and openness to other worlds are integrally related, just as developing a knowledge of self depends, in a large part, on a willingness to attend to alterity or difference ... Ethnography may depend on auto/biography, but the auto/biography of the researcher also gets hitched up to the ethnographic process with results that must be uncertain. (Johnson et al., 2004, pp. 206–8)

ACTIVITY 10.2

- Outline the benefits of self-reflexive research as outlined in the passage above.
- Now identify some of the reasons that, according to Johnson et al., inform the need for self-reflection to be supplemented by the insights and experiences of others.

Although ethnographic research has a long tradition in cultural studies and has been a powerful tool in enabling marginalized and underrepresented groups to have a voice in the analysis of their culture, it is important to note that in Johnson et al.'s account the emphasis on the uses of ethnography is tempered by a stress on the necessity for a process of self-reflection on the part of the researcher. This is important since it is all too easy to assume that powerful testimony or telling social interaction observed in the field amounts to evidence of a meaning or value that is shared within a given cultural group. As Bastleer et al. remind us, ethnography, however enlightened and politically self-conscious, cannot escape the problems affecting all academically based social investigation: how to take account, within the 'neutral' forms and procedures of the analysis, of the immensely powerful and pervasive ideologies that shape all practical languages and cultures; how and with what authority and on whose behalf to interpret the lives, experiences, and meanings of others. (Bastleer et al., 1985, p. 146)

In moving away from an epistemological practice, which sought to explain cultural activity in terms of its underlying 'laws' or structures, to an ontological one, interested in questions of identity and the subject in process, Angela McRobbie, one of the practitioners whose work has moved the subject in this direction, has argued that

> Identity could be seen as dragging cultural studies in to the 1990s by acting as a kind of guide to how people see themselves, not as class subjects, not as psychoanalytic subjects, but as active agents whose sense of self is projected onto and expressed in an expansive range of cultural practices, including texts, images, and commodities. If this is the case, then the problem in cultural studies today . . . is the absence of references to real existing identities in the ethnographic sense . . . The site of identity formation in cultural studies remains implicitly in and through cultural commodities and texts rather than in and through the cultural practices of everyday life . . . [I]t is necessary that we somehow move away from the binary opposition which still haunts cultural studies, that is, the distinction between text and lived experience, between media and reality, between culture and society. (McRobbie, 1992, p. 730)

In a sense, cultural studies is, like the cultures it seeks to understand, simply becoming more self-referential (McGuigan, 1992, pp. 207–50). Cultural studies has moved away from institutional and political analyses and towards a study of identity. Informed by the issues we have examined above, we can now turn to some work on the place of technology in modern culture. We begin by reprising the legacy of cultural studies work on TV since this provides a useful starting point, in terms of underlying issues of approach, to the analysis of individuals' uses of technology within their culture.

Twentieth-Century Technology: Cultural Studies of TV

Thirty years ago cultural studies tended to see TV as something which sought to impose ideological positions upon a largely passive audience: the nature of the analogue medium meant that viewers watched television rather than interacting with it as they might with today's digital multi-channel outputs. Studies such as Brunsdon and Morley's (1978) analysis of the early-evening BBC TV news show *Nationwide* stressed the ways in which the medium sought to shape and construct itself in line with the beliefs and values of its ideal audience; the show created an idealized spectator and, the study suggests, worked by trying to position its actual viewers in this role. More positive accounts of TV from this period still tended to see the medium as controlling its audience. Here is Graeme Turner's summary of Fiske and Hartley's work in their influential *Reading Television* (1978).

Reading 10.3

Fiske and Hartley approach television as an oral, rather than a literate, medium . . .

> Every medium has its own unique set of characteristics, but the codes which structure the language of television are much more like those of speech than of writing. Any attempt to decode a television text as if it were a literary text is thus not only doomed to failure but is also likely to result in a negative evaluation of the medium based on its inability to do a job to which it is in fact fundamentally unsuited. [Fiske and Hartley, 1978, p. 15]

Their description of the function of television draws on Hall's encoding/decoding model [see Hall, 1980, and chapter 3]:

> The internal psychological state of the individual is not the prime determinant in the communication of television messages. These are decoded according to individually learnt but culturally generated codes and conventions, which of course impose similar constraints of perception on the encoders of the messages. It seems, then, that television functions as a social ritual, overriding individual distinctions, in which our culture engages in order to communicate with its collective self. [ibid., p. 85]

Television, they suggest, performs a 'bardic function' for the culture. Just as the bard translated the central concerns of his day into verse, television renders our own everyday perceptions into its specialized language system. It serves the needs of the culture in particular ways: it addresses collective audiences rather than the individual; it is oral rather than literate; it operates as a centring discourse, appearing as the voice of the culture with which individuals can identify; and it takes its place in the cycle of production and reproduction of the culture's dominant myths and ideologies. Fiske and Hartley divide television's bardic function into categories that include the articulation of a consensus about reality; the implication of individuals into membership of the culture; the celebration, explanation, interpretation, and justification of the doings of individuals within the society; the demonstration of the practical adequacy of the culture's ideologies and mythologies, and, conversely, the exposure of any practical inadequacy resulting from changed social conditions; and the guarantee of audience members' status and identity. There is some overlap in these categories, but the general notion of the bardic function continues to be useful. (Turner, 1992, pp. 101–2)

ACTIVITY 10.3

- What do you think the differences are between systems of communication based upon speech and those based upon writing?
- How far can TV today be seen as a speech-based form of communication? What is the 'grammar' of TV (its rules of organization)? What about forms (bragging, gossip, proclamations, etc.)? Is there a vocabulary of TV which differs between programmes? Try comparing a TV adaptation of a classic novel with an episode of a soap opera, for example. (For a useful guide on how to analyse TV see Selby and Cowdery, 1995.)
- Fiske and Hartley were writing before the advent of the remote control: given this technology and the proliferation of channels in the digital era, how far would you want to argue that the 'internal psychological state of the individual' has become a major factor in TV communication?
- How far do you think the idea of a 'bardic function' remains viable today? Think about state, legal and sporting events broadcast on TV (e.g., coverage of the attacks on the USA on 9/11, the role of al-Jazeera TV in coverage of the Iraq War, election broadcasts, international sporting events) and the ways in which these might fit into Fiske and Hartley's categories. Take other types of TV programme, like a quiz show, the Oprah Winfrey show, or even a soap opera, and think about the extent to which these can be discussed as possessing a 'bardic function', translating contemporary cultural concerns.

The institution of TV

Here is Stuart Price's discussion of TV as an institution.

Reading 10.4

What is the meaning of the term 'institution'? It is all too easy to attempt to explain the term by giving an *example* of a familiar media institution, like the BBC, rather than a *definition*. In *A Dictionary of Communication and Media Studies* (1989,

p. 87), Watson and Hill define institution quite differently, as a 'term generally applied to patterns of behaviour which are established, approved and usually of some permanence'.

Here we have an idea which might help us to break the habit of imagining institutions simply as large buildings in Central London. 'Patterns of behaviour' suggests that there is a human dimension to all institutions. In *Mass Communication Theory* (1987), McQuail writes that various media have become institutionalised, which means that (p. 37) 'they have acquired a stable form, structure and set of functions and related public expectations.'

The key to both definitions is to be found in words like 'patterns' and 'structure', 'established' and 'stable'. In other words, institutions are bodies which have a settled structure and a set way of functioning. Alvarado, Gutch and Wollen (1987, p. 48) use the definition employed by Raymond Williams:

> Institution is one of several examples of a noun of action or process which became, at a certain stage, a general and abstract noun describing something apparently objective and systematic; in fact, in the modern sense, an *institution*.

These authors create no surprises when they insist (p. 49) that:

> . . . no text without production and without audience is possible, and to teach about institutions is to teach about the relations . . . between those three.

Here, the idea of institution as a *relationship* is stressed – a relationship between production, text and audience. (Price, 1993, pp. 297–8)

One way of thinking about TV's relationship with its audience is in terms of its supposed 'bardic function'. If this function exists, the range of programmes ought to reflect what culture regards as significant and relevant: that is, they ought to reflect 'a consensus about reality' (Turner, 1992, p. 102).

ACTIVITY 10.4

- Price's account of TV as institution is one that stresses interaction between viewer and channel. You could explore this by drawing up a table of the main stations' output over a week and then filling in details of what you watched as a percentage of the output of that programme type.
- You could also collect data from friends and colleagues; in order to provide a broader picture you should try to ensure that your survey covers people of different ages, genders and ethnicities.
- You can find detailed data on UK TV viewing at the Broadcasters' Audience Research Board's website, www.barb.co.uk.

You may find that there are patterns in your results which indicate assumptions about the role and function of TV made by a particular age or socio-economic group. For more detailed work in a slightly different vein, you could try observing a single subject watching a taped programme and noting all the things which they do in addition to watching the TV. The following extract, from Marie Gillespie's study of the ways in which South Asian families in west London in the 1980s viewed and used home videos, offers insights into the complex use to which technologies can be put with relation to questions of identity and community.

Reading 10.5

In Southall [west London] the rapid expansion of the home video market needs to be considered not only as providing an extension to an already important and dynamic film culture [consisting of popular Hindi films, known as Bollywood films, shown in local cinemas] but also very much a response on the part of a black community to life in Britain. Southall, like many other black communities, has come into existence in the first instance as a result of racist immigration and housing policies. Such communities have developed as sanctuaries against the racism they experience. The exclusion and marginalization of many people in Southall from mainstream British society, coupled with the failure to provide adequate leisure/culture facilities, has . . . contributed to the development of an important home video culture . . .

For the older members of the community, nostalgia is a key element in the pleasure experienced through film. In one particularly moving account by a man in his seventies, tears welled in his eyes as he recounted: 'When we see black-and-white films it reminds us of our childhood, our school days, our school mates, of what we were thinking, of what we did do, of our heroes . . . and I tell you this gives us great pleasure.' The films would appear to act as a form of collective popular memory and some parents are able to convey a sense of their past in India to their children . . .

Various degrees of scepticism are registered among the boys [interviewed by Gillespie] about parents' attempts to artificially maintain a culture through film: 'Parents want their children to maintain certain religious values, beliefs and customs but that doesn't mean that Indian films are necessarily going to educate them in that way. They may well do the opposite . . . I think the moral standards in most recent films is pretty appalling.' But clear distinctions are made between religion and a sense of cultural identity and whilst firmly upholding the Sikh faith one boy claims: 'Parents use the films to represent their culture to their children but that will not work because those are not my roots, that place [India] has nothing to do with me anymore.'

Many parents lament what they see as a process of progressive cultural loss in each generation of children. Looking to the past they attempt to re-create traditional culture. Meanwhile young people, with eyes to the future, are busy re-creating something new. The striving after cultural continuity and the negotiation of cultural identity are thus inescapably dialectical processes and they must, moreover, be seen in the widest possible context. The notion of viewing as a social activity which takes place in families needs to be extended to include more detailed explorations of the wider social, cultural, and ideological contexts and uses of the VCR. (Gillespie, 1993)

ACTIVITY 10.5

Identify some further ways in which people use technology to construct new identities or to reassert traditional identities. Think about the role of newer technologies like DVDs: how does the newer technology work to give us greater flexibility in how we use the cultural content? Today India is seen as 'the next Asian superpower', wooed by presidents (http://observer. guardian.co.uk/world/story/0,,1718111,00.html). Given the markedly different connotations of India today, it seems unlikely that Southall mothers are dragooning their children to watch the latest Bollywood movie for its celebration of traditional values. What kind of films did your parents encourage you to watch when you were younger? Can you identify any latent ideological significance in their recommendations?

Gillespie's work showed how one group of people were able to adapt a technology to serve a social end. In today's era of pervasive digital media culture we are all becoming 'screenagers': visually literate consumers operating in a digitally mediated culture (Rushkoff, 1997, p. 3). Rushkoff suggests that mediating multiplicity is an essential skill for survival in today's culture. Darley has suggested that the advent of mass-market digital culture has seen the development of a particular kind of consumer, 'playful seekers after style, spectacle and visceral thrills, prepared in the main to be perceptually (and physically), rather than intellectually active. On the whole such spectators are receivers and sorters of immediate sensuous impressions' (Darley, 2000, p. 173).

ACTIVITY 10.6

- Does Darley's analysis hold up when applied to Web-based digital media or interactive personal technology like MP3 players or cellphones?
- Think carefully about the extent of our control of such devices. What are its limits? Can they be circumvented?

To illustrate the ways in which new technology can impact on every aspect of contemporary life, we now briefly consider some innovations in the ways we can interact using portable technology.

Living with Technology

Contemporary Western culture is fundamentally shaped by technology. Think about the ways in which our homes, clothes, mobility and leisure activities all rely upon some form of technology: whether it is the power station converting gas to electrical power or the refrigerator that keeps our food fresh, Western culture is a hundred per cent reliant upon technology. Today there is a growing trend for technology to be ever more intimately involved in our day-to-day lives, to become something that is used at a personal level to interact with our culture. For example, most of us have a cellphone that means (for a price) we can keep in touch with friends, family or business associates almost irrespective of where we are. Technology enables us to radically transcend temporal zones and contributes to the shaking up of our sense of space and place (cf. reading 5.4, p. 135). In the marketing of portable technological devices, much play is made on issues of personal choice and independence: we choose, we decide, we are in control – or so the manufacturers and digital networks would have us believe. Today's digital technology means that – again for a price – we can all become producers of new media content with our own syndicated show on the Web – with a laptop, wi-fi, an MP3 device and a digital video camera we can set ourselves up as broadcasters using web-space for pod- or video-casting. Apple Computers' iLife 06 software suite, for example, was marketed as

> the easiest way to make the most out of every bit of your digital life. Use your Mac to collect, organize and edit the various elements. Transform them into mouth-watering masterpieces with Apple-designed templates. Then share the magic moments in beautiful books, colorful calendars, dazzling DVDs, perfect podcasts, and attractive online journals. All starring you. (www.apple.com/ilife/, accessed 10 June 2007)

ACTIVITY 10.7

- List all the personal portable technological items you own, e.g., iPod, cellphone, digital camera, laptop computer.
- Which do you have within a metre of where you are now?
- For each device, estimate how often you use it in a typical 24-hour period.
- Now get an older friend or relative, perhaps a parent or grandparent, to answer the three questions above.

My (Tim Middleton's) 90-year-old grandmother owns rather different personal portable technology devices to me: apart from a TV remote control the only portable device we could think of that she owns was a personal alarm that, when activated, would call a carer in the case of a fall. My sixty-something father owns a cellphone, but he only turns it on when he wants to make a call and consequently uses it less than once a week. As a forty-something, my own use of personal portable technology is rather more extensive, with items like cellphones, Palm Pilot, iPod and laptop used several times a day and digital cameras used every week. This variation in usage will not just be down to age (economic factors will clearly be at work too), but it is suggestive of the greater penetration of personal technology into the lives of young people: doubtless the readers of this book will be making greater use of a range of personal technology than its authors do. That is not to say the young have a monopoly on using such equipment: viewed from a broad perspective heart-pacemakers and digital hearing aids are also portable personal technology, and more likely to be found in or on older people. But 'clever' cellphones and MP3 players that let you watch your favourite TV show are hardly cutting-edge. For real innovation one possible next step is harnessing the latent power of wearable technology. MIT's Media Lab has been developing what it calls Socially-Intelligent Wearables.

Reading 10.6

[C]ell phones are soon expected to become the most popular consumer device on the planet. About half of the 800 million cell phones shipped in 2005 were more powerful than Pentium 1 computers. By quantifying the behavior of cell phone users it now seems possible to predict answers to questions like whom they got along with, what movie they enjoyed, how well they spoke, or even what product they might buy.

This real-time information could be used for feedback and training, to customise experiences and interactions with machines, take images or annotate conversations, or even connect friends and colleagues with appropriate privacy restrictions.

The GroupMedia project evolved from our work at the Wearable Computing Group, a.k.a. Borglab, driven by the need for more perceptual socially-aware applications for cellphones and PDAs. We measure speech speaking styles (speech feature processing), head-nodding, body motion (accelerometry) and physiology (galvanic skin response) to understand interest in conversations, effectiveness of elevator pitches, movie audience reactions, speed-dating, focus groups, and group interaction dynamics. (http://groupmedia.media.mit.edu/, accessed 10 June 2007)

One example of a socially intelligent application of technology is the 'Jerk-O-Meter' software for use on cellphones:

Reading 10.7

Research Profile: Jerk-O-Meter

Profile By Anmol Madan, Research Associate

Have you ever had the experience where you call someone up and he or she doesn't seem to be paying attention to you?

The Jerk-O-Meter (or JerkoMeter) is a real-time speech feature analysis application that runs on your VOIP [Voice over Internet Protocol] phone or cell phone that remedies precisely that experience. It uses speech features that measure activity and stress (and soon empathy) from your tone of voice and speaking style, to predict if you are 'being a jerk' on the phone. The phone displays appropriate messages, and can also be set up to inform the person on the other end of the line that you're extremely busy. The messages range from 'Stop being a jerk!' to 'Wow, you're a smooth talker,' based on your performance. The application is currently designed to analyze only the user's conversation, and not the person at the other end of the line. The Jerk-O-Meter is the work of Anmol Madan, a PhD candidate at the MIT Media Laboratory, and Dr. Alex (Sandy) Pentland, a pioneer in wearable and socially aware computing.

The mathematical models for the Jerk-O-Meter were derived from several research studies at the Media Lab. These studies evaluated how a person's speaking style could reflect his or her interest in a conversation, in going out on a date, or perhaps even in buying a particular product. Our results show that a person's speaking style and 'tone of voice' can predict objective outcomes (e.g. interest in a conversation, or in going out on a date) with 75–85% accuracy . . .

The Jerk-O-Meter is just one possible implementation of the underlying technology, which has much broader applications in areas such as customized user experiences, consumer research, advertising, marketing, movies and television audiences, call centers, and various consumer and corporate applications. An important implication is that computers and cell phones may now understand people better, just as other people do. Instead of users adapting their habits to work with computers or cell phones, these devices could support us in the ways that we naturally communicate.

The current version of the Jerk-O-Meter is a research prototype, and runs in Linux on the Zaurus VOIP phone. Ron Caneel, alum of the research group, wrote part of the code to extract the activity and stress levels in real time. From a technical perspective, the Jerk-O-Meter could easily be converted into a downloadable application for a cell phone.

Jerk-O-Meter is an academic research project and is not commercially available at this time. (www.media.mit.edu/press/jerk-o-meter/, accessed 25 June 2006)

For further information see www.media.mit.edu/wearables/lizzy/.

ACTIVITY 10.8

- Think about the ways in which you use your cellphone to communicate. How many calls did you not bother to answer in the last few days? Did you text someone when you could not be bothered to speak to them in person?
- Looking at your phone's call records, who are the people you phone most often? Is this group the same as those whom you text most frequently? Can you identify patterns in this personal data? Do you call one group more than another or interact with one group at a particular time of the day?
- Now we want to spread the net a little wider and reflect upon your daily and weekly use of new digital technologies. For each day over a seven-day period we would like you to keep a detailed log, on the pattern of table 10.1, of your usage of a number of devices and systems. At the same time we'd like you to get at least two other people, ideally of different ages to you, to complete the same exercise.
- Once you have collected your data you can go on to analyse it. We suggest you plot some simple graphs to record your usage of different devices, the frequency of your use and the social networks in relation to which you used them. You can then compare this data to that generated by the people you asked to complete the survey.
- Having conducted your research into types of technology and the frequency with which it is used, you can move on to examine what the technology is used for. You can develop this study by conducting ethnographic research on the subjects who completed the week-long log for you, perhaps interviewing the people who completed the survey and detailing such quantitative data as age, gender, ethnicity, employment status and income. You may also want to gather qualitative data via interviews with your subjects about their use of the various items in the survey. Remember that research involving human participants raises many ethical issues, and you must reflect on these before you start the research process (see Denzin and Lincoln, 1994; Denzin, 1997; Bryman, 2001).
- If you are doing this work as part of a course you can compare your results with your classmates'.

Working with the Web

In the late nineteenth century the hottest technology was the newly invented radio (Marvin, 1988, p. 157), a wireless system that, at the time, was seen 'as

Table 10.1   Log of personal technology usage

Device	Activity	Day and start time	Duration of use	Category of use: personal, work, college, family, other (define)
Mobile phone	Outgoing voice call Outgoing SMS Outgoing video or photo message Incoming voice call Incoming SMS Incoming video or photo message			
Personal computer	Web browsing Purchasing from an online store (specify store and category of item(s)) Other, e.g., podcasting; blogging (specify)			
MP3 player	Listening to music			
Other, e.g., GPS system, satellite navigation system	E.g., using for hiking or mountain biking; in car			

a future means of personal communication'. Today's digital media culture means that 'the future of personal communication . . . [is] again connected to wireless technologies (Wise, 2000, p. 81). The wi-fi world of many Western societies means that personal computing is now truly personal. William Gibson's prescient vision of cyberspace as 'mass-mediated phantasm' has come to pass (Gibson, 1984, p. 51). The rise of blogging and the growth of the online encyclopaedia 'Wikipedia' might be taken as examples of the mass-mediated nature of much of the Web; both are indicative of the way in which new technology has begun to break down the hold of traditional media and information organizations. During recent military conflicts in Kosovo and Iraq the Web has been as much part of the action as events in the 'real' world. On a more personal note, the Web enables millions of people to tell the story of their own life, whether it is in Baghdad (http://dear_raed.blogspot.com; also see http://en.wikipedia.org/wiki/Salam_Pax) or Boston (www.boston-online.com/Blogs). From a cultural studies perspective these applications of technology to everyday (or not so everyday in Salam Pax's case) life create 'a form of media which facilitates the "reflexive presentation of a self" [form] that has been used both as a means of advocacy by the marginalised and disadvantaged and as a means of presenting an idealised self to the world' (Cheung, 2004, p. 56). Viewed in this light blogs – 'a website where entries are written in chronological order and displayed in reverse chronological order' (http://en.wikipedia.org/wiki/Blog, accessed 10 June 2007) – are further examples of reflexive self-presentation. As this technology becomes more ubiquitous, more and more people are becoming actively engaged in the online presentation of self.

The World Wide Web – the network of data that you can read via browser software like Firefox or Apple Computer's Safari – has rapidly become a part of the culture of contemporary western societies. Print-based advertisements for new commodities routinely carry details of the product's associated webpages which offer further opportunities for consumers to interact with the business or service in question. While the Web has become a part of our culture it is sometimes hard to work out what aspect of our culture it most connects with. Is it a place that we tend to turn to for leisure? Is it something that we use to build and maintain social networks? Is it somewhere we act as consumers? Is it somewhere we are creators, adding content in a way that was not possible with analogue communication systems like TV? It is, of course, associated with activities in all of these areas and more; this is where studying the Web from a cultural studies perspective starts to get complicated.

Reading 10.8

Is there anything Distinctive about Researching the Web?

Webpages are complex artefacts that can be written, read, used or consumed, and therefore despite their apparently virtual nature, they are sometimes compared to other designed products that have a more traditional material form, such as a book or DVD. Although it is possible to do a fine-grained reading of an individual webpage as a cultural text, as if it were a written paper document, it is equally feasible to take a broad view of the way in which the Web is becoming part of global culture and commerce. In the methodological terms, the former project could be conducted entirely through online observation without ever gathering the opinions of those who created the webpages. In contrast, for a study of global contexts, it is likely that reference to secondary sources would be necessary, perhaps accompanied by interviews with those in relevant international organisations. Yet even though the Web is often portrayed as a global medium, it may involve experiences that take on a distinctive local flavour, such as Web browsing at an internet café in one particular town or neighborhood. For this type of project, a researcher might use a place based ethnography including extensive participant observation. (Wakeford, 2004, p. 35)

ACTIVITY 10.9

- One useful way of understanding the culture of the Web is to try and understand the way its component parts link up. Touchgraph will enable you to explore the links between sites on the Web or to track the links between works listed in Amazon.com and other webpages (www.touchgraph.com). Choose a website that relates to some aspect of contemporary culture that you care about and enter its URL at Touchgraph.
- What can you say about the resulting data? Did it make connections that you had not anticipated? As Wakeford warns (2004, p. 40), one risk of this system is that it emphasizes 'technological links, rather than the ones that show a human centred network'.
- To further refine your approach to working with the Web, you may like to look at the resources and links on Web-based research at the Association of Internet Researchers website (www.aoir.org) and the Pew Internet and American Life project (www.pewinternet.org).

As we have already mentioned, one especially active aspect of human-centred Web-based culture is the use of podcasting. We will conclude our discussion of technology and culture by looking a little more closely at this cultural phenomenon.

ACTIVITY 10.10

Read the Wikipedia entry on podcasting at http://en.wikipedia.org/wiki/Podcasting.

- Using the Web find out more about the range of podcasting activity: www.podcast.net and Apple Computers' ITunes site (www.apple.com/itunes/podcasts/) are good sources for a range of podcasts. Take one category and listen to some examples. See, for example, those offered by the New York Museum of Modern Art at www.moma.org/visit_moma/audio.html.
- It will be helpful if you look at some of the images they are discussing. How far does the podcast help you to understand the image? Is comprehension the prime purpose of the podcast?
- You might want to use Touchgraph (www.touchgraph.com) to see how many sites on the Web link with MOMA's podcast.

ACTIVITY 10.10

- You could consider who the intended audience for these podcasts are. What do you think the gallery is trying to achieve by making this content available in this format? What factors inform its choice of works on which it has provided podcasts? What are the social and economic implications of its use of this material?

Many cultural commentators working on the Web and its culture suggest that the best way to study its varied phenomena is from the inside. Today's technology means that it is relatively easy to set up your own podcast using proprietary software like that within Apple Computers' iLife, and if you are not a Mac user Google listed over 35 million items when searched for 'podcast software': however you get online we hope to hear your work on the Web soon.

Conclusions

In reflecting on the impact of technology on aspects of contemporary Western culture, we have, of course, examined only a tiny, and some might say rather unenlightening, aspect of our modern technologically influenced culture. Many of the applications of technology we have talked about here are not essential to life and, from some perspectives, have a dubious or debilitating impact on our culture and society: for two influential commentators much digital technology has informed 'the recline of western civilization' (Kroker and Weinstein, 1994, p. 2), turning us to screen-based or hand-held devices that act as ungainly intermediaries in simulated acts of human interaction.

There are, of course, many areas in which new digital technology is genuinely benefiting human life, whether it is solar-powered digitally monitored water pumps in sub-Saharan Africa or the next generation of digital hearing aids. What we have tried to emphasize in this chapter is that in the end it is not the technology itself that cultural studies is interested in, but rather what it does to us and to our interaction with the society in which we live and the cultural contexts in which we make meanings that help us to better understand ourselves.

Conclusion

We hope that you have found things in this book that have enriched and enhanced your study of culture and set you thinking about the areas you would like to explore in more detail.

If you have worked through some or all of the chapters in this book, you will know by now that we are much more interested in the processes by which culture can be studied than we are in arguing for a particular approach or theoretical position. You will also be aware that we have particular areas of interest and that these have shaped our account of how you might set about studying culture.

This book has sought to equip you with a range of approaches to some of the main aspects of contemporary culture in the world today. We have tried to look at material from across the cultural terrain, focusing our discussions on people, places and practices that seem to us to be significant in any approach to the study of our culture. As teachers of cultural studies we have, inevitably, engaged in debates within the subject area, and this book's emphasis on the need to reflect upon the relationship between a still dominant high culture and that of everyday life, and its concern to establish a dialogue with the traces of the cultures of different epochs which still inform our society today, are just two of the ways in which we have tried to make a case for areas that are often marginalized or neglected in introductions to cultural studies.

Where Next?

If you have been reading this book as part of a programme of study in a college or university then the answer to this question may well seem to be mapped out for you. Whether or not this is the case, we would like to make a few suggestions about the ways in which you might want to follow up the arguments and ideas introduced in this work. It may be that the areas we highlight below are not the ones that caught your interest or attention, and if this is the case we refer you to the further reading suggestions for the chapter dealing with the topics that particularly interested you.

The following suggestions provide some ways of further refining and developing your approach to the study of culture:

- Follow the debates about the nature, focus and use of cultural studies in academic journals such as *Cultural Studies, Feminist Review, Journal of Popular Culture, Postmodern Culture, Theory, Culture and Society, Signs: Journal of Women in Culture and Society* and *Women's Studies International Forum.* You will also find articles and reports on items of relevance to cultural studies in the mainstream press, although these are often sensationalized and rely on 'sound-bite' reporting.
- Questions of cultural value have been touched upon a number of times in this book and provide an area of intense debate within cultural studies. Works which have important things to say about this issue include Steven Connor, *Theory and Cultural Value* (Oxford: Blackwell, 1992), John Frow, *Cultural Studies and Cultural Value* (Oxford: Oxford University Press, 1995) and Jim McGuigan, *Cultural Populism* (London: Routledge, 1992). For an approach that focuses upon the ways in which the issue of cultural values arises in relation to responses to film and TV adaptations of 'classic' literary works see the essays in Deborah Cartmell et al. (eds), *Pulping Fictions: Consuming Culture across the Literature/Media Divide* (London: Pluto Press, 1996).
- Cultural studies has, by and large, embraced postmodern theory in its account of contemporary culture, and many introductory works rely upon postmodernist assumptions which are not always debated. The following works will help you come to your own conclusions: Lawrence Cahoone, *From Modernism to Postmodernism: an Anthology* (Oxford: Blackwell, 1996), Steven Connor, *Postmodernist Culture: an Introduction to Theories of the Contemporary* (Oxford: Blackwell, 1989), Terry Eagleton, *The Illusions of Postmodernism* (Oxford: Blackwell, 1996), Scott Lash and Jonathan Friedman (eds), *Modernity and Identity* (Oxford: Blackwell, 1992), and Charles Lemert (ed.), *Social Theory: the Multicultural and Classic Readings*, 3rd edn (Boulder, CO: Westview, 2004).
- The cultural legacy of imperialism and colonialism and the cultures of post-colonialism are further key areas of debate. You can explore some of

the issues in this complex field via the essays in Bill Ashcroft, Gareth Griffiths and Helen Tiffin (eds), *The Post-colonial Studies Reader* (London: Routledge, 1995) or Patrick Williams and Laura Chrisman, *Colonial Discourse and Post-colonial Theory: a Reader* (Hemel Hempstead: Harvester Wheatsheaf, 1993). Two important books in this field worth reading in their own right are Homi Bhabha, *The Location of Culture* (London: Routledge, 1994) and Edward Said, *Culture and Imperialism* (London: Chatto and Windus, 1993). For a focus on the culture of British imperialism see, among others, the essays in John M. MacKenzie, *Imperialism and Popular Culture* (Manchester: Manchester University Press, 1986), and the primary-source texts in Elleke Boehmer, *Empire Writing* (Oxford: Oxford University Press, 1998).

- One area we have not focused on in great detail is the question of how cultural artefacts are produced and distributed. The part played by multinational and global corporations, such as Sony or Rupert Murdoch's News Corporation, in producing what we can see, listen to, participate in and so on is an important topic. You could explore the ways in which the global media is organized and how it is shaped by international, national and local politics. Useful texts to get you started include P. du Gay (ed.), *Production of Cultures/Cultures of Production* (London: Sage/Open University, 1997), M. Real, *Exploring Media Culture: a Guide* (London: Sage, 1996), J. Street, *Politics and Popular Culture* (Cambridge: Polity Press, 1998) and K. Thompson, *Cultural Regulation and Media* (London: Sage/ Open University, 1997).

References and Further Reading

Chapter 1

Arnold, M. (1869) *Culture and Anarchy.* London: Cambridge University Press.

Bourdieu, P. (1984) *Distinction: a Social Critique of the Judgement of Taste,* trans. R. Nice. Cambridge, MA: Harvard University Press.

Clifford, J. (1993) On collecting art and culture. In S. During (ed.), *The Cultural Studies Reader.* London: Routledge.

du Gay, P. et al. (eds) (1997) *Doing Cultural Studies: the Story of the Sony Walkman.* London. Sage/Open University.

Ford, B. (ed.) (1992) *The Cambridge Cultural History of Britain. Volume 9: Victorian Britain.* Cambridge: Cambridge University Press.

Hoggart, R. (1957) *The Uses of Literacy.* Harmondsworth: Penguin.

Houghton, W. (1957) *The Victorian Frame of Mind 1830–1870.* New Haven, CT, and London: Yale University Press.

Jordan, G. and Weedon, C. (1995) *Cultural Politics: Class, Gender, Race and the Postmodern World.* Oxford: Blackwell.

Kuper, A. and Kuper, J. (eds) (1985) *The Social Science Encylopedia.* London: Routledge.

Leavis, F. R. (1930) *Mass Civilization and Minority Culture.* Cambridge: Minority Press.

Leavis, Q. D. (1932) *Fiction and the Reading Public.* London: Chatto and Windus.

Macdonald, D. (1957) A theory of mass culture. In B. Rosenberg and D. Manning White (eds), *Mass Culture: the Popular Arts in America.* New York: Macmillan.

Ortner, S. (1974) Is female to male as nature is to culture? In M. Z. Rosaldo and L. Lamphere (eds), *Women, Culture and Society.* Stanford, CA: Stanford University Press.

Said, E. (1993) *Culture and Imperialism.* London: Vintage.

Storey, J. (1993) *An Introductory Guide to Cultural Theory and Popular Culture.* London: Harvester Wheatsheaf.

Strinati, D. (1995) *An Introduction to Theories of Popular Culture.* London: Routledge.

Williams, R. (1958a) Culture is ordinary. Reprinted in A. Gray and J. McGuigan (eds, 1993), *Studying Culture: an Introductory Reader.* London: Edward Arnold.

Williams, R. (1958b) *Culture and Society: Coleridge to Orwell.* London: Chatto and Windus.

Williams, R. (1961) *The Long Revolution.* London: Chatto and Windus.

Williams, R. (1976) *Keywords: a Vocabulary of Culture and Society.* London: Fontana.

Chapter 2

African Rights (1994) *Rwanda: Death, Despair and Defiance.* London: African Rights.

Althusser, L. (1971) Ideology and ideological state apparatuses. In *Lenin and Philosophy and Other Essays*, trans. B. Brewster. London: New Left Books.

Birke, L. (1992) Transforming biology. In H. Crowley and S. Himmelweit (eds), *Knowing Women: Feminism and Knowledge.* Cambridge: Polity Press.

Bordo, S. (1993) *Unbearable Weight: Feminism, Western Culture and the Body.* Berkeley: University of California Press.

Carby, H. (1982) White woman listen! Black feminism and the boundaries of sisterhood. In Centre for Contemporary Cultural Studies, *The Empire Strikes Back: Race and Racism in 70s Britain.* London: Hutchinson.

Cashmore, E. and Troyna. B. (1990) *Introduction to Race Relations.* London: Falmer Press.

Cohen, R. and Kennedy, P. (2000) *Global Sociology.* Basingstoke: Palgrave.

Coward, R. (1984) *Female Desire: Women's Sexuality Today.* London: Paladin.

Crowley, H. and Himmelweit, S. (eds) (1992) *Knowing Women: Feminism and Knowledge.* Cambridge: Polity Press.

Daly, M. (1979) *Gyn/Ecology: the Metaethics of Radical Feminism.* London: The Women's Press.

Fanon, F. (1986) *Black Skins, White Masks* (trans. C. L. Markman). London: Pluto.

Featherstone, M., Hepworth, M. and Turner, B. S. (eds) (1991) *The Body: Social Process and Cultural Theory.* London: Sage.

Freud, S. (1933) New introductory lectures on psychoanalysis. In J. Strachey (ed.), *The Standard Edition of the Complete Works of Sigmund Freud, volume 22.* London: Hogarth Press.

Gates, H. L., Jr (1986) *'Race', Writing and Difference.* Chicago: Chicago University Press.

Giddens, A. (1990) *The Consequences of Modernity*. Cambridge: Polity Press.

Gilroy, P. (1987) *'There Ain't No Black in the Union Jack': the Cultural Politics of Race and Nation*. London: Hutchinson.

Glissant, E. (1992) Caribbean discourse: reversion and diversion. In A. J. Arnold and K. Drame (eds), *Caribbean Discourse: Selected Essays*. Charlottesville: University Press of Virginia.

Haaken, J. (2002) Cultural amnesia: memory, trauma and war. In *Signs: Journal of Women in Culture and Society*, 28(1).

Hammad, S. (2002) Composites. In *Signs: Journal of Women in Culture and Society*, 28(1).

Haythorne, E. (1990) *On Earth to Make the Numbers Up*. Castleford: Yorkshire Art Circus.

Heron, L. (ed.) (1985) *Truth, Dare, Promise: Girls Growing up in the Fifties*. London: Virago.

hooks, b. (1996) *Bone Black: Memories of Girlhood*. London: The Women's Press.

Jordan, G. and Weedon, C. (1995) *Cultural Politics: Class, Gender, Race and the Postmodern World*. Oxford: Blackwell.

Kureishi, H. (1990) *The Buddha of Suburbia*. London: Faber and Faber.

Marx, K. (1859) *A Contribution to the Critique of Political Economy*. Reprinted in *Marx/Engels: Selected Works in One Volume*. London: Lawrence and Wishart (1968).

Mercer, K. (1990) Welcome to the jungle: identity and diversity in postmodern politics. In *Identity, Community, Culture, Difference*. London: Lawrence and Wishart.

Minh-ha, Trinh T. (1989) *Woman, Native, Other: Writing, Postcoloniality, and Feminism*. Bloomington: Indiana University Press.

Robins, K. (1997) What in the world's going on? In P. du Gay (ed.), *Production of Culture/Cultures of Production*. London: Sage/Open University.

Rutherford, J. (ed.) (1990) *Identity: Community, Culture, Difference*. London: Lawrence and Wishart.

Shilling, C. (1993) *The Body and Social Theory*. London: Sage.

Shilling, C. (1997) The body and difference. In K. Woodward (ed.), *Identity and Difference*. London: Sage.

Simons, M. and Bleiman, B. (1987) *More Lives*. London: ILEA English Centre.

Stanley, L. (1992) *The Auto/biographical I: the Theory and Practice of Feminist Auto/biography*. Manchester: Manchester University Press.

Stevens, R. (1994) Evolutionary origins of identity. In J. Anderson and M. Ricci (eds), *Society and Social Science: a Reader*. Milton Keynes: Open University.

Weeks, J. (1990) The value of difference. In J. Rutherford (ed.), *Identity: Community, Culture, Difference*. London: Lawrence and Wishart.

Woodward, K. (ed.) (1997) *Identity and Difference*. London: Sage/Open University.

Chapter 3

Allen, R. C. (ed.) (1987) *Channels of Discourse*. Chapel Hill and London: University of North Carolina Press.

Barthes, R. (1967) *Elements of Semiology*. London: Jonathan Cape.

Barthes, R. (1973) *Mythologies*. London: Granada.

Belsey, C. (1980) *Critical Practice*. London: Methuen.

Benveniste, E. (1971) *Problems in General Linguistics*. Coral Gables, FL: University of Miami Press.

Berger, J. (1972) *Ways of Seeing*. London: BBC/Penguin.

Betterton, R. (ed.) (1987) *Looking On: Images of Femininity in the Visual Arts and Media*. London: Pandora.

Bobo, J. (1988) *The Color Purple*: black women as cultural readers. Reprinted in Dines and Humez (1995).

Bonner, F., Goodman, L., Allen, R., Janes, L. and King, C. (eds) (1992) *Imagining Women: Cultural Representations and Gender*. Cambridge: Polity Press.

Branston, G. and Stafford, R. (1996) *The Media Student's Book*. London: Routledge.

Coward, R. (1984) *Female Desire: Women's Sexuality Today*. London: Paladin.

Dines, G. and Humez, J. M. (eds) (1995) *Gender, Race and Class in Media: a Textreader*. London: Sage.

Duncker, P. (1992) *Sisters and Strangers: an Introduction to Contemporary Feminist Fiction*. Oxford: Blackwell.

Dyer, R. (1983) Seen to be believed: some problems in the representation of gay people as typical. *Studies in Visual Communication*, 9(2). Reprinted in Dyer (1993).

Dyer, R. (1993) *The Matter of Images: Essays in Representation*. London: Routledge.

Fiske, J. (1987) *Television Culture*. London: Routledge.

Foucault, M. (1972) *The Archaeology of Knowledge*. London: Tavistock.

Foucault, M. (1973) *The Birth of the Clinic*. London: Tavistock.

Foucault, M. (1975) *Discipline and Punish: the Birth of the Prison*. London: Allen Lane.

Foucault, M. (1978) *The History of Sexuality*. Harmondsworth: Penguin.

Frederickson, G. (1987) *The Black Image in the White Mind*. Hanover, NH: Wesleyan University Press.

Gates, H. L. (1988) *The Signifying Monkey*. Oxford: Oxford University Press.

Gledhill, C. (1984) Klute I: a contemporary film noir and feminist criticism. In E. A. Kaplan (ed.), *Women in Film Noir*. London: British Film Institute.

Golby, J. (1986) *Culture and Society in Britain 1850–1890*. Oxford: Oxford University Press/The Open University.

Gray, A. and McGuigan, J. (eds) (1993) *Studying Culture: an Introductory Reader*. London: Edward Arnold.

Grossberg, L. (1984) Strategies of Marxist cultural interpretation. *Critical Studies in Mass Communication*, 1.

Hall, S. (1990) Encoding/decoding in television discourse. In S. Hall, D. Hobson, A. Lowe and P. Willis (eds), *Culture: Media: Language*. London: Hutchinson. Reprinted in S. During (ed., 1993), *The Cultural Studies Reader*. London: Routledge.

Hall, S. (1992) The West and the rest. In S. Hall and B. Gieben (eds), *Formations of Modernity*. Cambridge: Polity Press/Open University.

Hall, S. (1997) *Representation: Cultural Representations and Signifying Practices*. London: Sage/Open University.

hooks, b. (1992) *Black Looks: Race and Representation*. Boston: South End Press.

Isaacs, S. (1948) *Childhood and After*. London: Routledge and Kegan Paul.

Levack, B. (1995) *The Witch-hunt in Early Modern Europe*, 2nd edn. New York: Longman.

Mackenzie, J. (ed.) (1986) *Imperialism and Popular Culture*. Manchester: Manchester University Press.

McClintock, A. (1995) *Imperial Leather*. London: Routledge.

McCracken, E. (1993) *Decoding Women's Magazine: from 'Mademoiselle' to 'Ms'*. London: Macmillan.

McDonald, M (1995) *Representing Women: Myths of Femininity in the Popular Media*. London: Edward Arnold.

Morley, D. (1989) Changing paradigms in audience studies. In E. Seiter (ed.), *Rethinking Television Audiences*. Chapel Hill: University of North Carolina Press.

O'Sullivan, T., Hartley, J., Saunders, D. and Fiske, J. (1983) *Key Concepts in Communication*. London: Methuen.

Said, E. (1978) *Orientalism*. Harmondsworth: Penguin.

Seiter, E. (1990) Different children, different dreams: racial representation in advertising. Reprinted in Dines and Humez (1995).

Showalter, E. (1997) *Hystories: Hysterical Epidemics and Modern Culture*. New York: Columbia University Press.

Spence, J. (1980) What do people do all day? Class and gender in images of women. *Screen Education*, 29. Reprinted in Spence (1995).

Spence, J. (1995) *Cultural Sniping: the Art of Transgression*. London: Routledge.

Saussure, F. de (1974) *Course in General Linguistics*, trans. W. Baskin. London: Fontana.

Williamson, J. (1978) *Decoding Advertisements: Ideology and Meaning in Advertising*. London: Marion Boyars.

Chapter 4

Ascherson, N. (1987) 'Heritage' as vulgar English nationalism. *Observer*, 29 November; and Why 'heritage' is right-wing. *Observer*, 8 November.

Barthes, R. (1973) *Mythologies*. London: Granada.

Baxendale, J. and Pawling, C. (1996) *Narrating the Thirties: a Decade in the Making, 1930 to the Present*. Basingstoke: Macmillan.

Benjamin, W. (1973) *Illuminations*. London: Collins.

Calder, A. (1992) *The Myth of the Blitz*. London: Pimlico.

Clarke, J., Crichter, C. and Johnson, R. (eds) (1979) *Working Class Culture: Studies in History and Theory*. London: Hutchinson.

Giles, J. and Middleton, T. (1995) *Writing Englishness 1900–50: an Introductory Sourcebook on National Identity*. London: Routledge.

Hewison, R. (1987) *The Heritage Industry: Britain in a Climate of Decline*. London: London University Press.

Jenkins, K. (1991) *Re-thinking History*. London: Routledge.

Johnson, R. (1982) *Making Histories: Studies in History-writing and Politics*. London: Hutchinson.

Marwick, A. (1970) *The Nature of History*. London and Basingstoke: Macmillan.

Marwick, A. (1986) Introduction to history. *Unit 1–3 A102, Arts Foundation Course*. Milton Keynes: Open University.

Paxman, J. (1998) *The English: a Portrait of a People*. London: Michael Joseph.

Rowbotham, S. (1973) *Hidden from History*. London: Pluto Press.

Samuel, R. (1994) *Theatres of Memory*. London: Verso.

Smith-Rosenberg, C. (1985) *Disorderly Conduct: Visions of Gender in Victorian America*. New York: Knopf.

Spence, J. (1980) What do people do all day? Class and gender in images of women. *Screen Education*, 29. Reprinted in J. Spence (1995), *Cultural Sniping: the Art of Transgression*. London: Routledge.

Steedman, C. (1992) *Past Tenses: Essays on Writing Autobiography anti History*. London: Rivers Oram.

Thompson, E. P. (1963) *The Making of the English Working Class*. Harmondsworth. Penguin.

Tosh, J. (1991) *The Pursuit of History: Aims, Methods and New Directions in the Study of Modern History*. London and New York: Longman.

White, H. (1973) *Metahistory: the Historical Imagination in Nineteenth Century Europe*. Baltimore: Johns Hopkins University Press.

Williams, R. (1976) *Keywords: a Vocabulary of Culture and Society*. London: Fontana.

Wright, P. (1985) *On Living in an Old Country: the National Past in Contemporary Britain*. London: Verso.

Chapter 5

Agnew, J. (1993) Representing space: space, scale and culture in social science. In J. Duncan and D. Ley (eds), *Place/Culture/Representation*. London: Routledge.

Allen, J. P. and Turner, E. (1997) *The Ethnic Quilt: Population Diversity in Southern California*. Northridge: Center for Geographical Studies, California State University, Northridge.

Barnes, T. J. and Duncan, J. (1992) *Writing Worlds: Discourse, Text and Metaphor in the Representation of Landscape.* London: Routledge.

Best, S. and Kellner, D. (1991) *Postmodern Theory: Critical Interrogations.* London: Macmillan.

Bhabha, H. (1994) *The Location of Culture.* London: Routledge.

Boehmer, E. (1995) *Colonial and Postcolonial Literature: Migrant Metaphors.* Oxford: Oxford University Press.

Bondi, L. (1993) Locating Identity Politics. In M. Keith and S. Pile (eds), *Place and the Politics of Identity.* London: Routledge.

Cosgrove, D. and Domosh, M. (1993) Author and authority: writing the new cultural geography. In J. Duncan and D. Ley (eds), *Place/Culture/Representation.* London: Routledge.

Davis, M. (1994) Cannibal city: Los Angeles and the destruction of nature. In R. Ferguson (ed.), *Urban Revisions: Current Projects for the Public Realm.* Cambridge, Mass.: MIT Press.

Davis, M. (1998) *City of Quartz: Excavating the Future in Los Angeles.* London: Pimlico.

Davis, M. (1999) *Ecology of Fear: Los Angeles and the Imagination of Disaster.* New York: Vintage Books.

de Certeau, M. (1984) *The Practice of Everyday Life.* Berkeley: University of California Press.

DeMarco, G. (1988) *A Short History of Los Angeles.* San Francisco: Lexikos.

Domanick, J. (1994) *To Protect and Serve: the LAPD's Century of War in the City of Dreams.* New York: Pocket Books.

Duncan, J. and Ley, D. (eds) (1993) *Place/Culture/Representation.* London: Routledge. (See especially 'Introduction: representing the place of culture', pp. 1–24.)

During, S. (ed.) (1993) *The Cultural Studies Reader.* London: Routledge. (See especially part 2, 'Space and time', pp. 135–73.)

Fiske, J. (1992) Cultural studies and the culture of everyday life. In L. Grossberg, C. Nelson and P. Treichler (eds), *Cultural Studies.* London: Routledge.

Foucault, M. (1986) Of other spaces. *Diacritics*, 16 (Spring).

Foucault, M. (1993) Space, power and knowledge. In During, S. (ed.).

Herbert, Steve (1997) *Policing Space: Territoriality and the Los Angeles Police Department.* Minneapolis: University of Minnesota Press.

Harvey, D. (1989) *The Condition of Postmodernity.* Oxford: Blackwell.

Jackson, P. (1994) *Maps of Meaning: An Introduction to Cultural Geography.* London: Routledge.

Jameson, F. (1984) Postmodernism, or the cultural logic of late capitalism. *New Left Review*, 146.

Joyce, J. (1993) *A James Joyce Reader* (London: Penguin).

Keil, R. (1998) *Los Angeles: Globalization, Urbanization and Social Struggles.* London: Wiley-Academy.

Keith, M. and Pile, S. (eds) (1993) *Place and the Politics of Identity.* London: Routledge.

Klein, N. M. (1997) *The History of Forgetting: Los Angeles and the Erasure of Memory*. London: Verso.

Kowinski, W. S. (1985) *The Malling of America: an Inside Look at the Great Consumer Paradise*. New York: Pantheon.

Laclau, E. (1990) *New Reflections on the Revolutions of our Time*. London: Verso.

Lave, J. (1988) *Cognition in Practice*. Cambridge: Cambridge University Press.

Lefebvre, H. (1991) *The Production of Space*. Oxford: Blackwell.

Massey, D. (1991) A global sense of place. *Marxism Today*, June. Reprinted in A. Gray and J. McGuigan (eds, 1993), *Studying Culture: an Introductory Reader*. London: Edward Arnold.

McWilliams, C. (1979) *Southern California: an Island on the Land*. Salt Lake City: Peregrine Smith.

Morris, M. (1988) Things to do with shopping centres. In S. Sheridan (ed.), *Grafts: Feminist Cultural Criticism*. London: Verso.

Ryan, S. (1994) Inscribing emptiness. In C. Tiffin and A. Lawson (eds), *De-Scribing Empire*. London: Routledge.

Scott, M. (1949) *Metropolitan Los Angeles: One Community*. Los Angeles: Haynes Foundation.

Smith, N. and Katz, C. (1993) Grounding metaphor: towards a spatialized politics. In M. Keith and S. Pile (eds).

Soja, E. (1989) *Postmodern Geographies: the Reassertion of Space in Critical Social Theory*. London: Verso.

Soja, E. (1996) *ThirdSpace: Journeys to Los Angeles and Other Real-and-Imagined Places*. Oxford: Blackwell.

Soja, E. (2000) *Postmetropolis: Critical Studies of Cities and Regions*. Oxford: Blackwell.

Soja, E. and Hooper B. (1993) The spaces that difference makes: some notes on the geographical margins of the new cultural politics. In M. Keith and S. Pile (eds).

Vujakovic, P. (1995) The Sleeping Beauty complex: maps as texts in the construction of national identity. In T. Hill and W. Hughes (eds), *Contemporary Writing and National Identity*. Bath: Sulis Press.

Waldinger, R. and Bozorgmehr, M. (eds) (1996) *Ethnic Los Angeles*. New York: Russell Sage Foundation.

Williams, R. (1965) *The Long Revolution*. London: Penguin.

Williams, R. (1977) *Marxism and Literature*. Oxford: Oxford University Press.

Willis, S. (1991) *A Primer for Daily Life*. London: Routledge.

Chapter 6

Apostolopoulos, Y., Leivadi, S. and Yiannakis, A. (eds) (1996) *The Sociology of Tourism: Theoretical and Empirical Investigations*. London: Routledge.

Berman, M. (1982) *All That is Solid Melts into Air: the Experience of Modernity*. New York: Simon and Schuster.

Bourdieu, P. (1984) *Distinction*. London: Routledge and Kegan Paul.

Cohen, E. (1996) A phenomenology of tourist experiences. In Y. Apostolopoulos, S. Leivadi and A. Yiannakis (eds), *The Sociology of Tourism: Theoretical and Empirical Investigations*. London: Routledge.

Cohen, R. and Kennedy, P. (2000) *Global Sociology*. Basingstoke: Palgrave.

Crystal, E. (1989) Tourism in Toraja (Sulawesi, Indonesia). In V. L. Smith (eds), *Hosts and Guests* (2nd edn). Philadelphia: University of Pennsylvania Press.

Davis, F. (1979) *Yearning for Yesterday*. New York: Free Press.

Davis, S. G. (1996) The theme park: global industry and cultural form. *Media, Culture and Society*, 18.

Dicks, B. (2003) *Culture on Display: The Production of Contemporary Visibility*. Maidenhead: Open University Press.

English Heritage (2005) Interactive Guide to English Heritage CD-Rom.

Feifer, M. (1985) *Going Places*. London: Routledge.

Friedman, J. (1990) Being in the world: globalization and localization. In M. Featherstone (ed.), *Global Culture: Nationalism, Globalization and Modernity*. London: Sage.

Glasser, R. (1975) Life force or tranquilizer? *Society and Leisure*, 7(3).

Harrison, D. (1992) Tradition, tourism and modernity in Swaziland. In D. Harrison (ed.), *Tourism and the Less Developed Countries*. Chichester: Wiley.

Harrison, D. (1995) Tourism, capitalism and development in less developed countries. In L. Sklair (ed.), *Capitalism and Development*. London: Routledge.

Hewison, R. (1987) *The Heritage Industry: Britain in a Climate of Decline*. London: Methuen.

Hewison, R. (1989) Heritage: an interpretation. In D. Uzzell (ed.), *Heritage Interpretation. Volume 1: The Natural and Built Environment*. London: Belhaven Press.

Kirshenblatt-Gimblett, B. (1998) *Destination Culture: Tourism, Museums and Heritage*. Berkeley: University of California Press.

Lanfant, M.-F., Allcock, J. B. and Bruner, G. M. (eds) (1995) *International Tourism*. London: Sage.

MacCannell, D. (1976) *The Tourist: a New Theory of the Leisure Class*. New York: Schocken Books.

McGuigan, J. (1996) *Culture and the Public Sphere*. London: Routledge.

McKean, P. F. (1989) Towards a theoretical analysis of tourism: economic dualism and cultural involution in Bali. In V. L. Smith (ed.), *Hosts and Guests* (2nd edn). Philadelphia: University of Pennsylvania Press.

Mugerauer, R. (2001) Openings to Each Other in the Technological Age. In N. AlSayaad (ed.), *Consuming Tradition, Manufacturing Heritage*. London: Routledge.

National Trust (1993) *Mr Straw's House: an Illustrated Souvenir*. National Trust Enterprises.

Picard, M. (1995) Cultural heritage and tourist capital: cultural tourism in Bali. In M.-F. Lanfant, J. B. Allcock and G. M. Bruner (eds), *International Tourism*. London: Sage.

QPD (Quality Paperbacks Direct) (2005) *QPD Review* (October).

Rozenberg, D. (1995) International tourism and utopia: the Balearic islands. In M.-F. Lanfant, J. B. Allcock and G. M. Bruner (eds) *International Tourism*. London: Sage.

Sen, A. (2004) Asian values and the West's claim to uniqueness. In C. Lemert (ed.), *Social Theory: the Multicultural and Classic Readings*. Boulder, CO, and Oxford: Westview Press.

Smith, V. L. (eds) (1989) *Hosts and Guests* (2nd edn). Philadelphia: University of Pennsylvania Press.

Urry, J. (2002) *The Tourist Gaze*. London, California and New Delhi: Sage.

Volkman, T. A. (1984) Great performances: Toraja cultural identity in the 1970s. *American Ethnologist*, 11(1).

World Tourism Organization. *Tourism Market Trends, 2004*. www.world-tourism. org/.

Wright, P. (1985) *On Living in an Old Country*. London: Verso.

Chapter 7

Barker, E. (1947) An attempt at perspective. In E. Barker (ed.), *The Character of England*. Oxford: Clarendon Press.

Barry, P. (2002) *Beginning Theory: an Introduction to Literary and Cultural Theory*. Manchester: Manchester University Press.

Bourdieu, P. (1986) *Distinction: a Social Critique of the Judgement of Taste*, trans. R. Nice. Cambridge, MA: Harvard University Press.

Brooker, P. and Widdowson, P. (1986) A literature for England. In R. Colls and P. Dodds (eds), *Englishness: Politics and Culture 1880–1920*. London: Croom Helm.

Bullen, J. B. (1988) *Post-impressionists in England*. London: Routledge.

Carpenter, E. (1908) *The Intermediate Sex: a Study of Some Transitional Types of Men and Women*.

Clark, K. and Holquist, M. (1984) *Mikhail Bakhtin*. Cambridge, MA: Harvard University Press.

Colls, R. and Dodds, P. (eds) (1986) *Englishness: Politics and Culture 1880–1920*. London: Croom Helm.

Crowther, M. A. (1992) The tramp. In R. Porter (ed.), *Myths of the English*. Cambridge: Polity Press.

Dawson, G. (1994) *Soldier Heroes*. London: Routledge.

de Certeau, M. (1984) *The Practice of Everyday Life*. Berkeley: University of California Press.

Dellamora, R. (1996) Homosexual scandal and compulsory heterosexuality in the 1890s. In L. Pykett (ed.), *Reading Fin de Siècle Fictions.* London: Longman.

Eagleton, T. (1987) The end of English. *Textual Practice,* 1(1).

Fiske, J. (1989) *Reading the Popular.* London: Unwin Hyman.

Fiske, J. (1991) *Understanding Popular Culture.* London: Unwin Hyman.

Flint, K. (1984) *Impressionists in England.* London: Routledge.

Ford, F. M. (1907) Extract from *The Spirit of the People.* In J. Giles and T. Middleton (1995).

Forster, E. M. (1971) *Maurice.* Harmondsworth: Penguin.

Frith, S. (1991) The good, the bad, and the indifferent: defending culture from the populists. *Diacritics,* 21(4).

Frow, J. (1995) *Cultural Studies and Cultural Value.* Oxford: Oxford University Press.

Giles, J. and Middleton, T. (1995) *Writing Englishness 1900–50: an Introductory Source-book on National Identity.* London: Routledge.

Grahame, K. (1983) *The Wind in the Willows.* Oxford: World's Classics.

Green, P. (1959) *Kenneth Grahame: a Study of His Life, Work and Times.* London: John Murray.

Harrison, C. and Wood, J. (eds) (1992) *Art in Theory.* Oxford: Blackwell.

Hirschkop, K. and Shepherd, D. (eds) (1989) *Bakhtin and Cultural Theory.* Manchester: Manchester University Press.

HMSO (1994) *English in the National Curriculum: Draft Proposals, May 1994.* London: HMSO.

Holden, P. and Ruppel, R. J. (eds) (2003) *Imperial Desire: Dissident Sexualities and Colonial Literature.* Minneapolis: University of Minnesota Press.

Holquist, M. (1990) *Dialogism: Bakhtin and His World.* London: Routledge.

Hughes, R. (1993) *The Culture of Complaint: the Fraying of America.* Oxford: Oxford University Press.

Humphries, S. and Gordon, P. (1996) *A Man's World.* London: BBC Books.

Johnson, R., et al. (2004) *The Practice of Cultural Studies.* London: Sage.

Knowles, J. (1996) Marxism, new historicism, cultural materialism. In R. Bradford (ed.), *Introducing Literary Studies.* London: Harvester.

Koestenbaum, W. (1989) *Double Talk.* London: Routledge.

Lal, V. (1996) *South Asian Cultural Studies.* Delhi: Manohar.

Ledger, S. (1997) *The New Woman: Fiction and Feminism at the Fin de Siècle.* Manchester: Manchester University Press.

Marriott, J. (1996) Sensation of the abyss: the urban poor and modernity. In M. Nava and A. O'Shea (eds), *Modern Times: Reflection on a Century of English Modernity.* London: Routledge.

Mason, M. (1994) *The Making of Victorian Sexuality.* Oxford: Oxford University Press.

McCracken, S. (1998) *Pulp: Reading Popular Fiction.* Manchester: Manchester University Press.

McGuigan, J. (1992) *Cultural Populism*. London: Routledge.

Montgomery, M. et al. (1992) *Ways of Reading: Advanced Reading Skills for Students of English Literature*. London: Routledge.

Newbolt Committee (1921) *The Teaching of English in England*. London: HMSO.

Pykett, L. (1995) *Engendering Fictions*. London: Arnold.

Schwarz, B. (1996) Night battles: hooligan and citizen. In M. Nava and A. O'Shea (eds), *Modern Times: Reflection on a Century of English Modernity*. London: Routledge.

Sedgwick, E. (1985) *Between Men: English Literature and Male Homosocial Desire*. New York: Columbia University Press.

Sedgwick, E. K. (1994) *Epistemology of the Closet*. London: Penguin.

Showalter, E. (1991) *Sexual Anarchy*. London: Bloomsbury.

Storey, J. (1993) *An Introductory Guide to Cultural Theory and Popular Culture*. London: Harvester Wheatsheaf.

Storey, J. (1996) *Cultural Studies and the Study of Popular Culture*. Edinburgh: Edinburgh University Press.

Taylor, M. (1989) *Lads: Love Poetry of the Trenches*. London: Constable.

Todorov, T. (1984) *Mikhail Bakhtin: The Dialogical Principle*, trans. W. Godzich. Manchester: Manchester University Press.

Twitchell, J. B. (1992) *Carnival Culture: the Trashing of Taste in America*. New York: Columbia University Press.

Weeks, J. (1981) *Sex, Politics and Society*. London: Longman.

Weeks, J. (1989) The idea of sexual minorities. In R. Samuel (ed.), *Patriotism: the Making and Unmaking of British National Identity. Volume 2: Minorities and Outsiders*. London: Routledge.

Williams, R. (1963) *Culture and Society, 1780–1950*. London: Chatto and Windus.

Williams, R. (1976) *Keywords: a Vocabulary of Culture and Society*. London: Fontana.

Williams, R. (1981) *Culture*. London: Fontana.

Williams, R. (1993) Culture is ordinary. In A. Gray and J. McGuigan (eds), *Studying Culture: an Introductory Reader*. London: Edward Arnold.

Chapter 8

Althusser, L. (1971) Ideology and ideological state apparatuses. In *Lenin and Philosophy and Other Essays*, trans. B. Brewster. London: New Left Books.

Anzaldúa, G. (1987) La conciencia de la mestiza/towards a new consciousness. In *Borderlands/La Frontera: the New Mestiza*. San Francisco: Spinsters/Aunt Lute.

Bordo, S. (1990) Reading the slender body. In M. Jacobus, E. Fox Keller and S. Shuttleworth (eds), *Body/Politics: Women and the Discourse of Science.* New York and London: Routledge.

Butler, J. (1990) *Gender Trouble: Feminism and the Subversion of Identity.* London: Routledge.

Crawford, R. (1985) A cultural account of 'health' – self-control, release, and the social body. In J. McKinlay (ed.), *Issues in the Political Economy of Health Care.* New York: Methuen.

Crowley, H. and Himmelweit, S. (eds) (1992) *Knowing Women: Feminism and Knowledge.* Cambridge: Polity Press.

Douglas, M. (1966) *Purity and Danger: an Analysis of Concepts of Pollution and Taboo.* London: Routledge.

Duffy, C. A. (1994) *Selected Poems*: Harmondsworth: Penguin.

Eagleton, M. (ed.) (1996) *Feminist Literary Theory: a Reader*, 2nd edn. Oxford: Blackwell.

Easthope, A. and McGowan, K. (eds) (1992) *A Critical and Cultural Theory Reader.* Buckingham: Open University Press.

Featherstone, M., Hepworth, M. and Turner, B. S. (eds) (1991) *The Body: Social Process and Cultural Theory.* London: Sage.

Foucault, M. (1967) *Madness and Civilization.* London: Tavistock.

Foucault, M. (1973) *The Birth of the Clinic.* London: Tavistock.

Foucault, M. (1975) *Discipline and Punish: the Birth of the Prison.* London: Allan Lane.

Fuss, D. (1989) *Essentially Speaking: Feminism, Nature and Difference.* London: Routledge.

Hall, S. (1996) Signification, representation, ideology: Althusser and the post-structuralist debates. In J. Curran, D. Morley and V. Walkerdine (eds), *Cultural Studies and Communications.* London: Edward Arnold.

Hill Collins, P. (2000) *Black Feminist Thought: Knowledge, Consciousness and the Politics of Empowerment.* New York: Routledge.

hooks, b. (1991) *Yearning: Race, Gender and Cultural Politics.* London: Turnaround (also extracted in Eagleton, 1996).

Howson, A. (2003) *The Body in Society: an Introduction.* Cambridge: Polity.

Kristeva, J. (1986) A question of subjectivity (interview with Susan Sellers). *Women's Review*, 12 (also extracted in Eagleton, 1996).

Lacan, J. (1949) *Ecrits: a Selection*, trans. Alan Sheridan. London: Tavistock and Norton.

Martin, E. (1991) The egg and the sperm: how science has constructed a romance based on stereotypical male-female roles. *Signs: Journal of Women in Culture and Society*, 16.

Martin, E. (1992) Body narratives, body boundaries. In L. Grossberg, C. Nelson and P. Treichler (eds), *Cultural Studies.* New York: Routledge.

Minsky, R. (1992) Lacan. In H. Crowley and S. Himmelweit (eds), *Knowing Women: Feminism and Knowledge.* Cambridge: Polity Press.

Moi, T. (ed.) (1986) *The Kristeva Reader*. Oxford: Blackwell.

Moi, T. (ed.) (1987) *French Feminist Thought: a Reader*. Oxford: Blackwell.

Nicholson, L. (ed.) *Feminism/Postmodernism*. New York: Routledge.

Oliver, K. (ed.) (2000) *French Feminism Reader*. Lanham, MD: Rowman and Littlefield.

Oliver, K. and Walsh, L. (2005) *Contemporary French Feminism*. Oxford Readings in Feminism. New York: Oxford University Press.

Rosen, T. (1983) *Strong and Sexy: the New Body Beautiful*. London: Columbus Books.

Shilling, C. (1993) *The Body and Social Theory*. London: Sage.

Shilling, C. (1997) The body and difference. In K. Woodward (ed.), *Identity and Difference*. London: Sage.

Shilling, C. (2004) *The Body in Culture, Technology and Society*. London: Sage.

Sterling, A. F. (2001) *Sexing the Body: Gender Politics and the Construction of Sexuality*. New York: Basic Books.

Turner, B. S. (1992) *Regulating Bodies: Essays in Medical Sociology*. London: Routledge.

Weeks, J. (1989) *Sex, Politics and Society: the Regulation of Sexuality since 1800*. London: Longman.

Weeks, J. (2003) *Sexuality*. Key Ideas Series. London: Routledge.

Chapter 9

Adorno, T. (1991) *The Culture Industry: Selected Essays on Mass Culture*, ed. J. M. Bernstein. London: Verso.

Adorno, T. and Horkheimer, M. (1947) The culture industry: enlightenment as mass deception. In *Dialectic of Enlightenment*. London: Verso.

Baudrillard, J. (1988) *Selected Writings*. Cambridge: Polity Press.

Bordo, S. (1990) Reading the slender body. In M. Jacobus, E. Fox Keller and S. Shuttleworth (eds), *Body/Politics: Women and the Discourse of Science*. New York and London: Routledge.

Bordwell, D., Steiger, J. and Thompson, K. (1985) *The Classical Hollywood Cinema: Film Style and Mode of Production to 1960*. New York: Columbia University Press.

Bourdieu, P. (1978) How can one be a sports fan? *Social Science Information*, 17(6).

Braham, P. (1997) Fashion: unpacking a cultural production. In P. du Gay (ed.), *Production of Culture/Cultures of Production*. London: Sage/Open University.

Drakulic, S. (1992) *How We Survived Communism and Even Laughed*. London: Vintage.

du Gay, P. (ed.) (1997) *Production of Culture/Cultures of Production*. London: Sage/Open University.

du Gay, P. et al. (eds) (1997) *Doing Cultural Studies: the Story of the Sony Walkman*. London: Sage/Open University.

During, S. (ed.) (1993) *The Cultural Studies Reader.* London: Routledge.

Dyer, R. (1979) The role of stereotypes. In J. Cook and M. Lewington (eds), *Images of Alcoholism.* London: British Film Institute.

Fiske, J. (1987) *Television Culture.* London: Routledge.

Giddens, A. (1990) *The Consequences of Modernity.* Cambridge: Polity Press.

Gillespie, M. (1989) Technology and tradition – audio-visual culture among South Asian families in West London. *Cultural Studies*, 3(2). Reprinted in A. Gray and J. McGuigan (eds, 1993), *Studying Culture: an Introductory Reader.* London: Edward Arnold.

Gomery, D. (1976) Writing the history of the American film industry: Warner Bros and sound. *Screen*, 17(2).

Grossberg, L. (1984) Strategies of Marxist cultural interpretation. *Critical Studies in Mass Communication*, 1.

Gullestad, M. (1992) *The Art of Social Relations: Essays on Culture, Social Action and Everyday Life in Modern Norway.* Oslo: Scandinavian University Press.

Gullestad, M. (1996) *Everyday Life Philosophers: Modernity, Morality and Autobiography in Norway.* Oslo: Scandinavian University Press.

Hartley, J. (1982) *Understanding News.* London: Methuen.

Hebdige, D. (1979) *Subculture: the Meaning of Style.* London: Methuen.

King, A. (ed.) (1991) *Culture, Globalization and the World System.* Basingstoke: Macmillan.

Klein, N. (2000) *No Logo.* London: Flamingo.

Lury, C. (1996) *Consumer Culture.* Cambridge: Polity Press.

McRobbie, A. (1996) *More!* New sexualities in girls' and women's magazines. In J. Curran, D. Morley and V. Walkerdine (eds), *Cultural Studies and Communications.* London: Edward Arnold.

Marcuse, H. (1964) *One Dimensional Man.* London: Routledge.

Miller, D. (1997) Consumption and its consequences. In H. Mackay (ed.), *Consumption and Everyday Life.* London: Sage/Open University.

Miller, D. (1998) Coca-Cola: a black sweet drink from Trinidad. In D. Miller (ed.), *Material Cultures.* London: University College London Press.

Morley, D. (1986) *Family Television: Cultural Power and Domestic Leisure.* London: Comedia.

Morley, D. (1992) *Television, Audiences and Cultural Studies.* London: Routledge.

Moore, S. (1997) What girl power means. *Independent*, 14 November.

Nava, M., Blake, A., MacRury, I. and Richards, B. (eds) (1997) *Buy This Book: Studies in Advertising and Consumption.* London: Routledge.

Packard, V. (1957) *The Hidden Persuaders.* London: Longmans, Green and Co.

Perkins, T. E. (1979) Rethinking stereotypes. In M. Barrett, P. Corrigan, A. Kuhn and J. Wolff (eds), *Ideology and Cultural Production.* London: Croom Helm.

Porter, R. (1993) Baudrillard: history, hysteria and consumption. In C. Rojek and B. S. Turner (eds), *Forget Baudrillard?* London and New York: Routledge.

Raban, J. (1974) *Soft City.* London: Fontana.

Radway, J. (1987) *Reading the Romance: Women, Patriarchy and Popular Literature.* London: Verso.

Schatz, T. (1981) *Hollywood Genres: Formulas, Filmmaking, and the Studio System.* New York: Random House.

Selby, K. and Cowdery, R. (1995) *How to Study Television.* Basingstoke: Macmillan.

Storey, J. (1996) *Cultural Studies and the Study of Popular Culture: Theories and Methods.* Edinburgh: Edinburgh University Press.

Thompson, K. (ed.) (1997) *Media and Cultural Regulation.* London: Sage/Open University.

Turner, G. (1993) *Film as Social Practice.* London: Routledge.

Veblen, T. (1899) *The Theory of the Leisure Class: an Economic Study of Institutions.* New York: Macmillan.

Williams, R. (1976) *Keywords: a Vocabulary of Culture and Society.* London: Fontana.

Chapter 10

Alvarado, M., Gutch, R. and Wollen, T. (1987) *Learning the Media.* London: Macmillan.

Bastleer, J. et al. (1985) *Rewriting English: Cultural Politics of Gender and Class.* London: Methuen.

Batelle, J. (2005) *The Search: How Google and Its Rivals Rewrote the Rules of Business and Transformed our Culture.* New York: Nicolas Brealey Publishing.

Brunsdon, C. and Morley, D. (1978) *Everyday Television: Nationwide.* London: BFI.

Bryman, A. (ed.) (2001) *Ethnography.* 4 vols. London: Sage. (See especially vol. 3: *Issues in Ethnography.*)

Burnett, R. and Marshall, D. P. (2003) *Web Theory: An Introduction.* London: Routledge.

Castells, M. (2004) *The Power of Identity.* The information age: economy, society and culture, vol. 2. Oxford: Blackwell.

Cheung, C. (2004) Identity construction and self-presentation on personal homepages: emancipatory potentials and reality constraints. In D. Gauntlett and R. Horsley (eds), *Web-Studies,* 2nd edn. London: Arnold.

Darley, A. (2000) *Visual Digital Culture: Surface Play and Spectacle in New Media Genres.* London: Routledge.

De Kerckhove, D. (1995) *The Skin of Culture: Investigating the New Electronic Reality.* London: Kogan Page.

Denzin, N. (1997) *Interpretive Ethnography: Ethnographic Practice for the 21st Century.* London: Sage.

Denzin, N. and Lincoln, E. (eds) (1994) *Handbook of Qualitative Research.* London: Sage.

Ebo, B. (ed.) (1998) *Cyberghetto or Cybertopia? Race, Class, and Gender on the Internet.* Westport, CT: Praeger.

Fiske, J. and Hartley, J. (1978) *Reading Television*. London: Methuen.

Friedman, T. (2005) *The World is Flat: a Brief History of the Twenty First Century*. London: Allen Lane.

Gauntlett, D. and Hill, A. (1999) *TV Living: Television, Culture and Everyday Life*. London: Routledge.

Gauntlett, D. and Horsley. R. (2004) *Web-Studies*, 2nd edn. London: Arnold.

Gibson, W. (1984) *Neuromancer*. London: Victor Gollancz.

Gillespie, M. (1989) Technology and tradition: audio visual culture among south Asian families in west London. In A. Gray and J. McGuigan (eds, 1993), *Studying Culture: an Introductory Reader*. London: Edward Arnold. First published in *Cultural Studies*, 3(2).

Hall, S. (1980) Encoding/decoding in television discourse. In S. Hall et al. (eds), *Culture: Media: Language*. London: Hutchinson.

Herman, A. and Swiss, T. (2000) *The World Wide Web and Contemporary Cultural Theory*. London: Routledge.

Johnson, R. et al. (2004) *The Practice of Cultural Studies*. London: Sage.

Johnson, S. (2005) *Everything Bad is Good for You: How Popular Culture is Making us Smarter*. London: Allen Lane.

Kroker, A. and Weinstein, D. (1994) *Data Trash: the Theory of the Virtual Class*. Montreal: New World Perspectives.

Marvin, C. (1988) *When Old Technologies were New*. Oxford: Oxford University Press.

McGuigan, J. (1992) *Cultural Populism*. London: Routledge.

McLuhan, M. (1964) *Understanding Media*. New York: McGraw.

McQuail, D. (1987) *Mass Communication Theory*. London: Sage.

McRobbie, A. (1992) Post-Marxism and cultural studies: a post-script. In Lawrence Grossberg, Cary Nelson, Paula A. Treichler et al. (eds), *Cultural Studies*. New York: Routledge.

Morley, D. (1992) *Television Audiences and Cultural Studies*. London: Routledge.

Price, S. (1993) *Media Studies*. London: Pitman.

Rushkoff, D. (1997) *Children of Chaos: Surviving the End of the World as We Know It*. London: Flamingo.

Selby, K. and Cowdery, R. (1995) *How to Study Television*. London: Macmillan.

Shade, L. R. (2002) *Gender and Community in the Social Construction of the Internet*. New York: Peter Lang.

Turner, G. (1992) *British Cultural Studies: an Introduction*. London: Routledge.

Watson, J. and Hill, A. (1989) *A Dictionary of Communication and Media Studies*. London: Arnold.

Wakeford, N. (2004) Developing methodological frameworks for studying the World Wide Web. In D. Gauntlett and R. Horsley (eds), *Web-Studies*, 2nd edn. London: Arnold.

Wise, R. (2000) *Multimedia: a Critical Introduction*. London: Routledge.

Bibliography

This bibliography provides a range of general titles, readers and reference books which should prove useful as starting points for further study.

Readers

Anon. (1994) *The Polity Reader in Cultural Theory*. Cambridge: Polity Press.

Baehr, H. and Gray, A. (eds) (1996), *Turning It On: a Reader in Women and Media*. London: Edward Arnold.

Curran, J., Morley, D. and Walkerdine, V. (eds) (1996) *Cultural Studies and Communications*. London: Edward Arnold.

Dines, G. and Humez, J. M. (eds) (1995) *Gender, Race and Class in Media: a Text-reader*. London: Sage.

During, S. (ed.) (1993) *The Cultural Studies Reader*. London: Routledge.

Easthope, A. and McGowan, K. (eds) (1992) *A Critical and Cultural Theory Reader*. Buckingham: Open University Press.

Eagleton, M. (ed.) (1996) *Feminist Literary Theory: a Reader*, 2nd edn. Oxford: Blackwell.

Franklin, S., Lury, C. and Stacey, J. (eds) (1991) *Off-centre: Feminism and Cultural Studies*. London: HarperCollins.

Gray, A. and McGuigan, J. (eds) (1993) *Studying Culture: an Introductory Reader*. London: Edward Arnold.

Grossberg, L., Nelson, C. and Treichler, P. (eds) (1992) *Cultural Studies*. New York: Routledge.

Skeggs, B. (1995) *Feminist Cultural Theory: Process and Production*. Manchester: Manchester University Press.

Storey, J. (ed.) (1994) *Cultural Theory and Popular Culture: a Reader*. London: Harvester.

Introductory texts

Baldwin, E., Longhurst, B., Smith, G., McCracken, S. and Ogborn, M. (2003) *Introducing Cultural Studies*. London: Prentice Hall.

Barker, C. (2004) *Cultural Studies: Theory and Practice*. London: Sage.

Bonner, F., Goodman, L., Allen, R., Janes, L. and King, C. (eds) (1992) *Imagining Women: Cultural Representations and Gender*. Cambridge: Polity Press.

Branston, G. and Stafford, R. (1996) *The Media Student's Book*. London: Routledge.

Crowley, H. and Himmelweit, S. (eds) (1992) *Knowing Women: Feminism and Knowledge*. Cambridge: Polity Press.

Sardar, Z. and Loon, B. V. (1997) *Cultural Studies for Beginners*. Cambridge: Icon Books.

Selby, K. and Cowdery, R. (1995) *How to Study Television*. Basingstoke: Macmillan.

Storey, J. (1993) *An Introductory Guide to Cultural Theory and Popular Culture*. London: Harvester Wheatsheaf.

Storey, J. (2003) *Cultural Studies and the Study of Popular Culture: Theories and Methods*. Edinburgh: Edinburgh University Press.

Strinati, D. (1995) *An Introduction to Theories of Popular Culture*. London: Routledge.

Turner, G. (1990) *British Cultural Studies: an Introduction*. London: Routledge.

Reference books

These are some examples, but browsing in the reference section of a library will suggest many others.

The Concise Oxford English Dictionary (formerly *The Concise Oxford Dictionary*), various editions. Oxford: Oxford University Press.

Cook, C. and Stevenson, J. (1988) *The Longman Handbook of Modern European History 1763–1985*. London: Longman.

Cook, C. and Stevenson, J. (1988) *The Longman Handbook of British History 1714–1987*. London: Longman.

Drabble, M. (ed.) *The Oxford Companion to English Literature*. Oxford: Oxford University Press.

Kuper, A. and Kuper, J. (eds) (1985) *The Social Science Encylopedia*. London: Routledge.

Riff, M. A. (ed.) (1987) *Dictionary of Modern Political Ideologies*. Manchester: Manchester University Press.

Rose, P. (ed.) (1995) *The Penguin Book of Women's Lives*. Harmondsworth: Penguin.

Walker, J. (ed.) (annual) *Halliwell's Film Guide*. London: HarperCollins.

Williams, R. (1976) *Keywords: a Vocabulary of Culture and Society*. London: Fontana.

Index

9/11
    memorialization of in culture
        109–13
    Suheir Hammad reflects on 38–9

Adorno, Theodor
    consumption 248–9
    mass culture 248–9
agency 31
    and ethics of appropriation 261–4
Agnew, James, on locale, location and
        place 125–6
Althusser, Louis
    individuals and ideologies 43, 214
    and Jacques Lacan 225
anti-humanism 212–13
    see also humanism
Anzaldúa, Gloria, on *la mestiza*
        219–20
Araeen, Rasheed, on cultural identity
        34–6
Arnold, Matthew
    Culture and Anarchy 8–10
    Edward Said on 25–7, 189, 192,
        196, 249
    high culture 11
    mass culture 13–14
autobiography 57–9
    Caroline Steedman on history and
        101–2

Bakhtin, Mikhail 179
    analysis of culture 187–9
Barker, Ernest, on English masculinity
        204
Barthes, Roland, on culture and myth
        113–14
Bath Spa University 127–8
Baudrillard, Jean
    on advertising 250–1
    on consumption 261–3
Bourdieu, Pierre
    Fiske on 185
    habitus 252–5, 263
Brontë, Charlotte, *Jane Eyre* 73–4, 83

Clifford, James, on the modern art
        culture system 12–13
consumption
    and identity 257–64
    and place 243–5
    theories of 238–9, 246–56
cultural geography
    reading of Los Angeles 137–45
    shopping and 130–6, 243–5
    theories of 121–6
    tourist places 159–61
cultural studies
    and ethnography 269–70
    history of 2
    US and South Asian trends 180

culture
  Chinese   28–9
  and civilization   8–12
  defined by Stuart Hall   62
  literary   189–95
  mass   13–17
  Raymond Williams on   6–8, 18–20,
    181
  and society   18–25
  and symbolization   29

De Certeau, Michel, as theorist of
    everyday life   186–7
De Kerckhove, Derrick, on late 20th-
    century Western cultural trends
    266–8
diaspora   53–4
discourse   25
  and representation   72–83
  and subjectivity   225–7
Duffy, Carol Ann, 'Recognition' 217–19
Durkheim, Emile, on the sacred and the
    profane   157–8
Dyer, Richard
  power and representation   88–9
  representation of gay identity   83–5

Englishness
  heritage culture and   116–19
  masculinity and homosexuality in
    197–205
  and a sense of the past   116
epistemology   94
ethnography   269–70

Fiske, John
  Bourdieu and everyday life   185–7
  consumption   263–4
  de Certeau and place   131
  and John Hartley on television
    272–3
Ford, Ford Madox, on English
    masculinity   204

Foucault, Michel
  and discourse   72
  discursive construction of subjectivity
    214
  heterotopia   123
  the subject and discourse   225–6

gender
  social constructivist approaches
    42–5
  sociobiological approach   45–9
Gibson, William, on cyberspace   281
globalization   51–3, 149, 174–7
Grahame, Kenneth, *The Wind in the
    Willows*   179, 197–209

Hall, Stuart
  culture and representation   65–7
  defines culture   62
  encoding and decoding   65–7, 272
  race and subjectivity   227–8
heterotopia   123–4
history
  heritage   116–18
  popular memory   102–15
  post-structuralist approaches
    98–101
  tourism and heritage   168–73
Hoggart, Richard, on mass culture
    15–17, 117
homosociality   205–8
hooks, bell, on homosexuality   43–4
Horkheimer, Max, and Theodor
    Adorno, on consumption   248–9
humanism   33
  see also anti-humanism   212–13

identity
  Angela McRobbie on   271
  crisis of in modernity   49–57
  Ernesto Laclau on   122
  essentialist and non-essentialist
    perspectives   38

and place   121–6
social constructivist approaches
    40–8
identity politics   55–7
interpellation
    in advertising   69
    defined   43

Johnson, Richard, on 'person research'
    method   269–70
Joyce, James, *A Portrait of the Artist as a
    Young Man*   120

Kristeva, Julia, on the semiotic
    223–5
Kureishi, Hanif, *The Buddha of Suburbia*
    50

Lacan, Jacques
    contrasted with physiological
        approach to subjectivity   230
    on subjectivity   221–3
Laclau, Ernesto, on identity   122
language
    encoding   69–70
    and representation   63–4
    signs and signifiers   63–5
    and subjectivity   220–4
Leavis, F. R. and Q. D., criticism of
    mass culture   14
Lefebvre, Henri, on the production of
    space   129–30
liberalism   33

Macdonald, Dwight, on mass culture
    14–16
Marcuse, Herbert, on false needs of
    consumer culture   248
Marwick, Arthur, on three meanings of
    'history'   92–4
Massey, Doreen, on time-space
    compression   135–6
materialist view of society   41

McRobbie, Angela, on identity
    formation   271
mediated place   161
memory *see* popular memory
Minh-ha, Trinh, on subjectivity
    39–40, 214
myth
    as distortion   116
    and popular memory   109–10
    Roland Barthes, *Mythologies*   113–14
    as system of representation   67–8

Ortner, Sherry, on gender and culture
    28–9

popular memory
    as history   103–9
    Raphael Samuel on   105–6

Samuel, Raphael
    heritage culture   118–19
    popular memory   105–6
Said, Edward, on Matthew Arnold's
    cultural politics   26–8
semiotics   76
Soja, Edward
    critique of 'innocent spatiality'   124
    on racial diversity in Los Angeles
        139
Spence, Jo, on the politics of
    representation   86–7
Storey, John
    Marxist accounts of consumption
        246–7
    Raymond Williams's definition of
        culture   181
subjectivity
    and the body   228–35
    decentred   214–15
    and discourse   225–7
    fragmented or multiple   215–19
    Jacques Lacan on   221–3
    and language   220–4

subjectivity (*cont'd*)
   social and material factors   37–8
   summary of main theories   236–7
   Trinh Minh-ha on   39–40

technology
   cultural studies of TV   271–6
   personal technology   277–9
   World Wide Web   282–4
Thompson, E. P., on presentation of the
   working class   96–8
tourism
   and heritage   168–73
   history of   152–5
   and identity   162–7
   as social practice   156–9
Turner, Graeme, on Fiske and Hartley's
   Reading Television   272–3

Veblen, Thorstein, on consumption
   248–50

White, Haydn, histories and chronicles
   99–101
Williams, Raymond
   the consumer   246
   cultural analysis based on study of
     relationships   122–3
   culture   6–8, 18–20
   definition of consumption
     239–40
   definition of culture   180–2
   definition of institution   274
   legacy for cultural materialist
     criticism   196–7
   structures of feeling   22–5
World Tourism Organization   154–6